Theodore Roosevelt

AMERICAN PRESIDENTS REFERENCE SERIES

Theodore Roosevelt

MARIO R. DINUNZIO

Providence College

CQ PRESS

A Division of Congressional Quarterly Inc.
Washington, D.C.

CQ Press
1255 22nd Street, N.W., Suite 400
Washington, D.C. 20037

202-729-1900; toll-free, 1-866-4CQ-PRESS (1-866-427-7737)

www.cqpress.com

⊚ The paper used in this publication exceeds the requirements of the American National Standard for Information Sciences— Permanence of Paper for Printed Library Materials, ANSI Z39.48-1992.

Cover illustration by Talia Greenberg
Design by Karen Doody
Composition by Auburn Associates, Inc., Baltimore, Md.
Editorial development by the Moschovitis Group, Inc.,
    New York, N.Y.

Printed and bound in the United States of America

07 06 05 04 03   5 4 3 2 1

Library of Congress Cataloging-in-Publication Data

DiNunzio, Mario R.
    Theodore Roosevelt / Mario R. DiNunzio.
       p. cm.—(American presidents reference series)
Includes bibliographical references and index.
    ISBN 1-56802-764-8 (alk. paper)
    1. Roosevelt, Theodore, 1858–1919. 2. Presidents—United
States—Biography. 3. United States—Politics and
government—1901–1909. I. Title. II. Series.
    E757.D58 2003
973.91'1'092—dc21

                                            2003009251

Contents

Documents

Preface

Theodore Roosevelt led what he called "the strenuous life," pursuing one great adventure after another: ranching in the Dakota Territory, fighting in Cuba, big-game hunting in Africa, exploring in the Amazon, becoming president of the United States. He felt compelled to write about each chapter of his life, sometimes with candor, sometimes with an eye to shaping public opinion. The result is a rich record. Some of his letters, essays, and even public messages were intended for posterity as much as for his immediate audience. Thus Roosevelt bequeathed to scholars a massive body of writing beyond his official pronouncements as president. His works fill twenty volumes, including his autobiography, several other books, and hundreds of speeches and journal articles. They stand as a valuable source of his interpretation of the issues and events about which he felt deeply. Because he wrote his own speeches and presidential messages, those documents offer insights into the style and substance of his thought. They also challenge the reader, calling for careful judgment about his ideas and motives.

Recorded in the six chapters of this book are the important events of his life before and after the presidency, his electoral history, his presidential policies and moments of crisis, and his relations with important national institutions. They show a man who could be alternately impulsive and thoughtful, unforgiving and tolerant, combative and gentle, even childlike. His presidency, with its successes and failures, can be measured against the performance of others who held the office, but his personality and style were unique.

Chapter 1 provides a biographical sketch of Roosevelt from his birth on October 27, 1858, to his death on January 6, 1919. Among other key events, the chapter looks at his childhood; his political emergence in the New York legislature; the death of his first wife, Alice; his rejuvenation in the Dakota wilds; and his exploits as the leader of the Rough Riders in Cuba. Chapter 2 examines the political landscape and electoral strategies that led Roosevelt to victory as a state legislator, governor, vice president, and president. The chapter also explores his relationship to political party bosses like Thomas Platt and Roosevelt's reelection defeat as the presidential nominee of the Progressive Party. Chapter 3 explains the policies of the Roosevelt administration, such as its efforts to reduce the power of trusts, its leadership on race relations and environmental conservation, and its support of railroad regulation and consumer protection. This chapter also looks at Roosevelt's "big stick" foreign policies. Chapter 4 explores the significant crises that affected the nation and the Roosevelt administration, including the Brownsville Incident, the attempted assassination of Roosevelt, the coal strike of 1902, and the challenges that led to the construction of the Panama Canal. Chapter 5 delves into Roosevelt's relationships with other political and governmental institutions like the press, his cabinet, Congress, the Supreme Court, and the military. Finally, in Chapter 6 readers will find highlights of Roosevelt's retirement, death, and legacy. Recounted here are the important events of his later years, including his safari to Africa, Nobel Peace Prize, Bull Moose candidacy, and stance against President Woodrow Wilson during and shortly after World War I.

Each chapter includes a bibliographic essay and excerpts of historic documents. Each document—whether letter, speech, presidential message, Supreme Court case, or legislation—is introduced by an explanatory headnote that puts it in the context of the narrative. Appendixes provide a brief description of the notable figures during the Roosevelt presidency, a chronology of Roosevelt's life, and a list of Roosevelt's cabinet members.

I am grateful to Valerie Tomaselli for her thoughtful guidance of this work and to Catherine E. Carter, Eleanora von Dehsen, Joanne S. Ainsworth, and Molly Lohman, all skilled editors who were unfailingly helpful. Special thanks go to Keith M. Lewison, whose research talents and masterful shepherding of files and documents kept the project on track. Any flaws in the telling of this story are mine; credit for the vitality and the drama recorded here belong to Theodore Roosevelt.

Mario R. DiNunzio
Providence College

President Roosevelt inspects Yellowstone National Park in 1903. Protecting the park from commercial development and ecological destruction had been a priority of Roosevelt's since 1894.

Introduction

The presidency of Theodore Roosevelt recast the role of the chief executive in American government and established a new agenda for "progressive," or "liberal," politics in the United States. Roosevelt led the way to the twentieth century's more activist presidency, dedicated to leading and bending the congressional will to fulfill executive designs for the nation. Most earlier presidents, with a few notable exceptions like George Washington, Andrew Jackson, and Abraham Lincoln, were content to administer (see the other biographies in this series); Roosevelt was determined to lead. He served at a critical point in the history of the United States. By the end of the nineteenth century the emergence of corporate giants and the concentration of wealth among finance capitalists had altered the relations of power everywhere in the industrial world. Private economic decisions generated immediate and broad public consequences. The relation of governments to that kind of power was inevitably destined to change. Some governments settled on socialist solutions, Marxist to one degree or another. Others responded with ideas that one day spawned varieties of fascism. The American response was an attempt at the democratic regulation of capitalism, and the first architect of that response was Theodore Roosevelt.

Roosevelt was an extraordinary man of extraordinary talents. An avid reader with a prodigious memory, he ranks with Thomas Jefferson and

Woodrow Wilson among the best educated of American presidents. He once considered a career in science, and as an amateur he became expert in ornithology and other animal life. Politics aside, he would be known today as an interesting and successful historian. His work as a journalist and political commentator was both highly partisan and broadly influential. The Smithsonian Institution was the beneficiary of his year-long African hunt for game specimens, and the Brazilian government dubbed an Amazon tributary Rio Roosevelt in recognition of his successful exploration of unknown and dangerous territory. In Cuba he fought with skill and fearless courage leading the Rough Riders to victory in battle during the Spanish-American War. In his life outside politics he amassed a record of achievement rare among men and unmatched among statesmen.

Among all his varied interests, his great passion was politics. Roosevelt was a thoroughly political animal. He had a keen eye for power. Finding the law in service to corporate interests uncongenial, he was determined to join what he called the "governing classes," where power resided. Defying the custom of most of his patrician contemporaries to remain aloof, he leapt into the gritty politics of New York City and quickly won the respect and support of ward bosses and citizens high and low. Once in the political world, he revealed an uncanny ability to weave through the often grimy maze of local and state politics, enjoying success but remaining independent and uncorrupted. He managed to infuriate the leadership of his own party but also to retain his influence and standing. He was, until 1912, steadfast in his political loyalty to the "regulars" who controlled the Republican Party, while prodding and pushing for enlightened change. An instinctive psychologist, Roosevelt understood men and their motives and knew how to move them. When his own powers of persuasion fell short, his adept manipulation of the press and public opinion often left his adversaries no choice but cooperation. A combination of intense partisanship and fierce ambition made him a dangerous foe. The trail of defeated duelists was a long one. His political skill and charismatic energy drew armies of loyal supporters, some of whom saw presidential potential early on, and most of whom remained faithful for a lifetime.

His agenda for change was one of the magnets that attracted that kind of support. Roosevelt was a reformer in spite of himself. He railed against the "goo-goos" and "do-gooders," but from his first term in the New York State Assembly he insisted on pushing his party to support resolutions against corrupt practices and, on occasion, against abusive social conditions. He admired men of achievement and wealth but despised their thoughtless disregard for the common good. He feared that these "malefactors of great wealth," the "criminal rich," would incite the masses to revolt. But neither was he a populist. He distrusted organized power among the masses, was suspicious of labor unions, and thought the Populist Party dangerous. Experience and his own pragmatic instincts sharpened his understanding of capitalist indifference to the commonweal and the genuine needs of the laboring classes. By the close of his presidency, and even more avidly in 1912, he was converted to a program of reform that anticipated and, in part, inspired the New Deal and the twentieth-century liberal agenda. As president he faced a steadfastly conservative establishment in Congress. It took all of his political ingenuity, popular appeal, and even occasional ruthlessness to wring concessions from the old guard of his party. He compromised when necessary; stood firm when firmness promised results. The product was a series of precedents that transformed the presidency and altered the relationship of the government to American capitalist enterprise.

Roosevelt also applied an understanding of the uses of power and his political vision to crafting a new role for the United States in the world. Years before he became president he championed the cause of a strong navy as the key to American influence in the hemisphere and the world. It was an imperialist world in which the major powers were already competing in an arms race. For Roosevelt, to be weak in that world was to be vulnerable. Imperialist adventure tempted him, and his attitude toward war fit that age of romantic nationalism. The war with Spain in 1898 was an opportunity not to be missed. That war also propelled the United States more deeply into the world of imperialism with the acquisition of the Philippine Islands. Roosevelt was pleased with the acquisition but later supported the idea of Philippine independence and backed away from the notion of a colonial empire. He did continue to insist on the need for the United States to exercise hemispheric responsibility. He considered it essential to build an isthmian canal and proclaimed that the "corollary" to the Monroe Doctrine was to keep Europe out of the Americas. At times his diplomacy, notably in relation to Panama, was heavy-handed and by some measures brutal. But the picture of Roosevelt wielding a "big stick" in diplomacy is something of a distortion. There were fewer and shorter interventions in Latin America under Roosevelt than under his two immediate successors, and his relations with major powers like Japan were marked by restraint, finesse, and some prescience. He was a realist in world affairs and remained convinced that building American power would serve as a deterrent to war.

When he returned from his African safari in 1910, the former president was distressed by what he considered a turn away from the progressive program he had bequeathed to his successor, William Howard Taft. There can be little doubt that his passionate desire to return to the presidency drove his criticism of Taft and the old guard of his party. His motives—ambition, a sense of betrayal, and the conviction that a modern America demanded greater economic and social justice for its people—will likely never be entirely unraveled. But his discontent drove him into the unaccustomed role of party rebel. When he failed to capture the party nomination in 1912, he cried foul and justified his rebellion. Had he waited, the nomination for president in 1916 was probably his for the taking. But Roosevelt had spent a lifetime seizing opportunity; waiting fit him poorly. His Bull Moose campaign was the last leg of his journey from a rather conventional conservatism to a kind of impassioned liberalism, which some of his former party associates considered radical.

Roosevelt met unaccustomed defeat in 1912 and was never quite reconciled to its consequences. He clung to a slim hope that 1916 would open the White House doors again, but while he was welcomed back into the Republican Party, he was not fully trusted or forgiven for his revolt. Turning to journalism again he kept the nation apprised of his thoughts and its duties. With the outbreak of World War I he could scarcely disguise his frustration at being out of the action, politically and militarily. His old partisanship exploded in continuous, fiery, and sometimes unfair attacks on President Wilson. Wilson faced unprecedented complexities in steering a powerful but neutral nation through the shoals of wartime diplomacy. Except for his decision to go to war, little that Wilson did escaped Roosevelt's lash, and his role in opposing Wilson's League of Nations initiative added little credit to his record. For an excellent discussion of how Roosevelt's opposition to the League of Nations affected his record, see Kendrick A. Clements and Eric A. Cheezum, *Woodrow Wilson* (Washington, D.C.: CQ Press, 2003).

The life and presidency of Theodore Roosevelt offer a formidable but compelling challenge to the student of history. One must confront the mysteries of a complex personality, the contradictions of a pragmatic and flexible mind, and the struggles of a presidency in an era of transition. He was a man of prodigious talent and of human failings. This volume is an effort to examine his work in its own time and in the context of the constraints, prejudices, and demands of the era. The conclusion here and the consensus of many historians, both critics and admirers (who are sometimes one and the same), hold the presidency of Theodore Roosevelt among the most important in the history of the United States.

Roosevelt and his second wife, Edith, pose with their children in 1895. A sixth child would be born two years later.

CHAPTER ONE

A Strenuous Life

Biographical Sketch

Americans have always been fascinated by their presidents. They enthrone no royalty but shower royal attention on the heads of state. Press and public invest them with a larger-than-life stature and expect the heroic; so they are naturally disappointed when their leaders prove to be quite human. Most presidents, in fact, have been rather ordinary men. Nevertheless, historians devote great energy to their study. As a result we know a great deal about most presidents, but few, except Lincoln and perhaps Franklin Roosevelt, have drawn more historical inquiry than Theodore Roosevelt. Each generation revisits his story, but for all we know about him, he remains a difficult person to understand and defies simple characterization.

Some scholars listed him among the greatest of presidents; others saw an unstable and perhaps dangerous leader. These two views, incidentally, were commonly held among his contemporaries, including members of his own party. Robert Dallek wrote that Roosevelt made the conduct of foreign affairs part of "the progressive struggle to advance morality, democracy, law and social order" (Dallek 1983, 61). Conceding that Roosevelt was among the most skilled presidents in the conduct of foreign affairs, Howard K. Beale argued that trouble lay in his imperialist values and that his desire for power set American foreign policy in a perilous direction (Beale 1956, 393–394). At least in part the reason for conflicting judgments lay with Roosevelt himself. He was an extraordinarily complex personality who invited differing assessments. Some historians could not resist the temptation of Freudian psychohistory and suggested a certain instability in Roosevelt owing to an uncontrollable drive to overcome his physical weakness as a boy (Pringle [1931] 1956, 4). Richard Hofstadter also implied that Theodore Roosevelt was somewhat hypocritical—a conservative who only posed as a progressive (Hofstadter 1954, 206ff.). Recent biographers, such as H. W. Brands and Edmund Morris, have been much kinder, and most lean toward a judgment of flawed greatness (Brands 1997; Morris 2001). To understand him, then, demands an understanding of the complexities and contradictions of his times and of his extraordinary life.

EARLY YEARS

Theodore Roosevelt was born to privilege. His father, Theodore Roosevelt Sr., was so successful in business that he retired as a relatively young man to devote himself to charitable causes in New York City. The Roosevelts had been New Yorkers since the first of them had settled in Manhattan in 1649. His mother, Martha (Mittie) Bulloch, was a beautiful southern belle the senior Roosevelt met on a trip to Georgia. Both parents had strong personalities and a profound and enduring influence on young Theodore. He idolized his father and in his *Autobiography* described him as "the best man I ever knew," who "combined strength and courage with gentleness" (Roosevelt 1926, 20:9). Teedie, as the family dubbed him, was the second of four children (he had an older sister Anna [Bamie] as well as a younger brother and sister, Elliott and Corinne). He was born on October 27, 1858, in the family home at 28 East 20th Street. Bouts of asthma, suffered from his earliest days, continued to plague him throughout his youth. Those bouts and a parade of other ailments left him a frail child, and at times his parents worried for his survival. In view of his delicate health they kept the boy out of school, and his education came by way of tutors until he entered Harvard. Sharply intelligent, Theodore developed a precocious interest in natural history, and before he was ten he recorded his observations in notebooks. Soon he graduated to collecting live specimens of frogs, snakes, and field mice, much to the distress of the household.

In 1869 the family sailed to Europe for a year-long grand tour during which Roosevelt fell ill repeatedly. On the return to New York, doctor's advice and the encouragement of his parents led him to begin a regimen of bodybuilding exercises, hoping to build resistance to the asthma and other afflictions. Slowly his health improved and attacks of illness struck less frequently. Meanwhile his interest in natural history persisted, and he became quite expert in his study of birds and adept at taxidermy, the odors from which also strained family patience. His collection of stuffed birds and mammals grew with his talent. Another family tour in 1872 brought the Roosevelts to Europe, North Africa, the Middle East, and down the Nile in Egypt. When they returned Theodore was fifteen. He resumed bodybuilding with more intensity and studied hard with an eye on admission to Harvard. Both efforts were successful. He remained thin of frame but stronger and healthier, and in the fall of 1876 he was ready for Harvard.

HARVARD, HONORS, AND ALICE

His college career was in some ways a forecast of his future. He was full of action, enjoyed a full social life, was invited to join prestigious clubs, including the Porcellian Club, and excelled in his studies. He became editor of the *Harvard Advocate,* the college literary magazine, beginning a lifelong passion for writing. Testimony to his improving health and dogged interest in "manly" pursuits was his signing up for boxing lessons. He eventually held his own in intramural bouts. He also found time to hunt in nearby woodlands, collecting more trophies for his collection.

In his sophomore year one of the great sorrows of his life left him shattered. In December, Theodore Senior died suddenly at the age of forty-six. Grief stayed with the young Roosevelt through his college years and sorrow much longer. It was characteristic of him that despite his pain, he resumed his active life at Harvard and redoubled his scholarly efforts. In his senior year, dissatisfied with available accounts, he began a book about the navy in the War of 1812. The work was completed a year later and published as *The Naval War of 1812* to friendly reviews. It was the best of his work as a historian and remains a respected source on the subject (see Document 1.1). Despite an active extracurricular life and the family tragedy, Roosevelt was admitted to the Phi Beta Kappa honors society and graduated with high honors.

The only unhappy episode of his senior year came in March, after a routine physical examination. The physician gave Roosevelt bad news.

He was suffering from heart trouble severe enough that he would have to live quietly without physical strain or vigorous activity. He should organize his life and choose a profession accordingly. The startled doctor then heard the young man lash out that he would defy those instructions even if it meant a short life. He could not live as an invalid. Roosevelt continued the strenuous life he loved, and his heart, stouter than the doctor imagined, carried him through Dakota winters, war, elephant hunting in Africa, exploring in Brazil, and a long and intense political career.

The Harvard years were important to Roosevelt's life for another reason. In his junior year he met a seventeen-year-old beauty from Chestnut Hill in Boston, Alice Hathaway Lee. He was instantly in love. He pursued a resistant Alice month after month undeterred by her coolness toward him. His ardor and persistence worked on Alice, and by January 1880, she agreed to marry him. Both families thought it a good match, uniting distinguished names from Boston and New York. They married on his birthday, October 27, 1880.

JOINING THE GOVERNING CLASS

Roosevelt was ecstatic in his new married life and driven to establish a career. His first thoughts pointed toward the law. Settling with his bride in New York in the new family home at 6 West 57th Street, he enrolled at Columbia University Law School. But after an earnest effort he realized that the study of the law did not appeal to him. He noted the gap between legal standards and his understanding of justice and abandoned law school. More attractive was the political scene. He began to frequent Morton Hall, the clubhouse of the Republicans of the Twenty-first District. The society boy hobnobbed with the local politicians, most of whom were from a distinctly different social stratum. His reception was chilly at first, but he soon won their respect and even a measure of friendship. This talent for winning over people very different from himself would serve him well in the future. Morton Hall was the door to his new vocation, politics. At the behest of the district leader, Joe Murray, Roosevelt ran for the post of assemblyman in the New York legislature and won the November election with over 60 percent of the votes (see Chapter 2). Theodore Roosevelt was now a politician.

This new career did not sit well with many among his family and friends. The years after the Civil War were among the most corrupt in the political history of New York and the nation. The "best people" thought politics a low business, not a proper activity for men of their class. The well-to-do, of course, played at politics with money and the influence it bought, but discreetly in the background, not as candidates. An office seeker in the Twenty-first District needed to solicit support not only among the patricians of Fifth Avenue but also among the plebeians in the saloons and shops of the grubbier neighborhoods. So some of his coterie frowned on Roosevelt's indiscretion. He responded to his critical friends that he "intended to be one of the governing class" (Roosevelt 1926, 20:59). Roosevelt wanted to be at the center of action, and politics was where the action was.

At twenty-three Roosevelt was the youngest member of the New York State Assembly. He began his first political venture as a solidly conservative and faithful party man, voting against raises for firemen and policemen and against a two-dollar minimum wage for government workers. He was suspicious of "do-good" reformers, whom he thought impractical. But he also showed that, given sufficient evidence, he could be drawn to support a necessary reform. The tension between his conservative instincts and the attraction of more liberal ideas stayed with him into the presidency and after. When, in 1882, a bill was introduced designed to improve the horrid working conditions of cigar makers toiling in overcrowded city tenements, Roosevelt expected to vote against the measure as an unwarranted government intrusion. Union leader Samuel Gompers persuaded the young legislator to tour the tenements to see for himself the vile conditions under which even children were forced to work. Roosevelt was sickened by what he witnessed and became a champion of the bill to improve the lot of the cigar makers. At first he failed but finally saw the law passed during his third term, though it was later declared unconstitutional by an industry-friendly state court.

Always sensitive to political corruption, Assemblyman Roosevelt was appalled to learn that a judge of the New York State Supreme Court, T. R. Westbrook, was a pawn of the notoriously corrupt financier Jay Gould, using his position on the court to advance Gould's thievery. In March 1882, Roosevelt rose in the assembly to call for the impeachment of Westbrook. At first blocked by the judge's defenders, Roosevelt refused to let go, and by detailed accusations, press attention, and repeated appeals to the body, won approval for an investigation (see Document 1.2). Eventually, well-placed bribes generated a report from the investigating committee that recommended against impeachment (Morris 1979, 180). Roosevelt lost the battle but won statewide respect for his stand on corruption and for his skill and courage in the assembly.

Legislative terms in the assembly ran for one year. The freshman stood for reelection in 1882 and won easily, even in the year when the Democrat Grover Cleveland swept into the governorship by a large margin. Roosevelt was elected again in the fall of 1883. In the assembly Roosevelt was irrepressible and openly ambitious. Some of his actions brought ridicule from his colleagues in both parties, which he felt keenly but did not allow to deflect him from the causes he embraced. Isaac Hunt, one of his close friends in Albany, remarked, "Such a super-abundance of animal life was hardly ever condensed in a human being" (McCullough 1981, 266). He wanted to establish himself as a party leader and even made a run to be Speaker of the assembly. That failed, but although he exasperated the party leadership with his penchant for legislative combat and his perception of reality in terms of good and evil, he also earned their respect. Respect extended even to some of the Democrats. His strong party loyalty did not prevent him from supporting some of Governor Cleveland's initiatives, and in an important battle the two were allies.

Cleveland had become governor as a fighter against corruption. Now he struggled for the passage of a civil service reform law for New York, a bill Roosevelt earnestly favored. Roosevelt, who seldom praised Democrats, was impressed, and his respect for Cleveland grew proportionately. The act could not pass without Republican votes, and the governor enlisted Roosevelt to help (see Document 1.3). Working together they garnered enough votes to pass the measure in May 1883. Such victories drew national attention to Cleveland and won Roosevelt praise and recognition across the state.

GRIEF BEYOND WORDS

Alice accompanied Roosevelt to Albany during the winter of his first term in 1882, but for the next two sessions she remained in New York City and he shuttled from Albany on weekends. He counted himself the happiest of men in his life with Alice. He bought a hundred-acre parcel of land in Oyster Bay on Long Island, and with Alice he made plans for a large and comfortable country home that would one day be called Sagamore Hill. Roosevelt wanted a large family and was delighted with news that a baby was due in February 1884. With success in politics, the comforts of prosperity, and a baby coming, life was good. But the joy was not to last.

In Albany for an assembly session on February 13, Roosevelt received a telegram announcing the birth of his daughter the previous night with the news that all was well. He was still enjoying the congratulations of his colleagues when a second message urged him to return to the city immediately. When he arrived at 57th Street, he found his beloved Alice barely conscious, dying of Bright's disease, a degenerative disease of the kidneys. In another bedroom lay his mother, dying of typhoid fever. Alice had seemed well up to the time of delivery, and his mother had been suffering what was thought to be a cold. Now both barely clung to life. In the early hours of February 14, Valentine's Day, Mittie Roosevelt died with her son by her side. In his grief he returned to his wife's room. That afternoon Alice died in his arms; she was twenty-two years old.

His sorrow was inconsolable. During the past three years, he could not disguise the happiness of his marriage to Alice. Now he wrote, "The light has gone out of my life" (McCullough 1981, 287). In the days after the funeral, the always voluble Roosevelt was uncharacteristically silent. That was understandable; more strange was his response to the memory of his love. Except for a brief memorial statement he wrote, he never spoke of her again. Letters were destroyed and he removed photographs and mementos from scrapbooks in what appeared to be an attempt to erase her from his life (Morris 1979, 243–244). Years later when he wrote his autobiography, he made no mention of Alice and never spoke of her to his daughter. He left the baby, named Alice, in the care of his sister Bamie, and for some months remained distant from the child. But the two eventually grew close and remained so. By the time he became president, she was a beautiful young woman who moved with ease and a sharp tongue in Washington society. She married Congressman Nicholas Longworth in 1906 and remained an important figure in Washington social circles until her death in 1980 at the age of ninety-six.

PARTY MAN

Within days of the funeral service for his wife and mother, Roosevelt was back in Albany, burying himself in the details of the legislature's work. If there was a sadness about him, it did nothing to deflect the limitless energy he threw at his work. He divided his time between Assembly chores in Albany and the chairmanship of the City Investigating Committee inquiring into corruption in New York City. He delivered several thousand pages of data to Albany, distilled them into a final report, and guided a series of resulting bills to passage. When the session ended he leapt into the politics of the party's presidential nomination.

By the nomination season in 1884 the Republican Party had fractured itself into one division of "Stalwarts," who fought civil service reform and backed President Chester Arthur, and another, the "Half-breeds," moderate reformers who supported James G. Blaine. Both men and their backers were tainted by rumors of corruption. Roosevelt joined a group of unaligned Republicans to work for the nomination of the honest and able George Edmunds, senator from Vermont. At the Chicago convention in June, he joined forces with a young Henry Cabot Lodge of Massachusetts in behalf of Edmunds; the association with Lodge was to endure for a lifetime. In the end Blaine won the nomination to the great distress of reform-minded Republicans for whom Blaine was unacceptable. These "Mugwumps," led by important reformers like Carl Schurz and E. L. Godkin, let it be known that they would vote for an honest Democrat for president. It was an offer too tempting for the Democrats to ignore; they chose Grover Cleveland, whose reputation as an honest governor had been boosted by some of Roosevelt's work in the New York Assembly. It was an irony that Roosevelt could not have missed. But along with Lodge, he refused to join the revolt. He was a loyal party man (see Document 1.4). He respected Cleveland but, given his association of the party with disloyalty during the Civil War and his experience fighting Tammany Hall in New York City, he despised the Democrats. He not only declined to support Cleveland as the rebels hoped, but in the fall actively campaigned for the election of Blaine. Cleveland became president, and Roosevelt thought his political future was damaged, but he did not regret his party orthodoxy.

THE COWBOY FROM MANHATTAN

During the time between the assembly sessions of 1883 and 1884 Roosevelt traveled to the Bad Lands of Dakota Territory for a taste of the West while it was still somewhat wild. There he invested in two cattle ranches along the Little Missouri River. In the summer of 1884 he returned to Dakota, checking on his investments and hunting the game of the plains. He extended the hunting trip to Wyoming for elk and on to Montana, where he proudly shot his first grizzly bear. One result of that trip was a new book, *The Lordly Buffalo,* which he published the following year (see Document 1.5). As the 1884 election season approached, a still-grieving Roosevelt decided not to stand for the legislature again, and after Blaine's defeat, he resolved to return to his Elkhorn ranch near the town of Medora (in what is now North Dakota) to live the life of a prairie cattleman (see Document 1.6).

He threw himself into the ranch work with his characteristic vigor and enthusiasm. The hard life of tending and driving cattle, sleeping outdoors, and enduring the often bitter Dakota weather was therapeutic for Roosevelt. He grew in girth and muscle and emerged from the experience healthier than he had ever been. In the process he won the respect of the hardened cowboys who had initially greeted him with condescending labels like "four-eyes" and "dude." That respect turned to high esteem in the spring of 1886, when local events drew him into a new adventure. By then he was chairman of the local stockmen's association and a deputy sheriff. When thieves stole his boat tied up on the river edge by the Elkhorn ranch house, Roosevelt bristled with anger and felt obliged as a deputy to pursue the thieves. With two companions he set out on a trek across 150 miles of rugged and still winter-chilled Dakota countryside on the trail of the outlaws. They caught up with them far down river, ambushed them, and marched them another 150 miles to the next large town for trial (Roosevelt 1926, 1:379ff.). Although Roosevelt thrived in the work of a ranchman, his investment did not. Disastrous weather, especially in the winter of 1886–1887, effectively ended his career as a cattleman at a substantial financial cost.

During the three years of his Dakota adventures, the cowboy returned to New York from time to time. On one of these visits in the fall of 1885, he chanced to meet Edith Carow. The two were childhood playmates and later sweethearts, until Alice captured his heart. He had not seen Edith in the months since Alice died. Now the attraction and intimacy of the past rekindled, and he spent much of that winter in her company. Roosevelt's stringent moral code frowned on the idea that widowers should remarry, but love conquered his scruples and soon they were engaged.

The year 1886 was one of courtship and, once more, politics. Hunting for a candidate to run for mayor, New York City Republicans settled on Roosevelt, and he reluctantly accepted, although he knew election was unlikely. It was a three-way race, and at twenty-eight, Roosevelt was the youngest man ever to run for the office of mayor of New York (see Document 1.7). In November he came in third, behind the Democratic candidate, businessman Abram S. Hewitt, and an independent, radical reformer, Henry George (see Chapter 2).

Just days after the election, the engaged couple left New York for London, where they were married on December 2. After a honeymoon trip to France and Italy, they returned to New York in late March to the news of the disastrous winter in Dakota that cost him so dearly. Roosevelt made up for some of his losses through his writing career, which continued unabated with the completion of books (biographies, histories, and hunting stories) and the publication of essays and hunting accounts in popular journals. The joys of his new marriage were brightened further with the birth of Theodore Jr., "Ted," in September 1887. Other children followed at a brisk pace. Roosevelt believed that large families were a personal and civic duty, and by 1897 he was the father of six. Alice and Ted were joined by Kermit, Ethel, Archibald, and Quentin.

Politics beckoned again in 1888, when Benjamin Harrison challenged President Cleveland. Roosevelt was pleased with Harrison's nomination and volunteered to make a series of stump speeches in key western states. Although Harrison failed to win the popular vote, the electoral count made him president. Henry Cabot Lodge, now an influential congressman, lobbied to find a place in the administration for his friend from New York. In his first attempt he failed to persuade Secretary of State James G. Blaine to offer him a post in the State Department. Roosevelt's reputation preceded him. Despite his help in the campaign of 1884, Blaine thought Roosevelt's temperament and tendency to seek quick action unsuited to the more thoughtful and nuanced demands of diplomacy (Miller 1992, 203). Turning to Harrison himself, Lodge had better success. Sharing some of Blaine's qualms, the president offered Roosevelt a job on the federal Civil Service Commission. Although he had hoped for more, Roosevelt quickly accepted.

ON THE NATIONAL SCENE

As one of three civil service commissioners Roosevelt became an important player in Washington politics. Using his acute sense of drama and timing to become the focus of action, as always, he drew wide press attention. With little resistance from his colleagues, Republican Charles Lyman and Democrat Hugh Thompson, he quickly assumed the role of leader and just as promptly sparked a controversy. Although the Pendleton Act of 1883 introduced the concept of merit in awarding federal jobs, most government officials were still politically appointed; less than a quarter were named through the civil service system. Furthermore, such rules as were provided by the law were enforced with leisurely indifference. The new commissioner set out to change this. He scoured commission records, and within days of taking office, issued a report citing negligence and fraud in the employment practices of the federal Customs House in New York City. Only weeks later he launched an investigation of irregularities in post offices across much of the Midwest and ordered the offending employees dismissed. His powers as a commissioner were limited to recommendations, but exposure in the press encouraged compliance; the men were fired.

That energetic dedication to duty earned the newcomer the enmity of Postmaster General John Wannamaker, one of the major financial contributors to Harrison's election campaign and guardian of much administration patronage. He was especially irate because of the publicity Roosevelt drew to his investigations and did what he could to frustrate the work of the avid commissioner. For the rest of Harrison's term, Roosevelt continued his crusade to make the commission an effective organ of reform despite administration resistance. In the process he exasperated Harrison and battled defiantly against Wannamaker. Carefully gathering irrefutable evidence before striking, Roosevelt succeeded in publicly embarrassing Wannamaker. The *New York Times* reported, "The exposure he has suffered from Mr. Roosevelt is merciless and humiliating, but it is clearly deserved" (quoted in Morris 1979, 452). Although he was a willing backer of the regular party machine, Roosevelt could not abide corruption, even, perhaps especially, in his own party. His often expressed disdain for professional reformers could not disguise the strong impulses toward reform he displayed from the start of his life in politics.

When Grover Cleveland defeated Harrison in their rematch in 1892, Roosevelt expected to be replaced but held on to the hope that the president might keep him on. With some discreet inquiries and enlisting the help of Carl Schurz, one of the 1884 Mugwumps and a Cleveland ally, his wish came true when Cleveland reappointed him. The president shared

Roosevelt's abhorrence of corruption; he was aware of the troubles Roosevelt had visited on his own party, and he needed one Republican on the commission. In February 1893, as he was about to join the Cleveland administration, Roosevelt called for Congress to increase the appropriation for the commission so that it might do its work more effectively (Roosevelt 1926, 14:88ff.). Roosevelt was grateful for political and financial reasons to stay at his post, and he was pleased that he could remain in Washington, in whose political and social circles he loved to move.

Roosevelt's commission success and the pleasures of his life in Washington were marred by family troubles. His brother Elliott, two years his junior and once much admired by him, had never settled into productive work and over the years had become heavily dependent on alcohol. Marriage to Anna Hall, a beautiful New York socialite, provided no remedy; the problem grew worse and extended into drug use. Neither the arrival of children nor the repeated exhortations of his older brother could move Elliott to change. Binges became frequent and he was given to abandoning his family for extended periods. Confinement in rehabilitation clinics brought only temporary interludes of sobriety. In December 1892, Anna was stricken with diphtheria and died at the age of twenty-nine. Elliott, struggling in one of his sober spells, now abandoned himself to alcoholism again. Through these trials Theodore alternated between anguished concern and fiery condemnation. He feared scandal would taint the family name and, not incidentally, his own public reputation. A paternity claim against Elliott by a former maid was settled privately. By the winter of 1894 Elliott had drunk himself to death. Years later, Theodore, acting in his brother's place, gave Elliott's daughter, Eleanor, away in marriage to a distant cousin from the upstate and Democratic side of the family, Franklin Delano Roosevelt.

Through these troubles, Roosevelt continued his civil service work but grew increasingly restless in the job. He was ready for a new challenge. In 1894 he declined another run for mayor of New York City, and when a reform candidate, William Strong, won the election as an independent, Roosevelt thought he had lost a chance, confident he could have won the election. But Strong's election did create a new opportunity for him. The new mayor offered and he quickly accepted a position on the city's Board of Police Commissioners.

Leaving Washington was difficult for Roosevelt. Beyond the politics, he had enjoyed a stimulating social life with friends and some of the elite of Washington society. The Roosevelts entertained members of the cabinet, congressional leaders and diplomats, writers and scientists. Lodge was closest to him, but he could also count among his close friends the historian Henry Adams, who once described Roosevelt as "pure act," and John Hay, once personal secretary to Lincoln and soon to be secretary of state. Dinners at the homes of Hay and Adams near the White House were full of intelligence and wit, politics and gossip. They were good times. Cecil Spring-Rice, who had stood as best man at the Roosevelts' London wedding and was now serving at the British embassy was a frequent guest. But duty and opportunity called elsewhere, and Roosevelt returned to New York and a spectacular run as a commissioner of police.

To lead the New York City police was a daunting task in 1895. The crime rate was appalling and corruption was endemic. Impoverished immigrants were flooding into the city; neighborhoods were changing rapidly, and in much of the city the streets were unsafe after dark. Roosevelt knew the city well and saw the job as a chance to shine. As he had in the Civil Service Commission in Washington, he assumed the leadership of the board and made a quick and decisive stroke for authority. He forced the retirement of the police chief, Thomas Byrnes, who had used the position to enrich himself.

Soon after settling into the post, Roosevelt renewed his acquaintance with the journalist Jacob Riis, who wrote *How the Other Half Lives* in 1890, an exposé of the horrid conditions of the slums. They became close friends, with Riis acting as his street-smart adviser. One night the commissioner decided to see for himself how his men were conducting themselves on duty. Virtually in disguise with his hat pulled down and his coat collar pulled up and Riis by his side, he walked the streets of lower Manhattan. The trip was revealing. He found patrolmen consorting with prostitutes, drinking in saloons, asleep, and otherwise neglecting their duties. Punishments were prompt and effective. The men of the force quickly learned that Roosevelt would not stand for this behavior, nor would he tolerate police corruption or the selective enforcement of laws. Roosevelt's public image blossomed with his careful cultivation of press coverage for his nighttime tours.

Less popular was his decision to enforce the city's Sunday closing law for liquor establishments, until then genially ignored. In a city where much of the population regarded beer and wine almost as food, his ruling caused an uproar. Roosevelt was not a prohibitionist, but he insisted this was a matter of respect for the law. He justified his action in an essay in the magazine *Forum* in a futile attempt to turn opinion (see Document 1.8). When saloonkeepers found ingenious ploys to get around the law (many began serving snacks and other "food" because restaurants were exempt from the law), Roosevelt's campaign was derailed. Meanwhile political enemies multiplied. Both Republican and Democratic politicians, knowing their constituents were among the purveyors and consumers of drink, resented his righteous enforcement of the statute. The influential Republican boss, Thomas C. Platt, said so publicly, fearing voter backlash against the party because of the Republican commissioner. Roosevelt understood the need for party backing if he were to advance, and he saw his political future in jeopardy. Although his police work increased his fame, he was aware that he could not remain in that work much longer.

As the 1896 election season approached, Roosevelt favored Congressman Thomas Reed, Speaker of the House, over William McKinley for the presidential nomination. But when McKinley got the nod, he climbed on the bandwagon. As he had in the past for other Republican candidates, he took to the road, blasting Democratic and Populist nominee William Jennings Bryan as a radical danger to the nation. If the country did not see Bryan as quite that dangerous (he won 6.5 million votes), it did favor McKinley with 7.1 million. A happy but anxious Roosevelt waited for news of his hoped-for reward for campaigning: a return to the national scene. He was now more than ready to abandon his seat on the police commission. Months passed, McKinley was inaugurated, but no news came. Again it was Lodge who intervened for his friend, but McKinley hesitated. The president and his closest adviser, Sen. Mark Hanna, R-Ohio, knew Roosevelt's tendency to impulsive and sensational action and worried that he might be troublesome in the administration. In addition to McKinley's reluctance, an appointment was held up by the doubts of Boss Platt, who was torn between supporting a man he did not much like and getting that man out of New York. Finally, some weeks after the inauguration, Roosevelt's anxiety was relieved. McKinley relented and with some misgivings named him assistant secretary of the navy.

For Roosevelt it was the perfect appointment. He had continued his interest in naval power since the publication of his book on the War of 1812. In 1888 he was invited to give a lecture at the Newport Naval War College, and in 1890 he wrote a highly favorable review of Alfred Thayer

Mahan's book, *The Influence of Sea Power upon History,* in the *Atlantic Monthly.* Mahan's work matched Roosevelt's conviction that the United States needed a strong navy to play a larger role in the world. The two men, together with Lodge, constituted a kind of pronavy lobby working for that end. His new appointment now put Roosevelt in a key position to do something about building a powerful navy. Strategic considerations aside, the new job placed him where he wanted to be, back in Washington.

In the conclusion of his review of Mahan's book, Roosevelt wrote, "We need a large navy, composed not merely of cruisers, but containing also a full proportion of powerful battleships, able to meet those of any other nation" (Roosevelt 1926, 12:272). He carried this thought with him into the Navy Department. Only days in office he wrote a confidential letter to Mahan reciting his strategy goals. Apprehensive of the growing power of Japan in the Pacific, he made a case for the immediate annexation of Hawaii. He called Cleveland's refusal to do so a "colossal crime." (His wish was realized when Hawaii was annexed two months later in June.) Given a free hand he would already have ended Spanish control of Cuba, and he saw the current upheaval there as an opportunity for just such a move.

The American navy at that time was already growing, but it was still smaller than the navies of any major European power. He told Mahan the United States should launch a building program for a dozen additional battleships. He delivered a similar message in a speech at the Naval War College in June, insisting that building military strength, especially naval power, was the way to deter potential enemies and avoid war (see Document 1.9). The speech drew national attention, thrilled the convinced who lavished praise on the speaker, and worried the more pacific who thought preparation for war would make it more likely.

With his strategic outlook fully developed, Roosevelt set out to fulfill its demands. This required the cooperation, or at least the acquiescence, of his superior, Secretary of the Navy John D. Long. The secretary was quickly impressed by Roosevelt's detailed knowledge of naval armaments and tactics. Their relationship from the start was warmly cordial, and, not given to overwork, Long was content to leave much of the detail of the department's work to his assistant, who could not have been more willing or pleased to take up the burden. Long frequently escaped the torrid summer heat of Washington for the cooler breezes of New

England with Roosevelt's encouragement. During these absences, Roosevelt was effectively acting secretary and a whirlwind of activity, issuing orders on his own authority and planning for possible operations. On at least three occasions he visited McKinley to discuss naval strategy, including operations should there be war with Spain over Cuba. He also maneuvered to get George Dewey appointed commander of the Asiatic Squadron. Long, grateful for the heavy load of work that Roosevelt carried, usually tolerated the assistant secretary's tendency to overreach.

At 9:40 p.m. on February 15, 1898, the world of Theodore Roosevelt changed. The USS *Maine,* on a courtesy visit to Havana Harbor, exploded, killing 262 sailors. The jingoist "yellow press" immediately blamed Spain and called for war. Cooler judgments awaited an investigation into the cause of the disaster. Roosevelt wanted war. He assumed Spanish treachery sank the *Maine* and longed for action. A few days later Secretary Long left his assistant in charge of the department for the day while he kept a medical appointment. Quickly assuming full authority as acting secretary, Roosevelt cabled Dewey in the Pacific ordering him to Hong Kong. Should war break out Dewey was instructed to sail to the Philippines for "offensive operations" (Morison 1951, 1:784–785). He sent other messages to naval forces around the world, issued a series of directives putting the navy on a war footing, and ordered massive supplies of guns and ammunition. Long was astonished and somewhat offended when he learned of all this on his return the next day, but he allowed the orders to stand.

President McKinley was reluctant to go to war. He was caught in a crossfire of salvos from those, like Roosevelt, insisting on war and from the other side, the anti-imperialist movement as well as many business interests who thought war would be disruptive to the economy. Finally in April the president conceded to the more aggressive and called on Congress to declare war on Spain.

To War and Glory

Once war was declared, there was no doubt in Roosevelt's mind: he would go to Cuba to fight. For him this was the chance of a lifetime; it seemed, in fact, that he had spent his life preparing for this moment by conquering one physical challenge after another. No urging to the contrary could deflect his will. He brushed aside the arguments friends and family listed to keep him at home. He was now almost forty years old and the father of six children, the youngest of whom was only months old. His eyesight was weak, his physical condition was past its prime, and, it was pointed out, he could be important to the war effort in the position he held. None of this tempered his resolve. Edith, recognizing the inevitable, surrendered to his dream.

When McKinley issued a call for volunteers, Roosevelt persuaded Secretary of War Russell A. Alger to grant him a commission as a lieutenant colonel under his friend Col. Leonard Wood to raise a regiment of the First U.S. Volunteer Cavalry. As soon as this was made public, a flood of volunteers applied to join the regiment. Wood and Roosevelt sifted through thousands of applications for the best men they could find. The chosen included men from a wide range of backgrounds, from manicured Ivy League university graduates to range-hardened western cowboys. Soon dubbed the Rough Riders, the contingent gathered outside San Antonio, Texas, in mid-May for organization and training. By the end of the month Washington ordered the regiment to Tampa, Florida, to await embarkation. There, Roosevelt spent a few frustrating weeks before bureaucratic confusion and the complexities of moving thousands of men were overcome. Meanwhile, Dewey, sailing from Hong Kong as soon as war was declared, had defeated a Spanish fleet guarding Manilla and had taken the Philippines. Roosevelt worried that the war might end before he could reach it. At last, on June 14, American forces set sail for Cuba.

Just two days after landing in Cuba, the Rough Riders saw their first action at Las Guásimas, dislodging an entrenched Spanish force. In the fierce firefight at least a dozen Rough Riders were killed, one while standing next to Roosevelt. News reports of the victory reached American newspapers, and Roosevelt's star was on the rise. Awaiting more action, his troops struggled against the discomfort of the ferocious Cuban summer heat and command confusion that left them short of supplies. But they had achieved victory and morale was high.

The day of glory came for Roosevelt on July 1, in what he described as his "crowded hour" (see Document 1.10). Orders came to assault Kettle Hill, where a large Spanish force was dug in. Roosevelt led his troops through brush and high grass while Spanish bullets sliced at them with an eerie buzzing whistle. Roosevelt posed an easy target because he insisted on remaining mounted on his horse, Little Texas, as he urged his men forward. "I had intended to go into action on foot as at Las Guasimas, but the heat was so oppressive that I found I should be quite unable to run up and down the line and superintend matters unless I was mounted; and, moreover, when on horseback, I could see the men better and they could see me better" (Roosevelt 1926, 11:82). The Rough Riders routed the Spanish troops and took the hilltop, Roosevelt leading the charge and killing one of the last defenders with a pistol shot. With only a brief pause to survey the scene, Roosevelt spied American troops about a thousand yards away assaulting San Juan Hill. Shouting to his troops to follow, the colonel stormed down the slope to join in the attack. By nightfall San Juan Hill was also taken, and Roosevelt was able to look down from that height to the town of Santiago. The Americans laid siege to the city, and by July 17, the Spanish capitulated.

The colonel's exploits were duly noted by reporters in the field and much applauded at home. Exposed as he was and with men cut down all around him, Roosevelt came out of the battle with only a scratch where a bullet grazed his arm. This in a struggle in which the Rough Riders suffered among the heaviest casualties of any cavalry unit in Cuba. Destiny or dumb luck, Roosevelt came out of the war a national hero and in one piece.

When the war ended there were unexplained delays in evacuating the troops, many of whom were suffering from the heat, their wounds, and mosquito-borne disease. Roosevelt convinced a group of officers to send a letter to the president urging immediate evacuation to avoid disaster. Leaping over the chain of command enraged the generals and Secretary of War Alger and probably accounted for the refusal of the Army to recommend Roosevelt for the Medal of Honor. (That slight was not redressed until Congress made the award posthumously in January 2001.) A few days after the officers' protest, the troops boarded transports and sailed to the healthier climate of Montauk on Long Island. Roosevelt disembarked to a hero's welcome. His daring leadership and fearlessness in the face of enemy fire won him the enduring respect and loyalty of his men, and press coverage of those exploits made him a national hero.

GOVERNOR ROOSEVELT

While waiting out a period of quarantine at Montauk, his path to the governorship was being prepared. The Republican governor, Frank

Black, was embroiled in an embezzlement scandal, and the party turned to the war hero with a reputation for integrity to head the ticket in the upcoming elections (see Chapter 2). With the help of the Republican boss, Sen. Thomas C. Platt, Roosevelt won the nomination easily, and following a whistle-stop tour across the state accompanied by his Rough Riders, won a close contest in November.

For Platt, Roosevelt's victory did not come without regrets. From his experience in the state assembly, Roosevelt had learned to work with party leaders, even with some of less than model reputations, while still maintaining his own ethical standards and independence. Platt soon learned he could not control his own creation, and conflict between the boss and the governor came quickly. Platt chose a nominee for super-intendent of public works unacceptable to the new governor who was brash enough to reject the choice. Platt was furious, but Roosevelt was adroit. He submitted a slate of four names of acceptable nominees to Platt and invited him to choose. Platt took the option and the first crisis passed without serious damage. With this kind of skillful maneuver Roosevelt crafted a delicate but functional working relationship with Platt and the Republican machine. A realist in such associations Roosevelt consulted frequently with Platt, deferring to the boss when he could, resisting when necessary. The two men developed a mutual, if grudging respect; still there were inevitable clashes.

When the legislature convened in 1899, a proposal was made to levy a franchise tax on corporations holding monopolies in public service industries such as transportation and electric power. The governor thought the measure fair given the monopoly nature of the industries and the profits they reaped. Businessmen, especially in New York City, feared the influence of local political machines in setting the tax rates and per-haps demanding bribes for fair treatment. Platt, whose services to the cor-porations were much appreciated by the business community, was appalled and so informed the governor. In an exchange of letters the boss attacked and the governor defended (Morison 1951, 2:1004ff.). With Roosevelt's support and some agile political moves, the franchise tax passed. Roosevelt defended the law in his message to the legislature in January 1900. In the same message he advocated the regulation of public utilities and large cor-porations, conservation measures including the regulation of the lumber industry, worker compensation for job injuries, and improvements in the state civil service system (see Documents 1.11 and 1.12).

Roosevelt, who disdained organized reformers, was constructing a reform platform. Boss Platt was alarmed and he had no stomach for continuous battles with Roosevelt. The governor had to go. President McKinley's vice president, Garret Hobart, died in 1899, and Platt now thought a perfect place to exile Roosevelt was in the vice presidency. He set his machine to work to win that prize for his troublesome colleague. Roosevelt languished in the vice presidency, but not for long. In a matter of months tragedy transformed him from a powerless officer-in-waiting to president of the United States (see Chapter 2).

MR. PRESIDENT

The White House years were the happiest of Roosevelt's life. He enjoyed the trappings of office and loved being the center of attention, although he suffered criticism badly. He welcomed the power and used it with skill and imagination. Energized by crises, he usually remained cool under pressure; mistakes tended to come at calmer moments. He steered a course to guide the country into the new realities of modern industrial capitalism with a sense of justice and the common good, and to lead the nation to a new and larger role in world affairs (see Chapters 3 and 4). In the end he was pleased with the results and thought his victories far outweighed his losses. And when the time came he hated to leave.

The Roosevelts brought a new vitality to the presidential residence. The White House was, of course, filled with children and their requisite toys and pets. This was a new experience for the staff, unaccustomed to youthful presidents and their lively progeny. Although the president suspended his professional writing career while in office, he did continue many of the habits and pastimes he long enjoyed. He found welcome escape from official duties in occasional hunting trips, including one in Mississippi in 1902 that became the stuff of legend. Nearing the end of a disappointing hunt, one of his party managed to disable a small bear and offered it up for the president to shoot. Looking at the scrawny and injured animal, Roosevelt refused. News reports spread the story of his compassion, and before long, small stuffed bears appeared in the toyshops, and the "teddy bear" added more color to the Roosevelt mythology.

Sagamore Hill also provided a place of refuge from Washington, but not entirely from its pressures, as the work followed him to Oyster Bay.

When he could not escape the capital, he nevertheless insisted on a regimen of physical activity with tennis on the White House grounds; swims in the Potomac; horseback riding, often at galloping speeds that frightened companion riders; and sparring matches in a makeshift boxing ring in the mansion. Only Edith could restrain him and not always successfully. One of his boxing bouts cost him the sight of his left eye, a disability he carefully kept secret. He was keenly interested in new inventions and always retained an almost childlike hunger for new experiences. During the White House years he managed a short flight in a new and somewhat fragile flying machine. He delighted in the joyride, but he also immediately saw the military potential in flight and ordered the navy to study the possibilities. He was equally intrigued by his short trip in a small submarine, whose controls he managed as it traveled submerged in Long Island Sound.

White House social life was naturally full of formal dinners and entertainments for the diplomatic corps, the cabinet, and leading members of Congress and the judiciary. Many of his old friends like Lodge, John Hay, Henry Adams, and Cecil Spring-Rice visited, as on occasion did international celebrities, writers and artists like H. G. Wells and Augustus Saint-Gaudens.

When Roosevelt left the presidency behind, he was fifty years old and still physically fit and mentally sharp. Although initially pleased that his friend and protégé William Howard Taft succeeded him, he was deeply reluctant to abandon center stage. In the years that followed, the fortunate convergence of events, the lucky breaks, and the uncanny timing that marked his rise to power eluded him (see Chapter 6). He continued to draw much attention, but always in the wings. African hunting and Brazilian exploring filled his life with adventures that few men experience. He resumed his writing career to great applause and with welcome financial rewards. But his political star would not rise again. His 1912 break with Taft and the Republican Party he had so loyally served led him to champion a liberal agenda with which the country would take years to catch up. His durable obsession that drove him to repeated attacks on President Wilson, unattractive for its venom, was fueled by personal animosity and perhaps in part by his frustration at being out of the action.

Roosevelt never gave up the dream of a political rebirth, and even as he felt his health declining, he looked forward in his last days to the election of 1920. Given the political circumstances, it might indeed have been his year. But by 1919 the "strenuous life" he commended to all had taken its toll. The American presidency would have to wait for another Roosevelt.

BIBLIOGRAPHIC ESSAY

Theodore Roosevelt has been a popular subject for biographers. Among the large body of works, the most informative are some older works by those who knew him, and several excellent scholarly biographies published in recent years. These include the following: H. W. Brands, *T.R.: The Last Romantic* (New York: Basic Books, 1997); this careful study focuses principally on his political career. Kathleen Dalton, *Theodore Roosevelt: A Strenuous Life* (New York: Alfred A. Knopf, 2002), the most recent biography, pays special attention to the influence of women in Roosevelt's personal and political life. William Henry Harbaugh, *The Life and Times of Theodore Roosevelt* (New York: Collier Books, 1963), is among the most scholarly of the biographies and still very useful. Nathan Miller, *Theodore Roosevelt: A Life* (New York: William Morrow, 1992), is a generally sympathetic biography. Edmund Morris, *The Rise of Theodore Roosevelt* (New York: Ballantine Books, 1979), the solidly researched and engagingly written first volume of a projected three-volume biography, recounts Roosevelt's life up to the moment he became president. Edmund Morris, *Theodore Rex* (New York: Random House, 2001), the second volume of the projected three, is a finely detailed history of the presidential years. Aloysius A. Norton, *Theodore Roosevelt* (Boston: Twayne, 1980), is a helpful source on Roosevelt's career as a writer. Henry Pringle, *Theodore Roosevelt: A Biography* (1931; reprint, New York: Harcourt Brace, 1956), a prize-winning biography dating from the 1930s, often criticizes the president's policies and politics. William Roscoe Thayer, *Theodore Roosevelt: An Intimate Biography* (New York: Grosset and Dunlap, 1919), is a sympathetic treatment by a friend of forty years. Owen Wister, *Roosevelt: The Story of a Friendship* (New York: Macmillan, 1930), offers the intimate details and personal insights of a Harvard classmate.

Also helpful concerning the prepresidential years are Jay Stuart Berman, *Police Administration and Progressive Reform: Theodore Roosevelt as Police Commissioner of New York* (Westport, Conn.: Greenwood Press, 1987); G. Wallace Chessman, *Governor Theodore Roosevelt: The Albany Apprenticeship*

(Cambridge: Harvard University Press, 1965); Paul H. Jeffers, *Commissioner Roosevelt: The Story of Theodore Roosevelt and the New York City Police, 1895–1897* (New York: J. Wiley and Sons, 1994); Virgil C. Jones, *Roosevelt's Rough Riders* (Garden City, N.Y.: Doubleday, 1971). David McCullough provides an intimate history of the Roosevelt family before the presidency in *Mornings on Horseback* (New York: Simon and Schuster, 1981).

Document 1.1   *The Naval War of 1812* (1881)

While still a student at Harvard, Roosevelt began his study of the navy in the War of 1812 and completed The Naval War of 1812 *in the year after graduation. The book was well received by critics and remained an important and respected source on the subject. Roosevelt later joined with Henry Cabot Lodge and Alfred Thayer Mahan to lobby for a stronger navy for the United States, and his interest in a strong navy remained with him for the rest of his career. This excerpt describes the famous battle between the USS Con-stitution (Old Ironsides) and HMS Guerriere.*

On August 2d the *Constitution* made sail from Boston and stood to the eastward, in hopes of falling in with some of the British cruisers. She was unsuccessful, however, and met nothing. Then she ran down to the Bay of Fundy, steered along the coast of Nova Scotia, and thence toward Newfoundland, and finally took her station off Cape Race in the Gulf of St. Lawrence, where she took and burned two brigs of little value. On the 15th she recaptured an American brig from the British sloop-ship *Avenger*, though the latter escaped; Captain Hull manned his prize and sent her in. He then sailed southward, and on the night of the 18th spoke a Salem privateer which gave him news of a British frigate to the south; thither he stood, and at 2 P.M. on the 19th, in lat. 410 30′ N. and 550 W., made out a large sail bearing E. S. E. and to leeward, which proved to be his old acquaintance, the frigate *Guerriere,* Captain Dacres. It was a cloudy day and the wind was blowing fresh from the northwest. The *Guerriere* was standing by the wind on the starboard tack, under easy canvas; she hauled up her courses, took in her topgallantsails, and at 4.30 backed her maintopsail. Hull then very deliberately began to shorten sail, taking in topgallantsail, staysails, and flying jib, sending down the royal yards and putting another reef in the topsails. Soon the Englishman hoisted three ensigns, when the American also set his colors, one at each masthead, and one at the mizzen peak.

The *Constitution* now ran down with the wind nearly aft. The *Guerriere* was on the starboard tack, and at 5 o'clock opened with her weather guns, the shot falling short, then wore round and fired her port broadside, of which two shots struck her opponent, the rest passing over and through her rigging. As the British frigate again wore to open with her starboard battery, the *Constitution* yawed a little and fired two or three of her port bow guns. Three or four times the *Guerriere* repeated this maneuver, wearing and firing alternate broadsides, but with little or no effect, while the *Constitution* yawed as often to avoid being raked, and occasionally fired one of her bow guns. This continued nearly an hour, as the vessels were very far apart when the action began, hardly any loss or damage being inflicted by either party. At 6.00 the *Guerriere* bore up and ran off under her topsails and jib, with the wind almost astern, a little on her port quarter; when the Constitution set her maintopgallantsail and foresail, and at 6.05 closed within half pistol-shot distance on her adversary's port beam. Immediately a furious cannonade opened, each ship firing as the guns bore.

By the time the ships were fairly abreast, at 6.20, the *Constitution* shot away the *Guerriere's* mizzenmast, which fell over the starboard quarter, knocking a large hole in the counter, and bringing the ship round against her helm. Hitherto she had suffered very greatly and the *Constitution* hardly at all. The latter, finding that she was ranging ahead, put her helm aport and then luffed short round her enemy's bows, delivering a heavy raking fire with the starboard guns and shooting away the *Guerriere's* mainyard. Then she wore and again passed her adversary's bows, raking with her port guns. The mizzenmast of the *Guerriere,* dragging in the water, had by this time pulled her bow round till the wind came on her starboard quarter; and so near were the two ships that the Englishman's bowsprit passed diagonally over the *Constitution's* quarter-deck, and as the latter ship fell off it got foul of her mizzen-rigging, and the vessels then lay with the *Guerriere's* starboard bow against the *Constitution's* port, or lee quarter-gallery. The Englishman's bow guns played havoc with Captain Hull's cabin, setting fire to it; but the flames were soon extinguished by Lieutenant Hoffmann. On both sides the boarders were called away; the British ran forward, but Captain Dacres relinquished the idea of attacking when he saw the crowds of men on the American's decks. Meanwhile, on the *Constitution,* the boarders and marines gathered aft, but such a heavy sea was running that they could not get on the *Guerriere*. Both sides suffered heavily from the closeness of the musketry fire; indeed, almost the entire loss on the *Constitution* occurred at this juncture. As Lieutenant Bush, of the marines, sprang upon the taffrail to leap on the enemy's decks, a British marine shot him dead; Mr. Morris, the first lieutenant, and Mr. Alwyn, the master, had also both leaped on the taffrail, and both were at the same moment wounded by the musketry fire. On the *Guerriere* the loss was far heavier, almost all the men on the forecastle being picked off. Captain Dacres himself was shot in the back and severely wounded by one of the American mizzentopmen, while he was standing on the starboard forecastle hammocks cheering on his crew; two of the lieutenants and the master were also shot down. The ships gradually worked round till the wind was again on the port quarter, when they separated, and the *Guerriere's* foremast and mainmast at once went by the board, and fell over on the starboard side, leaving her a defenseless hulk, rolling her main-deck guns into the water. At 6.30 the *Constitution* hauled aboard her tacks, ran off a little distance to the eastward, and lay to. Her braces and standing and running rigging were much cut up and some of the spars wounded, but a few minutes sufficed to repair damages, when Captain Hull stood under his adversary's lee, and the latter at once struck, at 7.00 P.M., just two hours after she had fired the first shot. On the part of the *Constitution*, however, the actual fighting, exclusive of six or eight guns fired during the first hour, while closing, occupied less than 30 minutes. The tonnage and metal of the combatants have already been referred to. The *Constitution* had, as already said, about 456 men aboard, while of the *Guerriere's* crew, 267 prisoners were received aboard the *Constitution;* deducting 10 who were Americans and would not fight, and adding the 15 killed outright, we get 272; 28 men were absent in prizes. The loss of the *Constitution* included Lieutenant William S. Bush, of the marines, and six seamen killed, and her first lieutenant Charles Morris, Master John C. Alwyn, four seamen, and one marine, wounded. Total, seven killed and seven wounded. Almost all this loss occurred when the ships came foul, and was due to the *Guerriere's* musketry and the two guns in her bridle-ports.

Source: Theodore Roosevelt, *The Works of Theodore Roosevelt,* national ed. (New York: Charles Scribner's Sons, 1926), 6:75–79.

Document 1.2   Investigation of Judge Westbrook, Speech in the New York Assembly, April 6, 1882

Although still a freshman legislator and only in his early twenties, Roosevelt took on the financial and political bigwigs of New York by insisting on the investigation of judicial fraud and collusion with corrupt business interests. Against the odds he won an investigation of charges against Judge T. R. Westbrook of the State Supreme Court. Eventually, well-placed bribes led to a report exonerating the judge, but the accompanying newspaper publicity broadcast Roosevelt's name across the state as a courageous young legislator.

Mr. Speaker, I have introduced these resolutions fully aware that it was an exceedingly important and serious task I was undertaking, and fully aware it would need proofs to substantiate before I would have a right to ask the gentlemen of this House to pass these resolutions. I do not make them on such general statements made in the newspapers. I make them on specific charges against the gentlemen named in the resolution.

These suits were brought as you all know against a fraudulent company—the Manhattan Elevated Railroad. That was a company that had a nominal stock of two million dollars—really of one hundred thousand dollars—that is, it possessed but five per cent of its nominal wealth. An agreement was concluded by that company with two other bonafide companies by which they purchased the right to run their own roads—I am quoting from the opinion of the present attorney-general Russell—they purchased the franchise of running their own roads; that is, they purchased nothing. This whole transaction was stigmatized by the Honorable Judge James Emott, of New York, in August of 1880, as a fraud pure and simple. The men who were mainly concerned in this fraud are known throughout New York as men whose financial dishonesty is a matter of common notoriety. I make that statement deliberately; that the three or four wealthy stock-gamblers who are interested in those roads were men who would barely be trusted in financial operations by any reputable business man.

Under such circumstances, almost confessed fraud having been perpetrated on a number of the stockholders by these three or four directors, it would have behooved the judiciary and the gentlemen who held the highest office in the gift of the people of this state to have handled it with peculiar care. A suit was brought in May last, I think, by the attorney-general against the Manhattan corporation. Mr. Burton Harrison was employed to investigate the affair. His report was absolute and conclusive that it was a fraudulent corporation, that it had no legal existence. It could have none when only five per cent of its stock had been paid in, and for a corporation that had only five per cent of its stock paid in to assume an additional debt of thirteen million dollars and to shift that on the community at large, was an absolute fraud. Under such circumstances the attorney-general acted properly in bringing a suit declaring the corporation to be illegal. Without any reason he suddenly discontinued this suit, and after two days brings another admitting the legality of the corporation and merely declaring that it was insolvent, an objection that he knew would be much easier over-come than the one first raised. The reason for discontinuing that suit has never been explained. It never ought to have been discontinued. It was a gigantic fraud and ought to have been stopped. It was an absolute wrong against the interests of the people for the attorney-general to change his suit and at the same time to allow any set of wealthy swindlers to escape the consequences of their misdeeds. One of the men employed by the attorney-general was also employed by the very man he was looking after, I believe, by Jay Gould.

Judge Westbrook's share in the transaction did not come in until about June 13, when the suit was brought before him. He then expressed in his opinion strongly and emphatically that it was a swindle from the begin-ning. These are all matters of record; they are no newspaper charges; you can see them from the recorded proceedings of the court. Then there was a petition to have receivers appointed. Four men were named by the pres-ident of the Manhattan Company, the very company whose issue was in existence, to be receivers. After twenty-four hours' delay—practically after only three or four hours delay—the judge appointed as receivers two men, one of whom was the vice-president of the Wabash Railroad, of which Jay Gould was president, and who was reputed to be Mr. Gould's clerk; the other was one of Gould's lawyers: a man who had, early in the season, pro-cured an injunction against the city to prohibit it from collecting taxes from these railroads. The fact that the taxes had not been collected was one of the grounds on which the suit for dissolving the corporation was brought. In other words, the judge appointed a receiver to take care of the interest of the people who had been employed to prevent the people from getting their taxes from the company. Those two receivers ought never to have been appointed by any judge who cared for the purity of the office which he fined. At the same time the judge had appointed one of his relatives to take a certain position in the affairs of the company. It is not of record that he ever performed any work. He received one thousand dollars. This statement is made on the authority of a man who can be subpoenaed and brought before the committee to testify under oath to what he said. It is no loose statement whatever.

At the same time the receivers petitioned for leave to issue certificates of indebtedness. The judge granted that petition in Gould's office; while holding court in the office of one of the men whom common repute holds, and as I think holds correctly, was nothing but a wealthy shark, especially in the attitude he had taken toward the people about these very suits. Those certificates were issued on such terms as to make it impossible they could be taken up. The Manhattan stock at that time was only eighty-six per cent. The judge allowed these certificates, to the extent of one million dollars, to be issued, but all should be taken at six per cent or none be taken; all be taken at par or none be taken. It was an absolute impossibility they should be taken up. The issue of the order was simply ridiculous.

The affair went on, and on the 21st of October the judge declared, in a speech, that the corporation was a swindle—declared it emphatically, without any reserve. Four days after, he does not write, but telegraphs, an order allowing the road to go out of the hands of the receivers back into the hands of the Manhattan Company, which by that time had become synonymous with getting into the hands of Jay Gould, Cyrus W. Field, and Russell Sage. That is, four days after he said it was a swindle, he puts the whole road in the hands of the swindlers. That is an absolute fact, and can be verified by matters of record. . . .

We have a right to demand that our judiciary should be kept beyond reproach, and we have a right to demand that, if we find men against whom there is not only suspicion, but almost a certainty that they have had collusion with men whose interest was in conflict with those of the public, they shall at least be required to bring positive facts with which to prove there has not been such collusion, and they ought themselves to have been the first to demand such an investigation. It was a matter of great astonishment to me that during the three months that have elapsed such an investigation has not been asked. I was aware it ought to have been done by a man of more experience than myself, but as nobody else chose to demand it I certainly would in the interest of the Commonwealth of New York. I shall move to amend my resolution by allowing the committee to employ a stenographer and summon witnesses before them at a sitting held in New York. This is a most important investigation and it should be treated with due weight. I hope my resolution will prevail.

Source: Theodore Roosevelt, *The Works of Theodore Roosevelt,* national ed. (New York: Charles Scribner's Sons, 1926), 14:7–11.

Document 1.3   The New York Civil-Service Reform Bill, Assembly Speech, April 9, 1883

Often an irritant to his own party leadership in Albany in advocating reforms, Roosevelt cooperated with Governor Grover Cleveland in working toward the passage of a state civil service law. When Roosevelt became governor himself in 1898, he worked to strengthen the original legislation.

The bill merely proposes to do for the city of New York what the Pendleton bill has done for the United States. Its aim is to take the civil service out of the political arena, where it now lies festering, a reproach and a hissing to all decent men, and the most terrible source of corruption that exists in the city; and to apply to the municipal government the same business principles that obtain in every well-conducted private business. To relieve us from the evils under which we labor owing to the present system of appointment, for partisan reasons only, it is absolutely necessary that appointments should be made only after competitive examinations. This is the only way in which to shake off the hold that corrupt political rings and chieftains now have on the public through the civil service, which they and their predecessors have debauched until it has become a crying scandal. To the assertion that injustice may be done by these competitive appointments, I can only answer that for everyone such there are a hundred far grosser evils under the present system, and more than this.

My object in pushing this measure is less to raise the standard of the civil service than it is to take the office-holders as a body out of politics. It is a good thing to raise the character of our public employees, but it is better still to take out of politics the vast band of hired mercenaries whose very existence depends on their success, and who can almost always in the end overcome the efforts of men whose only care is to secure a pure and honest government, for in such a contest the discipline of regulars, fighting literally for their means of livelihood, is sure in the end to overcome the spasmodic ardor of volunteers.

The existence of these men as an organized body, existing only for their own selfish interests, is a standing menace to our free institutions, and it must and shall be removed before the people can decide the great public questions that arise purely on their merits, untrammeled by the base considerations that now surround them. And the law must apply to both parties alike. One party practicing it while the other did not would afford a parallel to a sparring-match in which one man struck foul blows and the other did not. The man who fought foul would win. My purpose is to make both parties fight fair, and when they do so the people will then, and then only, be able to decide each measure only with regard to the effect it will have on the welfare of the country.

Source: Theodore Roosevelt, *The Works of Theodore Roosevelt,* national ed. (New York: Charles Scribner's Sons, 1926), 14:23–24.

Document 1.4   The Independents Who Would Not Bolt, Speech to Young Republican Club of Brooklyn, October 18, 1884

Roosevelt often championed reform ideas during his career, but with the exception of the special circumstances in 1912, he always considered himself a staunch party man. He found a way to work with the party machine even when some of its operators were less than savory characters. In this speech he expressed his loyalty to the party nominee and refused to join the "Mugwump" revolt against the former senator James G. Blaine.

I am glad, for many reasons, that my first speech in the present campaign should be made under the auspices of the young Republicans of Brooklyn, who have won for themselves so honorable a name for their upright and fearless independence, and who have yet had the good sense to show that, though Independents, they are emphatically and distinctly Republicans, and that they mean to reform and not to destroy the party to which they belong.

There is nothing that I have more regretted in the present campaign than the fact that many of those with whom we were proud to act in time past, have now felt obliged to go over to the camp of those who are, as we firmly believe, the most bitter foes of the very principles which Independent Republicanism has so stoutly upheld. Beyond question, many of our brother Independents have done what they conscientiously believe to be right; most certainly. We cannot question the honesty of purpose and the sincerity of motive that actuate men like Carl Schurz, George William Curtis, and Horace White; but I think these gentlemen have been drawn into a course of action which, in the end, they must most bitterly regret, and into contact and companionship with men whom they must heartily despise, and I think they themselves would be among the first to see the evil results to the whole community that would inevitably follow in the fortunately exceedingly improbable event of their being able to accomplish the defeat of the Republican nominee.

One feature of their conduct is, however, certainly open to criticism, and that is the way they have attacked those of their fellow Republicans who have remained loyal to the party. I do not object to their considering themselves the salt of the earth, but I beg leave to differ from them when they assure us that the rest of the Republican world has absolutely lost its savor. . . . Without an exception all of the Independent Republicans who accomplished so much at Albany during the last two or three winters are loyal to the Republican party; and almost without an exception the same statement holds true of the band of Independents or Edmunds men who at the last State convention, held at Utica, achieved a victory for the cause of Independent Republicanism which is absolutely unparalleled in our political annals. . . .

We are not electing an irresponsible autocrat; we are merely selecting a President who is the servant of the people, and is more especially the servant of the party that elects him. I know that Mr. Blaine, if elected President, must represent the honesty and must obey the will of the mass of honest and upright Republicans who have nominated him and who will elect him. . . .

Source: Theodore Roosevelt, *The Works of Theodore Roosevelt,* national ed. (New York: Charles Scribner's Sons, 1926), 14:41–43.

Document 1.5   Hunting Trips of a Ranch Man, Excerpt from *The Lordly Buffalo* (1885)

With a prodigious memory and a passion for writing, Roosevelt let few important experiences in his life escape his pen. His love of hunting and of the outdoor life in general provided the topics of many books and essays for popular journals. In this excerpt he laments the destruction of the buffalo but cannot resist the temptation to experience the thrill of the hunt.

Gone forever are the mighty herds of the lordly buffalo. A few solitary individuals and small bands are still to be found scattered here and there in the wilder parts of the plains; and, though most of these will be very soon destroyed, others will for some years fight off their doom and lead a precarious existence either in remote and almost desert portions of the country near the Mexican frontier, or else in the wildest and most inaccessible fastnesses of the Rocky Mountains; but the great herds, that for the first three-quarters of this century formed the distinguishing and characteristic feature of the Western plains, have vanished forever.

It is only about a hundred years ago that the white man, in his march westward, first encroached upon the lands of the buffalo, for these animals had never penetrated in any number to the Appalachian chain of mountains. Indeed, it was after the beginning of the century before the inroads of the whites upon them grew at all serious. Then, though constantly driven westward, the diminution in their territory, if sure, was at least slow, although growing progressively more rapid. Less than a score of years ago the great herds, containing many millions of individuals, ranged over a vast expanse of country that stretched in an unbroken line from near Mexico to far into British America; in fact, over almost all the plains that are now known as the cattle region. But since that time their destruction has gone on with appalling rapidity and thoroughness; and the main factors in bringing it about have been the railroads, which carried hordes of hunters into the land and gave them means to transport their spoils to market. Not quite twenty years since, the range was broken in two, and the buffalo herds in the middle slaughtered or thrust aside; and thus there resulted two ranges, the northern and the southern. The latter was the larger but, being more open to the hunters, was the sooner to be depopulated; and the last of the great southern herds was destroyed in 1878, though scattered bands escaped and wandered into the desolate wastes to the southwest. Meanwhile, equally savage war was waged on the northern herds, and five years later the last of these was also destroyed or broken up. The bulk of this slaughter was done in the dozen years from 1872 to 1883; never before in all history were so many large wild animals of one species slain in so short a space of time.

The extermination of the buffalo has been a veritable tragedy of the animal world. . . .While the slaughter of the buffalo has been in places needless and brutal, and while it is greatly to be regretted that the species is likely to become extinct, and while, moreover, from a purely selfish standpoint, many, including myself, would rather see it continue to exist as the chief feature in the unchanged life of the Western wilderness; yet, on the other hand it must be remembered that its continued existence in any numbers was absolutely incompatible with anything but a very sparse settlement of the country; and that its destruction was the condition precedent upon the advance of white civilization in the West, and was a positive boon to the more thrifty and industrious frontiersmen. . . . From the standpoint of humanity at large, the extermination of the buffalo has been a blessing. The many have been benefitted by it; and I suppose the comparatively few of us who would have preferred the continuance of the old order of things, merely for the sake of our own selfish enjoyment, have no right to complain. . . .

One September I determined to take a short trip after bison. . . .

Shortly after midday we left the creek bottom, and skirted a ridge of broken buttes, cut up by the gullies and winding ravines, in whose bottoms grew bunch-grass. While passing near the mouth and to leeward of one of these ravines both ponies threw up their heads and snuffed the air, turning their muzzles toward the head of the gully. Feeling sure that they had smelt some wild beast, either a bear or a buffalo, I slipped off my pony and ran quickly but cautiously up along the valley. Before I had gone a hundred yards, I noticed in the soft soil at the bottom the round prints of a bison's hoofs; and immediately afterward got a glimpse of the animal himself, as he fed slowly up the course of the ravine, some distance ahead of me. The wind was just right, and no ground could have been better for stalking. Hardly needing to bend down, I walked up behind a small sharp-crested hillock and, peeping over, there below me, not fifty yards off, was a great bison bull. He was walking along, grazing as he walked. His glossy fall coat was in fine trim and shone in the rays of the sun, while his pride of bearing showed him to be in the lusty vigor of his prime. As I rose above the crest of the hill, he held up his head and cocked his tail to the air. Before he could go off, I put the bullet in behind his shoulder. The wound was an almost immediately fatal one, yet with surprising agility for so large and heavy an animal, he bounded up the opposite side of the ravine, heedless of two more balls, both of which went into his flank and ranged forward, and disappeared over the ridge at a lumbering gallop, the blood pouring from his mouth and nostrils. We knew he could not go far, and trotted leisurely along on his bloody trail; and in the next gully we found him stark dead, lying almost on his back, having pitched over the side when he tried to go down it. His head was a remarkably fine one, even for a fall buffalo. He was lying in a very bad position, and it was most tedious and tiresome work to cut it off and pack it out. The flesh of a cow or calf is better eating than is that of a bull; but the so-called hump meat—that is, the strip of steak on each side of the backbone—is excellent and tender and juicy. Buffalo meat is with difficulty to be distinguished from ordinary beef. At any rate, the flesh of this bull tasted uncommonly good to us, for we had been without fresh meat for a week; and until a healthy, active man has been without it for some little time, he does not know how positively and almost painfully hungry for flesh he becomes, no matter how much farinaceous food he may have. And the very toil I had been obliged to go through, in order to procure the head, made me feel all the prouder of it when at last it was in my possession.

Source: Theodore Roosevelt, *The Works of Theodore Roosevelt,* national ed. (New York: Charles Scribner's Sons, 1926), 1:185–206.

Document 1.6   Ranch Life and the Hunting Trail, Excerpt from *The Home Ranch* (1888)

Abandoning politics in late 1884, Roosevelt returned to his Elkhorn ranch near the town of Medora (in what is now North Dakota) to live the life of a prairie cattleman. He wrote of his experiences as a rancher with obvious pleasure. His eye for detail produced images of life in the West that drew his readers into a sense of sharing his experiences and kept his writings in demand.

My home-ranch lies on both sides of the Little Missouri, the nearest ranchman above me being about twelve, and the nearest below me about ten, miles distant. The general course of the stream here is northerly, but, while flowing through my ranch, it takes a great westerly reach of some three miles, walled in, as always, between chains of steep, high bluffs half a mile or more apart. The stream twists down through the valley in long sweeps, leaving oval wooded bottoms, first on one side and then on the other; and in an open glade among the thick-growing timber stands the long, low house of hewn logs.

Just in front of the ranch veranda is a line of old cotton-woods that shade it during the fierce heats of summer, rendering it always cool and pleasant. But a few feet beyond these trees comes the cut-off bank of the river, through whose broad, sandy bed the shallow stream winds as if lost, except when a freshet fills it from brim to brim with foaming yellow water. The bluffs that wall in the river-valley curve back in semicircles, rising from its alluvial bottom generally as abrupt cliffs, but often as steep, grassy slopes that lead up to great level plateaus; and the line is broken every mile or two by the entrance of a coulee, or dry creek, whose head branches may be twenty miles back. Above us, where the river comes round the bend, the valley is very narrow, and the high buttes bounding it rise, sheer and barren, into scalped hill peaks and naked knife-blade ridges.

The other buildings stand in the same open glade with the ranch-house, the dense growth of cottonwoods and matted, thorny underbrush making a wall all about, through which we have chopped our wagon roads and trodden out our own bridle-paths. The cattle have now trampled down this brush a little, but deer still lie in it, only a couple of hundred yards from the house; and from the door sometimes in the evening one can see them peer out into the open, or make their way down, timidly and cautiously, to drink at the river. The stable, sheds, and other outbuildings, with the hay-ricks and the pens for such cattle as we bring in during winter are near the house; the patch of fenced garden land is on the edge of the woods; and near the middle of the glade stands the high, circular horse corral, with a snubbing-post in the center, and a wing built out from one side of the gate entrance, so that the saddle band can be driven in without trouble. As it is very hard to work cattle where there is much brush, the larger cow corral is some four miles off on an open bottom.

A ranchman's life is certainly a very pleasant one, albeit generally varied with plenty of hardship and anxiety. Although occasionally he passes days of severe toil—for example, if he goes on the round-up he works as hard as any of his men—yet he no longer has to undergo the monotonous drudgery attendant upon the tasks of the cowboy or of the apprentice in the business. His fare is simple; but, if he chooses, it is good enough. Many ranches are provided with nothing at all but salt pork, canned goods, and bread; indeed, it is a curious fact that in traveling through the cow country it is often impossible to get any milk or butter; but this is only because the owners or managers are too lazy to take enough trouble to insure their own comfort. We ourselves always keep up two or three cows, choosing such as are naturally tame, and so we invariably have plenty of milk and, when there is time for churning, a good deal of butter. We also keep hens, which, in spite of the damaging inroads of hawks, bobcats, and foxes, supply us with eggs, and in time of need, when our rifles have failed to keep us in game, with stewed, roast, or fried chicken also. From our garden we get potatoes, and unless drought, frost, or grasshoppers interfere (which they do about every second year), other vegetables as well. For fresh meat we depend chiefly upon our prowess as hunters. . . .

A ranchman's work is, of course, free from much of the sameness attendant upon that of a mere cowboy. One day he will ride out with his men among the cattle, or after strayed horses; the next he may hunt, so as to keep the ranch in meat; then he can make the tour of his outlying camps; or, again, may join one of the round-ups for a week or two, perhaps keeping with it the entire time it is working. On occasions he will have a good deal of spare time on his hands, which, if he chooses, he can spend in reading or writing. If he cares for books, there will be many a worn volume in the primitive little sitting-room, with its log walls and huge fireplace; but after a hard day's work a man will not read much, but will rock to and fro in the flickering firelight, talking sleepily over his success in the day's chase and the difficulty he has had with the cattle; or else may simply lie stretched at full length on the elk hides and wolf skins in front of the hearthstone, listening in drowsy silence to the roar and crackle of the blazing logs and to the moaning of the wind outside.

Source: Theodore Roosevelt, *The Works of Theodore Roosevelt,* national ed. (New York: Charles Scribner's Sons, 1926), 1:294–296, 305–306.

Document 1.7   Candidate for Mayor, Campaign Speech, October 15, 1886

On Roosevelt's return from Dakota, he was persuaded by Republican leaders in New York City to make a run for mayor. Given the strength of the Democrats and the great respect commanded by their candidate, Abram S. Hewitt, Roosevelt knew the odds of victory were long. He had hoped, however, to do better than his weak third-place finish behind radical theorist Henry George.

The other day I happened to have a few spare moments, and I read the speech which Mr. Hewitt made at the meeting of the United Democrats. I could not read it before, for until the other day I had been occupied in reading the printed and lengthy letters which have been passing between him and Mr. George, and was struck by his statement, made with that modesty and diffidence for which he is noted, that every honest and respectable voter in the city of New York would vote for him. Now, if I am to judge by the faces of those who make up this meeting to-night, Mr. Abram Hewitt will find on the 3d of next November that the criminals of this city have polled an extraordinarily large and, what is more, a winning vote.

Gentlemen, I come before you on two distinct issues. I take direct issue with each of my competitors—one with one of them and one with the other. We hold in this campaign that we are not only the representatives of law and order, but we are also the representatives of radical municipal reform. At the same meeting to which I have already alluded Mayor Grace said that his chief objection to me as a candidate for mayor was that I am too radical a reformer. I am perfectly willing, gentlemen, to take that issue and make the fight on it alone, and I believe that you, all of you, think that there is a need of reform, radical reform, in the City Hall.

We have heard for the past ten days the wailing of Mr. Hewitt's managers, appealing for our votes in support of their candidate. This is a curious political alliance. We see the Tammany Hall heelers clasping hands with the heelers of the County Democracy, aided by that dull, feeble Chadband faction represented by *The Evening Post*. I read in a recent issue of that truthful sheet that we did not take issue with Henry George. That is not a correct statement. We emphatically take radical issue with Mr. George, and our past record entitles us to stand up in the fight against that theorist better than the Democrats. The fact is we don't fear the drawing away from us of any Republican votes by the George campaign. It is the Hewitt managers who fear that George will carry many Democratic votes out of their ranks. They know that he has shattered their machinery, and they hope by noise and clamor to impress the timid good with the belief that by voting for me they will elect Mr. George. We say that we stand directly against George's theories, and we are antagonistic to the practices of the supporters of Hewitt.

Gentlemen, we all know how we are served by the supporters of Mr. Hewitt who now hold office, many of whom hold their places, not because they serve the people, but because they serve some local political boss. We know many who are retained in office on account of their ability to influence an election or control a political convention. The time for radical reform has arrived, and if I am elected you will have it.

No honest and no competent city official need fear my election. I was partly instrumental in making the civil-service laws, and you may rest entirely assured that if I am elected mayor I shall see to it that they are strictly enforced. All sinecurists, dishonest and incompetent city officials have cause—very great cause—to fear my election. I am a strong party man myself, but if I am elected, as I feel I shall be, and I find a public servant who is dishonest, I will chop his head off if he is the highest Republican in this municipality.

I would like also to take issue emphatically with Mr. George when he says that he would make a better mayor for the working men than I would. I am, if I am anything, an American. I am an American from the crown of my head to the soles of my feet. If I take office I will take it as a freeman, as an equal to my fellow freemen, to serve loyally, honestly, and conscientiously every citizen of this great Commonwealth. I don't care what may be his politics, I don't care what may be his religion, I don't care what may be his color. I don't care who he is, so long as he is honest he shall be served by me. All I ask of him is that he discharge faithfully the duties of an American citizen, and I am his representative. If I am chosen I will have one ambition—which is lawful and honorable—to so comport myself as to earn the right to the respect and esteem of every citizen of the city of New York. I am the candidate for mayor nominated and indorsed by the citizens and the Republican party. If I am made mayor, I will be mayor of the city of New York.

Gentlemen, I won't detain you much longer, but I wish to state again that we stand against George on account of his theories and against Hewitt on account of the practices of his followers. We will not only try to preserve law and order, but we will endeavor to effect radical reform in the City Hall. We will show favor to no one party, but treat all parties alike as they stand. I will remain strong for my own party, yet shall see the chief magistracy used to promote no single party, but the welfare of the entire city. I don't know of any more promises which I can make. I will let my past record serve as an earnest for what I shall do in the future.

Source: Theodore Roosevelt, *The Works of Theodore Roosevelt*, national ed. (New York: Charles Scribner's Sons, 1926), 14:72–74.

Document 1.8   The Enforcement of the Sunday Drinking Law, *Forum*, September 1895

One of Roosevelt's least successful initiatives as New York City police commissioner was his attempt to enforce the Sunday closing law governing city saloons. The law had been largely ignored, but Roosevelt believed if it remained on the statute books it ought to be enforced. His effort earned him the hostility of leaders of both political parties, who worried about the backlash from their thirsty constituents. He defended himself in an essay in the popular magazine Forum.

The question at issue in New York City just at present is much more important than the question of a more or less liberal Sunday excise law. The question is as to whether public officials are to be true to their oaths of office, and see that the law is administered in good faith. The police board stands squarely in favor of the honest enforcement of the law. Our opponents of every grade and of every shade of political belief take the position that government officials, who have sworn to enforce the law, shall violate their oaths whenever they think it will please a sufficient number of the public to make the violation worth while. It seems almost incredible that in such a controversy it should be necessary to do more than state in precise terms both propositions. Yet it evidently is necessary. Not only have the wealthy brewers and liquor-sellers, whose illegal business was interfered with, venomously attacked the commissioners for enforcing the law; but they have been joined by the major portion of the New York press and by the very large mass of voters who put the gratification of appetite above all law. These men have not dared to meet the issue squarely and fairly. They have tried to befog it and to raise false issues. They have especially sought to change the fight from the simple principle of the enforcement of law into a contest as to the extent of the restrictions which should properly be placed on the sale of liquors. They do not deny that we have enforced the law with fairness and impartiality, but they insist that we ought to connive at lawbreaking.

Very many friends of the reform movement, and very many politicians of the party to which I belong, have become frightened at the issue thus raised; and the great bulk of the machine leaders of the Democracy profess to be exultant at it, and to see in it a chance for securing their own return to power. Senator Hill and Tammany in particular have loudly welcomed the contest. On the other hand, certain Republican politicians and certain Republican newspapers have contended that our action in honestly doing our duty as public officers of the municipality of New York will jeopardize the success of the Republican party, with which I, the president of the board, am identified. The implication is that for the sake of the Republican party, a party of which I am a very earnest member, I should violate my oath of office and connive at lawbreaking. To this I can only answer that I am far too good a Republican to be willing to believe that the honest enforcement of law by a Republican can redound to the discredit of the party to which he belongs. This applies as much to the weak-kneed municipal reformers who fear that we have hurt the cause of municipal reform as it does to the Republicans. . . .

The position of Senator Hill and the Tammany leaders, when reduced to its simplest terms, is merely the expression of the conviction that it does not pay to be honest. They believe that advocacy of lawbreaking is a good card before the people. As one of their newspapers frankly put it, the machine Democratic leaders intend to bid for the support of the voters on the ground that their party "will not enforce laws" which are distasteful to any considerable section of the public. . . .

All that we did was to take a law which was very much alive, but which had been used only for purposes of blackmail, and to do away entirely with the blackmail feature by enforcing it equitably as regards all persons. Looked at soberly, this scarcely seems a revolutionary proceeding; and still less does it seem like one which needs an elaborate justification. . . .

The clamor that followed our action was deafening; and it was also rather amusing in view of the fact that all we had done was to perform our obvious duty. At the outset the one invariable statement with which we were met was that we could not enforce the law. A hundred—aye, a thousand—times we were told by big politicians, by newspapers, by private individuals, that the excise law could not be enforced. . . .

The one all-important element in good citizenship in our country is obedience to law. The greatest crimes that can be committed against our government are to put on the statute-books, or to allow to remain there, laws that are not meant to be enforced, and to fail to enforce the laws that exist.

Mr. Jacob A. Riis, in a recent article, has put this in words so excellent that I cannot refrain from quoting them:

"That laws are made to break, not to obey, is a fact of which the street takes early notice, and shapes its conduct accordingly. Respect for the law is not going to spring from disregard of it. . . . We need an era of enforcement of law—less of pretense—more of purpose."

The police board is doing its best to bring about precisely such an era.

Source: Theodore Roosevelt, *The Works of Theodore Roosevelt,* national ed. (New York: Charles Scribner's Sons, 1926), 14:183–191.

Document 1.9   Washington's Forgotten Maxim, A Call for Military Strength, Address to the Naval War College, June 1897

An advocate of a stronger navy ever since his study of the War of 1812 (see Document 1.1), Roosevelt used his position as President William McKinley's assistant secretary of the navy to campaign for new construction, especially of battleships. As possible trouble with Spain over Cuba loomed, he pressed his case more urgently. In the address he anticipated an argument that would become a cold war staple: that military strength would serve as a deterrent rather than a cause of war.

A century has passed since Washington wrote "To be prepared for war is the most effectual means to promote peace." We pay to this maxim the lip loyalty we so often pay to Washington's words; but it has never sunk deep into our hearts. . . .

Preparation for war is the surest guaranty for peace. Arbitration is an excellent thing, but ultimately those who wish to see this country at peace with foreign nations will be wise if they place reliance upon a first-class fleet of first-class battleships rather than on any arbitration treaty which the wit of man can devise. Nelson said that the British fleet was the best negotiator in Europe, and there was much truth in the saying. Moreover, while we are sincere and earnest in our advocacy of peace, we must not forget that an ignoble peace is worse than any war. . . .

In building this navy, we must remember two things: First, that our ships and guns should be the very best of their kind; and second, that no matter how good they are, they will be useless unless the man in the conning tower and the man behind the guns are also the best of their kind. It is mere folly to send men to perish because they have arms with which they cannot win. . . .

Tame submission to foreign aggression of any kind is a mean and unworthy thing; but it is even meaner and more unworthy to bluster first, and then either submit or else refuse to make those preparations which can alone obviate the necessity for submission. I believe with all my heart in the Monroe Doctrine, and, I believe also that the great mass of the American people are loyal to it; but it is worse than idle to announce our adherence to this doctrine and yet to decline to take measures to show that ours is not mere lip loyalty. We had far better submit to interference by foreign powers with the affairs of this continent than to announce that we will *not* tolerate such interference, and yet refuse to make ready the means by which alone we can prevent it. In public as in private life, a bold front tends to insure peace and not strife. If we possess a formidable navy, small is the chance indeed that we shall ever be dragged into a war to uphold the Monroe Doctrine. If we do not possess such a navy, war may be forced on us at any time.

It is certain, then, that we need a first-class navy. It is equally certain that this should not be merely a navy for defense. Our chief harbors should, of course, be fortified and put in condition to resist the attack of an enemy's fleet; and one of our prime needs is an ample force of torpedo boats to use primarily for coast defense. But in war the mere defensive never pays, and can never result in anything but disaster. It is not enough to parry a blow. The surest way to prevent its repetition is to return it. . . .

Still more is it necessary to have a fleet of great battle-ships if we intend to live up to the Monroe Doctrine, and to insist upon its observance in the two Americas and the islands on either side of them. If a foreign power, whether in Europe or Asia, should determine to assert its position in those lands wherein we feel that our influence should be supreme, there is but one way in which we can effectively interfere. Diplomacy is utterly useless where there is no force behind it; the diplomat is the servant, not the master, of the soldier. . . .

We ask for a great navy, partly because we think that the possession of such a navy is the surest guaranty of peace, and partly because we feel that no national life is worth having if the nation is not willing, when the need shall arise, to stake everything on the supreme arbitrament of war, and to pour out its blood, its treasure, and its tears like water, rather than submit to the loss of honor and renown.

In closing, let me repeat that we ask for a great navy, we ask for an armament fit for the nation's needs, not primarily, to fight, but to avert fighting. Preparedness deters the foe, and maintains right by the show of ready might without the use of violence. Peace, like freedom, is not a gift that tarries long in the hands of cowards, or of those too feeble or too short-sighted to deserve it; and we ask to be given the means to insure that honorable peace which alone is worth having.

Source: Theodore Roosevelt, *The Works of Theodore Roosevelt,* national ed. (New York: Charles Scribner's Sons, 1926), 13:182–199.

Document 1.10   The Rough Riders, "The Cavalry at Santiago," Excerpt from *The Rough Riders* (1899)

Roosevelt led his Rough Riders in the bloodiest fighting of the Spanish-American War. Although he repeatedly exposed himself to the greatest danger and his regiment suffered heavy casualties in dead and wounded, he emerged from the battles healthy and unscathed. Astonished observers wondered at his invulnerability. His greatest triumph came in the assault on Kettle Hill recorded in his book, The Rough Riders, *published in 1899.*

The fight was now on in good earnest, and the Spaniards on the hills were engaged in heavy volley firing. The Mauser bullets drove in sheets through the trees and the tall jungle grass, making a peculiar whirring or rustling sound; some of the bullets seemed to pop in the air, so that we thought they were explosive; and, indeed, many of those which were coated with brass did explode, in the sense that the brass coat was ripped off, making a thin plate of hard metal with a jagged edge, which inflicted a ghastly wound. These bullets were shot from a 45-caliber rifle carrying smokeless powder, which was much used by the guerillas and irregular Spanish troops. . . .

While we were lying in reserve we were suffering nearly as much as afterward when we charged. I think that the bulk of the Spanish fire was practically unaimed, or at least not aimed at any particular man, and only occasionally at a particular body of men; but they swept the whole field of battle up to the edge of the river, and man after man in our ranks fell dead or wounded, although I had the troopers scattered out far apart, taking advantage of every scrap of cover. . . .

The instant I received the order I sprang on my horse and then my "crowded hour" began. The guerillas had been shooting at us from the edges of the jungle and from their perches in the leafy trees, and as they used smokeless powder, it was almost impossible to see them, though a few of my men had from time to time responded. We had also suffered from the hill on our right front, which was held chiefly by guerillas, although there were also some Spanish regulars with them, for we found their dead. I formed my men in column of troops, each troop extended in open skirmishing order, the right resting on the wire fences which bordered the sunken lane. Captain Jenkins led the first squadron, his eyes literally dancing with joyous excitement.

I started in the rear of the regiment, the position in which the colonel should theoretically stay. Captain Mills and Captain McCormick were both with me as aides; but I speedily had to send them off on special duty in getting the different bodies of men forward. I had intended to go into action on foot as at Las Guasimas, but the heat was so oppressive that I found I should be quite unable to run up and down the line and superintend matters unless I was mounted; and, moreover, when on horseback, I could see the men better and they could see me better.

A curious incident happened as I was getting the men started forward. Always when men have been lying down under cover for some time, and are required to advance, there is a little hesitation, each looking to see whether the others are going forward. As I rode down the line, calling to the troopers to go forward, and rasping brief directions to the captains and lieutenants, I came upon a man lying behind a little bush, and I ordered him to jump up. I do not think he understood that we were making a forward move, and he looked up at me for a moment with hesitation, and I again bade him rise, jeering him and saying: "Are you afraid to stand up when I am on horseback?" As I spoke, he suddenly fell forward on his face, a bullet having struck him and gone through him lengthwise. I suppose the bullet had been aimed at me; at any rate, I, who was on horseback in the open, was unhurt, and the man lying flat on the ground in the cover beside me was killed. . . .

By the time I had come to the head of the regiment we ran into the left wing of the Ninth Regulars, and some of the First Regulars, who were lying down; that is, the troopers were lying down, while the officers were walking to and fro. The officers of the white and colored regiments alike took the greatest pride in seeing that the men more than did their duty; and the mortality among them was great.

I spoke to the captain in command of the rear platoons, saying that I had been ordered to support the regulars in the attack upon the hills, and that in my judgment we could not take these hills by firing at them, and so as to attack the hill from that side. Captain Mills had already thrown three of the other troops of the regiment across this road for the same purpose. Wheeling around, I then again galloped toward the hill, passing the shouting, cheering, firing men, and went up the lane, splashing through a small stream; when I got abreast of the ranch buildings on the top of Kettle Hill, I turned and went up the slope. Being on horseback I was, of course, able to get ahead of the men on foot, excepting my orderly, Henry Bardshar, who had run ahead very fast in order to get better shots at the Spaniards, who were now running out of the ranch buildings. Sergeant Campbell and a number of the Arizona men, and Dudley Dean, among others, were very close behind. Stevens, with his platoon of the Ninth, was abreast of us; so were McNamee and Hartwick. Some forty yards from the top I ran into a wire fence and jumped off little Texas turning him loose. He had been scraped by a couple of bullets, one of which nicked my elbow, and I never expected to see him again. As I ran up to the hill, Bardshar stopped to shoot, and two Spaniards fell as he emptied his magazine. These were the only Spaniards I actually saw fall to aimed shots by anyone of my men, with the exception of two guerillas in trees.

Almost immediately afterward the hill was covered by the troops, both Rough Riders and the colored troopers of the Ninth, and some men of the First. . . . One Spaniard was captured in the buildings, another was shot as he tried to hide himself, and a few others were killed as they ran. . . .

No sooner were we on the crest than the Spaniards from the line of hills in our front, where they were strongly entrenched, opened a very heavy fire upon us with their rifles. They also opened upon us with one or two pieces of artillery, using time fuses which burned very accurately, the shells exploding right over our heads.

On the top of the hill was a huge iron kettle, or something of the kind, probably used for sugar-refining. Several of our men took shelter behind this. We had a splendid view of the charge on the San Juan blockhouse to our left, where the infantry of Kent, led by Hawkins, were climbing the hill. Obviously the proper thing to do was to help them, and I got the men together and started them volley-firing against the Spaniards in the San Juan blockhouse and in the trenches around it. We could only see their heads; of course this was all we ever could see when we were firing at them in their trenches. . . .

The infantry got nearer and nearer the crest of the hill. At last we could see the Spaniards running from the rifle-pits as the Americans came on in

that we must rush them. He answered that his orders were to keep his n
lying where they were, and that he could not charge without order;
asked where the colonel was, and as he was not in sight, said, "Then I
the ranking officer here and I give the order to charge"—for I did not w:
to keep the men longer in the open suffering under a fire which they cou
not effectively return. Naturally the captain hesitated to obey this orc
when no word had been received from his own colonel. So I said, "Th
let my men through, sir," and rode on through the lines, followed by t
grinning Rough Riders, whose attention had been completely taken (
the Spanish bullets, partly by my dialogue with the regulars, and partly
the language I had been using to themselves as I got the lines forwar
for I had been joking with some and swearing at others, as the exigenci
of the case seemed to demand. When we started to go through, howeve
it proved too much for the regulars, and they jumped up and came alon;
their officers and troops mingling with mine, all being delighted at th
chance. When I got to where the head of the left wing of the Ninth w:
lying, through the courtesy of Lieutenant Hartwick, two of whose colore
troopers threw down the fence, I was enabled to get back into the lan(
at the same time waving my hat, and giving the order to charge the hi
on our right front. Out of my sight, over on the right, Captains McBlai
and Taylor, of the Ninth, made up their minds independently to charg(
at just about this time; and at almost the same moment Colonels Carrol
and Hamilton, who were off, I believe, to my left, where we could see nei
ther them nor their men, gave the order to advance. But of all this I knew
nothing at the time. The whole line, tired of waiting, and eager to close
with the enemy, was straining to go forward; and it seems that different
parts slipped the leash at almost the same moment. The First Cavalry came
up the hill just behind, and partly mixed with my regiment and the Ninth.
As already said, portions of the Third, Sixth, and Tenth followed, while the
rest of the members of these three regiments kept more in touch with the
infantry on our left.

By this time we were all in the spirit of the thing and greatly excited by
the charge, the men cheering and running forward between shots, while
the delighted faces of the foremost officers, like Captain C. J. Stevens, of
the Ninth, as they ran at the head of their troops, will always stay in my
mind. As soon as I was in the line I galloped forward a few yards until I
saw that the men were well started, and then galloped back to help
Goodrich, who was in command of his troop, get his men across the road

their final rush. Then I stopped my men for fear they should injure their comrades, and called to them to charge the next line of trenches, on the hills in our front, from which we had been undergoing a good deal of punishment. Thinking that the men would all come, I jumped over the wire fence in front of us and started at the double; but, as a matter of fact, the troopers were so excited, what with shooting and being shot, and shouting and cheering, that they did not hear, or did not heed me; and after running about a hundred yards I found I had only five men along with me. Bullets were ripping the grass all around us, and one of the men, Clay Green, was mortally wounded. . . . I ran back, jumped over the wire fence, and went over the crest of the hill, filled with anger against the troopers, and especially those of my own regiment, for not having accompanied me. They, of course, were quite innocent of wrong-doing; and even while I taunted them bitterly for not having followed me, it was all I could do not to smile at the look of injury and surprise that came over their faces, while they cried out: "We didn't hear you, we didn't see you go, Colonel; lead on now, we'll sure follow you." I wanted the other regiments to come too, so I ran down to where General Sumner was and asked him if I might make the charge; and he told me to go and that he would see that the men followed. By this time everybody had his attention attracted, and when I leaped over the fence again, with Major Jenkins beside me, the men of the various regiments which were already on the hill came with a rush, and we started across the wide valley which lay between us and the Spanish entrenchments. . . . Long before we got near them the Spaniards ran, save a few here and there, who either surrendered or were shot down. When we reached the trenches we found them filled with dead bodies in the light blue and white uniform of the Spanish regular army.

Source: Theodore Roosevelt, *The Works of Theodore Roosevelt,* national ed. (New York: Charles Scribner's Sons, 1926), 11:78–89.

Document 1.11   Annual Message to the State Legislature of New York in Support of Civil Service, January 2, 1899

As a young legislator Roosevelt worked for the passage of the first New York civil service law. Given that history and his years on the federal Civil Service Commission, it is not surprising that his first message to the legislature as governor included a call for strengthening the existing system.

. . . The methods of appointment to the civil service of the State are now in utter confusion, no less than three systems being in effect in the city of New York, one in other cities, and one in the State at large. I recommend that a law be passed introducing one uniform practice for the entire State, and providing, as required by the Constitution, for the enforcement of proper civil-service regulations in the State and its subdivisions. This law should be modeled in its essential provisions upon the old civil-service law which was repealed by the civil service law now upon the statute-books. The inquiries I have made have satisfied me that the present law works badly from every standpoint, and the half-mark given upon the so-called fitness test represents not a competitive examination at all, but the individual preference of the appointing officer, or rather of the outsider who has requested the appointment. It would be much better to have it stated outright that this was the case and that the examination was merely a pass or non-competitive examination, instead of going through the farce of a nominally competitive examination which is not such in reality. Where there is a large list of eligibles, as is the case now on some registers, it is practically impossible for the appointing officer to examine the whole list, and if he tried, it would merely result in a great loss of time to him, and a loss of both time and money to the unfortunate candidates. Where competitive examinations are to be held, they should be competitive in fact and not in name only. . . . Where it appears after trial, or after careful investigation, that competitive examinations will not work well, then the places should be exempted from examination. . . . I do not make a fetish of written competitive examinations for admission to the civil service. There are situations where these written competitive examinations are not applicable at all. . . . Physical examinations, and technical examinations into the capacity of the man to do the work sought, should, wherever advisable, be used to supplement or even to supplant the written examination proper, and this written examination itself should be of as practical a type as possible, and directed to the special needs of the position sought. There is no need of discussing the advantages of the methods which we have grown to group together when we speak of civil-service reform. They have by long experience been proved to work admirably. In the postal service, for instance, the examinations for clerks, letter-carriers, and railway-mail clerks are entirely practical, and the application of the reformed system to the postal service has produced a very great improvement in the character of the work done. In the navy yards of the nation the benefit resultant upon taking the appointment and retention of navy-yard employees out of the hands of local politicians, and making them consequent upon fitness and good conduct only has resulted in an incredible improvement, not only in the character of the work done, but in saving of expense to the government. Our present navy would not have been able to do its duty in the war with Spain in the way that it actually did, had the government service in the navy-yard not been put upon a merit basis. What has succeeded in these great branches of the national service will surely succeed in the State service if given a proper trial.

Source: Theodore Roosevelt, *The Works of Theodore Roosevelt,* national ed. (New York: Charles Scribner's Sons, 1926), 15:18–20.

Document 1.12   Annual Message to the State Legislature of New York in Defense of the Franchise Tax, January 3, 1900

One of the many battles Governor Roosevelt fought with Republican boss Thomas C. Platt concerned the taxing of corporations that held monopoly franchises from the state and city governments. Roosevelt fought the party machine and won passage of the franchise tax in the legislative session of 1899. He made a point of defending the law as fair and just in his next annual message to the legislature.

. . . For years most . . . [local New York] franchises escaped paying their proper share of the public burdens. The last legislature placed on the statute-book a law requiring them to be treated as real estate for the purposes of taxation, the tax to be assessed and collected by the State assessors for the benefit of the localities concerned. This marks an immense stride in advance. Of course, at first, serious difficulties are sure to arise in enforcing it. The means for carrying it into effect are very inadequate. There may be delay before we get from it the substantial additions to the revenue which will finally accrue, and there may be disappointment to the enthusiasts who are so apt to hope too much from such legislation. But it will undoubtedly add largely to the public revenues as soon as it is fairly in operation, and the amount thus added will increase steadily year by year. The principle which this law establishes has come to stay. There will doubtless have to be additional legislation from time to time to perfect the system as its shortcomings are made evident in actual practice. But the corporations owning valuable public franchises must pay their full and proper share of the public burdens.

The franchise tax law is framed with the intent of securing exact and equal justice, no more and no less. It is not in any way intended as a means for persecuting or oppressing corporations. It is not intended to cut down legitimate dividends; still less to cut down wages or to prevent a just return for the far-sighted business skill of some captain of industry who has been able to establish a public service greatly to the advantage of the localities concerned, where before his time men of less business capacity had failed. But it is intended that property which derives its value from the grant of a privilege by the public shall be taxed proportionately to the value of the privilege granted. In enforcing this law, much tact, patience, resolution, and judgment will be needed. All these qualities the State Board of Tax Commissioners have thus far shown. Their salaries are altogether inadequate, for the new law has immensely increased not only their responsibilities, but their work. They should be given not only the needed increase for themselves, but also an appropriation for an additional number of clerks and experts.

During the year 1899 not a single corporation has received at the hands of the State of New York one privilege of any kind, sort, or description, by law or otherwise, to which it was not entitled, and which was not in the public interest; nor has corporate influence availed against any measure which was in the public interest. At certain times, and in certain places, corporations have undoubtedly exerted a corrupting influence in political life; but in this State for this year it is absolutely true, as shown by the history of every measure that has come before the legislature from the franchise tax down, that no corporate influence has been able to prevail against the interests of the public.

Source: Theodore Roosevelt, *The Works of Theodore Roosevelt,* national ed. (New York: Charles Scribner's Sons, 1926), 15:38–39.

President Roosevelt in Rhode Island during a tour of New England in 1902.

CHAPTER TWO

Campaigns and Elections

The assassination of William McKinley in the summer of 1901 lifted Theodore Roosevelt to the presidency only months after his inauguration as vice president. The occasion of his ascension was disheartening, but Roosevelt's ambition for high office had motivated him for some years, through his campaigns for New York State assemblyman, his unsuccessful bid for New York City mayor, and his race for governor.

BEGINNINGS IN POLITICS

Theodore Roosevelt had always wanted to be close to the action. Just a year after his graduation from Harvard in 1880, and to the distress of some of his relatives and friends who thought politics a dirty business, Roosevelt decided to test the political waters in New York City. He began to frequent the local Republican headquarters of the Twenty-first District. Although at first regarded as an upper-class rube, he won the respect of the local organization and was quickly asked to run for office.

The newcomer joined the Republican organization at a pivotal moment. In 1881 Joe Murray, a district leader, was ready to mount a challenge to the district boss, Jack Hess. Murray asked Roosevelt to stand for the state assembly against the candidate backed by Hess. A reluctant Roosevelt accepted, and in the showdown, Murray's forces prevailed.

The political neophyte initially conducted an unimaginative campaign, writing voters to ask their support without offering them any reason to do so. But the district leaders mobilized the party machinery, soliciting endorsements from Roosevelt's wealthy neighbors and promoting their candidate in the poor areas of the district. In November, Roosevelt won election 3,490 to 1,989. He was reelected in 1882, bucking a Democratic tide in the city, and won again the following year.

Although Roosevelt often dissented from party policies, especially when he suspected less-than-honest dealings, he remained a party man and consistently refused to join splinter groups of reformers he liked to call "do-gooders." He carried this attitude into national politics as well. For example, he fought against the nomination of James G. Blaine at the Republican convention of 1884, in part because Blaine was tainted by allegations of corruption. But when the party chose Blaine, Roosevelt hit the campaign trail and supported Blaine's candidacy with enthusiasm.

With some reluctance, and knowing the election odds were against him, Roosevelt accepted his party's call to run for the office of mayor of New York City in 1886. Despite a vigorous campaign effort, during which he called for reform of City Hall, he finished third in the race behind the winner, Abram S. Hewitt, a highly respected businessman who had the support of the city's commercial community as well as the backing of the Democratic machine (Tammany Hall), and the independent candidate, Henry George, a proponent of radical reform and the famous author of *Progress and Poverty*.

The mayoral race was Roosevelt's last election run until his campaign for governor in 1898, but the interim was not a pause in his life in politics. He served as delegate to the national conventions and worked unstintingly for Republican presidential candidates. In the election of 1888 Roosevelt traveled the campaign trail, speaking in key western states in support of Republican presidential hopeful Benjamin Harrison, and in 1896 he worked enthusiastically for William McKinley.

BECOMING GOVERNOR

Secretary of State John Hay once referred to the conflict in Cuba as a "splendid little war." It was that for Roosevelt, who emerged from battle unscarred and a hero of some of the fiercest fighting of the war. By the time the Rough Riders arrived at Montauk, New York, for demobilization in

August 1898 news of Roosevelt's exploits in Cuba had already made him something of a national hero, and he reveled in the attention. Particularly important was the notice of the New York State Republican machine, which was in trouble and facing an election in November. Party boss Thomas C. Platt needed a replacement for Governor Frank Black at the head of the Republican ticket. Scandal tarnished the Black administration when a million dollars allocated for improvements on the Erie Canal disappeared. Platt needed a clean and honest name to lead the ticket; that such a name should be attached to a war hero was a welcome bonus. Familiar with Roosevelt's independence and willfulness, Platt was not enthusiastic about the choice, but the scandal limited his options and political realism dictated his course. He sent one of his trusted men, Lemuel Quigg, to Montauk to offer the Colonel the prospect of the nomination for governor. Roosevelt welcomed the invitation. At about the same time, John Jay Chapman, a leader of the Independent Party fighting against Platt, also visited Roosevelt with an offer for his party's nomination. Chapman assumed Roosevelt would also be nominated by the Republicans, but if Roosevelt won the governorship, the nomination by the Independents would give the party influence in Albany in their fight against the Platt machine. For a time Roosevelt entertained both offers. After meeting with Platt, Roosevelt gave assurances that he would not assault the party machinery and accepted Platt's proffered nomination. Then, to Chapman's furious distress, he declined the Independent Party offer (see Document 2.1).

Nomination by the Republicans was now a mere formality, but trouble suddenly threatened the Roosevelt candidacy. It was discovered that Roosevelt had listed his residence as Washington, D.C., while he served as assistant secretary of the navy. The action helped him avoid paying some state taxes. New York law, however, required five years of continuous residence in the state for a candidate for governor. Was the Colonel eligible to run in 1898? After a brief panic, a troop of lawyers finessed the issue with complex argument and an ingenious reading of the law, and the nomination proceeded without further incident (Miller 1992, 317).

The Democrats, hoping to take advantage of Republican scandals concerning the missing Erie Canal funds, nominated Judge Augustus Van Wick of Brooklyn. Not nearly as well known as Roosevelt, Van Wick was reputed to be an honest man, and his lack of notoriety made him a smaller target for attack in contrast to the weight of scandal the Republicans were carrying into the election. In fact the early odds favored Van

Wick, despite Roosevelt's popularity as war hero. Early fumbling by party campaign managers made matters worse. By mid-October, Roosevelt decided to take personal charge of his campaign. He organized a whistle-stop train tour and crisscrossed the state accompanied by a party of volunteer Rough Rider veterans. With skill and undisguised enthusiasm, the crowd-pleasing Roosevelt made more than one hundred speeches in towns large and small (see Documents 2.2 and 2.3).

As the Democrats dwelled on the issue of Republican corruption and the missing million, Roosevelt shot back with charges of corruption in Tammany Hall, the label for the Democrats in New York City. Roosevelt was pleased with his tour, and the effort brought results. The returns on November 8 gave Roosevelt a close victory by 17,794 votes out of a total vote of more than 3.1 million. After celebrating at his Sagamore Hill home in Oyster Bay, the governor-elect prepared to move his growing family to Albany to begin a short but pivotal chapter of his political career.

Roosevelt was now governor of the most populous and important state in the nation. As in the past he understood that realism in politics would demand compromise and hard decisions, but he was, as always, determined to establish a record of honest administration (see Document 2.4). He governed well, and thoughts of even higher office were not unrealistic. But his sailing as governor was not entirely smooth; he had to deal with Platt and the Republican machine. The governor conferred with Platt often and worked to keep the relationship stiffly cordial, if not warm and friendly. But clashes were inevitable over political appointments and legislative initiatives. When reformers proposed a new franchise tax on corporations, for example, Roosevelt supported the measure and infuriated Platt, whose organization drew generous financial support from the big business community. The governor succeeded in pushing the measure through the legislature as a frustrated Platt looked on in disgust. Nor was the party leader pleased when Roosevelt supported the tightening of state civil service legislation. Platt's nomination of Roosevelt had kept the Republicans in power, but he deemed the expense exorbitant and the taste bitter. Something had to be done in anticipation of the next election. Roosevelt, eyeing a future presidential bid, wanted another term as governor; Platt wanted him out. As annoying as Roosevelt was to Platt, his popularity with the electorate was growing. He could not simply be dumped from the next state ticket without fatal damage to the party. Some new strategy was needed to rid the party of Roosevelt without the appearance of ingratitude or betrayal. Boss Platt soon found the answer.

MR. VICE PRESIDENT

As the election of 1900 approached, Platt knew that President McKinley was looking for a vice presidential nominee. Vice President Garret Hobart had died suddenly in November 1899, and McKinley needed an effective campaigner on his ticket. Here, Platt thought, was his chance to be rid of Roosevelt. What better place to bury his adversary than in the vice presidency? There he would be powerless and, most important, away from New York. Barring tragedy, vice presidents were seldom heard from again. Roosevelt, of course, knew that the office was traditionally a dead end; no vice president had been elected to the presidency since Martin Van Buren in 1836. He also knew it would be extremely difficult to be renominated for governor without Platt's support, and even if he succeeded, the idea of struggling against the political boss for another term was not appealing. When the subject of the vice presidency was first broached, Roosevelt rejected the idea (see Document 2.5). But Platt would not be deflected. In the unaccustomed role of cheerleading for Roosevelt, he set to work corralling delegates to the Republican National Convention for the governor's nomination to the second spot on the ticket.

There were obstacles besides Roosevelt's reluctance. McKinley himself was wary of the governor's independence and unpredictability, well demonstrated during his tenure as assistant secretary of the navy. Mark Hanna, U.S. senator from Ohio and the president's close friend and adviser, despised Roosevelt and resisted the idea of placing him on the ticket with all his energy. Platt knew he could count on the New York delegates, most of whom were as anxious to be rid of the governor as he was. He decided to work around Hanna by making a deal with the Ohio Republican leader, Matthew Quay. Quay headed the anti-Hanna Republicans in his state, of whom there were many. When Platt approached him, Quay was more than willing to line up support for Roosevelt to embarrass Hanna (Morris 1979, 727). As news of these maneuvers inevitably became known, Roosevelt continued to deny any interest in becoming vice president, insisting he would rather remain as governor.

At the start, Roosevelt's negative posture toward the vice presidential nomination was probably completely genuine. Whether it remained so is a matter of conjecture. It became clear to him that being nominated for governor again would mean an ugly fight with Platt and no assurance of success. His friend Henry Cabot Lodge, whose political advice Roosevelt usually took seriously, suggested he accept the vice presidential opportunity, but that if he truly wanted to avoid nomination, he should stay away from the Republican convention (see Document 2.6). Roosevelt ignored the caution about attending the convention, perhaps a clue that his resistance to being nominated was weakening. His arrival on the floor of the convention waving his Rough Rider–style hat set off a demonstration for the war-hero governor. Always responsive to the cheers of admirers, Roosevelt now probably reconciled himself to accepting the nomination. In contrast to the strong language of earlier denials of interest in nomination, he released a statement to the convention repeating that he preferred to remain governor of New York, but he worded the message in such muted terms that observers took it to mean he would accept if nominated (see Document 2.7). He also kept himself in the limelight by delivering an impassioned address to the convention seconding the nomination of McKinley (see Document 2.8).

Meanwhile, Platt's work behind the scenes had settled the issue to the great exasperation of Hanna. He is recorded as saying to his Republican colleagues, "Don't you realize that there's only one life between that madman and the presidency?" (Brands 1997, 397). But Hanna knew he was beaten and retreated into silence. When the roll call for the vice presidential nomination concluded, Roosevelt won the vote of every delegate but one, his own (see Document 2.9).

The Democrats again nominated William Jennings Bryan, and the now-crumbling Populist Party added its own endorsement. Bryan was a welcome target for the Republicans. McKinley remained in the background and left the campaigning to his supporters, especially his new running mate. Throwing himself into the battle with his usual inexhaustible energy, Roosevelt assaulted Bryan country, touring the western states as far as Colorado. He trumpeted the return of prosperity to the country now recovered from the recession of 1894. He was especially forceful in defending the American role in the Spanish-American War and blasted critics of the military suppression of insurrection in the Philippines, even suggesting disloyalty among the dissenters. Bryan he portrayed as a demagogue and extremist who would be a danger to the country if elected. He faulted the Democrat for advocating lower tariffs and an inheritance tax, and he ridiculed Bryan's continued insistence that the coinage of silver for cheap money was a key to the country's financial well-being. He countered Bryan's attacks on big business by offering his own criticism of the excesses of the trusts and citing his passage of the corporation franchise tax in New York (see Document 2.10).

Roosevelt traveled over twenty thousand miles in the campaign, making more than 650 speeches to enthusiastic crowds who came to see the Colonel as much as the candidate. As always, Roosevelt was a crowd pleaser, and appearing with a delegation of Rough Riders in tow also helped. The results were gratifying. The McKinley-Roosevelt ticket won 51.7 percent (7,219,193) of the nearly fourteen million votes cast. It was the largest Republican majority against the Democrats since 1872 (Ulysses S. Grant's reelection). Even Bryan's home state of Nebraska voted Republican. The electoral vote was a lopsided 292 to 155. Roosevelt, once reluctant to leave the governorship, now prepared to return to Washington. Boss Platt happily decided he would attend the inauguration in order to see Teddy "take the veil" (Morris 1979, 734).

The new vice president was predictably unsatisfied in his new office. He presided briefly over a short session of the Senate, somewhat bored and needing help with Senate protocol. Beyond that unexciting task, there was little for him to do. Politics, as often noted, is the art of the possible, but one must always be alert for the unexpected. The unexpected came in September 1901, while Roosevelt was tending to a speaking engagement in Vermont.

ASSASSINATION AND THE PRESIDENCY

On September 6, President McKinley stood in a receiving line at the Temple of Music of the Pan-American Exposition in Buffalo, New York. A young man extended a bandaged right hand concealing a revolver toward McKinley and fired two shots into the president's abdomen. Leon Czolgosz was quickly subdued and hustled away as McKinley lay bleeding. The assassin, about twenty-eight years old, had a history of instability. He had flirted with anarchist groups in Cleveland and Chicago but was unsuccessful in winning acceptance because of his strange personality. He moved to Buffalo in July and hatched his murderous plan when he saw news reports that the president would visit the exposition. With swift justice he was tried, found guilty, and executed before the end of October.

When news of the attack reached Roosevelt in Vermont, he rushed to Buffalo at the call of McKinley's staff. By the time he reached the city, the news seemed better. During the next few days, the president rallied and appeared to be recovering from his wounds. To reassure a worried nation Roosevelt was advised to join his family on a planned vacation in the Adirondack Mountains. The vice president did so and one day set out to climb Mount Marcy, genuinely relieved that the crisis seemed to have passed. Late in the day, on September 13, preparing to come down from the summit, he saw a messenger hurrying toward him through the mountain mist. He knew instinctively that his life was about to change. Infection the doctors could not control had spread through the president's abdomen, and now he was not expected to live. Roosevelt traveled through the night on a horse-drawn rig to reach the nearest rail station. When he reached the station he was greeted with the news that the president was dead (see Document 2.11). Roosevelt arrived in Buffalo in early afternoon, and soon after, in the library of a private home, Secretary of War Elihu Root, the senior cabinet member present, administered the oath of office. Theodore Roosevelt was president of the United States.

THE 1904 PRESIDENTIAL ELECTION

No one enjoyed being president more than Theodore Roosevelt. At forty-two he was the youngest man to hold the office, in full vigor and determined to establish a record of outstanding achievement. Despite substantial achievements in the office, he chafed a bit at the notion of being an "accidental president," and from the beginning he had his eye on 1904 and election in his own right. In anticipation of the election he made a national tour in 1903. He was greeted everywhere by admiring crowds, but still, he worried. Would applause for a reigning president translate into votes at the polls? He had proved himself a cunning and masterful political player; now he could boast of success as chief executive. Despite his wariness of an unpredictable electorate, he looked forward to the campaign.

Although public opinion seemed to give the president high marks, the more conservative elements of his own party marked a different scorecard. His use of phrases like "the criminal rich" did not endear him to the bigwigs and corporate contributors to the Republican Party. Roosevelt's often unrestrained language, designed to generate popular support, embarrassed and angered much of the party leadership. More frustrating, much as they distrusted Roosevelt, there was little they could do now to get rid of him. There was no "upstairs" to which he could be kicked. Even if they could nominate someone else, the spectacle of a party rejecting its own sitting president, and a popular one at that, would mean probable defeat at the polls. So conservatives and big business grumbled but muted their criticism and opened their wallets. One exception among Republican conservatives was Secretary of War Elihu Root, who defended the president to the old guard and acted as a liaison to ease the fears of the doubters.

Unreconstructed in his dislike for Roosevelt was Senator Hanna. Although he supported some of Roosevelt's initiatives in the Senate, Hanna never reconciled himself to Roosevelt in the presidency and despised his antibusiness posturing. As the election season approached, he hoped someone else, perhaps he, himself, could head the party ticket in 1904. His hope was derailed by an Ohio enemy, Sen. Joseph B. Foraker, who proposed that the Ohio state convention endorse the nomination of the president at its meeting in June 1903, a full year before the national convention (Brands 1997, 493). Hanna resisted, but faced with the choice of going along or publicly opposing the president's nomination, he quietly backed down. Roosevelt was infuriated by Hanna's effort (see Documents 2.12 and 2.13). But when the senator was mortally stricken with typhoid, a forgiving president visited his bedside, and the men reconciled shortly before Hanna's death in February 1904. With Hanna's challenge aborted, there was clear sailing to the nomination.

Brushing aside protests from old guard Republicans, Roosevelt insisted on naming a trusted ally, George B. Cortelyou, secretary of the new Department of Commerce and Labor, to be national party chairman in charge of the campaign. The president took firm control of the convention machinery. Elihu Root delivered the keynote address, reviewing the accomplishments of the administration, and Henry Cabot Lodge chaired the platform committee assuring Roosevelt's design for that document. Since the outcome was already certain, there were few fireworks at what was a rather dull convention. A brief roar of approval greeted Roosevelt's nomination, and a unanimous roll-call vote settled the matter. With the nomination of Sen. Charles W. Fairbanks, R-Ind., for vice president, a sop to the conservatives, the Republican ticket was filled.

The Democrats, whose only president since James Buchanan's election in 1856 was Grover Cleveland (1885–1889 and 1893–1897), yearned for a victory. They turned away from two-time loser Bryan and sought to project a more conservative cast in this election. There was a brief flurry of rumors that Cleveland would be lured from retirement, but this turned out to be little more than wishful thinking among his admirers in the party. Instead, at their convention in St. Louis in July, the Democrats turned to Alton B. Parker, chief justice of the New York Court of Appeals. Former senator Henry G. Davis of West Virginia was nominated as his running mate. It would have been difficult to choose anyone in sharper contrast to Roosevelt than Parker. Reserved, stolid, compared with Bryan, as conservative in his politics as he was in his private demeanor, he offered the Democrats an image of respectable solidity after the tumultuous campaigns of 1896 and 1900. Although the Democratic platform remained silent this election year on the issue of silver and cheap money, Parker announced his own firm support for the gold standard (see Document 2.14). Roosevelt had known Parker for years and regarded him with great respect. Acknowledging his potential appeal to conservative voters, perhaps even some from his own party, Roosevelt saw Parker as a dangerous opponent (Morison 1951, 4:852, 858; see Document 2.15). He worried, too, because some of the newspapers that had endorsed McKinley four years earlier now supported Parker.

This was to be a different campaign for Roosevelt. As a sitting president, custom dictated that he not actively campaign, and with some frustration, he reluctantly followed the tradition. But with the dependable Cortelyou as party chairman, the president closely directed the course of the campaign. Parker painted Roosevelt as erratic, sensational, and arbitrary and added the charge that the last four years had seen unprecedented executive encroachment on the legislative and judicial functions of government. Republicans responded by listing the administration's achievements: the Panama Canal treaty, prosecution of the Northern Securities trust, the Newlands Reclamation Act, the establishment of the Department of Commerce and Labor, the Elkins Anti-Rebate Act against unfair railroad practices, and the settlement of the anthracite coal strike in 1902. All of these Roosevelt could boast as personal victories (see Document 2.16).

The only serious trouble for his campaign came when Joseph Pulitzer's *New York World* broke the story that the country's biggest corporations were contributing heavily to the president's campaign chest (Pringle [1931] 1956, 249–252). Among the contributors were J. P. Morgan, John D. Rockefeller, and the railroad mogul E. H. Harriman. When Parker took up these charges in a campaign statement, Roosevelt's respect for his fellow New Yorker diminished. The president's campaign kept the money and responded that the amounts contributed were much smaller than those given to the McKinley campaign in 1900. The Roosevelt campaign raised $2.2 million, most of the money coming from corporations. Roosevelt was undoubtedly aware of the sources of his campaign's funds, but he bristled at any suggestion of improper influence and at least one of his contributors agreed. Steel magnate Henry Clay Frick later complained that businessmen had "bought the s.o.b., and then he didn't stay bought" (Miller 1992, 440).

The flap over money had little effect on the result. Roosevelt won in a landslide with 7.6 million votes to Parker's 5.1 million, sweeping every state outside the South and taking even traditionally Democratic Missouri. The electoral vote reflected the popular sweep, 336 to 140. Roosevelt was naturally delighted by the massive victory. But while basking in the euphoria of his triumph, Roosevelt made a stunning mistake he would come to regret deeply. Speaking to reporters as news of the victory became clear, Roosevelt shocked his family and colleagues when he announced that out of respect for the two-term tradition established by Washington, he would not again be a candidate for president. The statement was absolute and there could be no turning back from it. This needlessly made him a lame-duck president in his new term of office. With much still on his agenda in 1908 and reelection probable, his election night vow haunted him for years. He made no mention of his two-term pledge in his inaugural address, but called on the nation to recognize its blessings and face the responsibilities of power at home and in the world (see Documents 2.17 and 2.18).

LAST CAMPAIGN

In 1908 Roosevelt marked William Howard Taft, his secretary of war and trusted friend, as his successor, confident that Taft would continue his reforming policies. Taft had served Roosevelt loyally as secretary of war, and now the president used his influence in the party to secure the nomination for him. Both progressive and conservative Republicans accepted the choice happily. The progressives saw Taft as sympathetic to reform; conservatives were convinced he would be one of their own and certainly more manageable than Roosevelt had been. (Of the 14.8 million votes cast Taft won 51.6 percent to William Jennings Bryan's 43.0 percent.) In the years that followed, the progressives were the disappointed ones, and Roosevelt, too, thought Taft had surrendered to the old guard. Relations between the two men began to show strain from the earliest days of the Taft presidency. When Roosevelt went off on African safari in 1909, he was kept informed of political affairs by a stream of letters from home. The reports disappointed Roosevelt, creating the impression, somewhat unfairly, that Taft was a pawn of the old guard. Taft did fail to support progressive efforts to unseat the conservative and dictatorial Speaker of the House, Joseph Cannon, R-Ill., and offered little effective help in the struggle to lower tariff rates. Nevertheless, the president continued to initiate antitrust actions and built a respectable conservation record.

But by 1909 the reformers wanted much more, and Roosevelt did too. While in Africa, Roosevelt read a critique of progressivism, *The Promise of American Life*, by Herbert Croly. The book argued that progressives, like Thomas Jefferson, were too fearful of strong government. The modern nation now needed strong leaders at the head of an active government in order to meet the challenges of industrial America. Roosevelt agreed. When he returned to the United States in 1910, he spoke out about the nation's needs in words that frightened conservatives and were easily interpreted as critical of Taft. Henry Cabot Lodge cautioned him to cool his rhetoric lest he split the party. But Roosevelt ached to be president again, and as he became more and more committed to a progressive agenda, the idea of displacing Taft became irresistible.

By 1912, Roosevelt's relationship with Taft was shattered, and he decided to challenge the president for the Republican nomination. Progressives lined up behind Roosevelt and he won popular support in several of the new primary elections held in anticipation of the convention, including the primary in Taft's home state of Ohio. But the convention machinery, particularly the credentials committee, was controlled by conservatives loyal to Taft. Virtually all disputes over seating delegates were settled in favor of the president. Roosevelt was awarded only 19 of the

254 contested seats. The convention remained under the firm control of the party bosses, who, aside from their commitment to Taft, were less than anxious for the return of a Roosevelt presidency. Taft was nominated on the first ballot. Roosevelt was not simply disappointed at being passed over, he felt betrayed and thought he had been cheated at the convention (Brands 1997, 714). That conviction reversed his lifelong habit of loyalty to the Republican Party even when its leadership and decisions disappointed him. This time he bolted.

Roosevelt, now a hero to progressives, won the nomination of the hastily convened Progressive Party convention in Chicago in August. Many of those who cheered him at this convention were the very "do-gooder" types he had ridiculed years earlier. Now he was ready to carry their banner. He responded to their nomination with a confession of political faith, a rollicking speech outlining an agenda of reform that delighted his audience and struck conservative observers as dangerously radical. An attack on Wall Street was accompanied by proposals for labor reform that a younger Roosevelt would also have thought radical, including support for a minimum wage, workmen's compensation, the protection of women and children in the workplace, and old age pensions. He called for tariff revision, the extension of the primary system, and more government regulation of industry. In many ways his speech was an anticipation of the New Deal of his distant cousin Franklin Delano Roosevelt. At the finish he called out to the ecstatic gathering, "We stand at Armageddon, and we battle for the Lord" (Roosevelt 1926, 17:299; see Document 6.7).

The campaign was vintage Roosevelt. With the slogan, the New Nationalism, capturing nothing less than a new conception of the role of government, he barnstormed the country in search of votes. The most dramatic moment of the campaign came at a rally in Milwaukee on October 14. John F. Schrank, a deranged gunman, shot Roosevelt in the chest as he prepared to enter the hall. A folded copy of his speech and a metal eyeglass case kept the bullet from reaching his heart. With the bullet still in his chest, Roosevelt insisted on mounting the stage to deliver his speech to the stunned audience. News of his dramatic performance did not hurt the campaign. After a brief pause to allow Roosevelt to recover, the campaign resumed.

His principal challenger was not Taft but Woodrow Wilson, a Democrat also campaigning as a progressive but critical of Roosevelt's ideas about the need for a more powerful government. His slogan was the New Freedom. The race was between Wilson and Roosevelt, with Taft trailing a weak third. Wilson amassed nearly 6.3 million votes; Roosevelt won just over 4.1 million; Taft drew about 3.5 million. One might argue that by splitting the party Roosevelt cost Taft reelection, but that is unlikely. Wilson, Roosevelt, and the Socialist Eugene V. Debs, who polled 900,370 votes, called for varying degrees of reform from moderate to radical. Taft and the Republicans in 1912 represented the status quo. The country clearly favored change, and the bulk of Roosevelt supporters would more likely have turned to Wilson than to Taft.

This was Roosevelt's last campaign for president. After the election he returned to the Republican Party and continued to hope for a comeback, but his revolt was too fresh for any chance at the nomination by Republicans in 1916. In that year he supported the Republican candidate for president, a former associate justice of the Supreme Court, Charles Evans Hughes of New York, against Wilson, whom he came to dislike intensely. He mounted a campaign tour for Hughes, somewhat reluctantly, for he could never completely forgive the regulars of his party for rejecting him in 1912. After the election, Roosevelt remained active in political infighting and sharply critical of the Wilson administration until his death in January 1919.

BIBLIOGRAPHIC ESSAY

Among the useful sources for the history of Roosevelt's election campaigns, John Morton Blum, *The Republican Roosevelt* (Cambridge: Harvard University Press, 1977), is an important analysis of Roosevelt's political ideas and development. G. Wallace Chessman, *Governor Theodore Roosevelt: The Albany Apprenticeship* (Cambridge: Harvard University Press, 1965), and John A. Corry, *A Rough Ride to Albany: Teddy Runs for Governor* (New York: n.p., 2000) offer students detailed accounts of Roosevelt's Albany experience. John Gable, *The Bull Moose Years: Theodore Roosevelt and the Progressive Party* (Port Washington, N.Y.: Kennikat Press, 1978), is very helpful for the 1912 campaign. William Henry Harbaugh, *The Life and Times of Theodore Roosevelt* (New York: Collier Books, 1963; originally published as *Power and Responsibility: The Life and Times of Theodore Roosevelt* [New York: Farrar, Straus and Cudahy, 1961]), is indispensable for Roosevelt studies. For more detail on the Bull Moose campaign see Frank K. Kelly, *The Fight for the White House: The Story of 1912* (New York: Thomas Y. Crowell, 1961). Nathan Miller, *Theodore Roosevelt: A Life* (New York: William Morrow, 1992), is a solid biography but less detailed than H. W. Brands, *T.R.: The Last Romantic*, or the two volumes of a projected trilogy by Edmund Morris, cited below. George E. Mowry, *Theodore Roosevelt and the Progressive Movement* (Madison: University of Wisconsin Press, 1946), remains an important work on the relation of Roosevelt to the liberal movement.

In addition to key works above, the following are also cited in this chapter: H. W. Brands, *T.R.: The Last Romantic* (New York: Basic Books, 1997), is a most readable recent full biography. Elting E. Morison, ed., *The Letters of Theodore Roosevelt*, 8 vols. (Cambridge: Harvard University Press, 1951–1954), is an indispensable tool for Roosevelt studies. Edmund Morris, *The Rise of Theodore Roosevelt* (New York: Coward, McCann and Geoghegan, 1979), the first volume of a projected three-volume biography, is rich in anecdotes and intimate details of TR's political and personal life. Edmund Morris, *Theodore Rex* (New York: Random House, 2001), the second volume of the projected trilogy, continues the detailed and intimate style of the first volume. Henry F. Pringle, *Theodore Roosevelt* (1931; reprint, New York: Harcourt, Brace, 1956), one of the earliest scholarly studies of Roosevelt, holds up well with age and offers occasional praise and some strong skepticism about TR's motives and achievements. Theodore Roosevelt, *The Works of Theodore Roosevelt*, 20 vols., national ed. (New York: Charles Scribner's Sons, 1926–1927), comprises a treasury of Roosevelt writings that includes his historical studies, accounts of his hunting, exploring, and ranching experiences, his autobiography, and his published essays on politics and society.

Document 2.1   Roosevelt to John Jay Chapman, September 22, 1898

On Roosevelt's return from heroic fighting in Cuba in the summer of 1898, he was simultaneously courted for the gubernatorial nomination by Thomas C. Platt, leader of the regular Republicans in New York, and John Jay Chapman, leader of the reformist Independent Party. After giving Chapman some encouragement, Roosevelt declined the Independent Party offer in this letter.

My dear Mr. Chapman:

I hesitate to write to you while the independent nomination has not been formally offered me, but I am now receiving so many questions as to my intentions in the matter that I am not willing to wait longer.

My name will probably be presented for Governor at the Republican state convention at Saratoga on the 27th. If I am nominated then it will be on the same ticket with those who are named for the other state offices. . . .

It seems to me that I would not be acting in good faith toward my fellow candidates if I permitted my name to head a ticket designed for their over-throw, a ticket moreover which cannot be put up because of objections to the character or fitness of any candidates, inasmuch as no candidates have yet been nominated.

I write this with great reluctance, for I wish the support of every Independent. If elected Governor, I would strive to serve the State as a whole and to serve my party by helping it serve the State. I should greatly like the aid of the Independents, and I appreciate the importance of the Independent vote, but I cannot accept a nomination on terms that would make me feel disloyal to the principles for which I stand, or at the cost of acting with what seems to me to be bad faith toward my associates.

Again expressing my hearty appreciation of the honor you wish to confer upon me, and my regret that it comes in such a shape that I do not see my way clear to accept it.

Source: New York Tribune, September 25, 1898; also available in Elting E. Morison, ed., *The Letters of Theodore Roosevelt* (Cambridge: Harvard University Press, 1951), 2:877.

Document 2.2   Opening Address in the Campaign for Governor of New York, October 5, 1898

Roosevelt opened his campaign for governor with a speech that oddly directed most of its attention to national affairs, perhaps a clue to his ambition for office beyond the governorship. He reflects here his enduring interest in expanding naval arms and strengthening national defense. Regarding the scene in New York, he promised honest government in the face of recent scandals but offered little to suggest the progressive reform ideas current in other states at the time.

First and foremost, this campaign is a campaign for good government, for good government both in the nation and the State. If I am elected governor I shall try to make good the promises, both expressed and implied, made on behalf of my candidacy, for I shall try to so administer the affairs of the State as to make each citizen a little prouder of the State, and I shall do my best to serve my party by helping it serve the people. So far as in me lies, I shall see that every branch of the government under me is administered with integrity and capacity, and when I deal with any public servant, I shall not be very patient with him if he lacks capacity, and short indeed will be his shrift if he lacks integrity. I shall feel most deeply my responsibilities to the people, and I shall do my best to show by my acts that I feel it even more deeply than my words express.

There comes a time in the life of a nation, as in the life of an individual, when it must face great responsibilities, whether it will or no. We have now reached that time. We cannot avoid facing the fact that we occupy a new place among the people of the world, and have entered upon a new career. All that we can decide is whether we shall bear ourselves well or ill in following out this career. . . .

Greatness means strife for nation and man alike. A soft, easy life is not worth living, if it impairs the fibre of brain and heart and muscle. We must dare to be great; and we must realize that greatness is the fruit of toil and sacrifice and high courage. . . .

I should ask the people of this country to support the administration of President McKinley, if for no other reason, because, say what you like, the victory at the polls of the men who are opposing and denouncing his administration in this election will be interpreted abroad as meaning, on the part of America, a repudiation of the war from which we have just emerged triumphant. It will strengthen the hands of every hostile power which views with jealousy our victories in the Antilles and the Philippines; it will mean that the nations that now secretly and enviously wish to clip the wings of our pride will be emboldened. It will result in the partial undoing of what our army and navy have accomplished. It will mean the chance of grave complications, and the likelihood of our meeting obstacles when it comes to reaping the fruit of our triumph. You could get the benefits of the victories of Grant and Sherman only by re-electing Lincoln, and we will gain less than we ought to from this war if the administration is not sustained at these elections.

That the question of our national defenses is a very real question and may at any time become of vital moment has been brought home to all of us within the last six months.

This nation is a great peaceable nation, both by the temper of its people and by its fortunate geographical situation, and is freed from the necessity of maintaining such armaments as those that cramp the limbs of the powers of Continental Europe. Nevertheless, events have shown that war is always a possibility, even for us. Now, the surest way to avert war, if it can be averted, is to be prepared to do well if forced to go into war. If we don't prepare for war in advance, then other powers will have a just contempt for us. They will fail to understand that with us unreadiness does not mean timidity; and they may at any time do things which would force us to make war, and which they would carefully refrain from doing if they were sure we were ready to resent them. . . .

Our experience with the navy offers a case in point. Very soon after the Civil War we let our navy utterly run down, until on the seas we became of less moment than any third-rate power. In consequence we had occasionally to suffer from Spain, as in the *Virginius* affair, injuries which she would not have dreamed of inflicting had we been ready to retaliate.

Fifteen years ago we began to build up the navy. The first great service this new navy performed was in 1890, when by the mere fact of its existence it served to prevent war with Chile. Nothing but our having the ships and being ready to use them made Chile keep the peace, and as a mere matter of expense the war which the navy thus averted would have cost many times over more than the whole cost of the navy for the past fifteen years.

The second great service performed by the navy for the country was this year, when we were at last forced into war, and when our thoroughly prepared navy with its splendid material and splendid personnel at once gained for us the command of the seas, and thereby insured our victory. But let one who spent some very active months in helping make ready the navy for this war warn you against believing that even yet we have a navy equal in size to our national needs or our national greatness. Those who remember the panic into which our whole seacoast was thrown, at the outset of this war, will make up their minds that we need a powerful navy; not merely to protect our great interests—far greater now than ever before—in the islands of the ocean, but also to defend our own coasts. When I say defend, I wish it understood that I use the word in its proper sense, for the only defensive that is worth anything is the offensive. . . .

We want to build up our navy, exactly as the navy has been built up within the last fifteen years. We have got to show forethought, to spend the money that is necessary for the task. If we fail to exercise such fore-thought and to show such willingness to stand the necessary burdens year after year, we have got to thank ourselves if, when the strain comes, the down-right fighting capacity of the officers and the men has to be relied upon to make good the faults which would never have existed if we had an army of sufficient size and if we yearly put that army through maneuvers which would test it as an army and not as an aggregation of small units, each unit excellent in its way, but each utterly unaccustomed to work on a large scale with the others. We need a far larger regular army than we now have, and we need to have it trained on a larger scale than it has been trained for the last quarter of a century. We don't need it in the least for police purposes at home; we don't need it to preserve order, for our people are quite able to preserve order themselves; but we do need it to protect our interests abroad.

I doubt if there is an American to-day so ungenerous as not to appreciate the debt of gratitude he owes to the splendid officers and splendid men of the regular army, and we want to make our gratitude tangible by building up that regular army. . . .

So much for the steps that are necessary if we are to uphold the honor and maintain the interests of the nation abroad. But we can do neither one nor the other if we fail at home so to order the affairs of our national, State, and municipal households as to secure both our moral and material well-being, for, though material prosperity is indispensable, yet it cannot by itself atone for the lack of that higher and finer moral and spiritual excellence which ultimately counts for more than all else in the true life of a great nation.

It is because of the importance of material well-being that it is vital for our citizens to take no step which will seem to again reopen the question so happily settled at the last election. Above all we must do nothing to give the feeling that we may reverse our attitude on the question of a sound and stable currency; the question that comes closest to every man and especially every man of small means, who either works with his hands or depends on his trade or business for his bread. If by your votes you put in power men who fail to meet this issue—and to dodge it is quite as dangerous as, and very much meaner than, meeting it the wrong way—you will have struck a heavy blow at your own well-being; you will have done all in your power to set back the return of prosperity, and you will have only yourselves to thank if you suffer in consequence.

When I make a plea not to vote, directly or indirectly, for those who favor any form of fiat money, I appeal for the exercise of intelligence. But on this as on every other point, I also and most strongly appeal for the exercise of honesty. Honesty we must have; no brilliancy, no "smartness," can take its place. Indeed, in our home affairs, both in the State and in the municipality, it has always seemed to me that what we need is, not so much genius as the homely, every-day virtues of common sense and common honesty.

Of course there are many problems for the solution of which we need the best intellect of the Commonwealth. But for the ordinary public officer, what is necessary is to be watchful, energetic, broad-minded, and disinterested. Everyone will make mistakes, and when made the best remedy is cheerfully to recognize their existence and promptly proceed to undo them. If we proceed in this way; if we promptly punish men who misbehave and sternly refuse to let any consideration either of political or personal friendship be treated as an offset to wrong-doing, it is not very difficult to secure that honest administration which is indispensable if our Republic is to endure. No influence of any kind must avail to shield the wrong-doer, be he of high or low degree.

In dealing with our citizens it is always best, where possible, not to treat any one class apart. On most points the interests of the working man, of the man who toils with his hands, are simply those of all good American citizens. Yet he has special interests; interests that are peculiarly his. Wherever he can be helped he most certainly should be helped. Ordinarily, I firmly believe and shall ever insist, that the help that will most surely avail the man who works is self-help. But the history of the trades-unions has shown that very much can also be done by that form of self-help where many join together to help one another.

It is not well to teach anyone to rely mainly upon the State, for the State can never play any but a very subordinate part in a man's welfare. Primarily the man must rely on himself. Yet the fact remains that along certain lines a great deal can be gained by legislation. Legislation cannot make a man prosperous, for it cannot make him honest or thrifty or industrious, but it can sometimes secure the fruits of honesty, thrift, and industry to the rightful owners, and in this case it should be resorted to.

Yet, after all, it seems to me that the great lesson to be taught our people is the lesson both of brotherhood and of self-help. In our several ways each of us must work hard to do his duty, each must preserve his sturdy independence; and yet each must realize his duty to others. And to each who performs his duty, in whatever way, must be given the full measure of respect. . . .

Source: Theodore Roosevelt, *The Works of Theodore Roosevelt,* national ed. (New York: Charles Scribner's Sons, 1926), 14:290–297.

Document 2.3   Gubernatorial Campaign Speech, October 27, 1898

On Roosevelt's whistle-stop campaign for governor, he made dozens of speeches across the state. In this example, he appeals to labor with an exhortation to self-help, still conservative on labor issues. Concrete prolabor proposals would wait for his conversion to a more progressive political faith.

I am particularly pleased that in this election there is on the ticket with me a candidate who is essentially a representative of the wage-workers. I do not wish to be misunderstood. The first and most important consideration in pushing forward a candidate should be, is or is he not a good citizen? But we must recognize the fact that, aside from their general interest as citizens, special groups of citizens have special interests, and just at present, where, as in this case, we have a representative of the labor interests who is on other grounds peculiarly fitted for the position to which he is nominated, it is an additional advantage to have him elected because of his connection with the great groups of citizens who collectively can be called wage-workers.

More and more of late years we have grown to understand and sympathize with the objects of the men who have taken the lead in working for what are called the interests of labor. And more and more these men have become more reasonable in their demands and less suspicious of those who wish, as they too should wish, carefully to investigate every remedy proposed for any wrong before committing themselves in its favor. . . .

While we must always insist that the working man, whether he work with head or hands, must keep steadily in view the fact that he must rely mainly upon himself, upon his own thrift, energy, and honesty, rather than upon the State; yet we must also remember that very much can be done by working men acting in groups, and that the State, too, in some cases, can do a great deal. It can help make a working man of more value in the life and labor of the community, and when he does this it will work for the public welfare, as well as that of the working man himself.

It is to the interest of all of us to produce a high type of citizenship among all our people. And, therefore, the State, standing as the representative of all the people, is deeply concerned in producing a high type of citizenship and manhood. We must not lose sight of the fact that the individual himself is the most potent factor in bringing this about, nor yet of the other fact that the State, likewise, can do something toward producing this same result.

I am not going to promise you as much as other men would promise you. Those who make countless promises never keep all of them. But if I am elected governor of New York State I promise you this—and I will see to it that my promises are made as good as my words: That no man shall wrong the State; that the State shall wrong no man, whether he be rich or poor; that the laws passed to protect the interests of the working man are carried out to the letter; that creed, color, or nationality shall make no difference; that every man shall be treated according to his merits as a man; that every man shall have the fullest liberty the laws allow.

In my regiment of Rough Riders I had men from the North, South, East, and West; men of money and men without money. I treated the Northerner as I treated the Southerner; I treated the poor Rough Rider as I treated the rich Rough Rider; and so shall it be if I am elected governor—every man shall be treated on his merits as a man.

Source: Theodore Roosevelt, *The Works of Theodore Roosevelt,* national ed. (New York: Charles Scribner's Sons, 1926), 14:306–307.

Document 2.4   Inaugural Address, January 2, 1899

Governor Roosevelt, keenly aware of recent state scandals, chose morality in government as the theme of his inaugural. The demands of that theme spelled trouble with Republican boss Thomas C. Platt and the party regulars throughout his administration.

A very heavy responsibility rests upon the governor of New York State, a State of 7,000,000 inhabitants, of great wealth, of widely varied industries and with a population singularly diversified, not merely in occupation, but in race origin, in habits of life, and in ways of thought. It is not an easy task so to frame our laws that justice may be done to all alike in such a population, so many of whom have interests that seem entirely antagonistic. But upon the great and fundamental issues of good government there must always be a unity of interest among all persons who wish well to the Commonwealth. There is much less need of genius or of any special brilliancy in the administration of our government than there is need of such homely virtues and qualities as common sense, honesty, and courage. There are very many difficult problems to face, some of which are as old as government itself, while others have sprung into being in consequence of the growing complexity and steadily increasing tension of our social life for the last two generations. It is not given to any man, or to any set of men, to see with absolutely clear vision into the future. All that can be done is to face the facts as we find them, to meet each difficulty in practical fashion, and to strive steadily for the betterment both of our civic and our social conditions.

We must realize, on the one hand, that we can do little if we do not set ourselves a high ideal, and, on the other, that we will fail in accomplishing even this little if we do not work through practical methods and with a readiness to face life as it is, and not as we think it ought to be. Under no form of government is it so necessary thus to combine efficiency and morality, high principle and rough common sense, justice and the sturdiest physical and moral courage, as in a republic. It is absolutely impossible for a republic long to endure if it becomes either corrupt or cowardly; if its public men, no less than its private men, lose the indispensable virtue of honesty, if its leaders of thought become visionary doctrinaires, or if it shows a lack of courage in dealing with the many grave problems which it must surely face, both at home and abroad, as it strives to work out the destiny for a mighty nation.

It is only through the party system that free governments are now successfully carried on, and yet we must keep ever vividly before us that the usefulness of a party is strictly limited by its usefulness to the State, and that in the long run, he serves his party best who most helps to make it instantly responsive to every need of the people, and to the highest demands of that spirit which tends to drive us onward and upward.

It shall be my purpose, so far as I am given strength, to administer my office with an eye single to the welfare of all the people of this great Commonwealth.

Source: Theodore Roosevelt, *The Works of Theodore Roosevelt,* national ed. (New York: Charles Scribner's Sons, 1926), 15:3–4.

Document 2.5   Roosevelt to Thomas C. Platt on Vice Presidential Nomination, February 1, 1900

As the election of 1900 approached, Platt worked assiduously to get Roosevelt out of New York. In this letter to Platt, the governor firmly rejected the idea of a vice presidential nomination and listed his reasons, none of which deflected Platt from his task.

My dear Senator Platt:

I have, of course, done a great deal of thinking about the Vice-Presidency since the talk I had with you followed by the letter from Lodge. . . . I can't help feeling more and more that the Vice-Presidency is not an office in which I could do anything and not an office in which a man who is still vigorous and not past middle life has much chance of doing anything. As you know, I am of an active nature. In spite of all the work and all the worry—and very largely because of your own constant courtesy and consideration, my dear Senator—I have thoroughly enjoyed being Governor. I have kept every promise, expressed or implied, I made on the stump and I feel that the Republican party is stronger before the State because of my incumbency. Certainly everything is being managed now on a perfectly straight basis and every office is as clean as a whistle.

Now, I should like to be Governor for another term, especially if we are able to take hold of the canals in serious shape. But as Vice-President, I don't see there is anything I can do. I would be simply a presiding officer and that I should find a bore. As you know, I am a man of moderate means . . . and I should have to live very simply in Washington and could not entertain in any way as Mr. Hobart and Mr. Morton entertained. My children are all growing up and I find the burden of their education constantly heavier, so that I am by no means sure that I ought to go on in public life at all, provided some remunerative work offered itself. The only reason that I would like to go on is that as I have not been a money maker I feel rather in honor bound to leave my children the equivalent in a way of a substantial sum of actual achievement in politics or letters. Now, as Governor, I can achieve something, but as Vice-President I should achieve nothing. The more I look at it, the less I feel as if the Vice-Presidency offered anything to me that would warrant my taking it.

Source: Theodore Roosevelt Collection, Library of Congress; also available in Elting E. Morison, ed., *The Letters of Theodore Roosevelt* (Cambridge: Harvard University Press, 1951), 2:1156–1157.

Document 2.6   Roosevelt to Henry Cabot Lodge on
Vice Presidential Nomination, February 2, 1900

Roosevelt consulted his close friend Henry Cabot Lodge on political matters throughout his career. Lodge advised him to accept the vice presidential nomination Thomas C. Platt was working so hard to arrange for him. But in February 1900 Roosevelt was still adamant about wanting another term as governor as he explained in this letter to Lodge.

Dear Cabot:

With the utmost reluctance I have come to a conclusion that is against your judgement. I know that you looking at matters from the outside have a clearer vision than I have; yet in this case I think it is obscured by your personal friendship for and belief in me in what regard as my future career. . . .

You got me the chance to be civil service commissioner and Assistant Secretary of the Navy, and it was by your advice that I went into the police department. All three jobs were worth doing and I did them reasonably to my own satisfaction. Now the thing to decide at the moment is whether I shall try for the Governorship again, or accept the Vice-Presidency, if offered. I have been pretty successful as Governor. As I wrote you, with the Payne business settled as it has been, I have got the departmental work of the State on a really high plane of execution. I have committed myself to a great policy in reference to the canals. There is ample work left for me to do in another term,—work that will need all of my energy and capacity— in short, work well worth any man's doing. I understand perfectly that in New York with the Republican party shading on the one hand into corrupt politicians, and on the other hand, into a group of impracticables of the Godkin-Parkhurst type who are essentially quite as dishonest, the task of getting results is one of incredible difficulty, and the danger of being wrecked very great, and this without regard to one's own capacities. For instance, if the machine were very strong and could get the upper hand, they would undoubtedly like to throw me over, while the *Evening Post* style of independent always tends to be so angered at my securing good results along lines which he does not understand, that he will join Tammany to try to destroy me, as he did when I ran before. But this is simply the inevitable risk in such a State as this. It is not possible to count on a political career in New York as it is in Massachusetts, and the only thing to do is to face the fact, do good work while the chance lasts, and show good humor when, as inevitably must happen, the luck turns, and for no fault of one's own, one is thrown out. But in the Vice-Presidency I could do nothing. I am a comparatively young man yet and I like to work. I do not like to be a figurehead. It would not entertain me to preside in the Senate. I should be in a cold shiver of rage at inability to answer hounds like Pettigrew and the scarcely more admirable Mason and Hale. I could not *do* anything; and yet I would be seeing continually things that I would like to do, and very possibly would like to do differently from the way in which they were being done. Finally the personal element comes in. Though I am a little better off than the *Sun* correspondent believes, I have not sufficient means to run the social side of the Vice-Presidency as it ought to be run. I should have to live very simply, and would be always in the position of "poor man at a frolic." I would not give a snap of my fingers for this if I went in the Cabinet or as a Senator, or was doing a real bit of work; but I would want to consider it when the office is in fact merely a show office. So, old man, I am going to declare decisively that I want to be Governor and do not want to be Vice-President. Publicly I shall only say I don't want to be Vice-P. Edith bids me to say that she hopes you will forgive me!

Source: Henry Cabot Lodge, ed., *Selections from the Correspondence of Theodore Roosevelt and Henry Cabot Lodge: 1884–1918* (New York: Charles Scribner's Sons, 1925), 1:447–448.

Document 2.7   Statement to Republican Convention on the Vice Presidential Nomination, June 18, 1900

Perhaps after reflecting on the difficulty in being renominated for governor by the regulars and on the troubles with Thomas C. Platt that lay ahead if he remained in New York, Roosevelt's thinking about the vice presidency seems to have changed by the time the Republican convention met. He released this statement to the delegates in language so soft compared with his earlier protests that it suggested he was ready to submit to the inevitable.

In view of the revival of the talk of myself as a Vice Presidential candidate, I have this to say. It is impossible too deeply to express how touched I am by the attitude of those delegates, who have wished me to take the nomination. Moreover, it is not necessary to say how thoroughly I understand the high honor and dignity of the office, an office so high and so honorable that it is well worthy the ambition of any man in the United States. But while appreciating all this to the full, I nevertheless feel most deeply that the field of my best usefulness to the public and to the party is in New York State; and that, if the party should see fit to re-nominate me for Governor, I can in that position help the National ticket as in no other way. I very earnestly hope and ask that every friend of mine in the convention respect my wish and my judgement in this matter.

Source: Nicholas Murray Butler Collection, Columbia University; also available in Elting E. Morison, ed., *The Letters of Theodore Roosevelt* (Cambridge: Harvard University Press, 1951), 2:1337n.

Document 2.8   Seconding Speech for the Nomination of McKinley, June 21, 1900

Entering the convention hall with a wave of his Rough Rider–style hat and delivering a fervent nomination speech for President William McKinley, Roosevelt received roars of approval from the admiring delegates. At this point he must have known his performance could only encourage their support for his nomination as vice president.

Mr. Chairman and my fellow delegates, my beloved Republicans and Americans, I rise to second the nomination of William McKinley, the President who has had to face more numerous and graver problems than any other President since the days of the mighty Lincoln, and who has faced them. Four years ago the Republicans made William McKinley their nominee for President. The Republican nominee, even before a fortnight had passed, he had become the candidate not merely of all Republicans but of all Americans far-sighted enough to see where the true interests of the nation lay, and keenly sensitive to the national honor. Four years ago we were confronted with the gravest crisis which this nation has had to face since Appomattox was won and the civil war came to a close. We were confronted by a situation where, if our opponents had triumphed, it meant not only an immense aggravation of the existing and already well-nigh intolerable physical distress, but a stain on the national honor so deep that a generation would have had to pass away before it could have been wiped out.

We appealed to the nation to put William McKinley in the first place on the two simple issues that if he were elected prosperity would come to the country and the country's honor would be upheld at home and abroad. . . .

Well, we kept our word. The opportunity was given, and it was seized by American energy, ingenuity and thrift, with the result that this country now, as we sit here, has reached a pitch of prosperity never before attained in the nation's history. So it has been in foreign affairs. Four years ago the nation was uneasy because at our very doors an American Island was writhing in hideous agony under a worse than mediaeval despotism. We had our Armenia at our threshold. The situation in Cuba had become such that we could no longer stand quiet and retain one shred of self-respect. The President faced this duty as he faced all others. He exhausted every expedient to get Spain to withdraw peacefully from the island which she was impotent to do aught than oppress, and when every peaceful means had failed, we drew the sword and waged the most righteous and brilliantly successful foreign war that this generation has seen. . . .

This is what the nation has done during the three years of President McKinley's administration, and this is what he stands for and typifies. To him it has been given—and thrice blessed the man to whom such is given—to embody in his own personality all that is loftiest, most earnest, most disinterested in the Nation's hope, in the Nation's desire, and to represent the Nation's strength in the struggle for righteousness.

We have done so well that our opponents actually use the fact as an argument for turning us out. We have put our economic policy on a basis so stable, we have enacted such wise financial legislation that they turn to the wise and honest men who deserted them at the last election and beg them to come back and support them now because even if they do get in we will prevent them from doing the harm they would like to do. I am not exaggerating. That is the exact argument they use; and to all who might be affected by it let me address one word of warning. Wise legislation is vitally important, but honest administration is even more important. No matter how perfect our financial legislation, if the management of the national finances were entrusted to any man who would be acceptable to the Populistic Democracy of to-day, we should be plunged back into an abyss of shame, disgrace and business chaos.

Our opponents have not any more even the poor excuse of honesty for their folly. They have raved against trusts, they have foamed at the mouth in prating of impossible remedies they would like to adopt; and now in my own State we have discovered all of the chief leaders of the Democracy, including that leader before whom the other lesser leaders stand with bared heads and trembling knees in a trust which really is of infamous and perhaps of criminal character. These apostles of Democracy, these prophets of the new dispensation, have themselves been discovered in a trust through which they hope to wring fortunes for themselves from the dire needs of their poorer brethren. I pity the Democratic orator who in New York State this fall speaks the word "trusts."

Now for the Philippines. The insurrection still goes on because the allies in this country of the bloody insurrectionary oligarchy in Luzon have taught their foolish dupes to believe that Democratic success at the polls next November means the abandonment of the islands to the savages, who would scramble for the bloody plunder until some other strong civilized nation came in to do the work that we would have shown ourselves unfit to perform. Our success in November means peace in the islands. The success of our opponents means an indefinite prolongation of the present bloody struggle.

We nominate President McKinley because he stands indeed for honesty at home and for honor abroad; because he stands for the continuance of the material prosperity which has brought comfort to every home in the Union; and because he stands for that kind of policy which consists in making performance square with promise.

We stand on the threshold of a new century big with the fate of mighty nations. It rests with us now to decide whether in the opening years of that century we shall march forward to fresh triumphs or whether at the outset we shall cripple ourselves for the contest. Is America a weakling, to shrink from the world-work of the great world powers? No. The young giant of the West stands on a continent and clasps the crest of an ocean in either hand. Our nation, glorious in youth and strength, looks into the future with eager eyes and rejoices as a strong man to run a race. We do not stand in craven mood asking to be spared the task, cringing as we look on the contest. No. We challenge the proud privilege of doing the work that Providence allots us, and we face the coming years high of heart and resolute of faith that to our people is given the right to win such honor and renown as has never yet been vouchsafed to the nation of mankind.

Source: Theodore Roosevelt, *The Works of Theodore Roosevelt,* national ed. (New York: Charles Scribner's Sons, 1926), 14:342–345.

Document 2.9   Vice Presidential Acceptance Speech, June 21, 1900

Roosevelt addressed the delegates to the Republican convention to accept his nomination for vice president in which he urged his audience to reject the past and "go forward along the path of prosperity and high honor abroad."

I accept the honor conferred upon me with the keenest and deepest appreciation of what it means, and, above all, of the responsibility that goes with it. Everything that is in my power to do will be done to secure the reelection of President McKinley, to whom it has been given in this crisis of the national history to stand for and embody the principles which lie closest to the heart of every American worthy of the name.

This is very much more than a mere party contest. We stand at the parting of the ways, and the people have now to decide whether they shall go forward along the path of prosperity and high honor abroad, or whether they will turn their backs upon what has been done during the past three years; whether they will plunge this country into an abyss of misery and disaster, or, what is worse than even misery and disaster—shame. I feel that we have a right to appeal not merely to Republicans, but to all good citizens, no matter what may have been their party affiliations in the past, and to ask them, on the strength of the record that President McKinley has made during the past three years and on the strength of the threat implied in what was done in Kansas City a few days ago, to stand shoulder to shoulder with us, perpetuating the conditions under which we have reached a degree of prosperity never before attained in the nation's history and under which abroad we have put the American flag on a level where it never before in the history of the country has been placed. For these reasons I feel we have a right to look forward with confident expectation to what the verdict of the people will be next November, and to ask all men to whom the well-being of the country and the honor of the national name are dear to stand with us as we fight for prosperity at home and the honor of the flag abroad.

Source: Official Proceedings of the Twelfth Republican National Convention (Philadelphia: Dunlap Printing Company, 1900), 154–155.

Document 2.10   Campaign Speech for McKinley-Roosevelt Ticket, September 7, 1900

As Roosevelt began to tour the country for President William McKinley, he struck the main themes of the campaign: sound money, the distinction between good trusts and bad trusts, and unblushing nationalism. Here is an example of a typical Roosevelt speech, made at Grand Rapids, Michigan.

There are several great issues at stake in this campaign, but of course the greatest issue of all is the issue of keeping the country on the plane of material well-being and honor to which it has been brought during the last four years. I do not claim that President McKinley's admirable administration and the wise legislation passed by Congress which he has sanctioned are solely responsible for our present well-being, but I do claim that it is this administration and this legislation which have rendered it possible for the American people to achieve such well-being. I insist furthermore that the one and only way to insure wide-spread industrial and social ruin would be now to reverse the policy under which we have so prospered, and to try that policy of financial disgrace and economic disaster which we rejected in '96. Our opponents now advance the most extraordinary arguments that have ever been advanced in a presidential campaign by any party on behalf of its presidential nominee. They have reaffirmed specifically their entire '96 platform, and yet they insist vigorously that all they considered of most vital importance in '96 shall now be relegated to a subordinate place; and more extraordinary still, they actually ask that Mr. Bryan and a Democratic House be elected, because the Senate will remain Republican anyhow, so that the President and the House won't be able to do much harm.

Think of it, gentlemen! This is the position actually taken by not a few of our opponents, and especially by the men who know that Mr. Bryan's financial policy is utterly ruinous, but who want to give themselves some excuse for voting against President McKinley, because forsooth President McKinley has been too active in upholding the honor of the flag. Mr. Bryan himself is sufficiently strident when he talks about those figments of disordered brains, militarism and imperialism; yet he coos as mildly as a sucking dove when he whispers his unchanged devotion to free silver. Now it is worth while remembering that if the question of the unsettlement of our currency is raised in any campaign, it must be one of the paramount questions. The other day in accepting the Populistic nomination Mr. Bryan was careful to point out how little he and they differed in essentials on the greenback question. He is quite right. Both are believers in fiat money; what particular kind of fiat money is necessarily a minor detail. It makes no difference whether free silver or fiat money is championed as the first or second issue so long as it is championed at all, save that to subordinate it as an issue removes the last justification for raising the issue at all. The one element more essential than any other to the prosperity of a great civilized nation is a sound and stable currency. The only possible excuse for jeopardizing the prosperity of the whole nation by attacking its system of currency is a conviction so intense that the issue must of necessity be a burning one. If our opponents do not regard the silver issue as a paramount issue, then they have been guilty of gross wrong to their fellow countrymen in raising it at all.

As a matter of fact, it *is* paramount, and the attitude of the Populistic Democracy in trying to keep it out of sight east of the Mississippi, while insisting upon their adherence to it west of the Mississippi, is in itself enough to discredit them in the eyes of all good citizens, whether Republicans or genuine Democrats. Moreover, the attitude is entirely futile. The leaders among our opponents are doubtless uneasily conscious that their free-silver policy would be disastrous to the welfare of our country; but having played the part of demagogues they must now reap the fruits of their action. If they came into power, their mere possession of power would throw this country into convulsions of disaster. They would be obliged to make war upon the principles of sound finance. The victory of Mr. Bryan would mean such a strengthening of the foes of honest money as to powerfully impress every wavering mind in the Senate, so that free-silver legislation could probably pass both houses; and no secretary of the treasury who would accept office under Mr. Bryan could do anything but follow a course of action which would plunge our financial system into chaos. If the farmer, the business man, and the wage-worker want prosperity to continue, they must make up their minds that the incoming of Mr. Bryan would mean terrible and wide-spread disaster.

A word as to trusts. Beyond a question the great industrial combinations which we group in popular parlance under the name of trusts have produced great and serious evils. There is every reason why we should try to abate these evils and to make men of wealth, whether they act individually or collectively, bear their full share of the country's burdens and keep as scrupulously within the bounds of equity and morality as any of their neighbors. But wild and frantic denunciation does not do them the least harm and simply postpones the day when we can make them amenable to proper laws. Hasty legislation of a violent type is either wholly ineffective against the evil, or else crushes the evil at the expense of crushing even more of good. We need to approach the subject both with a firm resolution to abate the evils and in a spirit of hard common sense as we search for the means of abating them. One of the first things to obtain is publicity. We must be able by law to find out exactly what each corporation does and earns. This mere publicity itself will effect something toward remedying many evils. Moreover, it will give us a clearer idea as to what the remaining evils are, and will therefore enable us to shape our measures for attacking the latter with good prospects of success. Immoderate attack always invites reaction and often defeat. Moderation combined with resolution can alone secure results worth having.

Let me point out to you that within the last two years we have in New York established a franchise tax under which the corporations which owe most to the State, but who had hitherto largely escaped taxation, have been required to pay their just share of taxation. This law has resulted in putting upon the assessment books nearly two hundred millions of property which had theretofore escaped taxation. It represents ten times over more than our opponents ever did in that State, or so far as I know in any other State, have done to remedy the inequalities which can justly be complained of; and yet we did it without any demagogic outcry, and we did it in no anarchic spirit; but simply as the friends of order and liberty, of property and individual rights, who intended temperately but firmly to insist upon justice for all. In other words, we made our performance square with our promise. Contrast this with what our opponents in that State did. The leader of the Democratic party in my State and the gentleman who ran against me for governor on an antitrust platform and who served on the Committee on Resolutions at Kansas City which drew up their present platform, are both of them very loud in their denunciation of trusts. They say a great deal more against them than I should say, because I am hampered by the fact that I want to have my deeds always make good my words. When we come to deeds, however, we find that in a particularly flagrant trust, the Ice Trust, the two gentlemen referred to stand foremost among the stockholders, the same stockholders including a number of the New York City officials, and this in spite of the fact that the city itself has dealings with the trust. Such a condition of affairs calls for but scant comment from me. You can hope for but little from men who in other words play the demagogue about trusts, but you can hope for infinitely less when these very men join to public denunciation of trusts private ownership in them. . . .

Now a word specifically as to the Philippines. It is in connection with the Philippines that Mr. Bryan has chiefly harped upon the "consent of the governed" theory. As a matter of fact we cannot too clearly keep in mind that the success of the Aguinaldian rebels would mean not liberty for all Filipinos, but liberty for a certain bloodthirsty section to oppress a great majority of their fellow countrymen. Under Spanish rule the Filipinos were treated with intolerable cruelty. The Aguinaldian leaders have, wherever their power has extended, continued a system almost as bad. The chief victims of this system have been not the Americans but their fellow Filipinos; for their hatred and cruelty have been exhibited chiefly at the cost of their fellow countrymen who have had the good sense and genuine patriotism to realize that the true interests of the islands lay in the American Government. So far as I am aware not one competent witness who has actually known the facts believes the Filipinos capable of self-government at present, or believes that such an effort would result in anything but a horrible confusion of tyranny and anarchy. . . .

Remember that to surrender the Philippines now to a little band of military usurpers would be to surrender the islands to bloodshed and misery. Our stay in the islands is the condition precedent of peace. . . .

My fellow citizens, the truth as regards the present situation is simply and clearly that the American people now have to decide whether or not they will play the part of a great nation nobly and well. It is with the nation as with the individual. None of us respects the man whose aim in life is to avoid every difficulty and danger and stay in the shelter of his own home, there to bring up children unable to face the roughness of the world. We respect the man who goes out to do a man's work, to front difficulties and overcome them, and to train up his children to do likewise. So it is with the nation. To decline to do our duty is simply to sink as China has sunk. If we are to continue to hold our heads high as Americans, we must bravely, soberly, and resolutely front each particular duty as it arises, and it is because of the great truth contained in this principle that we appeal to every man, Northerner and Southern[er], Easterner and Westerner, whether his father fought under Grant or under Lee, whatever political party he may have belonged to in the past—to stand with us now when we ask that the hands of President McKinley be upheld, and that this nation instead of shrinking in unmanly terror from its duty, shall stride forward, to use its giant strength for the upholding of our honor and the interests of mankind in doing that part of the world's work which Providence has allotted to us.

Source: Theodore Roosevelt, *The Works of Theodore Roosevelt,* national ed. (New York: Charles Scribner's Sons, 1926), 14:346–359.

Document 2.11   On Becoming President, September 23, 1901

Although stunned by President William McKinley's assassination, in this excerpt from a letter to Henry Cabot Lodge, Roosevelt revealed he was undaunted in assuming the responsibilities of the presidency.

Dear Cabot:

It is a dreadful thing to come into the Presidency this way; but it would be a far worse thing to be morbid about it. Here is the task, and I have got to do it to the best of my ability; and that is all there is about it. I believe you will approve of what I have done and of the way I have handled myself so far. It is only a beginning, but it is better to make a beginning good than bad.

Source: Henry Cabot Lodge, ed., *Selections from the Correspondence of Theodore Roosevelt and Henry Cabot Lodge: 1884–1918* (New York: Charles Scribner's Sons, 1925), 1:506.

Document 2.12   On the Ohio Republican Endorsement, May 23, 1903

When an Ohio Republican faction opposed to Sen. Mark Hanna proposed to endorse Roosevelt at their state convention in June 1903, a year before the national convention, Hanna fought the idea. In the following letter to Henry C. Payne, Roosevelt's postmaster general and strong supporter, Roosevelt vented his anger at Hanna's maneuver.

My dear Mr. Payne:

I have regretted Senator Hanna's action in the Ohio Convention, and his last utterance is of course sheer nonsense and insincere nonsense at that.

I do not understand his saying that the Ohio Republicans could not with propriety at this time take the action concerning me which at a corresponding period in President McKinley's first administration Mr. Hanna was most anxious I should take, and which I did take. If Mr. Hanna is for me there could be no possible objection to his saying so. Of course he has a perfect right to be against me, but if such is the case his action should be based explicitly on that ground, and not on grounds which are foolish!

Source: Roosevelt Collection, Library of Congress; also available in Elting E. Morison, ed., *The Letters of Theodore Roosevelt* (Cambridge: Harvard University Press, 1951), 3:479–480.

Document 2.13   Exchange of Telegrams with Sen. Mark Hanna, May 27, 1903

Roosevelt passed on to Henry Cabot Lodge his exchange with Sen. Mark Hanna on the matter of the early Ohio Republican endorsement in 1903.

Dear Cabot:

For your private information I would like you to know that the following three telegrams passed between myself and Senator Hanna:

Cleveland, Ohio, May 23, 1903

The President, Seattle, Washington.

The issue which has been forced upon me in the matter of our State Convention this year endorsing you for the Republican nomination next year has come in a way which makes it necessary for me to oppose such a resolution. When you know all the facts I am sure you will approve my course.

M. A. Hanna

May 25, 1903

Hon. M. A. Hanna, Cleveland, Ohio.

Your telegram received. I have not asked any man for his support. I have had nothing whatever to do with raising this issue. Inasmuch as it has been raised of course those who favor my administration and my nomination will favor endorsing both and those who do not will oppose.

Theodore Roosevelt

Cleveland, Ohio, May 26, 1903

The President.

Your telegram of the 25th. In view of the sentiment expressed I shall not oppose the endorsement of your administration and candidacy by our State Convention. I have given the substance of this to the Associated Press.

M. A. Hanna

Source: Henry Cabot Lodge, ed., *Selections from the Correspondence of Theodore Roosevelt and Henry Cabot Lodge: 1884–1918* (New York: Charles Scribner's Sons, 1925), 2:18–20.

Document 2.14   Concerning Alton Parker, July 11, 1904

In a letter to his friend John Hay, the secretary of state, Roosevelt outlined his response to the statement of support for the gold standard by his Democratic challenger, Alton Parker. In election contests, Roosevelt often painted the opposition in colors less than honorable.

Dear John:

Apparently the "best thought" of New York, as typified by the newspapers which it prefers to read, feels that on high moral grounds of an inscrutable nature, they should condemn the Republicans for saying that sound money is an issue upon which they have opinions, and applaud the Democrats because they say that it is not an issue at the moment, and that therefore the views of their candidate on the subject do not count; this same candidate boasting of the fact that he has been regular, and has supported the cause of free silver in the last two elections, and therefore is entitled to the support of the free silverites, but inasmuch as his support was insincere, and he did not believe in the cause which he supported, he is therefore also entitled to the support of the gold Democrats. Literally this is the only opinion of Parker's on any current subject of which we now have knowledge, and he did not give this opinion until the convention had met and it became impossible for him to avoid giving it. His movement was most adroit, and he is entitled to hearty praise, from the standpoint of a clever politician, for what he has done. He did not refuse the nomination; he did not ask the Democrats to stand for gold; but he phrased his telegram so that they could answer that they did not regard the currency matter as one at issue, and that therefore his views on the subject did not concern them. If we Republicans did anything of this kind (which is unsupposable) we would rightfully be taunted by all of the virtuous mugwump crowd with insincerity, double-dealing, straddling, and everything else. But the same people who would thus attack us for doing this very thing, now become hysterical as they praise Parker and the Democracy. August Belmont and Cord Meyer, together with old Davis—whose nomination, as you say, was a very shrewd move—represent as unscrupulous financial interests as we have in this country; Dave Hill and Billy Sheehan represent all that is lowest in our political methods; and these are the men who are behind Parker—the men whom he represents and stands for—the men who found him, advertised him, and made him a candidate. . . .

Source: Roosevelt Collection, Library of Congress; also available in Elting E. Morison, ed., *The Letters of Theodore Roosevelt* (Cambridge: Harvard University Press, 1951), 4:851–853.

Document 2.15   Again on Alton Parker, July 14, 1904

Despite Roosevelt's popularity, he took nothing for granted in his 1904 campaign. In this letter to Henry Cabot Lodge he regarded Alton Parker as a serious and able challenger.

Dear Cabot:

I agree absolutely with what you say about Parker and the effect of his act when the convention was about to adjourn. It was a bold and skillful move. To say that he had any principles on the subject of gold is of course nonsense; for if so he would have inserted the gold plank in the New York Democratic platform. But then he was hunting for delegates and was exceedingly careful to offend no one. Now he played a perfectly safe but spectacular game and has attracted the good will of many decent people, and of course the hysterical adulation of the large neurotic class typified by the *Evening Post*. He has become a very formidable candidate and opponent; for instead of being a colorless man of no convictions he now stands forth to the average man—and this at an astonishingly small cost—as one having convictions compared to which he treats self-interest as of no account. He has, as you say, become a somebody instead of a nobody. I think that his act gave him all of Cleveland's strength without any of Cleveland's weakness, and made him, on the whole, the most formidable man the Democrats could have nominated. What the outcome will be I have not the slightest idea. Not only is Wisconsin, in my judgment, in a perilous situation, but so is West Virginia. John Kean seems satisfied about New Jersey; but no one can tell what reflex effect New York opinion will have in that State. In addition, of course, if we have failure of crops, or big labor troubles, into which they are always adroitly trying to bring me, we may encounter disaster in all the States of small margin. In short, I think we have a hard and uphill fight ahead of us. It is because of this feeling that I took an aggressive stand in my speech of acceptance. . . .

Source: Henry Cabot Lodge, ed., *Selections from the Correspondence of Theodore Roosevelt and Henry Cabot Lodge: 1884–1918* (New York: Charles Scribner's Sons, 1925), 2:89–90.

Document 2.16   Accepting the Republican Nomination, September 12, 1904

In 1904 Roosevelt followed the custom of the time, which frowned on a sitting president actively campaigning for reelection. He did, however, summarize the issues of the campaign in his letter of acceptance to Joseph G. Cannon,

Speaker of the House of Representatives and chairman of the Republican notification committee, aware that his words would be widely reported.

HON. J. G. CANNON, Chairman of the Notification Committee.

My dear Sir: I accept the nomination for the Presidency tendered me by the Republican National Convention, and cordially approve the platform adopted by it. In writing this letter there are certain points upon which I desire to lay especial stress.

It is difficult to find out from the utterances of our opponents what are the real issues upon which they propose to wage this campaign. It is not unfair to say that, having abandoned most of the principles upon which they have insisted during the last eight years, they now seem at a loss, both as to what it is that they really believe, and as to how firmly they shall assert their belief in anything. In fact, it is doubtful if they venture resolutely to press a single issue; as soon as they raise one they shrink from it and seek to explain it away. Such an attitude is the probably inevitable result of the effort to improvise convictions; for when thus improvised, it is natural that they should be held in a tentative manner.

The party now in control of the Government is troubled by no such difficulties. . . .

So well has the work been done that our opponents do not venture to recite the facts about our policies or acts and then oppose them. They attack them only when they have first misrepresented them; for a truthful recital would leave no room for adverse comment.

Panama offers an instance in point. Our opponents can criticize what we did in Panama only on condition of misstating what was done. The Administration behaved throughout not only with good faith, but with extraordinary patience and large generosity toward those with whom it dealt. It was also mindful of American interests. It acted in strict compliance with the law passed by Congress. Had not Panama been promptly recognized, and the transit across the Isthmus kept open, in accordance with our treaty rights and obligations, there would have ensued endless guerilla warfare and possibly foreign complications; while all chance of building the canal would have been deferred, certainly for years, perhaps for a generation or more. . . .

In addition to those acts of the Administration which they venture to assail only after misrepresenting them, there are others which they dare not overtly or officially attack, and yet which they covertly bring forward as reasons for the overthrow of the party. In certain great centers and with certain great interests our opponents make every effort to show that the settlement of the Anthracite Coal Strike by the individual act of the President, and the successful suit against the Northern Securities Company—the Merger suit—undertaken by the Department of Justice, were acts because of which the present Administration should be thrown from power. Yet they dare not openly condemn either act. They dare not in any authoritative or formal manner say that in either case wrong was done or error committed in the method of action, or in the choice of instruments for putting that action into effect. . . .

So far as the rights of the individual wage-worker and the individual capitalist are concerned, both as regards one another, as regards the public, and as regards organized capital and labor, the position of the Administration has been so clear that there is no excuse for misrepresenting it, and no ground for opposing it unless misrepresented. Within the limits defined by the National Constitution the National Administration has sought to secure to each man the full enjoyment of his right to live his life and dispose of his property and his labor as he deems best, so long as he wrongs no one else. It has shown in effective fashion that in endeavoring to make good this guaranty, it treats all men, rich or poor, whatever their creed, their color, or their birthplace, as standing alike before the law. Under our form of government the sphere in which the Nation as distinguished from the State can act is narrowly circumscribed; but within that sphere all that could be done has been done. All thinking men are aware of the restrictions upon the power of action of the National Government in such matters. Being ourselves mindful of them, we have been scrupulously careful on the one hand to be moderate in our promises, and on the other hand to keep these promises in letter and in spirit. Our opponents have been hampered by no such considerations. . . .

Conditions change and the laws must be modified from time to time to fit new exigencies. But the genuine underlying principle of protection, as it has been embodied in all but one of the American tariff laws for the last forty years, has worked out results so beneficent, so evenly and widely spread, so advantageous alike to farmers and capitalists and working men, to commerce and trade of every kind, that the American people, if they show their usual practical business sense, will insist that when these laws are modified they shall be modified with the utmost care and conservatism, and by the friends and not the enemies of the protective system. They cannot afford to trust the modification to those who treat protection and robbery as synonymous terms. . . .

Our opponents promise independence to the Philippine Islands. Here again we are confronted by the fact that their irreconcilable differences of opinion among themselves, their proved inability to create a constructive policy when in power, and their readiness, for the sake of momentary political expediency, to abandon the principles upon which they have insisted as essential, conspire to puzzle us as to whether they do or do not intend in good faith to carry out this promise if they are given control of the Government. . . . They have occupied three entirely different positions within fifty days. Which is the promise they really intend to keep? They do not know their own minds; and no one can tell how long they would keep of the same mind, should they by any chance come to a working agreement among themselves. . . .

We make our appeal to no class and to no section, but to all good citizens, in whatever part of the land they dwell, and whatever may be their occupation or worldly condition. We have striven both for civic righteousness and for national greatness; and we have faith to believe that our hands will be upheld by all who feel love of country and trust in the uplifting of mankind. We stand for enforcement of the law and for obedience to the law; our Government is a government of orderly liberty equally alien to tyranny and to anarchy; and its foundation-stone is the observance of the law, alike by the people and by the public servants. We hold ever before us as the all-important end of policy and administration the reign of peace at home and throughout the world; of peace, which comes only by doing justice.

Source: Theodore Roosevelt, *The Works of Theodore Roosevelt,* national ed. (New York: Charles Scribner's Sons, 1926), 16:372–405.

Document 2.17   Limiting Himself to One Full Term in Office, November 9, 1904

In the afterglow of his landslide victory, Roosevelt made what was probably the most serious mistake of his political career. His usually keen political instincts failed him when he effectively made himself a lame-duck president with the announcement that he would not be a candidate for president in 1908.

On the fourth of March next I shall have served three and a half years, and this three and a half years constitutes my first term. The wise custom which limits the President to two terms regards the substance and not the form. Under no circumstances will I be a candidate for or accept another nomination.

Source: Washington Evening Star, November 9, 1904, quoted in Edmund Morris, *Theodore Rex* (New York: Random House, 2001), 364.

Document 2.18   Inaugural Address, March 4, 1905
In Roosevelt's inaugural address he told his audience, "Much has been given us, and much will rightfully be expected from us."

My fellow-citizens, no people on earth have more cause to be thankful than ours, and this is said reverently, in no spirit of boastfulness in our own strength, but with gratitude to the Giver of Good who has blessed us with the conditions which have enabled us to achieve so large a measure of well-being and of happiness. To us as a people it has been granted to lay the foundations of our national life in a new continent. We are the heirs of the ages, and yet we have had to pay few of the penalties which in old countries are exacted by the dead hand of a bygone civilization. We have not been obliged to fight for our existence against any alien race; and yet our life has called for the vigor and effort without which the manlier and hardier virtues wither away. Under such conditions it would be our own fault if we failed; and the success which we have had in the past, the success which we confidently believe the future will bring, should cause in us no feeling of vainglory, but rather a deep and abiding realization of all which life has offered us; a full acknowledgment of the responsibility which is ours; and a fixed determination to show that under a free government a mighty people can thrive best, alike as regards the things of the body and the things of the soul.

Much has been given us, and much will rightfully be expected from us. We have duties to others and duties to ourselves; and we can shirk neither. We have become a great nation, forced by the fact of its greatness into relations with the other nations of the earth, and we must behave as beseems a people with such responsibilities. Toward all other nations, large and small, our attitude must be one of cordial and sincere friendship. We must show not only in our words, but in our deeds, that we are earnestly desirous of securing their good will by acting toward them in a spirit of just and generous recognition of all their rights. But justice and generosity in a nation, as in an individual, count most when shown not by the weak but by the strong. While ever careful to refrain from wrongdoing others, we must be no less insistent that we are not wronged ourselves. We wish peace, but we wish the peace of justice, the peace of righteousness. We wish it because we think it is right and not because we are afraid. No weak nation that acts manfully and justly should ever have cause to fear us, and no strong power should ever be able to single us out as a subject for insolent aggression.

Our relations with the other powers of the world are important; but still more important are our relations among ourselves. Such growth in wealth, in population, and in power as this nation has seen during the century and a quarter of its national life is inevitably accompanied by a like growth in the problems which are ever before every nation that rises to greatness. Power invariably means both responsibility and danger. Our forefathers faced certain perils which we have outgrown. We now face other perils, the very existence of which it was impossible that they should foresee. Modern life is both complex and intense, and the tremendous changes wrought by the extraordinary industrial development of the last half century are felt in every fiber of our social and political being. Never before have men tried so vast and formidable an experiment as that of administering the affairs of a continent under the forms of a Democratic republic. The conditions which have told for our marvelous material well-being, which have developed to a very high degree our energy, self-reliance, and individual initiative, have also brought the care and anxiety inseparable from the accumulation of great wealth in industrial centers. Upon the success of our experiment much depends, not only as regards our own welfare, but as regards the welfare of mankind. If we fail, the cause of free self-government throughout the world will rock to its foundations, and therefore our responsibility is heavy, to ourselves, to the world as it is to-day, and to the generations yet unborn. There is no good reason why we should fear the future, but there is every reason why we should face it seriously, neither hiding from ourselves the gravity of the problems before us nor fearing to approach these problems with the unbending, unflinching purpose to solve them aright.

Yet, after all, though the problems are new, though the tasks set before us differ from the tasks set before our fathers who founded and preserved this Republic, the spirit in which these tasks must be undertaken and these problems faced, if our duty is to be well done, remains essentially unchanged. We know that self-government is difficult. We know that no people needs such high traits of character as that people which seeks to govern its affairs aright through the freely expressed will of the freemen who compose it. But we have faith that we shall not prove false to the memories of the men of the mighty past. They did their work, they left us the splendid heritage we now enjoy. We in our turn have an assured confidence that we shall be able to leave this heritage unwasted and enlarged to our children and our children's children. To do so we must show, not merely in great crises, but in the everyday affairs of life, the qualities of practical intelligence, of courage, of hardihood, and endurance, and above all the power of devotion to a lofty ideal, which made great the men who founded this Republic in the days of Washington, which made great the men who preserved this Republic in the days of Abraham Lincoln.

Source: Theodore Roosevelt, *The Works of Theodore Roosevelt,* national ed. (New York: Charles Scribner's Sons, 1926), 15:267–269.

During the eighteenth and nineteenth centuries, no president while in office traveled outside the United States. Theodore Roosevelt broke this precedent when he visited Panama in 1906 to inspect the canal under construction.

CHAPTER THREE

Administration Policies

The policies of the Roosevelt administration were naturally shaped by Roosevelt's personal political philosophy, which itself was molded by his experience, class, and ambition. Roosevelt was a "regular" Republican who harbored reforming impulses in spite of himself. His style as a reformer was uniquely his own. From the time he entered politics as a state legislator in New York, he consistently supported the party organization. He tended to dismiss "do-good" reformers as unrealistic and, as he often tainted people he disliked, unmanly. Populists he scorned as dangerous. Yet he could also exasperate party leaders by introducing and promoting anticorruption and reform legislation. As a freshman legislator in Albany, he initiated a fight to investigate corruption in construction contracts and won against the resistance of the deeply annoyed leadership. As a member of the national Civil Service Commission he sternly rejected patronage influences. And as governor of New York, he drove Republican political boss Thomas C. Platt to distraction by insisting on appointing responsible and honest state officials and on taxing corporations. Nevertheless, little in his past record suggested sympathy for important social reform. In the legislature he voted against a two-dollar minimum wage for municipal workers and opposed raises for police and firefighters. He described a bill to limit the working day of streetcar conductors to twelve hours as socialistic.

Roosevelt's political instincts were conservative. He feared the mob and was suspicious of any attempt to organize the poorer classes politically. Hard work, self-help, and good citizenship were sufficient for anyone to improve his station in life. He saw labor unions as troublemakers and interpreted the farmers' populist movement of the 1890s as revolutionary. Yet he also despised the new class of super rich that dominated American economic life and, he thought, often fed the corruption of the political system. Both extremes were dangerous to the nation. He believed the powerful business barons were so greedy and thoughtless that, unchecked, they would drive the exploited working class to desperation and violence. Roosevelt had no quarrel with capitalism as a system. He admired the power of the moguls, but he hated their excesses. He wrote, "Of all forms of tyranny the least attractive and the most vulgar is the tyranny of mere wealth, the tyranny of a plutocracy" (Roosevelt 1926, 20:416).

These convictions informed his political philosophy and shaped his response to the pressing issues of his times. What was needed, he believed, was a mediating force to harness the extremes of capitalist greed and radical upheaval. He had no difficulty seeing himself as the honest broker guarding the nation's interests against damage by selfish contending forces. Modern capitalism created concentrated power, and the good of society demanded countervailing power. As president, Roosevelt can be understood as a man of conservative instincts, who was not reluctant to invest government with the means to act against selfish special interests that endangered the national good. Upon entering the presidency, then, he assumed a peculiar role of conservative as reformer, trying to balance his election success, party loyalty, and faith in free enterprise with justice and the national welfare.

In his first annual message to Congress, the new president offered clues to the direction of his administration (see Document 3.1). He paid tribute to the rapid growth and great achievements of American capital, and he cautioned against "ignorant" and "reckless" attacks on the trusts. But he also warned of the "real and grave evils" of business concentration. He conceded that business combinations, or trusts, should not be prohibited but then argued that they should be "supervised and within reasonable limits controlled." He even suggested that amending the Constitution might be necessary to give the government more power to regulate business. Roosevelt turned his words into action for a first strike against the unfettered power of the trusts.

THE NORTHERN SECURITIES CASE

Soon after taking office, Roosevelt conferred with his attorney general, Philander C. Knox, on antitrust strategy. He pressed Knox to find a suitable case for prosecution. The Sherman Anti-Trust Act of 1890 sought to outlaw "combinations in restraint of trade," but a business-friendly Supreme Court had consistently sided with the corporations and seemed to take the teeth out of the law. Perversely, the government and the courts often used this act aimed at trusts as a weapon against labor unions to break strike actions. No important trust had been prosecuted successfully since its passage. The federal government had not even initiated an antitrust suit against any giant corporation under the Sherman Anti-Trust Act since 1895. In *United States v. E. C. Knight*, the government lost when the Supreme Court distinguished between manufacturing and commerce and held the company immune from prosecution as a trust, despite the fact that the company controlled 90 percent of sugar refining in the country.

After rejecting numerous possible choices, Knox settled on the Northern Securities Company as a target that could be hit successfully as an illegal trust under the terms of the Sherman Act. This trust was, more accurately, a holding company, a corporation that brought other companies under its wing by holding a controlling portion of stock in the subsidiaries. If a holding company swallowed enough individual businesses in the same industry, it became sufficiently powerful to drive out the remaining competition, creating an effective monopoly.

Attorney General Knox was one of the country's most skillful corporation lawyers grown wealthy in the service of big business. He understood the complexities of trust organization, and now he stood ready to serve the president with the knowledge and skill so valued by his former clients. After diligent study, he was convinced that the Northern Securities Company qualified as a trust in restraint of trade and thus subject to prosecution.

The Northern Securities Company was a combination created to control rail traffic throughout the Northwest. A war for control of this traffic had pitted railroad magnate Edward H. Harriman, supported by financing from John D. Rockefeller, against James J. Hill and J. P. Morgan. These were among the most shrewd and powerful American capitalists, and they soon saw the advantages of cooperation over competition. They called a truce and agreed to combine their rail holdings, bringing together the Northern Pacific, the Great Northern, and the Chicago, Burlington, and Quincy lines. In the process they watered down the new company's stock, issuing more shares than the value of the holdings warranted, for great personal profit. The future promised more, for they now controlled railroading in a huge section of the country.

In February 1902 Knox announced the government's suit, and the shock waves reached Wall Street. J. P. Morgan traveled to Washington to see what could be done to fix things. At a meeting with Knox and Roosevelt in the White House, the leader of American finance confronted a new force, a government willing to act. The matter, he was told, would be settled in the courts. The case reached the Supreme Court in March 1904. To Roosevelt's delight, the Court found the trust in violation of the Sherman Act and sustained the lower court order for dissolution of the company by a vote of 5 to 4 (see Documents 3.2 and 3.3). In his majority opinion, Justice John Marshall Harlan rejected the argument that the company was merely the result of a stock transaction and therefore not an act of commerce. He insisted that all that was necessary under the Sherman Act was proof that trade was restrained by the combination. The defense argued that the company was chartered by the state of New Jersey and action against it would violate state sovereignty. Harlan again sided with the prosecution, holding that the states were subject to congressional control of interstate commerce under the Constitution. Among the dissenters was Justice Oliver Wendell Holmes Jr., whom Roosevelt had appointed to the Court in December 1902. Holmes argued that trusts were a product of successful competition and that Congress had overstepped its constitutional powers in trying to regulate them. The president had counted on Holmes's vote and was furious at his defection. Up to this time Roosevelt regarded Holmes with the greatest respect; now he described him as spineless as a banana (Dalton 2002, 291).

When the decision was handed down, stock prices tumbled and business leaders worried about what the government might do next. For the time being, their fears were exaggerated. The suit was intended to send a message, not to start a revolution. For all his bluster, Roosevelt was cautious and had a keen sense of timing. He did not want to be blamed for an economic collapse, and he wanted to be elected in 1904. He also knew he had to work with a very conservative Republican majority in Congress, dominated by staunchly probusiness Republican legislators like Speaker of the House Joseph Cannon of Illinois and Sens. Nelson Aldrich of Rhode Island, John C. Spooner of Wisconsin, and Mark Hanna of Ohio. No other important antitrust suits were brought during his first term. But Roosevelt's action against the Northern Securities Company had put teeth, pulled by the *Knight* case, back into the Sherman Act, and this was important for the future. Safely reelected, he instituted more than forty antitrust suits during his second term, taking on such giants as Rockefeller's Standard Oil (decided by the Supreme Court in the 1911 case *Standard Oil Co. v. United States*) and the American Tobacco Company (also decided by the Supreme Court in 1911 in *United States v. American Tobacco*). Although Presidents William Howard Taft and Woodrow Wilson would institute more suits against big business than he did, Roosevelt's reputation as a trustbuster stuck. That image survived his action during the financial panic of 1907. Fearing that the collapse of an important industrial firm, Tennessee Coal and Iron, would lead to bank failures and a general economic collapse, Roosevelt agreed to allow J. P. Morgan's U.S. Steel to buy Tennessee Coal and Iron without fear of prosecution as a trust (see Chapter 4).

The Northern Securities case and those that followed established the precedent and alerted the nation to the evil of trust control. Although trustbusting was an appropriate weapon, its usefulness was limited, and Roosevelt understood that more was needed. The public interest demanded that the power of capital should be supervised and regulated, and this was a task that could be effective only at the federal level of government. The consolidation of American business continued despite antitrust laws, but Roosevelt created a new role for the government as a regulating force in what, until his administration, had been a thoroughly unregulated economy.

BUSINESS REGULATION

Among the earliest initiatives toward business regulation in the Roosevelt years was the Elkins Act of 1903. For years congressional efforts to outlaw railroad rebates to favored customers had been frustrated. Special rates for large-volume shippers had given large companies an edge to help drive out competition. The Elkins Act prohibited such rebates and made both parties to such transactions subject to prosecution. This was an easy success on a relatively minor problem, in part because the railroads offered little resistance. There was growing public demand for more thoroughgoing railroad regulation, a demand given voice in Congress by a small but increasing number of progressive legislators. Roosevelt pushed for legislation to enlarge the enforcement powers of the Interstate Commerce Commission (ICC). The weak commission had been able to gather much data on railroad practices but lacked any effective powers of enforcement. In 1905 the bill to enlarge the powers of the ICC passed the House, but conservatives in the Senate killed the measure and simply established a committee to look into railroad issues. What seemed like an innocuous ploy actually produced evidence that substantiated the charges of abuse and unfair practices in the industry.

With public anger rising at railroad indifference to the public interest, and with a landslide reelection as mandate, Roosevelt was ready for a thrust at effective regulation. In his annual message in December 1905 (see Document 3.4), the president repeated with greater urgency his call for a law to harness the rail industry and related the issue to the general need for business regulation. First, he again paid tribute to the productivity of American industry but then quickly warned of the danger that very success had spawned. He defined the problem clearly as one of excessive power. Giant corporations had concentrated so much wealth and amassed such independent power in their hands that it was now necessary "to give to the sovereign—that is, to the government, which represents the people as a whole—some effective power of supervision . . . " (Roosevelt 1926, 15:271). The place to begin was with the railroads. He called for a law to give the ICC authority to regulate railroad rates. The law needed also to block the practice of special favors to favored shippers, including free tickets as well as rebates, which continued in disguised form despite the Elkins Act. In response, many bills emerged in the House of Representatives. Roosevelt favored the version sponsored by the Iowa Republican William P. Hepburn, which empowered the ICC to set reasonable railroad rates. The lower house responded quickly and almost with one voice, passing the measure 346 to 7. Trouble came in the Senate.

There, Nelson Aldrich of Rhode Island led the opposition. Aldrich was one of the most conservative Republicans in the Senate, a fierce defender of business and banking interests, a champion of high tariffs, and a relentless enemy of even the most modest efforts at government regulation. He read the Hepburn bill as an assault on the cherished pieties of *laissez-faire*. Presidential intimate Henry Cabot Lodge joined the defenders of the faith, as did Philander Knox, so recently the president's ally as attorney general, but now a newly made senator from Pennsylvania and orthodox conservative. On the other side was a small contingent of progressive Republicans who sought the cooperation of like-minded Democrats. Aldrich, a master of senatorial infighting, realized the measure could not be defeated outright and sought to weaken it to insignificance. By parliamentary maneuvering he arranged crippling amendments. In a gesture calculated to rile the president, he consigned the bill to the floor leadership of Benjamin "Pitchfork" Tillman, a Democrat from South Carolina and famously hostile to the president. Although Tillman favored regulation, his appointment anticipated trouble with the White House and disarray in the Senate. The results of the trick, however, disappointed Aldrich in the end.

As the debates and legislative ploys continued, it became clear that any hope for passage would require compromise. The most serious objection to the bill concerned the courts. The House version restricted court involvement to narrow questions of law. Conservatives wanted to grant the courts power to review the rates set by the ICC. Roosevelt originally favored a restricted role for the courts, but given the political realities of the Senate, he now supported compromise. With his approval, Sen. William Allison, R-Iowa, a friend of the legislation, introduced an amendment enlarging the authority of the courts over rates (Morison 1952, 5:210–211). The compromise cleared the way for passage. By a vote of 71 to 3 on March 18, 1906, the Hepburn Act introduced the first significant government regulation of the railroads. The ICC was now responsible for ensuring reasonable rates. The act extended the government's authority to pipelines, storage facilities, and other functions related to transportation, and it required railroads to adopt uniform bookkeeping procedures.

All were not happy with the product. Old guard conservatives were irate, their earlier misgivings about Roosevelt now confirmed. Hostile as they were, there was also public opinion to be considered. Reluctant to be seen as defenders of railroad interest at all costs, especially after the compromise, most quietly agreed to final passage. On the other side, the fervently progressive Robert M. La Follette, a recent addition to the Senate from Wisconsin, vehemently opposed the compromise for weakening the bill, a view shared by many of his progressive colleagues. Compromise and all, Roosevelt beamed at his victory, which he regarded as a good beginning.

Roosevelt's commitment to business regulation grew steadily stronger. Before leaving office he urged Congress to make ICC supervision of railroads much stronger and to extend its jurisdiction to telephone and telegraph companies. His last annual message recognized that antitrust prosecutions could not and should not wipe out all giant enterprises. Instead the government should assume "full power and control" to prevent "every form of improper favoritism or other wrong doing" (Roosevelt 1926, 15:491). Roosevelt had traveled a long way from his youthful conservatism.

FOOD AND DRUG REFORM

Roosevelt's journey continued with more regulatory efforts after passage of the Hepburn Act. The need for regulation went beyond railroads and giant corporations to action against irresponsible business practices that endangered public well-being. Food producers had long been suspected of dishonest and unhealthy practices. Dangerous substances found their way into patent medicines; spices and other food products were regularly adulterated to stretch profits. The muckrakers, a label Roosevelt himself attached to journalists who uncovered the worst of business excesses, exposed the sins of the food and drug industry. The most famous exposé of the meat packing industry was Upton Sinclair's novel *The Jungle*, published in 1906 (see Document 3.5). Sinclair rendered a sordid picture of filthy plant conditions, rodent contamination, doctoring and reuse of spoiled meats, and other disgusting habits of the industry. Both the novel and the public outcry it stirred drew Roosevelt's attention.

Efforts to clean up the food industry preceded the publication of *The Jungle*. For years a team from the Department of Agriculture led by Harvey W. Wiley struggled in a losing battle to protect food supplies. Even the conservative American Medical Association advocated corrective legislation. Proposals for reform died in Congress, usually in the Senate. With the shock of Sinclair's work still fresh, Roosevelt ordered an investigation. An earlier inquiry by Agriculture Department officers more friendly to the industry than Wiley had turned up little that was disturbing. Now a group appointed by the president found conditions in the industry deplorable and provided evidence that Sinclair's accusations were justified. Roosevelt pressed for legislative remedies.

Albert J. Beveridge renewed the fight in the Senate. Beveridge, R-Ind., was a supporter of progressive causes, including railroad regulation, action against the trusts, and opposition to child labor. Now he called for the appropriation of more money for government food inspectors, the dating of canned meats, labeling to list contents, and the inspection of sanitary conditions of food packing plants. Aware of the fate of earlier bills on these subjects, Beveridge incorporated his ideas in a rider to an appropriations bill, forcing quick consideration. Friends of the food industry, including Speaker of the House Joseph Cannon and Rep. Joseph Wadsworth, R-N.Y., a stockbreeder passionately hostile to regulation, tried to weaken the Beveridge proposal beyond recognition and utility. More news reports of foul conditions in the industry and Roosevelt's release of findings from his own investigation forced die-hard conservatives to back away from all-out opposition and agree to compromise. Congress passed, and on June 30, 1906, Roosevelt signed, the Meat Inspection Act, which provided $3 million to support government inspection and mandated a dating system for canned meats. The reform momentum also pushed the passage of the Pure Food and Drug Act, which the president signed on the same day. This law barred adulterated or mislabeled food and drugs from interstate commerce (see Document 3.6).

Roosevelt had won another important victory, effectively maneuvering against a Congress generally dominated by conservatives, especially in the Senate. With help from the press, his own timely use of the presidential "bully pulpit" to inspire public support, and a flexibility that accommodated compromise, he beat the odds of winning against powerful industry lobbies and legislators tied too intimately to special interests. Improving conditions in the food industry was clearly important to the health and welfare of the country, and success boosted the president's popularity. But these laws also served the larger aim of transforming the character of the federal government according to Roosevelt's design. This was another step in creating an activist government willing to challenge the influence of private corporate power in the new century without dismantling the capitalist system.

LABOR RELATIONS

As with his policies toward capital, Roosevelt's ideas about labor grew steadily more progressive during his years in office. As noted, his attitude toward unions before he became president was unfriendly, if not hostile.

His changing perspective was undoubtedly influenced by the coal miners' strike of 1902 (see Chapter 4). With winter approaching and supplies of the nation's principal fuel growing short, the threat to the country brought presidential intervention. Roosevelt summoned both sides to the White House, the workers represented by union leader John Mitchell and the operators led by George F. Baer. The president found Baer and his colleagues unconscionably stubborn and railed against the blindness of management in the face of real danger of social unrest. The demands of Mitchell and the union he found moderate and justified.

Roosevelt was not sympathetic toward the socialist worker groups; he favored the "open shop," in which nonunion workers could be employed; and he had no patience for any resort to violence in labor disputes. He sent troops for brief periods to prevent strike violence in Arizona in 1902 and Nevada in 1906, actions that were taken as unfriendly to labor by union supporters. By the start of his second term his inclination on labor issues leaned increasingly toward the wage earners. He repeatedly asked Congress for a law providing compensation to workers injured on the job in areas of federal jurisdiction, finally winning passage of the Employers' Liability Act in 1906. When the Supreme Court declared the act unconstitutional in January 1908, an angry Roosevelt thought the 5–4 decision shortsighted and wrong. He pressed for and won reenactment of the law in 1908 with the "unconstitutional" provisions eliminated. By this time his agenda on behalf of worker rights was both progressive and prophetic. He called for restrictions on the use of the injunction as a tool to end strike actions. The Sherman Anti-Trust Act had provided the courts with the power to issue injunctions against conspiracies "in restraint of trade." Since then the courts defined strikes as such restraints, and the injunction was often used against labor when the object of the law was to attack monopolies. He continued to push for a constitutionally acceptable law providing workmen's compensation. He wanted an eight-hour law, an end to the evils of child labor, and regulation of the working conditions of women. He also sought federal authorization to investigate labor disputes. All of this was consistent with his vision of a larger role for the federal government as a mediating force in American life.

Although more progressives had been elected to Congress during his presidency, conservative strength was still too formidable to allow the passage of such reforms. After leaving office his sympathy for worker rights grew even stronger, and an even more progressive, some thought radical, program became part of the platform for his 1912 Bull Moose campaign (see Chapter 2).

CONSERVATION

Another national concern hugely important to Roosevelt and ripe for expansive government action was conservation. He had once considered a career as a naturalist, and since his youth he had been a skilled ornithologist. From his days as a Dakota rancher and western game hunter, Roosevelt had been sensitive to the uses and abuses of the nation's resources. His hunting trips through the West alerted him to the dangers of unrestrained exploitation. In January 1885, he became a founding member and first president of the Boone and Crockett Club. The organization brought together members interested in encouraging sport hunting, but it also dedicated itself to conservation efforts to protect the federal lands and large game of the West. The experience of his travels forced his attention on the need to husband water resources, and he supported irrigation projects in the arid regions of the country. As was true generally, Roosevelt was no radical on environmental issues. He did not object in principle to logging or grazing enterprises on federal lands, but to the excesses of those activities endangering the environment.

In his first annual message to Congress shortly after becoming president, Roosevelt raised an array of issues related to conservation (see Document 3.7). He urged forest protection through rational management and the strengthening of the Forest Bureau; authorization for the president to withdraw lands as forest reserves; restoration and proper management of habitat for the support of wild animals and plant life; federal engineering projects for water conservation and the reclamation and irrigation of arid lands. Much of this work was beyond the resources of the states acting alone, and he saw the national government as the principal agent for these projects.

With undisguised enthusiasm, Roosevelt threw his support to the Reclamation Act of 1902, which had originated with Sen. Francis G. Newlands, D-Nev. The bill proposed much of what was in the president's annual message. As he would experience repeatedly, he faced obstacles presented by private interest lobbies and conservatives in Congress. Speaker Joseph Cannon was especially opposed to federal involvement in such work and ignored a personal appeal from the president asking him not to oppose the measure (Morison 1951, 3:272–273). Virtually all western state legislators favored the bill; they gained strength from the votes of Democrats and from the president's influence. Despite the opposition, especially from eastern Republicans, Congress passed the act and a delighted president signed it in June (see Document 3.8). The law provided that monies derived from the sale of public land be used for reclamation as well as irrigation and flood control projects; as money became available these projects could begin without further congressional action. Eventually, millions of acres were protected from private exploitation, having been set aside for federal projects.

In 1905 Roosevelt shifted the Forest Bureau out of the Department of Agriculture and established it as the Forest Service under the Department of the Interior, appointing his conservationist ally and friend Gifford Pinchot as its chief. Pinchot had studied forestry in Europe, worked for private clients for a time and joined the forestry services of the federal government in 1896. That experience and a similar outlook on conservation made him a favorite of the president. Working with Pinchot and bypassing Congress, Roosevelt used executive authority to place more land out of the reach of mining, cattle, and lumber interests. Among the devices he used was the executive designation of important tracts as national parks. The commercial interests often strip-mined, overgrazed, and clear-cut untold acres, leaving behind an erosion-prone, devastated landscape. Those thus evicted fought back with what seemed to be some success, but the president outwitted his adversaries. In February 1907, lobbyists from the affected industries persuaded their friends in Congress to counterattack. A rider was attached to an agriculture bill restricting the president's power to draw more land into federal reserves. When the bill reached the White House, Roosevelt delayed and summoned Pinchot to provide a list of the best of the lands not yet reserved. By executive order he withdrew sixteen million acres from commercial use. With the orders safely executed, he then signed the agriculture bill with its now impotent rider.

Not yet fully satisfied with his conservation effort, Roosevelt called a national Conservation Conference to meet at the White House in May 1908. He brought the nation's governors together with leaders of the conservation movement. At its conclusion, the conference issued a report calling for a continuation of the president's policies (see Document

3.9). Roosevelt responded by establishing a National Conservation Commission and appointed Pinchot to be its leader. Before leaving office Roosevelt made one last ingenious move for conservation. Back in 1906 he had persuaded Congress to pass the Act for the Preservation of American Antiquities, designed to protect prehistoric and other national treasures. Now he used the authority granted him by that law to designate more than a dozen areas as national monuments, placing them beyond the picks and axes of commercial enterprise (see Document 3.10). Among the sites so designated were the Grand Canyon and Niagara Falls. When Roosevelt came into office, federal land reserves measured some 50 million acres; as he left office almost 200 million acres were in reserve. Roosevelt's use of presidential powers in these efforts was a virtuoso performance that delighted his friends and embittered his enemies.

Concern for environmental matters followed Roosevelt out of the White House. Gifford Pinchot continued as head of the Forest Service in the Taft administration. But in 1910, when Pinchot squabbled with Interior Secretary Richard Ballinger over Forest Service policy, Taft sided with his cabinet secretary and fired Pinchot. When Roosevelt, not yet returned from his African travels, heard the news he was irate. The episode added to his disillusionment with Taft and contributed to his eventual break with the president.

RACE RELATIONS

Roosevelt confronted some issues during his presidency that did not produce memorable legislation but that were important to his administration and the nation. Among these were matters concerning race relations. As with so much in the life and thought of Theodore Roosevelt, his convictions about race defy simple explanation. By twenty-first-century standards, he might be called a racist, but this would not be a fair characterization of his record. Like most of the educated of his day, Roosevelt was deeply influenced by Darwinian ideas that had been distorted in the social sciences into social Darwinism. In sophisticated journals, church pulpits, and university classrooms, the idea that social evolution had produced superior and inferior racial groupings was standard instruction delivered with all the authority of science but without excessive concern for evidence. Roosevelt's own writings on the achievements of the English-speaking peoples and the conquest of the American West indicate he had absorbed the prevailing dogmas. Superior people produced superior results. With some feeling he chided Americans of Anglo-Saxon and other Nordic roots for not reproducing themselves in sufficient numbers while lesser races and immigrant types were being distressingly prolific. He feared the result would weaken the strong bloodline of the American nation. At the start of the twentieth century, such beliefs were held as firmly by intellectuals as the untutored. The period from 1890 to the 1920s, an era dubbed "progressive" for its liberal thought and action, was also the worst period of race relations in the United States after the Civil War. Disfranchisement, segregation, and lynching were sanctioned or, in the case of lynching, largely ignored by the courts and the political system, especially but not exclusively in the South.

In Roosevelt's conduct as president in matters of race, there was much to praise and some to regret. Stronger than his conviction of white supremacy was his commitment to the ideals of freedom, fairness, and a perhaps too naive faith in bootstrap self-improvement. He firmly believed that the responsible, honest, and law-abiding citizen, black or white, blue blood or recent immigrant, deserved fair and equal treatment. That many blacks and immigrants fell short of these standards he found regrettable but not uncommon. His odd mix of prejudice and goodwill produced an equally odd mix in his performance as president.

On an evening in October 1902, Roosevelt invited Booker T. Washington, founder of the Tuskegee Institute in Alabama and the most influential African American leader in the country, to dine with him at the White House. Blacks had attended receptions at the executive mansion in the past, but none had ever been asked to dine privately with the president. Roosevelt was not unaware of the importance of symbolic gestures, and he must have known that Washington's visit would cause an outcry. But even he was surprised at the vehemence of the protests. That the president's wife, Edith, was seated at the table was taken as an insult to American womanhood. Across the South outrage spewed with unrestrained venom and ugly language. Newspapers, including some in the North, reported the social occasion as they would a criminal act. Such was the state of racial feeling in America in 1902. The president defended the dinner party as entirely proper, but the invitation was not repeated.

Roosevelt had great respect for Washington and his influence, especially in the South, among African Americans. One of the motives for the dinner invitation was to discuss his plans for strengthening the

Republican Party in the South by revising patronage policy. Because of an array of disfranchising devices that reduced black voting to insignificance, the one-party Democratic South offered little hope of victory to Republican candidates. But Republican state organizations could play an important role in the national party, especially with delegates to national conventions. The party in the South was controlled by a small number of officeholders appointed through Republican control of federal patronage. Roosevelt told Washington that he intended to appoint the best men he could find to such offices, black or white, even if that meant an occasional Democrat. His hope was to broaden the party base in the region, and not incidentally to strengthen his own influence there, looking forward to the nominating convention of 1904.

No racial issue in America in that era was as ugly or tragic as the practice of lynching. In the decade of the 1890s lynchings averaged 187.5 per year. The number declined by half in the first decade of the new century, but the proportion of incidents in the South increased from 82 percent to 92 percent, and overwhelmingly the victims were black (Woodward 1971, 351). There was little chance of legislative remedy, but Roosevelt did speak out against the practice, which he called "inhuman." When Governor Winfield Durbin moved decisively against race rioting sparked by lynching in Indiana in 1903, the president wrote congratulating him for his firm action and adding an impassioned condemnation of lynching. In the letter he knew would be made public, he referred to the "hideous forms so often taken by mob violence when colored men are the victims and—on which occasions the mob seems to lay most weight, not on the crime but on the color of the criminal" (Morison 1951, 3:540–543). He noted that the victims were frequently altogether innocent, and of the perpetrators, he added, "Whoever . . . has ever taken part in lawlessly putting to death a criminal by the dreadful torture of fire must forever have the awful spectacle of his own handiwork seared into his brain and soul. He can never again be the same man" (see Document 3.11). The atrocities and the president's urgent concern persisted. In December 1906 his annual message to Congress devoted several pages to the horror of lynching, which represented "a loosening of the bands of civilization" and "throws into prominence in the community all the foul and evil creatures who dwell therein" (see Document 3.12). Given the intensity of racial hostility of the time, there was little opportunism in Roosevelt's speaking out and much justice. His words may have made some contribution to the declining numbers, but lynching continued to plague the nation for another generation.

A less admirable chapter of Roosevelt's policies with regard to black Americans concerned the treatment of black soldiers in Brownsville, Texas (see Chapter 4). A racial incident between the soldiers and towns-people in August 1906 led to gunfire that left one local citizen dead and several wounded. After an investigation and when none of the soldiers among three companies of black troops was willing to inform on the shooters, Roosevelt ordered every man in the companies dishonorably discharged. Among them were six Medal of Honor winners.

Racial troubles of a different kind also drew the president's attention. On the West Coast, anger was increasing at the influx of Asian workers, hostility fueled by both racial and economic prejudices (see Chapter 4). In 1906, when the San Francisco School Board ordered the segregation of Asian students into one designated school, an embarrassed and angry Roosevelt assured Japan that the action in California did not represent American opinion or policy, and he lashed out at California officials. The troubles in San Francisco eased when the school board withdrew the segregation order. Then Roosevelt entered into what came to be known as the Gentlemen's Agreement with Japan. He promised no official discrimination against the Japanese living in the United States, and Japan agreed to restrain the emigration of Japanese workers.

A CHANGING PRESIDENCY

Roosevelt's wide-ranging initiatives, his vigorous and imaginative use of executive powers, and his sense of timing and openness to compromise earned him an enviable record of achievement. With these qualities he transformed the presidency and began the transformation of the role of the national government as the country faced new problems in a new century.

By the turn of the twentieth century, capitalism had undergone a defining change. Where once relatively small, owner-managed manu-facturing and commercial units were the rule, now finance capitalists commanding massive financial resources dominated multiple industries and exercised power over society undreamed of by their predecessors. For the first time private business decisions could change society in ways that only governments could do in the past. Capitalists like J. P. Morgan, for example, regularly exercised more power over economic matters than the president himself, and at times he did so indirectly over political matters as well. Among industrial nations the response to the new realities of modern capitalist power varied. Marxists sought revolution while the more democratically inclined wished for a more benign transition to some brand of socialism. On the right, the appealing solution was a supernationalism with government of unlimited authority; this answer later produced the vicious fascist experiments. The American response to modern capitalist power was an attempt to harness and regulate that power, to preserve a large measure of free enterprise balanced with legislative and executive oversight by an effective government.

That process of adjustment in the United States was begun by Theodore Roosevelt. During his tenure he set the precedents and began to transform the presidency and the federal government to counterbalance the pervasive influence of capitalism. His political ambitions, his prejudices against "plutocracy," a growing sensitivity to the condition of the working classes (although not fully expressed until after he left office), and his lingering conservative instincts drove his policies. He understood power and recognized the need for the exercise of power in the public interest. The conservative side of his presidential years can be understood because he admired the productivity of capitalism and the skill of its practitioners; he had no wish to undermine the system. But he also understood the narrowness of civic vision and thin concern for the mass of toilers who made production possible. The occasional philanthropist could be generous and humane; the system, driven primarily for the accumulation of profit and left unchecked, could not.

As Roosevelt saw the growing danger from an unharnessed capitalism, and as he came to better understand the needs of the working classes, he embraced a program of government regulation of business enterprise. (By the 1912 presidential campaign his agenda was a forecast of the massive changes that eventually came with the New Deal of President Franklin Roosevelt.) His vision of government was one of stewardship, with responsibility for husbanding the country's natural treasure and protecting the welfare and good order of a nation that, by his time in office, was a society of racial and ethnic diversity unprecedented in the history of the world. The domestic policies of Theodore Roosevelt's administration can better be understood in this context than through a vision of Roosevelt either as a progressive crusader for the common man or as a disguised conservative with no intention to seriously discomfort the economic ruling class.

FOREIGN POLICY

The role of the United States as an important world power was greatly expanded during the presidency of Theodore Roosevelt. His work in foreign affairs is sometimes described as "big stick" diplomacy, a label derived from his oft-quoted advice, "Speak softly and carry a big stick." The description distorts the president's performance. As in domestic politics, he often spoke loudly, and if he carried a big stick, he used it sparingly and with caution. Actually, fewer violent military actions occurred under Roosevelt than under almost any other president in the twentieth century. As always, he was a realist in his reading of world affairs and understood that international relations were relations of power governed by national self-interest. He planned and prosecuted American foreign policy accordingly.

In the 1890s the United States entered the world of imperialism, one in which European powers were engaged in a decades-long binge of expansionism in Africa and Asia. In that decade the United States acquired Guam, Hawaii, the Philippine Islands, Puerto Rico, and Samoa, despite the protests of anti-imperialist groups in the country. Even those of imperialist leanings had second thoughts about this kind of colonial expansion, especially given the costly insurrection against American presence in the Philippines that had begun in 1899. When that fighting receded in mid-1902, preparations began in anticipation of Philippine independence, and the United States acquired no further overseas territories (with the exception of the Virgin Islands, purchased from Denmark in 1916).

Roosevelt's direction of foreign policy was determined by several key motives. Primary was national security in a world engaged in an arms race. He related American security to Western hemispheric independence from European intervention, an idea as old as the Monroe Doctrine. In the Pacific he was concerned with the growing power of an industrializing and expansive Japan. His policies also sought to encourage the trading of American goods overseas. To help achieve these goals Roosevelt believed, as he had since his youth, that a strong navy was essential, and now he was in a position to shape directly the size and character of that navy. Throughout his presidency he repeatedly pressed Congress for appropriations to build a large battle fleet. With an ambitious program of construction, including two battleships per year plus cruisers and support ships, Roosevelt doubled the size of the navy while in office.

The first treaty of the Roosevelt administration was the result of negotiations begun by John Hay, President McKinley's secretary of state. He was a friend of the new president, and Roosevelt insisted that the elderly and ailing Hay continue in office. Hay had concluded, and in December 1901 the Senate ratified, the second Hay-Pauncefote Treaty, by which Great Britain ceded to the United States the right to build and control a canal linking the Atlantic and Pacific Oceans. The two countries had agreed to share such responsibilities in the Clayton-Bulwer Treaty of 1850. Seeking closer relations with the United States, Great Britain now surrendered its rights in such a project. Roosevelt was very much interested in pursuing the canal project, which became a landmark of his administration.

Two routes offered plausible locations for a canal, one across Nicaragua connecting a series of lakes, a second across the narrow isthmus of Panama, a province of Colombia. After extensive studies and discussions, Roosevelt favored the Panama site and negotiations began with Colombia. In 1903 the Hay-Herran Treaty settled the terms by which the United States would receive a ninety-nine-year lease on a six-mile-wide canal zone in exchange for a payment of $10 million plus a rental fee of $250,000 per year. The Senate quickly ratified the agreement, but in August, the Colombian legislature rejected the treaty, insisting on more money. An angry Roosevelt privately used words like "jack rabbits" and "extortionists" to describe the Colombians (Morison 1951, 3:566–567). Back channel intrigues and secret negotiations followed with parties interested in a canal route free of Colombian influence (see Chapter 4). Philippe Bunau-Varilla was an engineer who had been active in transferring construction rights from a now bankrupt French company to the United States. He served as a contact with Panamanians bent on revolt from Colombia. With judicious timing, Roosevelt ordered navy vessels and a contingent of marines to patrol the coast of Panama. All proceeded rapidly. The Panamanian rebels declared independence, American ships blocked Colombian forces sent to put down the rebellion, and the United States hastily recognized the new Republic of Panama. With little delay a treaty with Panama provided terms similar to those originally offered to Colombia. At home, there was some criticism in the press at the time and by historians later that a more benign course, continuing negotiations with Colombia, might have produced the desired results without the unseemly intrigue and revolution (Mowry 1958, 154). "The wine of national power had in this instance gone to Roosevelt's head. There was no need for such haste" (Dulles 1955, 74). A more recent view defends Roosevelt's diplomacy and shifts more responsibility to "recklessness" on the part of Colombia (Collin 1990, 329–338). Roosevelt, himself, was unrepentant. He consistently defended his actions as just, and years later he boasted that while others debated, "I took the Canal Zone . . ." (Pringle [1931] 1956, 233). Beyond the canal issue, other Latin American concerns absorbed Roosevelt's attention. Numerous countries in the region fell heavily in debt to European creditors, raising the threat of foreign intervention in the hemisphere. When Britain, Germany, and Italy sent warships to the coast of Venezuela to pressure for payment of debts in December 1903, Roosevelt successfully persuaded the parties to agree to arbitration to settle the matter (see Chapter 4). A similar threat in the Dominican Republic took a different turn.

That country, corruptly administered and heavily in debt, was threatened with intervention by several European nations. In December 1904 Roosevelt responded to the threat with a declaration that came to be known as the Roosevelt Corollary to the Monroe Doctrine (see Document 3.13). The corollary reserved to the United States the right to exercise a police power if flagrant "wrong doing or impotence" threatened foreign intervention in an American hemisphere nation. The Monroe Doctrine was now not only an admonition to Europeans to keep out of the Americas but also an assumption by the United States of the right to intervene in advance to prevent foreign intrusions. Clearly, the United States was asserting a policing role in the affairs of other nations on its own authority. Just as clearly, the threat to Latin America from Europe, vigorously expansionist for decades, was a plausible danger. This was a reflection of the new role of American power in world affairs and, as some interpreted it, a signal of American imperialism. Following the declaration, in January 1905, Roosevelt ordered American troops to Santo Domingo, the capital city of the Dominican Republic. The government in disarray there acceded to American control of its customs offices. Efficient administration free of corruption succeeded in retiring the foreign debt, and in 1907 American troops withdrew. The precedent for

American intervention was reaffirmed when turmoil in Cuba led to rebellion and the collapse of the Cuban government in 1906. Roosevelt sent troops to the island, appointed a new governor, and order was restored. The American troops remained until 1909.

The image of Roosevelt as an imperialist is easily exaggerated. Although he was bold, perhaps arrogant, in the exercise of American power over sovereign nations, the provocations and dangers, Panama aside, were real; no territory was annexed; casualties were minimal or nonexistent; and his actions, compared with the record of imperialist powers, were restrained. In fact, during the administrations of his successors, Presidents Taft and Wilson, interventions would be more frequent, longer lasting, and less benign.

One of Roosevelt's celebrated roles in foreign affairs was his performance as a peacemaker. Russia and Japan went to war in 1904, and Russia and the world were shocked at the solid beating the Japanese visited on Russian naval and land forces. The president saw American interests best served if neither side won a complete victory upsetting the balance of power in the region. He intervened, this time to make peace. In the summer of 1905, at Roosevelt's invitation, both sides agreed to a truce and peace talks at Portsmouth, New Hampshire. Roosevelt's mediation tempered the demands of a victorious Japan, causing some resentment in that country. The Treaty of Portsmouth ended the Russo-Japanese War, and for his role Roosevelt won the Nobel Peace Prize in 1906, the first president to do so.

Relations with Japan occupied the president in other ways. Roosevelt was concerned about the growing power of Japan in the Pacific and maneuvered on the one hand to ensure good relations and on the other to impress the Japanese with America's new status as a world power. Following the Gentlemen's Agreement of 1907, which settled the question of Japanese immigration to the West Coast, Roosevelt resolved on a friendly show of muscle. He ordered the navy to assemble a fleet for a two-year world cruise. The Great White Fleet of battle and support ships pointedly visited Japan to underscore the position of the United States as a Pacific power. Although there was some criticism in Congress and the press about this extravagant show, the American fleet was well received in Japan and other countries.

To strengthen still further relations with Japan, the president encouraged negotiations that resulted in the Root-Takahira Agreement in 1908 (see Chapter 4). Elihu Root, who began his service in the administration as secretary of war, was one of the president's most trusted advisers on both domestic politics and foreign matters. Root became secretary of state on the death of John Hay in July 1905. Roosevelt had worried about the vulnerability of the Philippines and what he thought was a Japanese desire to expand its influence in the Pacific. The Root-Takahira Agreement was a mutual pledge by the United States and Japan to respect their territories in the Pacific, the integrity of China, and the Open Door policy in China that John Hay had engineered in the hope of keeping access to Chinese markets open.

Relations with European powers were less intense than those with Japan. After decades of bitter memories of the War of 1812 and unhappiness over Britain's aid to the Confederacy during the Civil War, Anglo-American relations improved steadily. The British, wary of the growing power of Germany, worked actively to cultivate American goodwill, as indicated by the concession agreed to in the Hay-Pauncefote Treaty concerning the canal. Yet another British concession came in negotiations over the boundary between Alaska and Canada. In 1903 a commission was established to arbitrate the long-standing boundary dispute. The commission was made up of three Americans, two Canadians, and an English representative. Roosevelt tried to nudge the commission decision in his favor by suggesting that troops might be sent to occupy the disputed area if the results of arbitration were disappointing. His bluster was probably unnecessary. The British member of the commission, undoubtedly on instruction from his government, sided with the three Americans, and to the distress of the Canadians, the American claim was sustained.

The United States, following George Washington's exhortation to neutrality, had always steered clear of involvement in purely European politics. Roosevelt made an exception to the rule. With the rise of Germany as a great power, a complex alliance system and an arms race brought high tension to the European scene by the turn of the century. In 1905 France and Germany were tangled in a dispute over control of Morocco, a quarrel that it was feared could explode into a general war. On a request from the Germans, Roosevelt agreed to organize an international conference to settle the Moroccan crisis. At the January 1906 Algeciras Conference in Spain, the American delegation sided with the French, and Roosevelt used his influence to move the Germans to a settlement. There was some unhappiness in Congress and the press in the United States among those who worried that American participation in such an enterprise would break tradition and entangle the country in European conflict. Roosevelt, however, defended his action as a success in keeping the peace and enhancing the prestige of the United States among the great powers. Because Great Britain was an ally and supporter of France in the dispute, Roosevelt's diplomacy contributed further to closer relations with the British.

CONCLUSION

In both domestic policy and foreign affairs Roosevelt's public bluster and private outbursts of emotion masked a readiness to compromise to achieve what was possible and a caution and restraint dictated by realism. He relished the use of power and could on occasion wield it fiercely against domestic or foreign adversaries. He used the press to embarrass or pressure members of Congress, and he was not above bending the rules, as he did with Pinchot on the conservation issue. His short-tempered treatment of the Brownsville soldiers and his impatient dismissal of Colombia over the Panama treaty are difficult to defend. But his record, taken as a whole, is one of remarkable achievement. He wrung a long list of progressive laws from a reluctant and conservative Congress; he ushered the United States into the twentieth century as a world power; and he transformed the role of the national government and office of the presidency to better meet their modern responsibilities.

BIBLIOGRAPHIC ESSAY

The major biographical works offer detailed treatments of the policies Roosevelt followed during his administration. H. W. Brands, *T.R.: The Last Romantic* (New York: Basic Books, 1997), is a careful study focusing principally on his political career. Kathleen Dalton, *Theodore Roosevelt: A Strenuous Life* (New York: Alfred A. Knopf, 2002), the most recent biography, pays special attention to the influence of women in Roosevelt's personal and political life. William Henry Harbaugh, *The Life and Times of Theodore Roosevelt* (New York: Collier Books, 1963), is among the most scholarly of the biographies and still very useful. Nathan Miller, *Theodore Roosevelt: A Life* (New York: William Morrow, 1992), is a generally sympathetic biography. Edmund Morris, *Theodore Rex* (New York: Random House, 2001), the second volume of a projected three-volume biography, is a finely detailed history of the presidential years. Henry Pringle, *Theodore Roosevelt: A Biography* (1931; reprint, New York: Harcourt Brace, 1956), a prize-winning biography dating from the 1930s, is often critical of the president's policies and politics.

Important studies focusing on administration policies include John Morton Blum, *The Republican Roosevelt,* 2d ed. (Cambridge: Harvard University Press, 1977), a skillful and scholarly analysis of the president in action, and Lewis L. Gould, *The Presidency of Theodore Roosevelt* (Lawrence: University Press of Kansas, 1991), one of the best compact histories of the Roosevelt presidency. George E. Mowry, *The Era of Theodore Roosevelt* (New York: Harper and Brothers, 1958), a volume in the New American Nation series, offers a broad picture of the United States during the Roosevelt years and a friendly interpretation of his performance.

On foreign policy see the following books. Thomas A. Bailey, *Theodore Roosevelt and the Japanese American Crises* (Stanford: Stanford University Press, 1934), remains a rich and useful source. Howard K. Beale, *Theodore Roosevelt and the Rise of America to World Power* (Baltimore: Johns Hopkins University Press, 1956), offers a solid summary of major events. Richard H. Collin, *Theodore Roosevelt's Caribbean* (Baton Rouge: Louisiana State University Press, 1990), is a recent defense of the president's actions concerning Panama. Foster Rhea Dulles, *America's Rise to World Power, 1898–1954* (New York: Harper Brothers, 1955), is a volume in the New American Nation series. Raymond A. Esthus, *Theodore Roosevelt and Japan* (Seattle: University of Washington Press, 1966), updates Bailey's earlier work. Howard C. Hill, *Roosevelt and the Caribbean* (New York: Russell and Russell, 1965), is excellent on Roosevelt's Latin American policies. Frederick W. Marks III, *Velvet on Iron: The Diplomacy of Theodore Roosevelt* (Lincoln: University of Nebraska Press, 1979), is a successful effort to assess Roosevelt's foreign policy in the context of his times. William N. Tilchin, *Theodore Roosevelt and the British Empire* (New York: St. Martin's Press, 1997), provides a careful and thorough study of an important relationship.

Document 3.1   On the Trust Problem, First Annual Message, December 3, 1901

The business community did not fully trust Roosevelt when he assumed the presidency. He quickly tried to reassure Congress about his support for American business enterprise while at the same time warning that abusive practices could not go unchallenged.

. . . The tremendous and highly complex industrial development which went on with ever accelerated rapidity during the latter half of the nineteenth century brings us face to face, at the beginning of the twentieth, with very serious social problems. The old laws, and the old customs which had almost the binding force of law, were once quite sufficient to regulate the accumulation and distribution of wealth. Since the industrial changes which have so enormously increased the productive power of mankind, they are no longer sufficient.

The growth of cities has gone on beyond comparison faster than the growth of the country, and the up building of the great industrial centers has meant a startling increase, not merely in the aggregate of wealth, but in the number of very large individual, and especially of very large corporate, fortunes. The creation of these great corporate fortunes has not been due to the tariff nor to any other governmental action, but to natural causes in the business world, operating in other countries as they operate in our own.

The process has aroused much antagonism, a great part of which is wholly without warrant. It is not true that as the rich have grown richer the poor have grown poorer. On the contrary, never before has the average man, the wage-worker, the farmer, the small trader, been so well off as in this country and at the present time. There have been abuses connected with the accumulation of wealth; yet it remains true that a fortune accumulated in legitimate business can be accumulated by the person specially benefitted only on condition of conferring immense incidental benefits upon others. Successful enterprise, of the type which benefits all mankind, can only exist if the conditions are such as to offer great prizes as the rewards of success.

The captains of industry who have driven the railway systems across this continent, who have built up our commerce, who have developed our manufactures, have on the whole done great good to our people. Without them the material development of which we are so justly proud could never have taken place. Moreover, we should recognize the immense importance to this material development of leaving as unhampered as is compatible with the public good the strong and forceful men upon whom the success of business operations inevitably rests. The slightest study of business conditions will satisfy anyone capable of forming a judgment that the personal equation is the most important factor in a business operation; that the business ability of the man at the head of any business concern, big or little, is usually the factor which fixes the gulf between striking success and hopeless failure.

An additional reason for caution in dealing with corporations is to be found in the international commercial conditions of today. The same business conditions which have produced the great aggregations of corporate and individual wealth have made them very potent factors in international commercial competition. Business concerns which have the largest means at their disposal and are managed by the ablest men are naturally those which take the lead in the strife for commercial supremacy among the nations of the world. America has only just begun to assume that commanding position in the international business world which we believe will more and more be hers. It is of the utmost importance that this position be not jeopardized, especially at a time when the overflowing abundance of our own natural resources and the skill, business energy, and mechanical aptitude of our people make foreign markets essential. Under such conditions it would be most unwise to cramp or to fetter the youthful strength of our nation. . . .

The mechanism of modern business is so delicate that extreme care must be taken not to interfere with it in a spirit of rashness or ignorance. Many of those who have made it their vocation to denounce the great industrial combinations which are popularly, although with technical inaccuracy, known as trusts, appeal especially to hatred and fear. These are precisely the two emotions, particularly when combined with ignorance, which unfit men for the exercise of cool and steady judgment. In facing new industrial conditions, the whole history of the world shows that legislation will generally be both unwise and ineffective unless undertaken after calm inquiry and with sober self-restraint. Much of the legislation directed at the trusts would have been exceedingly mischievous had it not also been entirely ineffective. In accordance with a well-known sociological law, the ignorant or reckless agitator has been the really effective friend of the evils which he has been nominally opposing. In dealing with business interests, for the government to undertake by crude and ill-considered legislation to do what may turn out to be bad, would be to incur the risk of such far-reaching national disaster that it would be preferable to undertake nothing at all. The men who demand the impossible or the undesirable serve as the allies of the forces with which they are nominally at war, for they hamper those who would endeavor to find out in rational fashion what the wrongs really are and to what extent and in what manner it is practicable to apply remedies.

All this is true; and yet it is also true that there are real and grave evils, one of the chief being overcapitalization because of its many baleful consequences; and a resolute and practical effort must be made to correct these evils.

There is widespread conviction in the minds of the American people that the great corporations known as trusts are in certain of their features and tendencies hurtful to the general welfare. This springs from no spirit of envy or uncharitableness, nor lack of pride in the great industrial achievements that have placed this country at the head of the nations struggling for commercial supremacy. It does not rest upon a lack of intelligent appreciation of the necessity of meeting changing and changed conditions of trade with new methods, nor upon ignorance of the fact that combination of capital in the effort to accomplish great things is necessary when the world's progress demands that great things be done. It is based upon sincere conviction that combination and concentration should be, not prohibited, but supervised and within reasonable limits controlled; and in my judgment this conviction is right.

It is no limitation upon property rights or freedom of contract to require that when men receive from government the privilege of doing business under corporate form, which frees them from individual responsibility, and enables them to call into their enterprises the capital of the public, they shall do so upon absolutely truthful representations as to the value of the property in which the capital is to be invested. Corporations engaged in interstate commerce should be regulated if they are found to exercise a license working to the public injury. It should be as much the aim of those who seek for social betterment to rid the business world of crimes of cunning as to rid the entire body politic of crimes of violence. Great corporations exist only because they are created and safeguarded by our institutions; and it is therefore our right and our duty to see that they work in harmony with these institutions.

The first essential in determining how to deal with the great industrial combinations is knowledge of the facts—publicity. In the interest of the public, the government should have the right to inspect and examine the workings of the great corporations engaged in interstate business. Publicity is the only sure remedy which we can now invoke. What further remedies are needed in the way of governmental regulation, or taxation, can only be determined after publicity has been obtained, by process of law, and in the course of administration. The first requisite is knowledge, full and complete—knowledge which may be made public to the world.

Artificial bodies, such as corporations and joint stock or other associations, depending upon any statutory law for their existence or privileges, should be subject to proper governmental supervision, and full and accurate information as to their operations should be made public regularly at reasonable intervals.

The large corporations, commonly called trusts, though organized in one state, always do business in many states, often doing very little business in the state where they are incorporated. There is utter lack of uniformity in the state laws about them; and as no state has any exclusive interest in or power over their acts, it has in practice proved impossible to get adequate regulation through state action. Therefore, in the interest of the whole people, the nation should, without interfering with the power of the states in the matter itself, also assume power of supervision and regulation over all corporations doing an interstate business. This is especially true where the corporation derives a portion of its wealth from the existence of some monopolistic element or tendency in its business. There would be no hardship in such supervision; banks are subject to it, and in their case it is now accepted as a simple matter of course. Indeed, it is probable that supervision of corporations by the national government need not go so far as is now the case with the supervision exercised over them by so conservative a state as Massachusetts, in order to produce excellent results.

When the Constitution was adopted, at the end of the eighteenth century, no human wisdom could foretell the sweeping changes, alike in industrial and political conditions, which were to take place by the beginning of the twentieth century. At that time it was accepted as a matter of course that the several states were the proper authorities to regulate, so far as was then necessary, the comparatively insignificant and strictly localized corporate bodies of the day. The conditions are now wholly different and wholly different action is called for. I believe that a law can be framed which will enable the national government to exercise control along the lines above indicated, profiting by the experience gained through the passage and administration of the Interstate Commerce Act. If, however, the judgment of the Congress is that it lacks the constitutional power to pass such an act, then a constitutional amendment should be submitted to confer the power. . . .

Source: Theodore Roosevelt, *The Works of Theodore Roosevelt,* national ed. (New York: Charles Scribner's Sons, 1926), 15:87–93.

**Document 3.2   *Northern Securities Co. v. United States,*
March 14, 1904**
The Supreme Court delighted Roosevelt and shocked the trust builders with its decision in favor of the government in the Northern Securities *case. This high-profile case did little to slow the formation of giant holding companies, but it did establish the president's reputation as a trustbuster, set a precedent for government action, and opened the door to future prosecutions. Below is an excerpt from the majority opinion written by Justice John Marshall Harlan.*

We will not encumber this opinion by extended extracts from the former opinions of this court. It is sufficient to say that . . . certain propositions are plainly deducible and embrace the present case. Those propositions are:

That although the act of Congress known as the Anti-Trust Act has no reference to the mere manufacture or production of articles or commodities within the limits of the several States, it does embrace and declare to be illegal every contract, combination or conspiracy, in whatever form, of whatever nature, and whoever may be parties to it, which directly or necessarily operates *in restraint* of trade or commerce *among the several States or with foreign nations;*

That the act is not limited to restraints of interstate and international trade or commerce that are unreasonable in their nature, but embraces *all* direct *restraints* imposed by any combination, conspiracy or monopoly upon such trade or commerce;

That railroad carriers engaged in interstate or international commerce are embraced by the act;

That combinations even among *private* manufacturers or dealers whereby interstate or international commerce is restrained are equally embraced by the act;

That Congress has the power to establish *rules* by which *interstate and international* commerce shall be governed, and, by the Anti-Trust Act, has prescribed the rule of free competition among those engaged in such commerce;

That *every* combination or conspiracy which would extinguish competition between otherwise competing railroads engaged in *interstate trade or commerce,* and which would *in that way* restrain such trade or commerce, is made illegal by the act;

That the natural effect of competition is to increase commerce, and an agreement whose direct effect is to prevent this play of competition restrains instead of promotes trade and commerce;

That to vitiate a combination, such as the act of Congress condemns, it need not be shown that the combination, in fact, results or will result in a total suppression of trade or in a complete monopoly, but it is only essential to show that by its necessary operation it tends to restrain interstate or international trade or commerce and to deprive the public of the advantages that flow from free competition;

That the constitutional guarantee of liberty of contract does not prevent Congress from prescribing the rule of free competition for those engaged in *interstate and international* commerce; and,

That under its power to regulate commerce among the several States and with foreign nations, Congress had authority to enact the statute in question. . . .

It is said that whatever may be the power of a State over such subjects Congress cannot forbid single individuals from disposing of their stock in a state corporation, even if such corporation be engaged in interstate and international commerce; that the holding or purchase by a state corporation or the purchase by individuals, of the stock of another corporation, for whatever purposes, are matters in respect of which Congress has no authority under the Constitution. . . . It is unnecessary in this case to consider such abstract, general questions. The court need not now concern itself with them. . . .

Whether the free operation of the normal laws of competition is a wise and wholesome rule for trade and commerce is an economic question which this court need not consider or determine. Undoubtedly, there are those who think that the general business interests and prosperity of the country will be best promoted if the rule of competition is not applied. But there are others who believe that such a rule is more necessary in these days of enormous wealth than it ever was in any former period of our history. Be all this as it may, Congress has, in effect, recognized the rule of free competition by declaring illegal every combination or conspiracy in restraint of . . . commerce.

Indeed, if the contentions of the defendants are sound, why may not *all* the railway companies in the United States, that are engaged, under state charters, in interstate and international commerce, enter into a combination such as the one here in question, and by the device of a holding corporation obtain the absolute control throughout the entire country of rates for passengers and freight, beyond the power of Congress to protect the public against their exactions? The argument in behalf of the defendants necessarily leads to such results and places Congress, although invested by the people of the United States with full authority to regulate . . . commerce, in a condition of utter helplessness, so far as the protection of the public against such combinations is concerned. . . .

It was said in argument that the circumstances under which the Northern Securities Company obtained the stock of the constituent companies imported simply an investment in the stock of other corporations, a purchase of that stock; which investment, or purchase, it was contended was not forbidden by the charter of the company and could not be made illegal by any act of Congress. This view is wholly fallacious. . . . There was no actual investment, in any substantial sense, by the Northern Securities Company in the stock of the two constituent companies. . . . However that company may have acquired for itself the stock in the Great Northern and Northern Pacific Railway companies . . . all the stock it held or acquired in the constituent companies was acquired and held to be used in suppressing competition between those companies. It came into existence only for that purpose. . . .

Guided by these long established rules of construction, it is manifest that if the Anti-Trust Act is held not to embrace a case such as is now before us, the plain intention of the legislative branch of the Government will be defeated. If Congress has not, by the words used in the act, described this and like cases, it would, we apprehend, be impossible to find words that would describe them. . . .

The judgement of the court is that the decree below be and hereby is affirmed.

Source: Northern Securities Co. v. United States, 193 U.S. 197 (1904).

**Document 3.3   Justice Holmes's Dissent in
the *Northern Securities* Case, March 14, 1904**
*Roosevelt appointed Justice Oliver Wendell Holmes Jr. to the Supreme Court
in the expectation that his decisions would be supportive of the administration. When Holmes dissented in the* Northern Securities *case the president
was furious. Had Holmes's reasoning prevailed, antitrust prosecutions would
have been virtually impossible.*

. . . Great cases like hard cases make bad law. For great cases are called
great, not by reason of their real importance in shaping the law of the
future, but because of some accident of immediate overwhelming interest which appeals to the feelings and distorts the judgement. These immediate interests exercise a kind of hydraulic pressure which makes what previously was clear seem doubtful, and before which even well settled
principles of law will bend. What we have to do in this case is to find the
meaning of some not very difficult words.

The question to be decided is whether, under the act of July 2, 1890,
it is unlawful, at any stage of the process, if several men unite to form a corporation for the purpose of buying more than half the stock of each of two
competing interstate railroad companies, if they form the corporation, and
the corporation buys the stock. I will suppose further that every step is
taken, from the beginning, with the single intent of ending competition
between the companies. . . .

This act is construed by the Government to affect the purchasers of
shares in two railroad companies because of the effect it may have, or, if
you like, is certain to have, upon the competition of these roads. If such a
remote result of the exercise of an ordinary incident of property and personal freedom is enough to make that exercise unlawful, there is hardly any
transaction concerning commerce between the States that may not be made
a crime by the finding of a jury or a court. The personal ascendency of one
man may be such that it would give to his advice the effect of a command,
if they owned but a single share in each road. The tendency of his presence
in the stockholders' meetings might be certain to prevent competition, and
thus his advice, if not his mere existence, become a crime. . . .

According to popular speech, every concern monopolizes whatever
business it does, and if that business is trade between two States it monopolizes a part of the trade among the States. Of course the statute does not

forbid that. It does not mean that all business must cease. A single railroad down a narrow valley or through a mountain gorge monopolizes all the railroad transportation through that valley or gorge. Indeed every railroad monopolizes, in a popular sense, the trade of some area. Yet I suppose that no one would say that the statute forbids a combination of men into a corporation to build and run such a railroad between the States. . . .

A partnership is not a contract or combination in restraint of trade between the partners unless the well known words are to be given a new meaning invented for the purpose of this act. . . .The law, I repeat, says nothing about competition, and only prevents its suppression by contracts or combinations in restraint of trade, and such contracts or combinations derive their character as restraining trade from other features than the suppression of competition alone. To see whether I am wrong, the illustrations put in the argument are of use. If I am, then a partnership between two stage drivers who had been competitors in driving across a state line, or two merchants once engaged in rival commerce among the States whether made after or before the act, if now continued, is a crime. For, again I repeat, if the restraint on the freedom of the members of a combination caused by their entering into partnership is a restraint of trade, every such combination, as well the small as the great, *is* within the act. . . .

Source: Northern Securities Co. v. United States, 193 U.S. 197 (1904).

Document 3.4   On the Need for Railroad Regulation, Fifth Annual Message, December 5, 1905

Safely elected, Roosevelt launched his campaign to strengthen the federal government's regulatory powers. His message to Congress was a forecast of the passage of the Hepburn Act of 1906 for more effective railroad regulation.

. . . I am well aware of the difficulties of the legislation that I am suggesting, and of the need of temperate and cautious action in securing it. I should emphatically protest against improperly radical or hasty action. The first thing to do is to deal with the great corporations engaged in the business of interstate transportation. As I said in my message of December 6 last, the immediate and most pressing need, so far as legislation is concerned, is the enactment into law of some scheme to secure to the agents of the government such supervision and regulation of the rates charged by the railroads of the country engaged in interstate traffic as shall summarily and effectively prevent the imposition of unjust or unreasonable rates. It must include putting a complete stop to rebates in every shape and form. This power to regulate rates, like all similar powers over the business world, should be exercised with moderation, caution, and self-restraint; but it should exist, so that it can be effectively exercised when the need arises.

The first consideration to be kept in mind is that the power should be affirmative and should be given to some administrative body created by the Congress. If given to the present Interstate Commerce Commission, or to a reorganized Interstate Commerce Commission, such commission should be made unequivocally administrative. I do not believe in the government interfering with private business more than is necessary. I do not believe in the government undertaking any work which can with propriety be left in private hands. But neither do I believe in the government flinching from overseeing any work when it becomes evident that abuses are sure to obtain therein unless there is governmental supervision. It is not my province to indicate the exact terms of the law which should be enacted; but I call the attention of the Congress to certain existing conditions with which it is desirable to deal. In my judgment the most important provision which such law should contain is that conferring upon some competent administrative body the power to decide, upon the case being brought before it, whether a given rate prescribed by a railroad is reasonable and just, and if it is found to be unreasonable and unjust, then, after full investigation of the complaint, to prescribe the limit of rate beyond which it shall not be lawful to go—the maximum reasonable rate, as it is commonly called—this decision to go into effect within a reasonable time and to obtain from thence onward, subject to review by the courts. It sometimes happens at present not that a rate is too high but that a favored shipper is given too low a rate. In such cases the commission would have the right to fix this already established minimum rate as the maximum; and it would need only one or two such decisions by the commission to cure railroad companies of the practice of giving improper minimum rates. I call your attention to the fact that my proposal is not to give the commission power to initiate or originate rates generally, but to regulate a rate already fixed or originated by the roads, upon complaint and after investigation. A heavy penalty should be exacted from any corporation which fails to respect an order of the commission. I regard this power to establish a maximum rate as being essential to any scheme of real reform in the matter of railway regulation. The first necessity is to secure it; and unless it is granted to the commission there is little use in touching the subject at all.

Source: Theodore Roosevelt, *The Works of Theodore Roosevelt,* national ed. (New York: Charles Scribner's Sons, 1926), 15:274–276.

Document 3.5   Conditions in the Meat Packing Industry, Excerpt from Upton Sinclair's *The Jungle* (1906)

In The Jungle *Upton Sinclair wrote a fictional but realistic account of conditions in the meat packing industry that revolted the country and the president, who read the book and immediately saw its usefulness in the fight to pass a pure food law. Sometimes suspicious of muckraking writers, Roosevelt discovered that Sinclair's accusations were corroborated by the investigation prompted by the book's publication.*

And shortly afterward one of these, a physician, made the discovery that the carcasses of steers which had been condemned as tubercular by the government inspectors, and which therefore contained ptomaines, which are deadly poisons, were left upon an open platform and carted away to be sold in the city; and so he insisted that these carcasses be treated with an injection of kerosene—and was ordered to resign the same week! So indignant were the packers that they went farther, and compelled the mayor to abolish the whole bureau of inspection; so that since then there has not been even a pretense of any interference with the graft. There was said to be two thousand dollars a week hush money from the tubercular steers alone; and as much again from the hogs which had died of cholera on the trains, and which you might see any day being loaded into boxcars and hauled away to a place called Globe, in Indiana, where they made a fancy grade of lard.

Jurgis heard of these things little by little, in the gossip of those who were obliged to perpetrate them. It seemed as if every time you met a person from a new department, you heard of new swindles and new crimes. There was, for instance, a Lithuanian who was a cattle butcher for the plant where Marija had worked, which killed meat for canning only; and to hear this man describe the animals which came to his place would have been worthwhile for a Dante or a Zola. It seemed that they must have agencies all over the country, to hunt out old and crippled and diseased cattle to be canned. There were cattle which had been fed on "whisky-malt," the refuse of the breweries, and had become what the men called "steerly"— which means covered with boils. It was a nasty job killing these, for when you plunged your knife into them they would burst and splash foul-smelling stuff into your face; and when a man's sleeves were smeared with blood, and his hands steeped in it, how was he ever to wipe his face, or to clear his eyes so that he could see? It was stuff such as this that made the "embalmed beef" that had killed several times as many United States soldiers as all the bullets of the Spaniards; only the army beef, besides, was not fresh canned, it was old stuff that had been lying for years in the cellars.

. . . Anybody who could invent a new imitation had been sure of a fortune from old Durham, said Jurgis' informant; but it was hard to think of anything new in a place where so many sharp wits had been at work for so long; where men welcomed tuberculosis in the cattle they were feeding, because it made them fatten more quickly; and where they bought up all the old rancid butter left over in the grocery stores of a continent, and "oxidized" it by a forced-air process, to take away the odor, rechurned it with skim milk, and sold it in bricks in the cities! Up to a year or two ago it had been the custom to kill horses in the yards—ostensibly for fertilizer; but after long agitation the newspapers had been able to make the public realize that the horses were being canned. Now it was against the law to kill horses in Packingtown, and the law was really complied with— for the present, at any rate. Any day, however, one might see sharp-horned and shaggy-haired creatures running with the sheep and yet what a job you would have to get the public to believe that a good part of what it buys for lamb and mutton is really goat's flesh!

. . . There was another interesting set of statistics that a person might have gathered in Packingtown—those of the various afflictions of the workers. . . .

. . . and as for the other men, who worked in tank rooms full of steam, and in some of which there were open vats near the level of the floor, their peculiar trouble was that they fell into the vats; and when they were fished out, there was never enough of them left to be worth exhibiting,—sometimes they would be overlooked for days, till all but the bones of them had gone out to the world as Durham's Pure Leaf Lard!

Source: Upton Sinclair, *The Jungle* (New York: Doubleday, Page, 1906), 116–120.

Document 3.6   Pure Food and Drug Act (1906)

Despite conservative moves in Congress to block government regulation, progressive lawmakers, with Roosevelt's enthusiastic support, managed to pass detailed regulations to help eliminate contaminated and adulterated products from entering the nation's food and drug supplies. This was another important extension of government oversight for the general welfare.

AN ACT FOR PREVENTING THE MANUFACTURE, SALE, OR TRANSPORTATION OF ADULTERATED OR MISBRANDED OR POISONOUS OR DELETERIOUS FOODS, DRUGS, MEDICINES, AND LIQUORS, AND FOR REGULATING TRAFFIC THEREIN, AND FOR OTHER PURPOSES.

SECTION 1. Be it enacted by the Senate and House of Representatives of the United States of America in Congress assembled, That it shall be unlawful for any person to manufacture within any Territory or the District of Columbia any article of food or drug which is adulterated or misbranded, within the meaning of this Act; and any person who shall violate any of the provisions of this section shall be guilty of a misdemeanor, and for each offense shall, upon conviction thereof, be fined not to exceed five hundred dollars or shall be sentenced to one year's imprisonment, or both such fine and imprisonment, in the discretion of the court, and for each subsequent offense and conviction thereof shall be fined not less than one thousand dollars or sentenced to one year's imprisonment, or both such fine and imprisonment, in the discretion of the court. . . .

SECTION 7. That for the purposes of this Act an article shall be deemed to be adulterated:

In the Case of Drugs:

First. If, when a drug is sold under or by a name recognized in the United States Pharmacopoeia or National Formulary, it differs from the standard of strength, quality, or purity, as determined by the test laid down in the United States Pharmacopoeia or National Formulary official at the time of investigation: Provided, That no drug defined in the United States Pharmacopoeia or National Formulary shall be deemed to be adulterated under this provision if the standard of strength, quality, or purity be plainly stated upon the bottle, box, or other container thereof although the standard may differ from that determined by the test laid down in the United States Pharmacopoeia or National Formulary.

Second. If its strength or purity fall below the professed standard or quality under which it is sold.

In the Case of Confectionery:

If it contain terra alba, barytes, talc, chrome yellow, or other mineral substance or poisonous color or flavor, or other ingredient deleterious or detrimental to health, or any vinous, malt or spirituous liquor or compound or narcotic drug.

In the Case of Food:

First. If any substance has been mixed and packed with it so as to reduce or lower or injuriously affect its quality or strength.

Second. If any substance has been substituted wholly or in part for the article.

Third. If any valuable constituent of the article has been wholly or in part abstracted.

Fourth. If it be mixed, colored, powdered, coated, or stained in a manner whereby damage or inferiority is concealed.

Fifth. If it contain any added poisonous or other added deleterious ingredient which may render such article injurious to health:

Provided, That when in the preparation of food products for shipment they are preserved by any external application applied in such manner that the preservative is necessarily removed mechanically, or by maceration in water, or otherwise, and directions for the removal of said preservative shall be printed on the covering or the package, the provisions of this Act shall be construed as applying only when said products are ready for consumption.

Sixth. If it consists in whole or in part of a filthy, decomposed, or putrid animal or vegetable substance, or any portion of an animal unfit for food, whether manufactured or not, or if it is the product of a diseased animal, or one that has died otherwise than by slaughter.

Source: Pure Food and Drug Act, U.S. Statutes at Large 34 (1906): 768–772.

Document 3.7   On Conservation, First Annual Message, December 3, 1901

Conservation of natural resources stood as one of the prime goals of the Roosevelt administration. Immediately on taking office, Roosevelt alerted Congress to the needs and benefits of a broad program of conservation. In this effort he would persist to the last days of his time in office.

. . . Wise forest protection does not mean the withdrawal of forest resources, whether of wood, water, or grass, from contributing their full share to the welfare of the people, but, on the contrary, gives the assurance of larger and more certain supplies. The fundamental idea of forestry is the perpetuation of forests by use. Forest protection is not an end of itself; it is a means to increase and sustain the resources of our country and the industries which depend upon them. The preservation of our forests is an imperative business necessity. We have come to see clearly that whatever destroys the forest, except to make way for agriculture, threatens our well-being. . . .

The present diffusion of responsibility is bad from every standpoint. It prevents that effective cooperation between the government and the men who utilize the resources of the reserves, without which the interests of both must suffer. The scientific bureaus generally should be put under the Department of Agriculture. The president should have by law the power of transferring lands for use as forest reserves to the Department of Agriculture. He already has such power in the case of lands needed by the departments of War and the Navy.

The wise administration of the forest reserves will be not less helpful to the interests which depend on water than to those which depend on wood and grass. The water supply itself depends upon the forest. In the arid region it is water, not land, which measures production. The western half of the United States would sustain a population greater than that of our whole country today if the waters that now run to waste were saved and used for irrigation. The forest and water problems are perhaps the most vital internal questions of the United States.

Certain of the forest reserves should also be made preserves for the wild forest creatures. All of the reserves should be better protected from fires. Many of them need special protection because of the great injury done by livestock, above all by sheep. The increase in deer, elk, and other animals in the Yellowstone Park shows what may be expected when other mountain forests are properly protected by law and properly guarded. Some of these areas have been so denuded of surface vegetation by overgrazing that the ground breeding birds, including grouse and quail, and many mammals, including deer, have been exterminated or driven away. At the same time the water-storing capacity of the surface has been decreased or destroyed, thus promoting floods in times of rain and diminishing the flow of streams between rains.

In cases where natural conditions have been restored for a few years, vegetation has again carpeted the ground, birds and deer are coming back, and hundreds of persons, especially from the immediate neighborhood, come each summer to enjoy the privilege of camping. Some at least of the forest reserves should afford perpetual protection to the native fauna and flora, safe havens of refuge to our rapidly diminishing wild animals of the larger kinds, and free camping grounds for the ever-increasing numbers of men and women who have learned to find rest, health, and recreation in the splendid forests and flower-clad meadows of our mountains. The forest reserves should be set apart forever for the use and benefit of our people as a whole and not sacrificed to the shortsighted greed of a few.

The forests are natural reservoirs. By restraining the streams in flood and replenishing them in drought they make possible the use of waters otherwise wasted. They prevent the soil from washing, and so protect the storage reservoirs from filling up with silt. Forest conservation is therefore an essential condition of water conservation.

The forests alone cannot, however, fully regulate and conserve the waters of the arid region. Great storage works are necessary to equalize the flow of streams and to save the flood waters. Their construction has been conclusively shown to be an undertaking too vast for private effort. Nor can it be best accomplished by the individual states acting alone. Far-reaching interstate problems are involved; and the resources of single states would often be inadequate. It is properly a national function, at least in some of its features. It is as right for the national government to make the streams and rivers of the arid region useful by engineering works for water storage as to make useful the rivers and harbors of the humid region by engineering works of another kind. The storing of the floods in reservoirs at the headwaters of our rivers is but an enlargement of our present policy of river control, under which levees are built on the lower reaches of the same streams.

The government should construct and maintain these reservoirs as it does other public works. Where their purpose is to regulate the flow of streams, the water should be turned freely into the channels in the dry season to take the same course under the same laws as the natural flow.

The reclamation of the unsettled arid public lands presents a different problem. Here it is not enough to regulate the flow of streams. The object of the government is to dispose of the land to settlers who will build homes upon it. To accomplish this object water must be brought within their reach.

The pioneer settlers on the arid public domain chose their homes along streams from which they could themselves divert the water to reclaim their holdings. Such opportunities are practically gone. There remain, however, vast areas of public land which can be made available for homestead settlement, but only by reservoirs and main-line canals impracticable for private enterprise. These irrigation works should be built by the national government. The lands reclaimed by them should be reserved by the government for actual settlers, and the cost of construction should so far as possible be repaid by the land reclaimed. The distribution of the water, the division of the streams among irrigators, should be left to the settlers themselves in conformity with state laws and without interference with those laws or with vested rights. The policy of the national government should be to aid irrigation in the several states and territories in such manner as will enable the people in the local communities to help themselves, and as will stimulate needed reforms in the state laws and regulations governing irrigation.

The reclamation and settlement of the arid lands will enrich every portion of our country, just as the settlement of the Ohio and Mississippi valleys brought prosperity to the Atlantic States. The increased demand for manufactured articles will stimulate industrial production, while wider home markets and the trade of Asia will consume the larger food-supplies and effectually prevent Western competition with Eastern agriculture. Indeed, the products of irrigation will be consumed chiefly in upbuilding local centers of mining and other industries, which would otherwise not come into existence at all. Our people as a whole will profit, for successful home-making is but another name for the upbuilding of the nation.

Source: Theodore Roosevelt, *The Works of Theodore Roosevelt,* national ed. (New York: Charles Scribner's Sons, 1926), 15:102–106.

Document 3.8   The Newlands Reclamation Act, June 17, 1902

The first victory for the president's conservation policy came with the passage of this act, which withdrew huge tracts of public land from private exploitation. It also provided funds for water projects, especially in dry western states, which, incidentally, greatly benefited farmers and ranchers in the region.

An Act Appropriating the Receipts from the Sale and
Disposal of Public Lands in Certain States and Territories to
the Construction of Irrigation Works for the Reclamation of
Arid Lands.

Section 1. Be it enacted by the Senate and House of Representatives of
the United States of America in Congress assembled, That all moneys
received from the sale and disposal of public lands in Arizona, California,
Colorado, Idaho, Kansas, Montana, Nebraska, Nevada, New Mexico,
North Dakota, Oklahoma, Oregon, South Dakota, Utah, Washington, and
Wyoming, beginning with the fiscal year ending June thirtieth, nineteen
hundred and one, including the surplus of fees and commissions in excess
of allowances to registers and receivers, and excepting the five per centum
of the proceeds of the sales of public lands in the above States set aside by
law for educational and other purposes, shall be, and the same are hereby,
reserved, set aside, and appropriated as a special fund in the Treasury to be
known as the "reclamation fund," to be used in the examination and survey for and the construction and maintenance of irrigation works for the
storage, diversion, and development of waters for the reclamation of arid
and semiarid lands in the said States and Territories, and for the payment
of all other expenditures provided for in this Act: Provided, That in case
the receipts from the sale and disposal of public lands other than those realized from the sale and disposal of lands referred to in this section are insuf-
ficient to meet the requirements for the support of agricultural colleges
in the several States and Territories, under the Act of August thirtieth,
eighteen hundred and ninety, entitled "An Act to apply a portion of the
proceeds of the public lands to the more complete endowment and support of the colleges for the benefit of agriculture and the mechanic arts,
established under the provisions of an Act of Congress approved July second, eighteen hundred and sixty-two," the deficiency, if any, in the sum
necessary for the support of the said colleges shall be provided for from
any moneys in the Treasury not otherwise appropriated. . . .

Section 7. That where in carrying out the provisions of this Act it
becomes necessary to acquire any rights or property, the Secretary of the
Interior is hereby authorized to acquire the same for the United States by
purchase or by condemnation under judicial process, and to pay from the
reclamation fund the sums which may be needed for that purpose, and
it shall be the duty of the Attorney-General of the United States upon
every application of the Secretary of the Interior, under this Act, to cause

proceedings to be commenced for condemnation within thirty days from the receipt of the application at the Department of Justice.

Source: The Newlands Reclamation Act, U.S. Statutes at Large 32 (1902): 388–390.

Document 3.9   Declaration of the Conservation Conference, May 15, 1908

To marshal public opinion and political support for conservation, Roosevelt invited the nation's governors to a White House conference. The result was a ringing endorsement of his policies and actions and a call for more. This was another example of Roosevelt's skill in bringing public pressure to bear on an often reluctant conservative Congress.

We the Governors of the States and Territories of the United States of America, in Conference assembled, do hereby declare the conviction that the great prosperity of our country rests upon the abundant resources of the land chosen by our forefathers for their homes and where they laid the foundation of this great Nation.

We look upon these resources as a heritage to be made use of in establishing and promoting the comfort, prosperity, and happiness of the American People, but not to be wasted, deteriorated, or needlessly destroyed.

We agree that our country's future is involved in this; that the great natural resources supply the material basis on which our civilization must continue to depend, and on which the perpetuity of the Nation itself rests.

We agree, in the light of facts brought to our knowledge and from information received from sources which we can not doubt, that this material basis is threatened with exhaustion. Even as each succeeding generation from the birth of the Nation has performed its part in promoting the progress and development of the Republic, so do we in this generation recognize it as a high duty to perform our part; and this duty in large degree lies in the adoption of measures for the conservation of the natural wealth of the country.

We declare our firm conviction that this conservation of our natural resources is a subject of transcendent importance, which should engage unremittingly the attention of the Nation, the States, and the People in earnest cooperation. These natural resources include the land on which we live and which yields our food; the living waters which fertilize the soil, supply power, and form great avenues of commerce; the forests which yield the materials for our homes, prevent erosion of the soil, and conserve the navigation and other uses of our streams; and the minerals which form the basis of our industrial life, and supply us with heat, light, and power.

We agree that the land should be so used that erosion and soil-wash shall cease; that there should be reclamation of arid and semi-arid regions by means of irrigation, and of swamp and overflowed regions by means of drainage; that the waters should be so conserved and used as to promote navigation, to enable the arid regions to be reclaimed by irrigation, and to develop power in the interests of the People; that the forests which regulate our rivers, support our industries, and promote the fertility and productiveness of the soil should be preserved and perpetuated; that the minerals found so abundantly beneath the surface should be so used as to prolong their utility; that the beauty, healthfulness, and habitability of our country should be preserved and increased; that the sources of national wealth exist for the benefit of the People, and that monopoly thereof should not be tolerated.

We commend the wise forethought of the President in sounding the note of warning as to the waste and exhaustion of the natural resources of the country, and signify our high appreciation of his action in calling this Conference to consider the same and to seek remedies therefore through cooperation of the Nation and the States.

We agree that this cooperation should find expression in suitable action by the Congress within the limits of and coextensive with the national jurisdiction of the subject, and, complementary thereto, by the legislatures of the several States within the limits of and coextensive with their jurisdiction.

We declare the conviction that in the use of the natural resources our independent States are interdependent and bound together by ties of mutual benefits, responsibilities and duties.

We agree in the wisdom of future conferences between the President, Members of Congress, and the Governors of States on the conservation of our natural resources with a view of continued cooperation and action on the lines suggested; and to this end we advise that from time to time, as in his judgment may seem wise, the President call the Governors of the States and Members of Congress and others into conference.

We agree that further action is advisable to ascertain the present condition of our natural resources and to promote the conservation of the same; and to that end we recommend the appointment by each State of a Commission on the Conservation of Natural Resources, to cooperate with each other and with any similar commission of the Federal Government.

We urge the continuation and extension of forest policies adapted to secure the husbanding and renewal of our diminishing timber supply, the prevention of soil erosion, the protection of headwaters, and the maintenance of the purity and navigability of our streams. We recognize that the private ownership of forest lands entails responsibilities in the interests of all the People, and we favor the enactment of laws looking to the protection and replacement of privately owned forests.

We recognize in our waters a most valuable asset of the People of the United States, and we recommend the enactment of laws looking to the conservation of water resources for irrigation, water supply, power, and navigation, to the end that navigable and source streams may be brought under complete control and fully utilized for every purpose. We especially urge on the Federal Congress the immediate adoption of a wise, active, and thorough waterway policy, providing for the prompt improvement of our streams and the conservation of their watersheds required for the uses of commerce and the protection of the interests of our People.

We recommend the enactment of laws looking to the prevention of waste in the mining and extraction of coal, oil, gas, and other minerals with a view to their wise conservation for the use of the People, and to the protection of human life in the mines.

Let us conserve the foundations of our prosperity.

Source: Proceedings of a Conference of Governors in the White House, May 13–15, 1908 (Washington, D.C.: Government Printing Office, 1909), 192ff.

Document 3.10   Act for the Preservation of American Antiquities, June 8, 1906

Always adept at political maneuvering, Roosevelt, with the assistance of Chief Forester Gifford Pinchot, invoked this act intended to preserve antiquities in order to withdraw millions of acres of public land from commercial use. He did this only hours before legislation took effect limiting his power to withdraw more land.

AN ACT FOR THE PRESERVATION OF AMERICAN ANTIQUITIES
SECTION 1. Be it enacted by the Senate and House of Representatives of the United States of America, in Congress assembled, That any person who shall appropriate, excavate, injure, or destroy any historic or prehistoric ruin or monument, or any object of antiquity, situated on lands owned or

controlled by the Government of the United States, without the permission of the Secretary of the department of the government having jurisdiction over the lands on which said antiquities are situated, shall, upon conviction, be fined in a sum of not more than five hundred dollars or be imprisoned for a period of not more than ninety days, or shall suffer both fine and imprisonment, at the discretion of the court.

Section 2. That the President of the United States is hereby authorized, in his discretion, to declare by public proclamation historic landmarks, historic and prehistoric structures, and other objects of historic or scientific interest that are situated upon the lands owned or controlled by the Government of the United States to be national monuments, and may reserve as a part thereof parcels of land, the limits of which in all cases shall be confined to the smallest area compatible with the proper care and management of the objects to be protected: Provided, That when such objects are situated upon a tract covered by a bona fide unperfected claim or held in private ownership, the tracts, or so much thereof as may be necessary for the proper care and management of the object, may be relinquished by the Government, and the Secretary of the Interior is hereby authorized to accept the relinquishment of such tracts in behalf of the Government of the United States.

Section 3. That permits for the examination of ruins, the excavation of archaeological sites, and the gathering of objects of antiquity upon the lands under their respective jurisdictions may be granted by the Secretaries of the Interior, Agriculture, and War to institutions which they may deem properly qualified to conduct such examination, excavation, or gathering, subject to such rules and regulations as they may prescribe: Provided, That the examinations, excavations, and gatherings are undertaken for the benefit of reputable museums, universities, colleges, or other recognized scientific or educational institutions, with a view to increasing the knowledge of such objects, and that the gatherings shall be made for permanent preservation in public museums.

Source: American Antiquities Act, U.S. Statutes at Large 34(1906): 225.

Document 3.11   On Lynching, August 6, 1903

Taking the occasion of a lynching race riot in Indiana, the president wrote a letter of congratulations to Governor Winfield Taylor Durbin for his firm action in ending the violence. Knowing the letter would become public, Roosevelt added his condemnation of lynching as an abomination of justice and humanity.

My dear Governor Durbin:

Permit me to thank you as an American citizen for the admirable way in which you have vindicated the majesty of the law by your recent action in reference to lynching. I feel, my dear sir, that you have made all men your debtors who believe, as all farseeing men must, that the well-being, indeed the very existence, of the Republic depends upon that spirit of orderly liberty under the law which is as incompatible with mob violence as with any form of despotism. Of course mob violence is simply one form of anarchy; and anarchy is now, as it always has been, the handmaiden and forerunner of tyranny.

I feel that you have not only reflected honor upon the state which for its good fortune has you as its Chief Executive, but upon the whole nation. It is incumbent upon every man throughout this country not only to hold up your hands in the course you have been following, but to show his realization that the matter is one which is of vital concern to us all.

All thoughtful men must feel the gravest alarm over the growth of lynching in this country, and especially over the peculiarly hideous forms so often taken by mob violence when colored men are the victims—on which occasions the mob seems to lay most weight, not on the crime but on the color of the criminal. In a certain proportion of these cases the man lynched has been guilty of a crime horrible beyond description; a crime so horrible that as far as he himself is concerned he has forfeited the right to any kind of sympathy whatsoever. The feeling of all good citizens that such a hideous crime shall not be hideously punished by mob violence is due not in the least to sympathy for the criminal, but to a very lively sense of the train of dreadful consequences which follow the course taken by the mob in exacting inhuman vengeance for an inhuman wrong. In such cases, moreover, it is well to remember that the criminal not merely sins against humanity in inexpiable and unpardonable fashion, but sins particularly against his own race, and does them a wrong far greater than any white man can possibly do them. Therefore, in such cases the colored people throughout the land should in every possible way show their belief that they, more than all others in the community, are horrified at the commission of such a crime and are peculiarly concerned in taking every possible measure to prevent its recurrence and to bring the criminal to immediate justice. The slightest lack of vigor either in denunciation of the crime or in bringing the criminal to justice is itself unpardonable. . . .

But the fullest recognition of the horror of the crime and the most complete lack of sympathy with the criminal cannot in the least diminish our horror at the way in which it has become customary to avenge these crimes and at the consequences that are already proceeding therefrom. It is of course inevitable that where vengeance is taken by a mob it should frequently light on innocent people; and the wrong done in such a case to the individual is one for which there is no remedy. But even where the real criminal is reached, the wrong done by the mob to the community itself is well-nigh as great. Especially is this true where the lynching is accompanied with torture. There are certain hideous sights which when once seen can never be wholly erased from the mental retina. The mere fact of having seen them implies degradation. This is a thousandfold stronger when instead of merely seeing the deed the man has participated in it. Whoever in any part of our country has ever taken part in lawlessly putting to death a criminal by the dreadful torture of fire must forever after have the awful spectacle of his own handiwork seared into his brain and soul. He can never again be the same man. . . .

The nation, like the individual, cannot commit a crime with impunity. If we are guilty of lawlessness and brutal violence, whether our guilt consists in active participation therein or in mere connivance and encouragement, we shall assuredly suffer later on because of what we have done. The cornerstone of this republic, as of all free government, is respect for and obedience to the law. Where we permit the law to be defied or evaded, whether by rich man or poor man, by black man or white, we are by just so much weakening the bonds of our civilization and increasing the chances of its overthrow and of the substitution of a system in which there shall be violent alternations of anarchy and tyranny.

Source: Theodore Roosevelt Collection, Library of Congress; also available in Elting E. Morison, ed., *The Letters of Theodore Roosevelt* (Cambridge: Harvard University Press, 1951), 3:540–543.

Document 3.12   On Lynching, Sixth Annual Message, December 3, 1906

Roosevelt used his position to focus the attention of Congress and the nation on the horror of lynching, with what effect is difficult to tell. The ugly crime continued, with somewhat reduced numbers, during the Roosevelt years.

. . . I call your attention and the attention of the nation to the prevalence of crime among us, and above all to the epidemic of lynching and mob violence that springs up, now in one part of our country, now in another. Each section, North, South, East, or West, has its own faults; no section can with wisdom spend its time jeering at the faults of another section; it should be busy trying to amend its own shortcomings. To deal with the crime of corruption it is necessary to have an awakened public conscience, and to supplement this by whatever legislation will add speed and certainty in the execution of the law. When we deal with lynching even more is necessary. A great many white men are lynched, but the crime is peculiarly frequent in respect to black men. The greatest existing cause of lynching is the perpetration, especially by black men, of the hideous crime of rape—the most abominable in all the category of crimes, even worse than murder. Mobs frequently avenge the commission of this crime by themselves torturing to death the man committing it; thus avenging in bestial fashion a bestial deed, and reducing themselves to a level with the criminal.

Lawlessness grows by what it feeds upon; and when mobs begin to lynch for rape they speedily extend the sphere of their operations and lynch for many other kinds of crimes, so that two-thirds of the lynchings are not for rape at all; while a considerable proportion of the individuals lynched are innocent of all crime. . . .

Moreover, where any crime committed by a member of one race against a member of another race is avenged in such fashion that it seems as if not the individual criminal, but the whole race, is attacked, the result is to exasperate to the highest degree race feeling. There is but one safe rule in dealing with black men as with white men; it is the same rule that must be applied in dealing with rich men and poor men; that is, to treat each man, whatever his color, his creed, or his social position, with even-handed justice on his real worth as a man. White people owe it quite as much to themselves as to the colored race to treat well the colored man who shows by his life that he deserves such treatment; for it is surely the highest wisdom to encourage in the colored race all those individuals who are honest, industrious, law-abiding, and who therefore make good and safe neighbors and citizens. Reward or punish the individual on his merits as an individual. Evil will surely come in the end to both races if we substitute for this just rule the habit of treating all the members of the race, good and bad, alike. There is no question of "social equality" or "negro domination" involved; only the question of relentlessly punishing bad men, and of securing to the good man the right to his life, his liberty, and the pursuit of his happiness as his own qualities of heart, head, and hand enable him to achieve it.

Every colored man should realize that the worst enemy of his race is the negro criminal, and above all the negro criminal who commits the dreadful crime of rape; and it should be felt as in the highest degree an offense against the whole country, and against the colored race in particular, for a colored man to fail to help the officers of the law in hunting down with all possible earnestness and zeal every such infamous offender. Moreover, in my judgment, the crime of rape should always be punished with death, as is the case with murder; assault with intent to commit rape should be made a capital crime, at least in the discretion of the court; and provision should be made by which the punishment may follow immediately upon the heels of the offense; while the trial should be so conducted that the victim need not be wantonly shamed while giving testimony, and that the least possible publicity shall be given to the details.

The members of the white race on the other hand should understand that every lynching represents by just so much a loosening of the bands of civilization; that the spirit of lynching inevitably throws into prominence in the community all the foul and evil creatures who dwell therein. No man can take part in the torture of a human being without having his own moral nature permanently lowered. Every lynching means just so much moral deterioration in all the children who have any knowledge of it, and therefore just so much additional trouble for the next generation of Americans.

Source: Theodore Roosevelt, *The Works of Theodore Roosevelt*, national ed. (New York: Charles Scribner's Sons, 1926), 15:351–353.

Document 3.13   Roosevelt Corollary to the Monroe Doctrine

With trouble in some Latin American countries, including the Dominican Republic, threatening European intervention, Roosevelt clarified American policy with a corollary to the Monroe Doctrine. In two messages to Congress he made the case for the exercise of police powers by the United States in the hemisphere. He disclaimed acquisitive intentions but emphasized the need for action when corruption or mismanagement invited intervention by European powers.

FOURTH ANNUAL MESSAGE, DECEMBER 6, 1904

. . . It is not true that the United States feels any land hunger or entertains any projects as regards the other nations of the Western Hemisphere save such as are for their welfare. All that this country desires is to see the neighboring countries stable, orderly, and prosperous. Any country whose people conduct themselves well can count upon our hearty friendship. If a nation shows that it knows how to act with reasonable efficiency and decency in social and political matters, if it keeps order and pays its obligations, it need fear no interference from the United States. Chronic wrongdoing, or an impotence which results in a general loosening of the ties of civilized society, may in America, as elsewhere, ultimately require intervention by some civilized nation, and in the Western Hemisphere the adherence of the United States to the Monroe Doctrine may force the United States, however reluctantly, in flagrant cases of such wrongdoing or impotence, to the exercise of an international police power. If every country washed by the Caribbean Sea would show the progress in stable and just civilization which with the aid of the Platt amendment [which reserved to the United States the right to intervene to preserve Cuban independence] Cuba has shown since our troops left the island, and which so many of the republics in both Americas are constantly and brilliantly showing, all question of interference by this Nation with their affairs would be at an end. Our interests and those of our southern neighbors are in reality identical. They have great natural riches, and if within their borders the reign of law and justice obtains, prosperity is sure to come to them. While they thus obey the primary laws of civilized society they may rest assured that they will be treated by us in a spirit of cordial and helpful sympathy. We would interfere with them only in the last resort, and then only if it became evident that their inability or unwillingness to do justice at home and abroad had violated the rights of the United States or had invited foreign aggression to the detriment of the entire body of American nations. It is a mere truism to say that every nation, whether in America or anywhere else, which desires to maintain its freedom, its independence, must ultimately realize that the right of such independence can not be separated from the responsibility of making good use of it.

In asserting the Monroe Doctrine, in taking such steps as we have taken in regard to Cuba, Venezuela, and Panama, and in endeavoring to circumscribe the theater of war in the Far East, and to secure the open door in China, we have acted in our own interest as well as in the interest of humanity at large. There are, however, cases in which, while our own interests are not greatly involved, strong appeal is made to our sympathies. . . . But in extreme cases action may be justifiable and proper. What form the action shall take must depend upon the circumstances of the case; that is, upon the degree of the atrocity and upon our power to remedy it. The cases in which we could interfere by force of arms as we interfered to put a stop to intolerable conditions in Cuba are necessarily very few.

FIFTH ANNUAL MESSAGE, DECEMBER 5, 1905
. . . It must be understood that under no circumstances will the United States use the Monroe Doctrine as a cloak for territorial aggression. We desire peace with all the world, but perhaps most of all with the other peoples of the American Continent. There are, of course, limits to the wrongs which any self-respecting nation can endure. It is always possible that wrong actions toward this Nation, or toward citizens of this Nation, in some State unable to keep order among its own people, unable to secure justice from outsiders, and unwilling to do justice to those outsiders who treat it well, may result in our having to take action to protect our rights; but such action will not be taken with a view to territorial aggression, and it will be taken at all only with extreme reluctance and when it has become evident that every other resource has been exhausted.

Moreover, we must make it evident that we do not intend to permit the Monroe Doctrine to be used by any nation on this Continent as a shield to protect it from the consequences of its own misdeeds against foreign nations. If a republic to the south of us commits a tort against a foreign nation, such as an outrage against a citizen of that nation, then the Monroe Doctrine does not force us to interfere to prevent punishment of the tort, save to see that the punishment does not assume the form of territorial occupation in any shape. The case is more difficult when it refers to a contractual obligation. Our own Government has always refused to enforce such contractual obligations on behalf of its citizens by an appeal to arms. It is much to be wished that all foreign governments would take the same view. But they do not; and in consequence we are liable at any time to be brought face to face with disagreeable alternatives. On the one hand, this country would certainly decline to go to war to prevent a foreign government from collecting a just debt; on the other hand, it is very inadvisable to permit any foreign power to take possession, even temporarily, of the custom houses of an American Republic in order to enforce the payment of its obligations; for such temporary occupation might turn into a permanent occupation. The only escape from these alternatives may at any time be that we must ourselves undertake to bring about some arrangement by which so much as possible of a just obligation shall be paid. It is far better that this country should put through such an arrangement, rather than allow any foreign country to undertake it. To do so insures the defaulting republic from having to pay debt of an improper character under duress, while it also insures honest creditors of the republic from being passed by in the interest of dishonest or grasping creditors. Moreover, for the United States to take such a position offers the only possible way of insuring us against a clash with some foreign power. The position is, therefore, in the interest of peace as well as in the interest of justice. It is of benefit to our people; it is of benefit to foreign peoples; and most of all it is really of benefit to the people of the country concerned. . . .

Source: Theodore Roosevelt, *The Works of Theodore Roosevelt,* national ed. (New York: Charles Scribner's Sons, 1926), 15:256–258, 302–303.

In a bid to end the war between Russia and Japan, Roosevelt met with delegates from the two countries at the 1905 Portsmouth Conference. He won the Nobel Peace Prize for his successful effort.

CHAPTER FOUR

Crises and Flash Points

T he presidency of Theodore Roosevelt was packed with dramatic moments in domestic and foreign affairs. Legislative battles, diplomatic tensions, tradition-breaking and precedent-setting initiatives filled the president's calendar. Amazing energy, self-confidence, and sharp political instincts carried him through the almost constant pressures of the office. Roosevelt knew that his decisions were changing the course of American development; this he intended. Whatever the impact of the pressures on him personally (he seemed to sustain them without damage to health or pride), he thrived on the activity, and at the end of his service, he regretted leaving the job.

The first years of the twentieth century were pivotal in the development of modern America. During the preceding thirty years, technological innovation—the exploitation of electricity and petroleum, the dawn of the automobile age, steel frame construction, massive immigration—reconfigured the American city, initiated suburban growth, and dramatically altered the habits as well as the ethnic mix of the American people. Concurrently, concentrated wealth, trust organization, and an amiably cooperative political and judicial system transformed a manufacturing economy of modest scale into a structure of finance capitalism of prodigious power unimagined in a simpler age. Jim Crow laws and violence embittered race relations and ushered the painful legacy of human bondage into the new century. Great power politics impelled by

161

decades of avid imperialism inspired Americans by threat and example to a new role in the hemisphere and in the world. It was in many ways a new world, which defied traditional understanding and response. Generally, in the decades since Abraham Lincoln, presidents performed as rather docile administrators of the will of Congress. Roosevelt understood, almost instinctively, that the traditional was inadequate to the challenges of the modern; that the new economic, social, and political realities confronting the United States required a new kind of executive leadership to guide the nation through these challenges. From the start he relished the exercise of power, encouraged innovation, embraced new initiatives, and with applause from friends and carping from enemies, he made the presidency a center of action.

In the course of the day-to-day tests of his leadership, some issues exploded into crises that taxed his endurance and threatened his reputation, about which he was acutely sensitive. These challenges demanded wisdom and sometimes quick action to avoid embarrassment, failure, or disaster. His performance under pressure gives us a mixed picture of courage, good judgment, and political skill, as well as volatility, stubbornness, and miscalculation. Roosevelt was proud of his successes and in human fashion tended to rationalize his failures. After years of writing history, he fully appreciated the elements that build historical reputations. Accordingly, he often wrote public statements and private letters with an eye to establishing for posterity and future historians a convincing defense of his performance. For his contemporaries, the effort was unnecessary. When he left office the judgment of the country was highly favorable and his popularity was unquestioned. Had he been a candidate for reelection in 1908, he would most probably have won another term. The perspective of history has also been generally kind; although judgments of how well he handled crises have been mixed, the overall assessment of his leadership has been positive.

THE ASSASSINATION CRISIS

The assassination of President William McKinley propelled Theodore Roosevelt into the presidency in an atmosphere of national crisis. McKinley was the third president killed by gunfire in thirty-six years. The trauma of another murdered president stunned the nation, and the longing for stability and continuity was deeply felt. In the first days of transition all eyes were on the young man who was now the new president, looking for the proper balance of appropriate mourning and a professional competence that would suggest fitness for office.

His status as war hero and his reputation as a leader who, as governor, had stood up to the bosses in New York were well known and carried immediate public respect. Some politicians, even in his own party, were less impressed. Sen. Mark Hanna's gripe about the "cowboy" was inspired by a view of Roosevelt not Hanna's alone. His independent streak was not attractive to the party men, nor was his tendency to impulsive action. How would such instincts play out now that the power of the presidency was in his hands? Although there was little in his past record to suggest an assault on capital, leaders of big business shared the doubts of the politicians about his "dependability." Roosevelt was not unaware of these sentiments and of the delicate tensions of the moment. In the aftermath of the assassination Roosevelt performed with reassuring tact and confident authority.

At the first news of the attack on McKinley, Roosevelt rushed to Buffalo, New York, where the president had been shot. By the time he arrived the president's condition was stable and steadily improved over the next three days. On September 10 Roosevelt left the city as a signal to the country that the danger had receded and joined his family on vacation in the Adirondacks. The optimism was misplaced, and by the early hours of Saturday, September 14, 1901, McKinley was dead. The president's passing required a carefully measured response. The usually voluble Roosevelt, moved by conflicting emotions, carefully controlled his public statements.

Traveling through the night and morning, he arrived in Buffalo by early afternoon and went first to see Ida McKinley, the president's widow, who was too shaken to receive her husband's successor. Next, Roosevelt joined those members of the cabinet who were in Buffalo to tend to the official business of swearing in. Thinking to reassure the country, in the presence of the cabinet and a delegation of reporters, Roosevelt pledged to "continue unchanged McKinley's policies for the honor and prosperity of the country" (Roosevelt 1926, 20:340). Elihu Root, the secretary of war and senior cabinet member present, choked back tears and administered the oath of office. At forty-two, Theodore Roosevelt became the youngest president in American history, a distinction still his (forty-three-year-old John F. Kennedy was the youngest to be elected president).

In his first act as president, Roosevelt immediately called a cabinet meeting in which he requested that all members remain in office, another gesture signaling stability and continuity to the country. On Monday morning he boarded the funeral train carrying McKinley's body back to Washington. An unhappy Mark Hanna was aboard, grief stricken at the loss of his friend and painfully regretting that his warning about the "cowboy" had gone unheeded. Hanna would never be reconciled to the presence of Roosevelt in the White House and even now thought of alternatives for 1904 (see Chapter 2).

In the days that followed, Roosevelt reflected on the transition and was pleased. He wrote to his friend and sometime mentor, Henry Cabot Lodge, "I believe you will approve of what I have done and the way I have handled myself so far" (Morison 1951, 3:150). Roosevelt wanted to be president, but he had looked to a future elective opportunity. He was genuinely grieved by the death of McKinley, whom he respected greatly. But once the sensitive season of transition was over, he threw himself into the duties of the office and never looked back.

THE ANTHRACITE COAL STRIKE OF 1902

The anthracite coal strike of 1902 presented Roosevelt with one of the most difficult political challenges of his administration. By the late nineteenth century the industry was vital to the nation's transportation, productivity, and comfort. Anthracite production grew from a few thousand tons in 1820 to more than eight million tons by 1860, and by 1900 the country was heavily dependent on it. Anthracite mines were concentrated in Pennsylvania but extended to neighboring states as well. Worked by recently arrived immigrants, including children, the mines were hellish places of body-breaking work and constant danger, subject to leaks of volatile and lung-corrupting gasses. Working hours were long, wages kept steady at subsistence levels. Accidents from cave-ins and gas explosions were so commonplace that hundreds died in the mines each year and many more suffered disabling injuries in an age when workers' compensation for job injuries was still considered a radical notion by the captains of industry. Company stores and the necessities of housing and food ate most of a miner's wages and kept many in perpetual debt.

Unionization efforts met fierce resistance from management, and strikes failed to bring measurable improvement in wages or working conditions. When coal prices fell in the 1890s, operators felt justified in setting the meager wage rate still lower. With little left to lose, the United Mine Workers Union (UMW), although it counted only about 10,000 members on its rolls, called a strike in 1897. To the surprise of union leaders and the shock of owners, about 100,000 miners followed the union lead out of the pits. The action won the miners a modest wage adjustment and boosted union membership dramatically.

In Pennsylvania, unions had been broken years earlier, and the UMW had few members there. In 1898 twenty-eight-year-old John Mitchell became president of the union and set out to organize that region. Mitchell, religiously devout and long committed to labor's cause, was not regarded as a radical but as a talented organizer and leader of men. His success at recruiting union members encouraged him to call a strike for higher wages in September 1900. Workers were paid according to the tonnage brought up from the pits. Rates were low and the operators made a practice of adjusting the definition of pounds-in-a-ton to squeeze more production from the fixed rates. Mitchell's principal adversary was George F. Baer, president of the Philadelphia and Reading Railroad, spokesman for the mine operators, and impassioned hater of unions.

When the details of the UMW cause were laid out, they were persuasive enough to win popular support for the miners. The strike also came at a time to alarm the political supporters of the mine owners in a presidential election year. Most anxious was Mark Hanna. The close friend of the president and chairman of the Republican Party had one overriding objective in 1900: the reelection of William McKinley. Entering the political season with a strike threatening the nation's fuel supplies did not fit his election strategy. Because many of the mines were owned by railroad companies and many of them were tied to J. P. Morgan, Hanna solicited the financier's help to pressure the operators. Morgan's pressure forced the operators to give in to union demands for a 10 percent wage increase and, humiliating for Baer, to recognize the union. The effectiveness of arranging union action for maximum political impact was a lesson not lost on Mitchell.

Success swelled union membership, but the operators struck back. Under Baer's leadership, despite the earlier agreement, the operators refused to deal with the UMW. At some mines they blacklisted union activists, and they steadily increased the size of their private police forces. Mitchell bided his time until 1902, a congressional election year. Before calling a strike, he first contacted Hanna, hoping he could be persuaded to help, as he had in 1900. This time neither Hanna nor Morgan was concerned enough to assist. Then, at Mitchell's call, the miners voted overwhelmingly to strike early in May. This time the owners were ready, sending an army of armed guards to the pits and importing scabs to work the struck mines.

As the weeks passed, workers and their families suffered, even their low wages now gone. That hardship, the modesty of miner demands, and the brutality of the company strikebreakers created clear public sympathy for the union. In New York, Democrats called for the government to take over the mines. Writers, churchmen, and other public figures spoke out in support of the strikers. Additional help in generating public sympathy came from the narrow and astonishingly impolitic mind of George Baer. A few weeks into the strike he announced, "The rights and interests of the laboring man will be protected and cared for—not by the labor agitators, but by the Christian men to whom God in his infinite wisdom has given control of the property interests of the country" (Sullivan 1936, 2:426). Across the country Baer's piety was denounced, not the least from the pulpits of deeply offended clergy.

By June, President Roosevelt was paying close attention. He urged Hanna to intervene, but now Baer and the operators were bent on breaking the union's power and deaf to Hanna. The president worried about the damage of a long shutdown in such a basic industry. At this point, though, there was little he could do, Attorney General Philander Knox informed him, unless massive violence erupted. Such an event would not have unduly troubled the owners because it would likely have led to government intervention to force an end to the strike. Through the summer the price of coal, already in short supply, rose steadily to five and six times normal. By September, Republicans worried about the reaction of voters as congressional elections and cold weather loomed. Sen. Henry Cabot Lodge saw disastrous trouble for the party, especially in chilly New England. A winter without coal, the basic fuel of home and industry at the time, was unthinkable.

From the start of the dispute Roosevelt thought the operators unconscionably stubborn for refusing even to negotiate with Mitchell. Late in September, after conferring with members of the cabinet, including Knox and Elihu Root, the president called the warring parties to a meeting at the White House. This was an extraordinary action in an American labor dispute and another sign of a new kind of active presidency. In a telegram he invited Baer and other operators to meet with Mitchell. It was an invitation neither side could refuse. Mitchell, with a union delegation, and Baer leading a group of mine operators met with Roosevelt on the morning of October 3.

Roosevelt reviewed the crisis, emphasizing the danger to the welfare of the nation (see Document 4.1). He called on the parties to find some way to reopen the mines and then recessed the meeting until later in the day to give everyone time for thought. When discussions resumed, it was clear that Mitchell would agree to arbitration of a settlement by an independent group, but the operators would have none of it. Baer boldly lectured the president, insisting that the solution lay in government intervention to break the strike. The meeting broke up without a resolution, and Roosevelt feared he had failed. The conference was a revelation to the president. Mitchell struck him as a firm but reasonable and cooperative advocate; Baer's conduct he found so offensive he confessed wanting to throw him bodily out of the room. It had become clear to him that Baer and not the union was the obstacle to a settlement. Soon after the meeting Roosevelt proposed to Mitchell that the workers return to the mines and in return he would appoint a commission to arbitrate and work to get the owners to accept the findings. A skeptical Mitchell declined politely, noting that he had conceded much but the operators had not budged. Roosevelt could not disagree.

Deeply frustrated and acutely aware that inaction was not an option he could live with, the president contemplated a drastic move. He laid plans for the military to seize and reopen the mines. With increasing violence in the mining towns and shortages of coal growing more dangerous by the day, he brushed aside constitutional scruples about his authority to act in this way. He went as far as calling in Gen. J.M. Schofield to consult about seizing the mines. The general told the president he was ready to serve. As he prepared for action, Roosevelt made one more attempt at a more moderate solution. He authorized his secretary of war and confidant, Elihu Root, to travel to New York to speak unofficially with J.P. Morgan. Once again demonstrating his remarkable personal power, although unelected to any public office, Morgan persuaded the operators to relent and accept binding arbitration. On October 13, Morgan traveled to Washington to inform the president of the agreement and discuss details.

The situation now looked hopeful, but obstacles remained. The operators submitted a list of the kind of men who should make up the board of arbitration; no union representative made the roster. More delicate exchanges followed among Roosevelt, Morgan, the operators, and the union. Roosevelt found humor and satisfaction when he convinced the operators that their demand for a "distinguished sociologist" could be satisfied by the appointment of E. E. Clark, head of the railway conductors union. Apparently the label was more important than the person. Roosevelt's patience and persistence finally paid off when both sides agreed to the makeup of the commission.

As the commission met at the end of October, the miners returned to work. The flow of coal to the country resumed, the price of the fuel fell to more reasonable levels, and the specter of a killing winter faded. The commission dictated a 10 percent rise in wages and several work concessions demanded by the union, but it refused to bind the operators to a recognition of the union as the collective bargaining agent of the workers. Thus some satisfaction was had on both sides, but it was Roosevelt who emerged as the hero of this drama. His work drew rave reviews at home and even in European circles. The politically astute recognized that something important had happened besides the end of a strike. This was the first time an American president had become so actively involved in the details of a conflict between capital and labor. Precedent was established for the future, and the presidential office itself was now a more powerful instrument in the life of the nation.

TAKING PANAMA

The building of the Panama Canal was one of Theodore Roosevelt's proudest achievements. The decades-old dream, once completed, brought perpetual benefits to the United States and to world trade generally. But in achieving his goal, Roosevelt took steps that went to the edge, and by some judgments, crossed the line of proper international behavior (Dulles 1955, 74; Mowry 1958, 154).

After repeated negotiations with the British to abrogate the Clayton-Bulwer Treaty of 1850, the Hay-Pauncefote Treaty of 1901 cleared the way for the United States to construct an interocean canal (see Document 4.2). Secretary of State John Hay won major concessions for the United States, including not only the right to build and maintain the canal, but also the right to build fortifications. In return the United States agreed that passage through the canal would be open to all countries on equal terms. After extended discussion over the best site for the project, Panama was chosen and the expected course of action was to reach an arrangement with Colombia to cross its territory. Roosevelt began negotiations, and the early results were promising. The president first agreed to pay $40 million to a French company, Compagnie Nouvell du Canal de Panama, for canal construction rights it held from Colombia. The deal was engineered by Philippe Bunau-Varilla and William Nelson Cromwell, agents of the now bankrupt company. The Hay-Herran convention with Colombia, negotiated in early 1903, would have settled the project had not the Colombian legislature rejected the terms of the agreement in August as inadequate financially. Roosevelt was so appalled at the slight that he refused to reopen negotiations, a course that might have avoided the unseemly turmoil that followed.

During these negotiations, earlier discontent with the rule of Colombia in Panama resurfaced, and independence elements there saw an opportunity. Roosevelt capitalized on the situation. In the fall of 1903, working out of a hotel in New York, Bunau-Varilla and Cromwell made contact with the discontented Panamanians, sent money to feed revolutionary enthusiasm, and shuttled to Washington for talks that included Roosevelt himself. The details of Roosevelt's conversations remain obscure, but late in October several ships, including a contingent of Marines, were ordered into the neighborhood of Panama. On November 3, the day after the arrival of the USS *Nashville* off shore, revolution broke out in Panama. The governor and other officials were arrested; some were bribed into cooperation. A contingent of Colombian troops was dispatched to put down the uprising, but with the intervention of American forces, Colombian troops could not reach the rebels. Panama immediately declared its independence and Roosevelt recognized the new government, all within the space of three days. For canal interests, it was a splendid little revolt. Evidence to the contrary, Roosevelt vehemently denied that the United States had plotted the events and insisted that the revolution was genuine. He justified the intervention of American troops by citing the obligation of the United States in the face of trouble to guarantee free transit across the isthmus, based on an old treaty with Colombia.

Bunau-Varilla now appeared in Washington as a representative of the Republic of Panama, his French citizenship no obstacle. The

Hay-Bunau-Varilla Treaty, concluded in November, gave the United States rights in perpetuity to a ten-mile-wide canal zone (larger than the six miles offered earlier by Colombia) in return for a $10 million payment and an annual rental fee of $250,000 (see Document 4.3). In December, Roosevelt offered Congress his explanation of events and presented the treaty with Panama for ratification (see Document 4.4). The Senate ratified the Hay-Bunau-Varilla Treaty by a vote of 66 to 14 in February 1904.

Most American opinion applauded the Panama adventure, but despite the obvious advantages to the United States, there were protests in the press and especially among anti-imperialists in Congress and the country at large. Although many of the details of American complicity in inciting and supporting the revolution were not known, Roosevelt was attacked for haste, aggressiveness, and imperialist ambition. The president, as always, was sensitive to criticism and quick to defend himself. He told Congress that every effort was made to persuade Colombia to accept a reasonable arrangement, skipping over the haste with which he abandoned negotiations with that government. On aiding the revolution in Panama he said, "the United States would have been guilty of folly and weakness, amounting in their sum to a crime against the nation had it acted otherwise than it did" (Roosevelt 1926, 15:212). In private to family and friends he called his actions right and honorable and assaulted his newspaper critics as hysterical. Roosevelt persisted in justifying his role over the years. As late as 1911 in an address at the University of California, he candidly asserted, "If I had followed conventional, conservative methods, I should have submitted a dignified state paper to the Congress and the debate would have been going on yet, but I took the canal zone and let Congress debate" (Pringle [1931] 1956, 232–233).

Ultimately, the judgment of the United States government did not sustain Roosevelt's defense of his relations with Colombia. In 1914 the Wilson administration negotiated an agreement for the payment of $25 million to Colombia, a concession of regret over Panama. The Senate refused to concur for a time but, seeking better relations with Colombia, ratified the agreement in 1921 (see Document 4.5).

THE VENEZUELA CRISIS

Stability and good order were not common governing virtues in many Latin American countries at the turn of the twentieth century, Venezuela among them. Plagued by frequent revolts, social and political turmoil, and careless financial practices, Venezuela was a source of annoyance to European creditors and concern to the United States, given the American sensitivity to the Monroe Doctrine and the danger of European intervention. But President Roosevelt had little patience with Latin American countries that were cavalier about their obligations and said, "If any South American country misbehaves toward any European country, let that European country spank it" (Morison 1951, 3:116). Clarifying American policy, he told Congress the Monroe Doctrine was not concerned with commercial relations, and the United States would not feel obliged to protect a hemisphere nation against Europe unless there was a threat of territorial acquisition (see Document 4.6).

Nevertheless the situation in Venezuela presented a challenge to the administration, particularly because Germany was a principal player. In contrast to the recent warming of relations with Great Britain, relations with Germany had shown strains in recent years. Roosevelt, himself, thought an increasingly powerful and expansionist Germany might have ambitions in Latin America, and he regarded Germany as potentially dangerous to the United States. Into this atmosphere the Venezuela crisis erupted in 1902.

Venezuela had attracted European investments and borrowed heavily as well. Creditors saw their investments collapse and bond debts went unpaid. The dictatorial and unpopular government of Cipriano Castro maintained a casual indifference to these obligations and rejected the suggestions that his government enter into arbitration to settle claims. Patience exhausted, Britain and Germany (later joined by Italy) blockaded the principal Venezuelan ports and in the process sank or seized several of its naval vessels. The action stirred hostile public opinion in the United States over an apparent violation of the Monroe Doctrine, a reaction exacerbated when the Europeans bombarded port and military sites. At this point Washington offered its good offices and urged the parties to arbitrate their differences. The European powers requested that Roosevelt lead the arbitration, but the president declined and pressed for the controversy to be referred to the Court of International Justice in The Hague. That body had been established to prevent conflict in just such situations, and this episode is counted as one of its successes. After the blockaders' use of military force, Castro accepted the arbitration proposal. The creditor nations agreed, but historical controversy persists over Roosevelt's role in pressing the Germans to accept arbitration.

How crucial were Roosevelt's actions in settling the dispute? In the 1904 presidential campaign he maintained that the Venezuela crisis was one of his administration's finest hours. Years later, after the start of World War I, he narrated a version of events in which he claimed his pressure drove the reluctant Germans to the arbitration table. By his account, when the Germans at first declined, he threatened to send an American fleet under Adm. George Dewey, then in waters off Puerto Rico, to Venezuela against the blockade. Historians, unable to find clear documentation for his story, accused Roosevelt of fabrication to enhance his record or, perhaps, out of anti-German emotions fired by the war (Brands 1997, 468). However, recent studies tend to support the general lines of Roosevelt's recollections (Beale 1956, 401–402; Marks 1979, 37ff.).

THE BROWNSVILLE INCIDENT

The Twenty-fifth Infantry Regiment was a unit composed of black soldiers in those days of segregation in the military. In the summer of 1906, the regiment was sent to Fort Brown in Texas, just outside the city of Brownsville. White citizens of the town were not happy about the presence of the troops, and tension was not long developing. Racial incidents and fights ensued; a rumor accused a black soldier of striking a white woman. Fearing trouble, a cautious officer confined the men to camp on August 13. That night shots rang out in the city, and authorities soon discovered one man had been killed and a policeman wounded. The mayor and townspeople blamed the shooting on troops from the camp. The men were quickly assembled for roll call and all were accounted for. Their rifles were inspected and found clean. If they were guilty, the soldiers would have had to sneak back into camp undetected and clean their rifles in the dark of night, a difficult task. Authorities presented a collection of spent cartridges as evidence that the shots came from army rifles, but investigation later revealed that they had not been found scattered as would be expected from random firing, but gathered in one small area. In defense of the soldiers it was pointed out that boxes of empty cartridges from target practice were easily available at the camp to any visitor. The army investigation could not present evidence against any individual soldiers, and despite official urging, none of the men in the camp would name anyone as responsible. Several witnesses from the city claimed that they saw soldiers firing but could not identify any of them. The conclusion was that a dozen or so black soldiers, unnamed, were guilty. The matter was then referred to Washington.

Roosevelt was outraged by the incident and furious, despite the absence of convincing evidence, that no soldiers would testify to point out the guilty. He had worked to appeal to black voters and to build a stronger Republican Party in the South; he had entertained Booker T. Washington at the White House; and he had lashed out against lynching. Now this incident threatened to excite racial tensions and confirm white prejudices about black lawlessness. By late October he made up his mind on punishment. As a courtesy he called Booker T. Washington to the White House to tell him in advance of his decision. Washington was distressed at what he heard and asked the president to delay in announcing his action. Roosevelt refused. On November 5 he handed down a judgment against the entire contingent of troops and ordered dishonorable discharges for 167 soldiers. That 6 of the 167 men held the Medal of Honor and more than a dozen had been cited for bravery in combat did not temper the order. The dishonorable discharge eliminated the possibility of pensions, and the men were barred from reenlisting in the military.

Across the country the order was greeted with anger and deep sadness in black communities, where Roosevelt had been admired and considered a friend. Telegrams and letters of protest from blacks and whites only stiffened the president's resolve in the matter. He insisted that his action was necessary to maintain military discipline and good order (see Document 4.7).

The day after the order was announced, Roosevelt sailed for Panama to inspect work on the canal. While he was in Panama, petitioners appealed to Secretary of War William Howard Taft to suspend the discharge orders until the president returned to the country. Taft, reluctant to act on his own, relayed the request to Panama, but Roosevelt refused to be moved (Morison 1952, 5:498).

When Roosevelt returned to Washington, the issue remained alive. Sen. Joseph Foraker, a Republican from Ohio with aspirations for the party's presidential nomination in 1908, took up the cause of the black soldiers and called for a new investigation. Roosevelt insisted that race did not enter into his decision and affirmed his conviction that men from the camp were guilty. Foraker was undeterred. He presented arguments that civilians had done the shooting and passed the blame to the soldiers.

The debate continued in January 1907, at the annual Gridiron Club dinner at which speeches were off the record but inevitably leaked. There Roosevelt and Foraker debated, exchanging angry accusations, reports of which kept the issue in the public mind. A year later a Senate committee took yet another look at the incident. The committee was made up of five Democrats and four Republicans, including Foraker. In March the majority report upheld the president, with Foraker and his colleagues in the minority still insisting the troops were innocent.

A military court of inquiry in 1909 let the verdict stand. Nevertheless, the army later quietly allowed fourteen of the dismissed soldiers to reenlist. Whatever actually happened at Brownsville that August night, Roosevelt's summary judgment and his defensiveness afterward cast a shadow over his legacy. It is interesting that years later when Roosevelt penned his autobiography, he chose to ignore this chapter of his presidency entirely. The last act of the Brownsville incident was not written until 1972. In that year the army announced that its procedures did not sanction mass punishments, and the men of the Twenty-fifth Infantry were designated as honorably discharged.

THE FINANCIAL PANIC OF 1907

The American economy enjoyed phenomenal expansion after the Civil War. Once a debtor nation dependent on foreign money to finance industrial investment, by the end of the nineteenth century the United States was an industrial giant, surpassing Britain and Germany, for example, in railroad tonnage and steel production. That success produced such great fortunes that the financial houses of New York now sustained domestic growth and loaned money around the world. This remarkable growth came despite a seriously deficient banking system. There had been no effective banking legislation in the United States since the National Banking Act of 1863. That law created a system of chartered national banks but left the country without a central banking authority. An active economy requires sustained liquidity, that is, an adequate supply of money available for loans, to finance new development and to see companies through periods of declining income. Thus the expanding economy lacked a stabilizing influence during periods of turmoil that came inevitably with rapid growth. The results were periodic business failures, financial panics, and fear that the nation's economy would sink into depression, as indeed it did in 1873 and again in 1894.

Roosevelt was not expert in economics, and in contrast to the flood of ideas on so many subjects in his messages to Congress, he had little new to offer concerning the country's financial operations. He saw periods of financial uncertainty or disruption as a product of excessive speculation and shady corporate behavior. His critics in the business community preferred to blame his threats to the system by attacks on the trusts and his enthusiasm for passing regulatory legislation to handcuff the enterprising. In the summer of 1907, a federal court found the Standard Oil Company guilty of multiple counts of illegal rebates and fined the company $29 million. Although the decision was later overturned, for conservatives it stood as evidence that Roosevelt's policies were undermining business confidence. In October a serious convulsion in the financial world threatened to bring down the American economy and presented Roosevelt with one of the most difficult decisions of his presidency.

The failure of several industrial and financial firms caused uncertainty, and a sharp decline in stock prices in March signaled trouble. Banks, which often loaned money for stock purchases, also suffered the effects of uncertainty. Late in October, nervous depositors, agitated by rumors of impending collapse, created a run on a major New York bank, the Knickerbocker Trust Company, wanting their cash. Since much of the demanded money was out on loan, the bank could not satisfy the rush for payment and was forced to close its doors. Immediately the stock market dropped steeply and other banks trembled.

With panic spreading, Secretary of the Treasury George B. Cortelyou traveled to New York on October 23 to meet with J. P. Morgan, who was working with John D. Rockefeller and other financiers to shore up several threatened banks. Cortelyou agreed to deposit $25 million in government funds in New York banks. On the next day, with the stock market still falling, Roosevelt announced the deposit decision, hoping to restore investor confidence. For the moment collapse was evaded, but the next week sowed more rumors about impending failures. Another shock could easily convert panic into crash and extended depression. The trouble was not over.

Soon, news leaked that the Tennessee Coal and Iron Company was in difficulty. Worse, the New York brokerage house of Moore and Schley had invested so heavily in the company that the failure of Tennessee Coal and Iron could pull down this important financial institution with it. Such a disaster would inevitably spread to other institutions and threaten the economy itself. Behind the scenes, financiers worked frantically to find a solution, and they soon enlisted the president in their cause.

Elbert H. Gary and Henry C. Frick, officers of United States Steel Company, whose board of directors was dominated by Morgan, asked urgently to see the president early Monday morning, November 4. Morgan's men presented a plan to save Tennessee Coal and Iron from collapse and, not incidentally, to rescue Moore and Schley from bankruptcy. U.S. Steel would perform a public service by purchasing Tennessee Coal and Iron and assuming its debts. They told the president they would have preferred not to take over the troubled company, for there would be little gain in it for U.S. Steel, but the larger emergency demanded action (Strouse 1999, 586). Their purpose at the White House was to seek assurance that when the deal was consummated, the president would not launch an antitrust suit against U.S. Steel, already the largest trust in the country. The timing of the meeting for early morning was significant. The steel men insisted they needed an answer before the stock market opened at ten o'clock to stem the panic. Under pressure for a quick decision and fearful of the consequences of continued uncertainty, Roosevelt agreed to refrain from prosecution. The wires instantly carried the news to New York, and the market responded with a rally. The president was not entirely pleased with his decision but thought he had little alternative in view of the crisis. He later carefully explained his position to Attorney General Charles Bonaparte (see Document 4.8).

Democrats and some progressives of his own party charged him with coddling the capitalists. Certainly his promise not to prosecute ran counter to the image he had cultivated as a guardian of the public interest against the greed of the trust. Neither did Roosevelt appreciate being linked to Morgan as an ally. After the crisis had passed, critics charged that Roosevelt had been duped by Morgan and his associates. Investigations by both the Senate and the House in 1909 suggested the Morgan's intervention was more than an act of civic goodwill; it proved to be profitable for U.S. Steel with the added advantage of a guarantee of immunity for the giant trust. Neither Roosevelt nor Morgan had the last word in the affair. In 1911 President Taft, then under political attack by Roosevelt and feeling unbound by his predecessor's promise, initiated an antitrust suit against U.S. Steel. The Supreme Court later rejected the charge of monopoly and the suit failed. Years later, still compelled to respond to his critics, Roosevelt wrote a lengthy justification in his autobiography (see Document 4.9).

Roosevelt understood power and its uses, and this was reflected in his trust and regulatory policies. With the details of economics and finance he was less adept. Whether he was "taken" by Morgan remains uncertain, but this temporary alliance did not weaken his conviction of the need for government to harness the power of capital, nor did it diminish the distrust with which he was held by the capitalists.

SAN FRANCISCO RACISM AND THE CRISIS WITH JAPAN

President Roosevelt came into office acutely aware of the growing influence of Japan in Asia. He was both wary of Japan's growing power and anxious to nourish friendly relations. The Japanese believed Roosevelt had unduly favored Russia in the Treaty of Portsmouth ending the Russo-Japanese War in 1905, but that unhappiness paled when compared with the tensions that developed from anti-Japanese feeling in California. Exaggerating both number and effect, Americans on the West Coast, goaded by sensationalist newspapers and politicians, angrily resented the immigration of Asian workers, "coolies" in the jargon of the time. In 1902 Congress specifically excluded Chinese laborers from entry into the United States. Roosevelt did not protest this action, but he did object to discrimination against and exclusion of Chinese businessmen and students. The arrival of Japanese immigrants caused intensified distress among Californians. Few Japanese lived in the state before 1890; by 1900 their number reached twenty-four thousand. The increase is traced to the annexation of Hawaii, after which Japanese workers resident there could travel to the mainland without the need for passports. The California response was a model of fear-fed intolerance. The decades of prejudice against the Chinese were now refocused on the Japanese. Soon, racial prejudice was transformed into public policy.

In March 1905 the California legislature passed, without a dissenting vote, a resolution calling for restrictions on Japanese immigration. The resolution was framed in insulting terms, depicting the Japanese as immoral and prone to violence. When the news reached Washington, Roosevelt referred to the legislators as idiots and the resolutions as foolish and offensive. The president regarded the Japanese as a highly civilized and able people, but he was concerned that large numbers of Japanese laborers would incite social turmoil in the West and damage relations with the government of Japan. Nor were his cares eased when the Japanese-Korean Exclusion League was formed in May 1905 and soon enrolled more than seventy thousand members. Under pressure from the Exclusion League, the San Francisco School Board ordered all Asian students in the city segregated in a single school in October 1906. In Japan, the press and public opinion reacted to the news with expected outrage, and a few extreme voices recommended a military response. The official reaction was more moderate, citing traditional friendship with the United States and affirming the expectation that the offense would be remedied. To Secretary of State Elihu Root, the government communicated its displeasure.

Roosevelt watched the California convulsions with growing distress. He offered Baron Kentaro Kaneko, a Harvard classmate and now a special envoy from Japan, assurances that events on the West Coast did not represent American opinion and promised he would work to remedy matters. He sent his secretary of commerce and labor, Victor H. Metcalf, west to defuse the tension and get the segregation order rescinded. Metcalf succeeded at neither. The school board was resistant and the townspeople unmoved. Reporting to Congress in December, Roosevelt described the action of the San Francisco school officials as a "wicked absurdity" and reminded the lawmakers that Japan had contributed more money for the relief of the city after the recent earthquake disaster than any other country. Then he called for legislation to allow for Japanese naturalization as American citizens (see Document 4.10). Attentive to his words, the Japanese government was pleased, the Californians irate.

With no sign of cooperation or understanding coming from California, Roosevelt decided to act. Late in January 1907, consulting with the California senators and congressmen, he invited the San Francisco superintendent of schools and the head of the school board to come to Washington. The delegation was soon enlarged to include the entire board as well as Mayor Eugene E. Schmitz. The delegation met with Roosevelt and Root early in February. With a commitment by Roosevelt to help check the inflow of Japanese laborers, the Californians agreed to revoke the segregation order in March. That same month, a warning from Roosevelt prevented the lower house of the state legislature from extending segregation of Asians in schools throughout California (see Document 4.11).

Meanwhile, Roosevelt struggled to calm relations with Japan. He doubted conflict was imminent but worried about the vulnerability of Hawaii and the Philippines. It was clear that the San Francisco school crisis was an outgrowth of anger over the arrival of Japanese workers. The president directed negotiations with Japan seeking a solution to the immigration issue that would simultaneously calm California fears and avoid offense to Japan. Outright exclusion was not an acceptable solution. But with assurances that the school dispute would be resolved satisfactorily, there emerged the basis of an understanding if not a formal treaty. With Roosevelt's encouragement, in February 1907 Congress passed a new immigration bill giving the president authority to restrict immigration if the disruption of labor conditions in the United States was likely. Japan was especially sensitive to any proposals that specifically mentioned Japanese immigration. The bill made no such reference and, taken literally, applied to immigrants from any country. For its part, the Japanese government conceded that it would voluntarily restrict the granting of passports for emigration to the United States, with some exceptions for travel to Hawaii. In return for this cooperation, it was understood that Japanese nationals would not be subject to discrimination as they had been in the San Francisco schools. While this Gentlemen's Agreement did not carry the force of a treaty, Roosevelt was delighted and proud that he had been able to defuse this potentially explosive crisis (see Document 4.12).

The end of segregation in San Francisco in March 1907 calmed Pacific waters for a time, but a storm hit again in May, when anti-Japanese rioting broke out in San Francisco. Press frenzy spread rumors that war was coming. The violence was quickly controlled, and again Japanese and American officials worked together to contain the damage to diplomatic relations. Eventually, courts in California ordered the payment of several hundred thousand dollars in damages to victims of the rioting. With order restored, Roosevelt confessed that "nothing during my Presidency has given me more concern than these troubles" (see Document 4.13). Indeed, Roosevelt was forced to act again in the last weeks of his presidency when the California legislature took up a bill that would have barred noncitizen Japanese from owning property. With a public rebuke and private pressure on the governor, he succeeded in killing the measure.

As disruptive as the issues of racial discrimination and "coolie" labor were, they were not grievous enough to be a cause for war when neither country was so inclined. But although amicably settled, the tensions suggested to some, Roosevelt included, that future conflict between these two Pacific powers was not inconceivable. Acknowledging the futility of colonialism and the vulnerability of the Philippines, Roosevelt was convinced that the islands should be readied for independence. Meanwhile, the Gentlemen's Agreement seemed to do its work. After June 1907, the number of Japanese entering the United States dropped sharply, and by August 1908, more Japanese left the country than entered it.

Always alert for an opportunity at drama, Roosevelt hit on an idea to impress Japan and the world. Proud of his work in building up American naval forces, he ordered a fleet of battleships on a world tour, in part to demonstrate American power and in part as a friendly gesture. When the Great White Fleet, as it was labeled, arrived in Yokohama, Japan, in October 1908, it received a remarkably friendly welcome. This was repeated at stops around the world, and Roosevelt counted the trip as one of his great successes as president.

Even as the immigration crises were tormenting Washington, Roosevelt and Secretary of State Root sought to negotiate a firm pronouncement for friendly relations with Japan. During 1908, Root and Kogoro Takahira, Japanese minister to the United States, discussed a joint statement on key Pacific issues, and Roosevelt joined the discussions personally in October. The result was the Root-Takahira Agreement of November 30, 1908 (see Document 4.14). The two nations committed themselves to peaceful commerce in the Pacific, continuation of the open door in China, respect for the territorial integrity of China, and a pledge to negotiate any differences that threatened to disrupt good relations. This agreement and Roosevelt's work on the problems in California were important contributions, but they did not seal the bonds of enduring friendship with Japan. Racial hostility continued on the West Coast, and Japanese designs for expansion in the Pacific spelled future trouble.

Theodore Roosevelt responded to crises with a combination of skill and realism, the same qualities he brought to bear on his more routine duties. He remained alert to the limits of the possible, and he understood both the uses and the limits of his power. Few presidents have as fully appreciated the uses of press and public opinion or have as skillfully turned both to advantage. His realism was, on occasion, defeated by haste or emotion, as was probably the case in the Brownsville matter. But conceding his flaws and accounting for the number and complexity of the crises of his years in office, his presidency must rank highly on the scales of successful leadership.

BIBLIOGRAPHIC ESSAY

For the study of the major crises of the Roosevelt administration the following works on the subject are helpful: John Morton Blum, *The Republican Roosevelt*, 2d ed. (Cambridge: Harvard University Press, 1977), a skillful and scholarly analysis of the president in action. H. W. Brands, *T.R.: The Last Romantic* (New York: Basic Books, 1997), is a careful study focusing principally on his political career. Kathleen Dalton, *Theodore Roosevelt: A Strenuous Life* (New York: Alfred A. Knopf, 2002), the most recent biography, pays special attention to the influence of women in Roosevelt's personal and political life. Lewis L. Gould, *The Presidency of Theodore Roosevelt* (Lawrence: University Press of Kansas, 1991), is one of the best compact histories of the Roosevelt presidency. William Henry Harbaugh, *The Life and Times of Theodore Roosevelt* (New York: Collier Books, 1963), among the most scholarly of the biographies, is still very useful. Nathan Miller, *Theodore Roosevelt: A Life* (New York: William Morrow, 1992), is a generally sympathetic biography. Edmund Morris, *Theodore Rex* (New York: Random House, 2001), the second volume of a projected three-volume biography, is a finely detailed history of the presidential years. George E. Mowry, *The Era of Theodore Roosevelt* (New York: Harper and Brothers, 1958), offers a broad picture of the United States during the Roosevelt years and a friendly interpretation of his performance. Henry Pringle, *Theodore Roosevelt: A Biography* (1931; reprint, New York: Harcourt Brace, 1956), is a prize-winning biography dating from the 1930s, often critical of the president's policies and politics.

On labor issues see Sidney Lens, *The Labor Wars: From the Molly Maguires to the Sitdowns* (New York: Doubleday, 1973), an interesting treatment of the coal strike of 1902. Will Irwin, ed., *Letters to Kermit from Theodore Roosevelt, 1902–1908* (New York: Charles Scribner's Sons, 1946), offers "posterity letters" that Roosevelt liked to send his son Kermit to record his version of events like the coal strike settlement for the historical record.

On the Latin American crises, including the disputes over Panama and Venezuela, see Howard K. Beale, *Theodore Roosevelt and the Rise of America to World Power* (Baltimore: Johns Hopkins University Press, 1956). Richard H. Collin, *Theodore Roosevelt's Caribbean* (Baton Rouge: Louisiana State University Press, 1990), provides a recent defense of the president's actions concerning Panama. Foster Rhea Dulles, *America's Rise to World Power, 1898–1954* (New York: Harper and Brothers, 1955) is a volume in the New American Nation series. Howard C. Hill, *Roosevelt and the Caribbean*

(New York: Russell and Russell, 1965), is a solid review of Roosevelt's Caribbean policy. Frederick W. Marks III, *Velvet on Iron: The Diplomacy of Theodore Roosevelt* (Lincoln: University of Nebraska Press, 1979), is a successful effort to assess Roosevelt's foreign policy in the context of his times.

For an examination of the Brownsville incident see Thomas G. Dyer, *Theodore Roosevelt and the Idea of Race* (Baton Rouge: Louisiana State University Press, 1980); Ann J. Lane, *The Brownsville Affair* (Port Washington, N.Y.: Kennikat Press, 1971); John D. Weaver, *The Brownsville Raid* (New York: Norton, 1970); and C. Van Woodward, *Origins of the New South* (Baton Rouge: Louisiana State University Press, 1971).

On crises in the Pacific, useful works include Thomas A. Bailey, *Theodore Roosevelt and the Japanese-American Crises* (Stanford: Stanford University Press, 1934); and Raymond A. Esthus, *Theodore Roosevelt and Japan* (Seattle: University of Washington Press, 1966).

Document 4.1   On the Coal Strike, October 22, 1902

As the anthracite coal strike, called in May 1902, dragged on into the fall, Roosevelt's concern about a winter without coal was shared by party leaders, especially in New England and other northern states. When the crisis passed he shared with the governor of Massachusetts, Winthrop Murray Crane, some of the strategy that led to the strike settlement at the end of October.

My dear Governor:

. . . Of course when the strike began last May we all realized its importance. Senator Hanna and the Civic Federation tried to bring about a settlement on the basis of the operators conceding something and the miners abating a good deal of their demands. The effort, as you know, was fruitless, the operators being very bitter against what they termed the interference of politicians, and openly attributing the present trouble to the settlement two years previously at the time of McKinley's second election—this settlement having been brought about by Hanna.

After Hanna's failure I directed Carroll D. Wright to investigate and report. His report was made to me on June 20. I submitted it to Knox, who promptly told me that he did not think I had any concern with the affair and that he could not see what good would come of publishing the report. Accordingly I did not publish it until August. In the interval I broached the subject two or three times with Knox, who always remained firm in his position. The continuance of the strike rendered me uneasy as to the future, however, and moreover I felt that the time might come when I would have to act, and I finally decided, toward the end of August, to make the report public together with Knox's opinion as to my having no power or duty in the matter. The opinion was in language which did not stop me from acting if the circumstances changed. During September it became evident to me that the circumstances were changing and that I must be prepared to take some action. However, when I saw Knox, after my return from Indianapolis when laid up with my leg [which Roosevelt had recently injured while touring in Massachusetts], he was still firm in his previous opinion.

You then came on and saw me with Payne. Your account of the condition of things in Massachusetts and of the imminence of a coal famine made me realize that I must take action at once. About the same time Seth Low wrote me to much the same effect from New York, and a little investigation showed that we were in measurable distance of a very serious calamity. Of course I was receiving all the time all kinds of worthless statements and worthless advice from people of every degree. But your statements I knew I could depend upon. You were no alarmist, and when you saw the coal famine impending, with untold misery as the result, with the certainty of riots which might develop into social war to follow, I did not feel like longer delaying. Root, who had come back from stopping overnight with Hanna, shared your views. I had as yet no legal or constitutional duty—and therefore no legal or constitutional right—in the matter. But I felt that the crisis was not one in which I could act on the Buchanan principle of striving to find some constitutional reason for inaction; and obviously the first thing to do was to try to get the representatives of both sides together and see whether by an appeal to their patriotism I could bring about an agreement. On October 1 I sent out . . . telegrams, framed after consultation with Root and Knox. Knox had by this time returned from a visit to Pittsburgh, and, although he had not believed in my going into the matter, he acted as he always does in such cases—that is, the course or policy having been decided he did his very best to make it successful; and from this time on he and Root were my two (best) strongest helpers and advisers. . . .

Source: Theodore Roosevelt Collection, Library of Congress; also available in Elting E. Morison, ed., *The Letters of Theodore Roosevelt* (Cambridge: Harvard University Press, 1951), 3:359–360.

Document 4.2   The Hay-Pauncefote Treaty (1901)

The United States won a free hand in building the Panama Canal when the British gave up their rights to joint construction and fortification provided in the Clayton-Bulwer Treaty of 1850. The British were especially active after 1880 in cultivating American friendship, given the rise of a powerful Germany. This was one of the gestures to draw American goodwill. The Senate ratified the treaty in December 1901.

The United States of America and His Majesty Edward the Seventh, of the United Kingdom of Great Britain and Ireland, . . . being desirous to facilitate the construction of a ship canal to connect the Atlantic and Pacific Oceans, by whatever route may be considered expedient, and to that end to remove any objection which may arise out of the convention of the nineteenth of April, 1850, commonly called the Clayton-Bulwer treaty, to the construction of such canal under the auspices of the Government of the United States, without impairing the "general principle" of neutralization established in Article VIII of that convention, have . . . agreed upon the following articles:

ARTICLE I. The High Contracting Parties agree that the present treaty shall supersede the afore-mentioned Convention of the 19th April, 1850.

ARTICLE II. It is agreed that the canal may be constructed under the auspices of the Government of the United States either directly at its own cost, or by gift or loan of money to individuals or Corporations, or through subscription to or purchase of stock or shares, and that, subject to the provisions of the present Treaty, the said Government shall have and enjoy all the rights incident to such construction, as well as the exclusive right of providing for the regulation and management of the canal.

ARTICLE III. The United States adopts, as the basis of the neutralization of such ship canal, the following Rules, substantially as embodied in the Convention of Constantinople signed the twenty-eighth of October, 1888, for the free navigation of the Suez Canal, that is to say:

1. The canal shall be free and open to the vessels of commerce and of war of all nations observing these Rules, on terms of entire equality, so that there shall be no discrimination against any such nation, or its citizens or subjects, in respect of the conditions or charges of traffic or otherwise. Such conditions and charges of traffic shall be just and equitable.

2. The canal shall never be blockaded, nor shall any right of war be exercised nor any act of hostility be committed within it. The United States,

however, shall be at liberty to maintain such military police along the canal as may be necessary to protect it against lawlessness and disorder.

ARTICLE IV. It is agreed that no change of territorial sovereignty or of international relations of the country or countries traversed by the before-mentioned canal shall affect the general principle of neutralization or the obligation of the High Contracting Parties under the present Treaty. . . .

Source: William M. Malloy, ed., *Treaties, Conventions, etc.* (Washington, D.C.: Government Printing Office, 1910), 1:782–783.

Document 4.3   Convention with Panama for the Construction of a Canal (Hay-Bunau-Varilla Treaty), February 26, 1904

After playing a key role in the Panamanian revolt against Colombia, Philippe Bunau-Varilla, former agent of the Compagnie Nouvell du Canal de Panama, presented himself in Washington as a representative of the new government of Panama to negotiate treaty terms. An official delegation from Panama arrived after the treaty was signed, and although it is suspected they would have demanded more from the United States, they were not prepared to endanger the agreement and accepted Bunau-Varilla's work.

ARTICLE I. The United States guarantees and will maintain the independence of the Republic of Panama.

ARTICLE II. The Republic of Panama grants to the United States in perpetuity the use, occupation and control of a zone of land and land under water for the construction, maintenance, operation, sanitation and protection of said Canal of the width of ten miles extending to the distance of five miles on each side of the center line of the route of the canal to be constructed; the said zone beginning in the Caribbean Sea, three marine miles from mean low water mark, and extending to and across the Isthmus of Panama into the Pacific Ocean to a distance of three marine miles from mean low water mark, with the proviso that the cities of Panama and Colón and the harbors adjacent to said cities, which are included within the boundaries of the zone above described, shall not be included within this grant. The Republic of Panama further grants to the United States in perpetuity the use, occupation and control of any other lands and waters outside of the zone above described which may be necessary and convenient for the construction, maintenance, operation, sanitation and protection of the said Canal or of any auxiliary canals or other works necessary and convenient for the construction, maintenance, operation, sanitation and protection of the said enterprise.

The Republic of Panama further grants in like manner to the United States in perpetuity all islands within the limits of the zone above described and in addition thereto the group of small islands in the Bay of Panama, named Perico, Naos, Culebra and Flamenco.

ARTICLE III. The Republic of Panama grants to the United States all the rights, power and authority within the zone mentioned and described in Article II of this agreement and within the limits of all auxiliary lands and waters mentioned and described in said Article II which the United States would possess and exercise if it were the sovereign of the territory within which said lands and waters are located to the entire exclusion of the exercise by the Republic of Panama of any such sovereign rights, power or authority. . . .

ARTICLE V. The Republic of Panama grants to the United States in perpetuity a monopoly for the construction, maintenance and operation of any system of communication by means of canal or railroad across its territory between the Caribbean Sea and the Pacific Ocean. . . .

ARTICLE VIII. The Republic of Panama grants to the United States all rights which it now has or hereafter may acquire to the property of the New Panama Canal Company and the Panama Railroad Company as a result of the transfer of sovereignty from the Republic of Colombia to the Republic of Panama over the Isthmus of Panama and authorizes the New Panama Canal Company to sell and transfer to the United States its rights, privileges, properties and concessions as well as the Panama Railroad and all the shares or part of the shares of that company.

ARTICLE IX. The United States agrees that the ports at either entrance of the Canal and the waters thereof and the Republic of Panama agrees that the towns of Panama and Colón shall be free for all time so that there shall not be imposed or collected custom house tolls, tonnage, anchorage, lighthouse, wharf, pilot or quarantine dues or any other charges or taxes of any kind upon any vessel using or passing through the Canal or belonging to or employed by the United States, directly or indirectly, in connection with the construction, maintenance, operation, sanitation and protection of the main Canal, or auxiliary works, or upon the cargo, officers, crew or passengers of any such vessels, except such tolls and charges as may be imposed by the United States for the use of the Canal and other works, and except tolls and charges imposed by the Republic of Panama upon merchandise destined to be introduced for the consumption of the rest of the Republic of Panama, and upon vessels touching at the ports of Colón and Panama and which do not cross the Canal. . . .

ARTICLE XIV. As the price or compensation for the rights, powers and privileges granted in this convention by the Republic of Panama to the United States, the Government of the United States agrees to pay to the Republic of Panama the sum of ten million dollars ($10,000,000) in gold coin of the United States on the exchange of the ratification of this convention and also an annual payment during the life of this convention of two hundred and fifty thousand dollars ($250,000) in like gold coin, beginning nine years after the date aforesaid. . . .

ARTICLE XVIII. The Canal, when constructed, and the entrances thereto shall be neutral in perpetuity, and shall be opened upon the terms provided for by Section 1 of Article III of, and in conformity with all the stipulations of, the treaty entered into by the Governments of the United States and Great Britain on November 18, 1901. . . .

ARTICLE XXIII. If it should become necessary at any time to employ armed forces for the safety or protection of the Canal, or of the ships that make use of the same, or the railways and auxiliary works, the United States shall have the right, at all times and in its discretion, to use its police and its land and naval forces or to establish fortifications for these purposes.

Source: William M. Malloy, ed., *Treaties, Conventions, etc.* (Washington, D.C.: Government Printing Office, 1910), 2:1349–1356.

Document 4.4   Concerning Panama, Third Annual Message, December 7, 1903

From the start Roosevelt was determined to defend his actions in Panama from his critics in Congress and among anti-imperialist groups. He cast the best light on the adventure, insisting the results were necessary and just. He continued that defense without retreat for many years.

. . . By the act of June 28, 1902, the Congress authorized the President to enter into treaty with Colombia for the building of the canal across the Isthmus of Panama; it being provided that in the event of failure to secure such treaty after the lapse of a reasonable time, recourse should be had to building a canal through Nicaragua. It has not been necessary to consider this alternative, as I am enabled to lay before the Senate a treaty providing for the building of the canal across the Isthmus of Panama. This was the route which commended itself to the deliberate judgment of the Congress, and we can now acquire by treaty the right to construct the canal over this route. The question now, therefore, is not by which route the isthmian canal shall be built, for that question has been definitely and irrevocably decided. The question is simply whether or not we shall have an isthmian canal.

When the Congress directed that we should take the Panama route under treaty with Colombia, the essence of the condition, of course, referred not to the Government which controlled that route, but to the route itself; to the territory across which the route lay, not to the name which for the moment the territory bore on the map. The purpose of the law was to authorize the President to make a treaty with the power in actual control of the Isthmus of Panama. This purpose has been fulfilled. . . .

For four hundred years, ever since shortly after the discovery of this hemisphere, the canal across the Isthmus has been planned. For two score years it has been worked at. When made it is to last for the ages. It is to alter the geography of a continent and the trade routes of the world. We have shown by every treaty we have negotiated or attempted to negotiate with the peoples in control of the Isthmus and with foreign nations in reference thereto our consistent good faith in observing our obligations; on the one hand to the peoples of the Isthmus, and on the other hand to the civilized world whose commercial rights we are safeguarding and guaranteeing by our action. We have done our duty to others in letter and in spirit, and we have shown the utmost forbearance in exacting our own rights.

Last spring, under the act above referred to, a treaty concluded between the representatives of the Republic of Colombia and of our Government was ratified by the Senate. This treaty was entered into at the urgent solicitation of the people of Colombia and after a body of experts appointed by our Government especially to go into the matter of the routes across the Isthmus had pronounced unanimously in favor of the Panama route. In drawing up this treaty every concession was made to the people and to the Government of Colombia. We were more than just in dealing with them. Our generosity was such as to make it a serious question whether we had not gone too far in their interest at the expense of our own; for in our scrupulous desire to pay all possible heed, not merely to the real but even to the fancied rights of our weaker neighbor, who already owed so much to our protection and forbearance, we yielded in all possible ways to her desires in drawing up the treaty. Nevertheless the Government of Colombia not merely repudiated the treaty, but repudiated it in such manner as to make it evident by the time the Colombian Congress adjourned that not the scantiest hope remained of ever getting a satisfactory treaty from them. The Government of Colombia made the treaty, and yet when the Colombian Congress was called to ratify it the vote against ratification was unanimous. It does not appear that the Government made any real effort to secure ratification.

Immediately after the adjournment of the Congress a revolution broke out in Panama. The people of Panama had long been discontented with the Republic of Colombia, and they had been kept quiet only by the prospect of the conclusion of the treaty, which was to them a matter of vital concern. When it became evident that the treaty was hopelessly lost, the people of Panama rose literally as one man. Not a shot was fired by a single man on the Isthmus in the interest of the Colombian Government. Not a life was lost in the accomplishment of the revolution. The Colombian troops stationed on the Isthmus, who had long been unpaid, made common cause with the people of Panama, and with astonishing unanimity the new Republic was started. The duty of the United States in the premises was clear. In strict accordance with the principles laid down by Secretaries [Lewis] Cass and [William] Seward in the official documents above quoted, the United States gave notice that it would permit the landing of no expeditionary force, the arrival of which would mean chaos and destruction along the line of the railroad and of the proposed Canal, and an interruption of transit as an inevitable consequence. The de facto Government of Panama was recognized. . . .

The above recital of facts establishes beyond question: First, that the United States has for over half a century patiently and in good faith carried out its obligations under the treaty of 1846; second, that when for the first time it became possible for Colombia to do anything in requital of the services thus repeatedly rendered to it for fifty-seven years by the United States, the Colombian Government peremptorily and offensively refused thus to do its part, even though to do so would have been to its advantage and immeasurably to the advantage of the State of Panama, at that time under its jurisdiction; third, that throughout this period revolutions, riots, and factional disturbances of every kind have occurred one after the other in almost uninterrupted succession, some of them lasting for months and even for years, while the central government was unable to put them down or to make peace with the rebels; fourth, that these disturbances instead of showing any sign of abating have tended to grow more numerous and more serious in the immediate past; fifth, that the control of Colombia over the Isthmus of Panama could not be maintained without the armed intervention and assistance of the United States. In other words, the Government of Colombia, though wholly unable to maintain order on the Isthmus, has nevertheless declined to ratify a treaty the conclusion of which opened the only chance to secure its own stability and to guarantee permanent peace on, and the construction of a canal across, the Isthmus.

Under such circumstances the Government of the United States would have been guilty of folly and weakness, amounting in their sum to a crime against the Nation, had it acted otherwise than it did when the revolution of November 3 last took place in Panama. This great enterprise of building the interoceanic canal can not be held up to gratify the whims, or out of respect to the governmental impotence, or to the even more sinister and evil political peculiarities, of people who, though they dwell afar off, yet, against the wish of the actual dwellers on the Isthmus, assert an unreal supremacy over the territory. The possession of a territory fraught with such peculiar capacities as the Isthmus in question carries with it obligations to mankind. The course of events has shown that this canal can not be built by private enterprise, or by any other nation than our own; therefore it must be built by the United States.

Every effort has been made by the Government of the United States to persuade Colombia to follow a course which was essentially not only to our interests and to the interests of the world, but to the interests of Colombia itself. These efforts have failed; and Colombia, by her persistence in repulsing the advances that have been made, has forced us, for the sake of our own honor, and of the interest and well-being, not merely of our own people, but of the people of the Isthmus of Panama and the people of the civilized countries of the world, to take decisive steps to bring to an end a condition of affairs which had become intolerable. The new Republic of Panama immediately offered to negotiate a treaty with us. This treaty I herewith submit. By it our interests are better safeguarded than in the treaty with Colombia which was ratified by the Senate at its last session. It is better in its terms than the treaties offered to us by the Republics of Nicaragua and Costa Rica. At last the right to begin this great undertaking is made available. Panama has done her part. All that remains is for the American Congress to do its part, and forthwith this Republic will enter upon the execution of a project colossal in its size and of well-nigh incalculable possibilities for the good of this country and the nations of mankind.

Source: Theodore Roosevelt, *The Works of Theodore Roosevelt,* national ed. (New York: Charles Scribner's Sons, 1926), 15:202–213.

Document 4.5   United States Treaty with Colombia, April 6, 1914

Seeking better relations with Colombia in light of Roosevelt's actions in Panama, the Wilson administration negotiated a treaty providing for the payment of $25 million and other benefits to Colombia. Wilson's actions angered Roosevelt, and the Senate was at first reluctant to ratify the agreement but finally did so in 1921.

The United States of America and the Republic of Colombia, being desirous to remove all the misunderstandings growing out of the political events in Panama in November 1903; to restore the cordial friendship that formerly characterized the relations between the two countries, and also to define and regulate their rights and interests in respect of the interoceanic canal which the Government of the United States has constructed across the Isthmus of Panama, have resolved for this purpose to conclude a Treaty. . . .

ARTICLE I. The Republic of Colombia shall enjoy the following rights in respect to the interoceanic Canal and the Panama Railway, the title to which is now vested entirely and absolutely in the United States of America, without any incumbrances or indemnities whatever.

1. The Republic of Colombia shall be at liberty at all times to transport through the interoceanic Canal its troops, materials of war and ships of war, without paying any charges to the United States.

2. The products of the soil and industry of Colombia passing through the Canal, as well as the Colombian mails, shall be exempt from any charge or duty other than those to which the products and mails of the United States may be subject. The products of the soil and industry of Colombia, such as cattle, salt and provisions, shall be admitted to entry in the

Canal Zone, and likewise, in the islands and mainland occupied or which may be occupied by the United States as auxiliary and accessory thereto, without paying other duties or charges than those payable by similar products of the United States.

3. Colombian citizens crossing the Canal Zone shall, upon production of proper proof of their nationality, be exempt from every toll, tax or duty to which citizens of the United States are not subject. . . .

ARTICLE II. The Government of the United States of America agrees to pay at the City of Washington to the Republic of Colombia the sum of twenty-five million dollars, gold, United States money, as follows: The sum of five million dollars shall be paid within six months after the exchange of ratifications of the present treaty, and reckoning from the date of that payment, the remaining twenty million dollars shall be paid in four annual installments of five million dollars each.

ARTICLE III. The Republic of Colombia recognizes Panama as an independent nation and taking as a basis the Colombian Law of June 9, 1855, agrees that the boundary shall be the following: From Cape Tiburon to the headwaters of the Rio de la Miel and following the mountain chain by the ridge of Gandi to the Sierra de Chugargun and that of Mali going down by the ridges of Nigue to the heights of Aspave and from thence to a point on the Pacific half way between Cocalito and La Ardita.

In consideration of this recognition, the Government of the United States will, immediately after the exchange of the ratifications of the present Treaty, take the necessary steps in order to obtain from the Government of Panama the despatch of a duly accredited agent to negotiate and conclude with the Government of Colombia a Treaty of Peace and Friendship, with a view to bring about both the establishment of regular diplomatic relations between Colombia and Panama and the adjustment of all questions of pecuniary liability as between the two countries, in accordance with recognized principles of law and precedents. . . .

Source: William M. Malloy, ed., *Treaties, Conventions, etc.* (Washington, D.C.: Government Printing Office, 1910–1938), 3:2538–2540.

Document 4.6   The Roosevelt Corollary, First Annual Message, December 3, 1901

Roosevelt had little sympathy for Latin American states whose governments were corrupt and drove their countries deeply into debt. Although he rejected European intervention, in 1901 he left open the possibility of punitive action short of acquisition by creditor nations. In 1904 he clarified his position with what came to be known as the Roosevelt Corollary to the Monroe Doctrine (see Chapter 3).

. . . The Monroe Doctrine should be the cardinal feature of the foreign policy of all the nations of the two Americas, as it is of the United States. Just seventy-eight years have passed since President Monroe in his Annual Message announced that "the American continents are henceforth not to be considered as subjects for future colonization by any European power." In other words, the Monroe Doctrine is a declaration that there must be no territorial aggrandizement by any non-American power at the expense of any American power on American soil. It is in no wise intended as hostile to any nation in the Old World. Still less is it intended to give cover to any aggression by one New World power at the expense of any other. It is simply a step, and a long step, toward assuring the universal peace of the world by securing the possibility of permanent peace on this hemisphere.

During the past century other influences have established the permanence and independence of the smaller states of Europe. Through the Monroe Doctrine we hope to be able to safeguard like independence and secure like permanence for the lesser among the New World nations.

This doctrine has nothing to do with the commercial relations of any American power, save that it in truth allows each of them to form such as it desires. In other words, it is really a guarantee of the commercial independence of the Americas. We do not ask under this doctrine for any exclusive commercial dealings with any other American State. We do not guarantee any State against punishment if it misconducts itself, provided that punishment does not take the form of the acquisition of territory by any non-American power.

Our attitude in Cuba is a sufficient guarantee of our own good faith. We have not the slightest desire to secure any territory at the expense of any of our neighbors. We wish to work with them hand in hand, so that all of us may be up-lifted together, and we rejoice over the good fortune

of any of them, we gladly hail their material prosperity and political stability, and are concerned and alarmed if any of them fall into industrial or
political chaos. We do not wish to see any Old World military power grow
up on this continent, or to be compelled to become a military power ourselves. The peoples of the Americas can prosper best if left to work out their
own salvation in their own way.

Source: Theodore Roosevelt, *The Works of Theodore Roosevelt,* national ed. (New
York: Charles Scribner's Sons, 1926), 15:116–117.

Document 4.7   On the Brownsville Decision, November 7, 1906

*In response to the Brownsville incident during the summer of 1906, Roosevelt
ordered all 167 members of the Twenty-fifth Regiment dishonorably discharged. Roosevelt received appeals from around the country in behalf of the
soldiers, including a plea for reconsideration from the Massachusetts governor, Curtis Guild. Roosevelt refused and explained why to the governor.*

Your telegram received. The order in question will under no circumstances
be rescinded or modified. The action was precisely such as I should have
taken had the soldiers guilty of the misconduct been white men instead
of colored men. I can hardly believe that those who requested you to communicate with me were aware of the extreme gravity of the offense committed. Certainly only ignorance of the facts could justify such an appeal
to me. As for the concluding paragraph of your telegram in which you state
that the men in question do not desire to make any political capital by public attacks on me, I can only say that I feel the most profound indifference
to any possible attack which can be made on me in this matter. When the
discipline and honor of the American Army are at stake I shall never under
any circumstances consider the political bearing of upholding that discipline and that honor, and no graver misfortune could happen to the American Army than failure to punish in the most signal way such conduct as
that which I have punished in the manner of which you complain. There
has been the fullest and most exhaustive investigation of the case. To show
you how little the question of color enters into the matter, I need only
point out that when a white officer was alleged to be guilty in speaking of
the incident of commenting unfavorably on the black troops generally, I

directed an immediate investigation into his words and suitable proceedings against him should he prove to have been correctly quoted.

Source: Theodore Roosevelt Collection, Library of Congress; also available in Elting
E. Morison, ed., *The Letters of Theodore Roosevelt* (Cambridge: Harvard University
Press, 1952), 5:489–490.

Document 4.8 On the U.S. Steel Decision, November 4, 1907

Roosevelt was careful to explain to his attorney general, Charles Joseph Bona-
parte, his rationale for allowing U.S. Steel to take over the Tennessee Coal
and Iron Company during the financial panic of 1907. He did this in part
to clarify the record and in part to defend what seemed to some to be a con-
tradiction of his antitrust policy.

My dear Mr. Attorney General:

Judge E. H. Gary and Mr. H. C. Frick on behalf of the Steel Corporation
have just called upon me. They state that there is a certain business firm
(the name of which I have not been told, but which is of real importance
in New York business circles) which will undoubtedly fail this week if help
is not given. Among its assets are a majority of the securities of the Tennessee Coal Company. Application has been urgently made to the Steel
Corporation to purchase this stock as the only means of avoiding a failure.
Judge Gary and Mr. Frick inform me that as a mere business transaction
they do not care to purchase the stock; that under ordinary circumstances
they would not consider purchasing the stock because but little benefit will
come to the Steel Corporation from the purchase; that they are aware that
the purchase will be used as a handle for attack upon them on the ground
that they are striving to secure a monopoly of the business and prevent
competition—not that this would represent what could honestly be said,
but what might recklessly and untruthfully be said. They further inform
me that as a matter of fact the policy of the Company has been to decline
to acquire more than sixty per cent of the steel properties, and that this
purpose has been persevered in for several years past, with the object of
preventing these accusations, and as a matter of fact their proportion of
steel properties has slightly decreased, so that it is below this sixty per cent,
and the acquisition of the property in question will not raise it above sixty

per cent. But they feel that it is immensely to their interest, as to the interest of every responsible businessman, to try to prevent a panic and general industrial smashup at this time, and that they are willing to go into this transaction, which they would not otherwise go into, because it seems the opinion of those best fitted to express judgment in New York that it will be an important factor in preventing a break that might be ruinous; and that this has been urged upon them by the combination of the most responsible bankers in New York who are now thus engaged in endeavoring to save the situation. But they asserted they did not wish to do this if I stated that it ought not to be done. I answered that while of course I could not advise them to take the action proposed, I felt it no public duty of mine to interpose any objection.

Source: Theodore Roosevelt, *The Works of Theodore Roosevelt,* national ed. (New York: Charles Scribner's Sons, 1926), 20:430–431.

Document 4.9   Later Defense of the U.S. Steel Decision

Reviewing his presidency in his autobiography, Roosevelt was intent on defending his performance, particularly in matters that had drawn criticism. Clearly he thought that giving assurances to U.S. Steel that it would not be prosecuted for antitrust violations if it purchased the Tennessee Coal and Iron Company during the Panic of 1907 was one of these matters, and he enlarged on his earlier explanation to the attorney general.

Mr. Bonaparte received this note in about an hour, and that same morning he came over, acknowledged its receipt, and said that my answer was the only proper answer that could have been made, having regard both to the law and to the needs of the situation. He stated that the legal situation had been in no way changed, and that no sufficient ground existed for prosecution of the Steel Corporation. But I acted purely on my own initiative, and the responsibility for the act was solely mine.

I was intimately acquainted with the situation in New York. The word "panic" means fear, unreasoning fear; to stop a panic it is necessary to restore confidence; and at the moment the so-called Morgan interests were the only interests which retained a full hold on the confidence of the people of New York—not only the business people, but the immense mass of men and women who owned small investments or had small savings in the banks and trust companies. Mr. Morgan and his associates were of course fighting hard to prevent the loss of confidence and the panic distrust from increasing to such a degree as to bring any other big financial institutions down; for this would probably have been followed by a general, and very likely a world-wide, crash. The Knickerbocker Trust Company had already failed, and runs had begun on, or were threatened as regards, two other big trust companies. These companies were now on the fighting-line, and it was to the interest of everybody to strengthen them, in order that the situation might be saved. It was a matter of general knowledge and belief that they, or the individuals prominent in them, held the securities of the Tennessee Coal and Iron Company, which securities had no market value, and were useless as a source of strength in the emergency. The Steel Corporation securities, on the contrary, were immediately marketable, their great value being known and admitted all over the world as the event showed. The proposal of Messrs. Frick and Gary was that the Steel Corporation should at once acquire the Tennessee Coal and Iron Company, and thereby substitute, among the assets of the threatened institutions (which, by the way, they did not name to me), securities of great and immediate value for securities which at the moment were of no value. It was necessary for me to decide on the instant, before the Stock Exchange opened, for the situation in New York was such that any hour might be vital, and failure to act for even an hour might make all subsequent efforts to act utterly useless. From the best information at my disposal, I believed (what was actually the fact) that the addition of the Tennessee Coal and Iron property would only increase the proportion of the Steel Company's holdings by about four per cent., making them about sixty-two per cent. instead of about fifty-eight per cent. of the total value in the country; an addition which, by itself, in my judgment (concurred in, not only by the attorney-general but by every competent lawyer), worked no change in the legal status of the Steel Corporation. The diminution in the percentage of holdings, and production, has gone on steadily, and the percentage is now about ten per cent. less than it was ten years ago.

The action was emphatically for the general good. It offered the only chance for arresting the panic, and it did arrest the panic. I answered Messrs. Frick and Gary, as set forth in the letter quoted above, to the effect that I did not deem it my duty to interfere, that is, to forbid the action which more than anything else in actual fact saved the situation. The result justified my judgment. The panic was stopped, public confidence in the solvency of the threatened institution being at once restored.

Business was vitally helped by what I did. The benefit was not only for the moment. It was permanent. Particularly was this the case in the South. Three or four years afterward I visited Birmingham. Every man I met, without exception, who was competent to testify, informed me voluntarily that the results of the action taken had been of the utmost benefit to Birmingham, and therefore to Alabama, the industry having profited to an extraordinary degree, not only from the standpoint of the business, but from the standpoint of the community at large and of the wage-workers, by the change in ownership. The results of the action I took were beneficial from every standpoint, and the action in itself, at the time when it was taken, was vitally necessary to the welfare of the people of the United States.

I would have been derelict in my duty, I would have shown myself a timid and unworthy public servant, if in that extraordinary crisis I had not acted precisely as I did act. . . .

Source: Theodore Roosevelt, *The Works of Theodore Roosevelt,* national ed. (New York: Charles Scribner's Sons, 1926), 20:431–433.

Document 4.10   In Defense of the Japanese in America, Sixth Annual Message, December 3, 1906

Few problems gave the president as many headaches as the racial conflicts in California, especially because of their implications for relations with Japan. He took pains to emphasize the positive in U.S.–Japanese relations in this message to Congress, aware that the Japanese would take notice.

. . . I am prompted to say this by the attitude of hostility here and there assumed toward the Japanese in this country. This hostility is sporadic and is limited to a very few places. Nevertheless, it is most discreditable to us as a people, and it may be fraught with the gravest consequences to the nation. The friendship between the United States and Japan has been continuous since the time, over half a century ago, when Commodore Perry, by his expedition to Japan, first opened the islands to western civilization. Since then the growth of Japan has been literally astounding. There is not only nothing to parallel it, but nothing to approach it in the history of civilized mankind. Japan has a glorious and ancient past. Her civilization is older than that of the nations of northern Europe—the nations from whom the people of the United States have chiefly sprung. But fifty years ago Japan's development was still that of the Middle Ages. During that fifty years the progress of the country in every walk in life has been a marvel to mankind, and she now stands as one of the greatest of civilized nations; great in the arts of war and in the arts of peace; great in military, in industrial, in artistic development and achievement. Japanese soldiers and sailors have shown themselves equal in combat to any of whom history makes note. She has produced great generals and mighty admirals; her fighting men, afloat and ashore, show all the heroic courage, the unquestioning, unfaltering loyalty, the splendid indifference to hardship and death, which marked the Loyal Ronins; and they show also that they possess the highest ideal of patriotism. Japanese artists of every kind see their products eagerly sought for in all lands. The industrial and commercial development of Japan has been phenomenal; greater than that of any other country during the same period. At the same time the advance in science and philosophy is no less marked. The admirable management of the Japanese Red Cross during the late [Russo-Japanese] war, the efficiency and humanity of the Japanese officials, nurses, and doctors, won the respectful admiration of all acquainted with the facts. Thru the Red Cross the Japanese people sent over $100,000 to the sufferers of San Francisco, and the gift was accepted with gratitude by our people. The courtesy of the Japanese, nationally and individually, has become proverbial. To no other country has there been such an increasing number of visitors from this land as to Japan. In return, Japanese have come here in great numbers. They are welcome, socially and intellectually, in all our colleges and institutions of higher learning, in all our professional and social bodies. The Japanese have won in a single generation the right to stand abreast of the foremost and most enlightened peoples of Europe and America; they have won on their own merits and by their own exertions the right to treatment on a basis of full and frank equality. The overwhelming mass of our people cherish a lively regard and respect for the people of Japan, and in almost every quarter of the Union the stranger from Japan is treated as he deserves; that is, he is treated as the stranger from any part of civilized Europe is and deserves to be treated. But here and there a most unworthy feeling has manifested itself toward the Japanese—the feeling that has been shown in shutting them out from the common schools in San Francisco, and in mutterings against them in one or two other places, because of their efficiency as workers. To shut them out from the public schools is a wicked absurdity, when there are no first-class colleges in the land, including the universities and colleges of California, which do not gladly welcome Japanese students and on which Japanese students do not reflect credit. We have as much to learn from Japan as Japan has to learn from us; and no nation is fit to teach unless it is also willing to learn. Throughout Japan Americans are well treated, and any failure on the part of Americans at home to treat the Japanese with a like courtesy and consideration is by just so much a confession of inferiority in our civilization.

Our nation fronts on the Pacific, just as it fronts on the Atlantic. We hope to play a constantly growing part in the great ocean of the Orient. We wish, as we ought to wish, for a great commercial development in our dealings with Asia; and it is out of the question that we should permanently have such development unless we freely and gladly extend to other nations the same measure of justice and good treatment which we expect to receive in return. It is only a very small body of our citizens that act badly. Where the Federal Government has power it will deal summarily with any such. Where the several States have power I earnestly ask that they also deal wisely and promptly with such conduct, or else this small body of wrong-doers may bring shame upon the great mass of their innocent and right-thinking fellows—that is, upon our nation as a whole. Good manners should be an international no less than an individual attribute. I ask fair treatment for the Japanese as I would ask fair treatment for Germans or Englishmen, Frenchmen, Russians, or Italians. I ask it as due to humanity and civilization. I ask it as due to ourselves because we must act uprightly toward all men.

I recommend to the Congress that an act be passed specifically providing for the naturalization of Japanese who come here intending to become American citizens. One of the great embarrassments attending the performance of our international obligations is the fact that the Statutes of the United States are entirely inadequate. They fail to give to the National Government sufficiently ample power, thru United States courts and by the use of the Army and Navy, to protect aliens in the rights secured to them under solemn treaties which are the law of the land. I therefore earnestly recommend that the criminal and civil statutes of the United States be so amended and added to as to enable the President, acting for the United States Government, which is responsible in our international relations, to enforce the rights of aliens under treaties. Even as the law now is something can be done by the Federal Government toward this end, and in the matter now before me affecting the Japanese everything that it is in my power to do will be done, and all of the forces, military and civil, of the United States which I may lawfully employ will be so employed. There should, however, be no particle of doubt as to the power of the National Government completely to perform and enforce its own obligations to other nations. The mob of a single city may at any time perform acts of lawless violence against some class of foreigners which would plunge us into war. That city by itself would be powerless to make defense against the foreign power thus assaulted, and if independent of this Government it would never venture to perform or permit the performance of the acts complained of. The entire power and the whole duty to protect the offending city or the offending community lies in the hands of the United States Government. It is unthinkable that we should continue a policy under which a given locality may be allowed to commit a crime against a friendly nation, and the United States Government limited, not to preventing the commission of the crime, but, in the last resort, to defending the people who have committed it against the consequences of their own wrong-doing. . . .

Source: Theodore Roosevelt, *The Works of Theodore Roosevelt,* national ed. (New York: Charles Scribner's Sons, 1926), 15:385–388.

Document 4.11   Appeal to Save San Francisco School Settlement, March 11, 1907

When new racial incidents and anti-Asian legislation threatened to upset the San Francisco school settlement, Roosevelt warned the California governor, James Norris Gillett, of the damage that would result and urged that the prior agreements be respected.

My dear Governor Gillett:

My letter of March 9th was written before I saw in the papers the statement that one House of the California Legislature had past *[sic]* with practical or entire unanimity a bill including the Japanese with the Mongolians and other Asiatics for whom separate schools are to be established. I do not know the details of the legislation. If it is meant to be ineffective and simply an expression of opinion or assertion of an abstract right which it is not intended to enforce, then it is merely a foolish and wanton insult to Japan, and may have little effect save to make it more difficult on the part of the national Government to secure for California what California desires, and to keep on terms of cordial friendship, as it should keep, with a great and friendly nation.

If it is meant to be effective; if it is meant to destroy an agreement to which the Secretary of State and I were able to come with the entire California delegation in Congress, and with Mayor Schmitz and the entire School Board, then it is exceedingly mischievous. At the outset let me point out that this agreement not only commanded the hearty and unanimous support of all of the Senators and Representatives of California in Congress, but the hearty and unanimous support of Mayor Schmitz and the School Board, without regard to political party. . . .

Mayor Schmitz and the School Board proposed to us a plan with which we were entirely satisfied, this plan providing that all foreign children, whether Japanese or of other nationalities, should be kept in separate schools or classes when either their age or their lack of understanding of English rendered this course advisable. The School Board informed me with all emphasis that this entirely satisfied them; that this met every legitimate need of the situation and provided against all possible abuses or difficulties connected with the presence of the Japanese in the schools.

Now, whatever the legal rights of the situation may be, it is most unwise for the people of California to insist upon something which is absolutely useless, which works no possible benefit, and which cannot but be taken as insulting to a people with whom we have ancestral ties of friendship and with whom we wish to remain at peace. Moreover, any such insistence in a course of hectoring and insulting the Japanese renders nugatory what we have accomplished in providing for excluding Japanese laborers, skilled and unskilled. I was informed very early, by men professing to speak for, and as I have every reason to suppose actually speaking for, the labor organizations of San Francisco, that the real objection was to the incoming of Japanese laborers—this meaning, of course, to the incoming of the great mass of Japanese. They asserted unequivocally that the trouble was not with the attendance of the Japanese at the schools; that this was merely a symptom of the irritation. . . .

With the objects thus set forth I was able to express my entire sympathy, and my belief (which has been borne out by the facts) that the Japanese

Government would have no objection whatever to the carrying out of the proposed policy and would help us in thus carrying it out. Accordingly we past [sic] legislation which will enable us to secure the entire exclusion of Japanese laborers—which of course means the exclusion of an enormous majority of all the Japanese who now come here—the effectiveness of this legislation being conditioned upon the willingness of the Japanese Government to assent to our policy; and this willingness itself being conditioned upon our carrying out in good faith the announced purpose of the Administration at Washington, of the representatives from California in Congress, and of the Mayor and the School Board of San Francisco, to see that there was no discrimination against the Japanese as regards the schools—or of course as regards other matters. The Japanese Government are entirely willing, if their citizens who are here are treated as well as we treat the citizens of European or South American countries, to refuse to grant passports to any laborers to come to the United States. The legislation past [sic] by Congress enables me to keep out of the country all Japanese laborers who do not have such passports; that is, all who go to Hawaii, Mexico or Canada, or to any other place, and then seek to come here. The success of the plan therefore depends absolutely upon our treating Japan with the same fairness with which we expect her to treat us in return. The legislation becomes meaningless and inoperative and cannot be made of avail save on condition that Japan herself does not issue passports to her laborers to come here direct. This action of Japan's we can secure by agreement, but we cannot agree to secure it unless we ourselves act in a spirit of fairness and right dealing. . . .

The Administration is as earnestly and eagerly desirous of standing for California's needs as for the needs of every other section of the country. Not only are the interests and honor of the men of the Pacific Slope dear to me, but I am most anxious to meet, just so far as I can consistently with my duty to the rest of the country, every one of their desires. One of the members of my Cabinet is a Californian, devoted in his loyalty to every interest of his great and beautiful State. I have been able to bring about a solution of this question which secures every particle of what the Californians wish, and which secures it in a way which commands the hearty assent of the rest of the nation; and this in a manner honorable to the United States and honorable to the proud nation of Japan, with whom it must ever be one of our prime objects to remain on terms of self-respecting peace. This peaceful and honorable solution, which secures every object that California desires, is threatened only by the unwise acts of certain

Californians. Should these acts become effective, so as to bring to naught what has been done, all solution of the matter will be indefinitely delayed. If the agreement is carried out, all immigration of Japanese laborers will stop forthwith. If by the action of certain Californians themselves we are prevented from carrying it out, this immigration will go on unchecked. Nor, in my judgment, will this nation ever consent to the exclusion of Japanese laborers save on substantially the terms upon which we have now secured their exclusion; that is, upon condition of treating the citizens of Japan who come hither just exactly as we are content to have Japan treat our citizens who go to her shores; in other words to give to Japanese students, travelers, scientific and professional men, in short to all Japanese who are actually here, exactly the same treatment that we should expect Americans in Japan to receive. Such method of procedure is the only just method. Moreover, it is the only method consonant with maintaining friendly relations with the great Island Empire of Asia. When everything that the people of California desire in this matter can thus be secured by an honorable agreement which preserves the friendship between the two nations unbroken, the people of the United States as a whole have the right to expect that the object thus completely attained shall be attained in accordance with, and not in violation of, the steadfast policy of the United States to deal honorably with other powers and to endeavor to secure peace and friendship with them.

The exclusion of Japanese laborers from the United States will now become an accomplished fact unless unwise action is taken, such as legislation reflecting on the Japanese, which might deprive us of the necessary cooperation of the Japanese government, of which we are otherwise assured. If this is done it may be many years before exclusion can be secured.

Source: Theodore Roosevelt Collection, Library of Congress; also available in Elting E. Morison, ed., *The Letters of Theodore Roosevelt* (Cambridge: Harvard University Press, 1952), 5:610–614.

Document 4.12   The Gentlemen's Agreement, Settling the Japanese Immigration Issue (1908)

Slowing the flow of workers from Japan to California was part of the understanding that settled the racial crisis (see Documents 4.10 and 4.11). To achieve this goal without offending the Japanese, Roosevelt negotiated this agreement on Japanese immigration.

In order that the best results might follow from an enforcement of the regulations, an understanding was reached with Japan that the existing policy of discouraging emigration of its subjects of the laboring classes to continental United States should be continued, and should, by co-operation with the governments, be made as effective as possible. This understanding contemplates that the Japanese government shall issue passports to continental United States only to such of its subjects as are non-laborers or are laborers who, in coming to the continent, seek to resume a formerly acquired domicile, to join a parent, wife, or children residing there, or to assume active control of an already possessed interest in a farming enterprise in this country, so that the three classes of laborers entitled to receive passports have come to be designated "former residents," "parents, wives, or children of residents," and "settled agriculturists."

With respect to Hawaii, the Japanese government of its own volition stated that, experimentally at least, the issuance of passports to members of the laboring classes proceeding thence would be limited to "former residents" and "parents, wives, or children of residents." The said government has also been exercising a careful supervision over the subject of emigration of its laboring class to foreign contiguous territory.

Source: Report of the Commissioner General of Immigration (1908), 125; also available in Henry Steele Commager, ed., *Documents of American History,* 8th ed. (New York: Appleton-Century-Crofts, 1968), 2:45.

Document 4.13   Analysis of the Japanese Question, May 23, 1907
Baron Kentaro Kaneko was a friend and Harvard classmate of Roosevelt and a special emissary to the United States. This letter was part of the president's effort to explain American policy and reassure the Japanese of America's honorable intentions.

My dear Baron Kaneko:

. . . Nothing during my Presidency has given me more concern than these troubles. History often teaches by example and I think we can best understand just what the situation is and how it ought to be met by taking into account the change in general international relations during the last two or three centuries. During this period all the civilized nations have made great progress. During the first part of it Japan did not appear in the general progress, but for the last half century she has gone ahead so much faster than any other nation that I think we can fairly say that taking the last three centuries together her advance has been on the whole greater than that of any other nation. But all have advanced, and especially in the way in which the people of each treat the people of other nationalities. Two centuries ago there was the greatest suspicion and malevolence exhibited by all the people high and low of each European country for all the people high and low of every other European country, with but few exceptions. The cultivated people of the different countries, however, had already begun to treat with one another on good terms. But when, for instance, the Huguenots were exiled from France, and great numbers of Huguenot workmen went to England, and their presence excited the most violent hostility, manifesting itself even in mob violence among the English workmen. The men were closely allied by race and religion, they had practically the same type of ancestral culture, and yet they were unable to get on together. Two centuries have passed, the world has moved forward, and now there could be no repetition of such hostilities. In the same way a marvelous progress has been made in the relations of Japan with the Occidental nations. Fifty years ago you and I and those like us in the two countries could not have traveled in one another's countries. We should have had very unpleasant and possibly very dangerous experiences. But the same progress that has been going on as between nations in Europe and their descendants in America and Australia has also been going on as between Japan and the Occidental nations. Now gentlemen, all educated people, members of the professions, and the like, get on so well together that they not only travel each in the other's country, but associate on the most intimate terms. Among the friends whom I especially value I include a number of Japanese gentlemen. But the half century has been too short a time for the advance to include the laboring classes of the two countries as between themselves. Exactly as the educated classes in Europe among the several nations grew to be able to associate together generations before it was possible for such association to take place among the men who had no such advantages of education, so it is evident we must not press too fast in bringing the laboring classes of Japan and America together. Already in the fifty years we have completely attained the goal as between the educated and the intellectual classes of the two countries. We must be content to wait another generation before we shall have made progress enough to permit the same close intimacy between the classes who have had less opportunity for cultivation, and whose lives are less easy, so that each has to feel in earning its daily bread the pressure of the competition of the other. I have become convinced that to try to move too far forward all at once is to incur jeopardy of trouble. This is just as true of one nation as of the other. If scores of thousands of American miners went to Sakhalin, or of American mechanics to Japan or Formosa, trouble would almost certainly ensue. Just in the same way scores of hundreds of Japanese laborers, whether agricultural or industrial, are certain, chiefly because of the pressure caused thereby, to be a source of trouble if they should come here or in Australia; I mention Australia because it is part of the British Empire, because the Australians have discriminated against continental immigration in favor of immigration from the British Isles, and have in effect discriminated to a certain degree in favor of immigration from England and Scotland as against immigration from Ireland.

My dear Baron, the business of statesmen is to try constantly to keep international relations better, to do away with the causes of friction, and to secure as nearly ideal justice as actual conditions will permit. I think that with this object in view and facing conditions not as I would like them to be but as they are, the best thing to do is to prevent the laboring classes of either country from going in any numbers to the other. In a generation I believe all need of such prevention will have passed away; and at any rate this leaves free the opportunity for all those fit to profit by intercourse, to go each to the other's country. I have just appointed a commission on general immigration which will very possibly urge restrictive measures as regards European immigration, and which I am in hopes will be able to bring about a method by which the result we have in view will be obtained with the minimum friction.

Source: Theodore Roosevelt Collection, Library of Congress; also available in Elting E. Morison, ed., *The Letters of Theodore Roosevelt* (Cambridge: Harvard University Press, 1952), 5:671–672.

Document 4.14   The Root-Takahira Agreement, November 30, 1908

Concerned about the growing power of Japan in the Pacific and the vulnerability of the Philippines, Roosevelt directed Secretary of State Elihu Root to negotiate this understanding in which the two nations pledged to negotiate any differences that threatened to disrupt good relations. Below is a letter from the Japanese ambassador to Root.

Sir:

The exchange of views between us, which has taken place at the several interviews which I have recently had the honor of holding with you, has shown that Japan and the United States holding important outlying insular possessions in the region of the Pacific Ocean, the Governments of the two countries are animated by a common aim, policy, and intention in that region.

Believing that a frank avowal of that aim, policy, and intention would not only tend to strengthen the relations of friendship and good neighborhood, which have immemorially existed between Japan and the United States, but would materially contribute to the preservation of the general peace, the Imperial Government have authorized me to present to you an outline of their understanding of that common aim, policy and intention.

1. It is the wish of the two Governments to encourage the free and peaceful development of their commerce on the Pacific Ocean.

2. The policy of both Governments, uninfluenced by any aggressive tendencies, is directed to the maintenance of the existing status quo in the region above mentioned and to the defense of the principle of equal opportunity for commerce and industry in China.

3. They are accordingly firmly resolved reciprocally to respect the territorial possessions belonging to each other in said region.

4. They are also determined to preserve the common interest of all powers in China by supporting by all pacific means at their disposal the independence and integrity of China and the principle of equal opportunity for commerce and industry of all nations in that Empire.

5. Should any event occur threatening the status quo as above described or the principle of equal opportunity as above defined, it remains for the two Governments to communicate with each other in order to arrive at an understanding as to what measures they may consider it useful to take.

If the foregoing outline accords with the view of the Government of the United States, I shall be gratified to receive your confirmation.

I take this opportunity to renew to your excellency the assurance of my highest consideration.

K. Takahira.

Source: Papers Relating to the Foreign Relations of the United States, 1908 (Washington, D.C.: Government Printing Office, 1912), 510–511; reprinted in Henry Steele Commager, ed., *Documents of American History,* 8th ed. (New York: Appleton-Century-Crofts, 1968), 52–53.

Melvin W. Fuller (center) presided over the Supreme Court when it decided a series of cases determining the strength of the Sherman Anti-Trust Act.

CHAPTER FIVE

Institutional Relations

Theodore Roosevelt brought all of his well-honed political skills to bear in his relations with those institutions that affected his career and especially his presidency. He was most adept at cultivating and, on occasion, manipulating the press to his advantage in political campaigns and in fostering his policy initiatives. In relations with Congress the picture is one of mixed results. Considering the conservative makeup of both houses and the enormous influence of business lobbies during his tenure, he accomplished much against firm resistance. This required compromise that often disturbed progressives but without which little could have been gained. Over the courts he had much less control and was often frustrated by decisions beyond his influence. He enjoyed the warmest relations with the military establishment in his work as assistant secretary of the navy and as president. This was not surprising considering his persistent advocacy of armed strength as critically important to a larger role for the United States in the world. Big business mistrusted Roosevelt but saw the wisdom of occasional, if grudging, support; organized labor was cautious but increasingly appreciative as his understanding of labor's needs grew. In all his dealings with organized elements of American society he used the prestige of his office, his dynamism, and his political talents to maintain generally supportive and productive relations.

211

THE PRESS

The quality of relationships between presidents and the press has depended very much on the personality and skill of the president. Woodrow Wilson tended to be rather formal and stiff and somewhat suspicious of the press; the relationship was not a warm one. Franklin D. Roosevelt enjoyed jousting with reporters and held frequent news conferences. His self-confidence and political shrewdness encouraged him to deal with the press as a helpful tool for shaping public opinion. John F. Kennedy charmed the press corps with wit and intelligence. Richard M. Nixon regarded reporters with more than suspicion and often appeared ill at ease, testy, and awkward.

Theodore Roosevelt was masterful in handling the fourth estate. He was probably the most successful of the presidents in cultivating friendly attention and managing news reports written about him. He could recognize a good story; he was, after all, a storyteller himself, and he knew how to make headlines.

From his earliest political ventures as an assemblyman in Albany from 1882 to 1884, he developed his talent for good press relations. His youth, his willingness to challenge and annoy the leadership of his own party, and his sensational exposure of corruption and calls for reform all made for good copy. His brief career as a police commissioner in New York City (1895–1897) clearly illustrated his strategy and his success in shaping the news. On his first day in the job he dragged reporters off the street as he arrived at headquarters to tell them of his plans to clean up the department. He quickly won their confidence so that they were soon bringing *him* information about trouble in the streets of the city.

One of the men Roosevelt summoned on that first day was Jacob Riis, the crusading journalist already famous for his book *How the Other Half Lives*, which described the horrific conditions in New York tenements. Riis later recollected his experiences: "For two years we were to be together all day, and quite often most of the night, in the environment in which I had spent twenty years of my life. And these two were the happiest by far of them all" (Riis 1904, 131). With Riis on that first day was Lincoln Steffens, then writing for the *New York Evening Post*. He recalled Roosevelt drawing the two aside and saying, "Now, then, what shall we do?" (Steffens 1931, 257).

When Roosevelt went to war in Cuba in 1898, the press followed, and several correspondents stayed close to the Colonel, knowing good stories lay waiting. Among these was the writer Stephen Crane, author of *The Red Badge of Courage,* and Roosevelt's friend from police days, Richard Harding Davis of the *New York Herald.* Davis stayed especially close to Roosevelt, and he witnessed and reported on his fighting exploits and horseback bravery. By the time the Rough Riders returned to Montauk, New York, for quarantine and demobilization, Roosevelt was a national hero with the press speculating that he would run for governor.

As governor (1899–1900) Roosevelt took pains to keep the press close and friendly. Riis helped in the campaign and after the victory contributed to plans for reform legislation. Roosevelt regularly called reporters into his office, sometimes twice a day, feeding them background information otherwise unavailable to them. He used one of these sessions to announce his support for the franchise tax he knew would so disturb Republican boss Thomas C. Platt (see Chapter 1). The supportive stories that followed helped win public applause and generate pressure on the legislature. The reporters appreciated the governor's candid exchanges, and they were careful to respect "off the record" remarks, lest they face the governor's ire and exile. Their respect and admiration could at times verge on excess. The influential editor William Allen White generated some embarrassment for Roosevelt when his stories suggested that the governor could challenge incumbent William McKinley for the presidential nomination in 1900. Roosevelt saw that as a path to political disaster and made his support for McKinley clear.

By the time he became president in 1901, Roosevelt had sharpened his instincts in handling the press, and his experience became immediately useful. A revealing episode in Roosevelt's manipulation of the press came in the days after the assassination of McKinley. While still in Buffalo, Roosevelt suggested to Herman H. Kohlsaat, publisher of the *Chicago Times-Herald,* that he would fire Secretary of State John Hay and Treasury Secretary Lyman Gage. He had no intention of doing so and knew that Kohlsaat would protest. Roosevelt let the publisher believe he had persuaded him to change his mind and keep the men in the cabinet. Kohlsaat left the meeting feeling important and influential, precisely the effect Roosevelt sought (Morris 2001, 18–19).

Openness to reporters marked the Roosevelt presidency from the beginning. Frequent background sessions and interviews kept reporters busy. The president liked to pass on background leaks to reporters to test public response to ideas before they became official so that a sour reaction could bury a bad idea harmlessly. He was solicitous of reporters. For example, he was the first president to provide a press room inside the White House (Cornwell 1966, 17). Special favors fell to special friends in the corps. Riis often visited the White House and was one of the few journalists allowed to visit at Sagamore Hill. One result was his adulatory book, *Theodore Roosevelt the Citizen,* published in 1904. One of Roosevelt's favorite phrases to describe his policies, "a square deal," probably originated from a conversation with Steffens, another White House intimate. When Steffens launched an investigation of government operations in Washington, Roosevelt encouraged him and wrote a letter urging individuals to cooperate with him. "Please tell Mr. Lincoln Steffens anything whatever about the running of the government by or under the Executive that you know (not incompatible with the public interest) and provided only that you tell him the truth—no matter what it may be. I will see that you are not hurt. [Signed] Theodore Roosevelt" (Steffens 1931, 515).

Even as president Roosevelt was a great subject for endearing caricature by newspaper cartoonists. Most famous was the "teddy bear" incident (see Chapter 1). Clifford K. Berryman of the *Washington Post* captured the incident in a cartoon that sketched a benign Roosevelt taking pity on the vulnerable animal. That cartoon and its imitators set off the teddy bear fad still strong a century later.

Easy access, presidential candor, and a sense of closeness in the Washington press corps paid dividends in stories that cast Roosevelt as a dynamic leader and magnetic personality. Benjamin "Pitchfork" Tillman, U.S. senator from South Carolina and no friend of the president, thought that the press had helped make Roosevelt the most popular president in American history (*Washington Evening Star,* January 17, 1906, quoted in Morris 2001, 430).

Roosevelt did set rules and limits that he insisted the reporters had to respect. He expected information offered in confidence to be kept out of print. If that rule was broken, the offending reporter was consigned to the Ananias Club, the president's term for being banned from access. He could be sharp with reporters who filed stories he did not like, and he was known to deny statements he made if they reflected badly on him in print. On one occasion he ordered a blackout on the *Boston Herald* for a story that his children were cruelly chasing a turkey on White House grounds. He demanded and got a retraction from the paper, which wanted to remain in his good graces. Although access was quite free in

Washington, Roosevelt earnestly protected family privacy at Sagamore Hill. Reporters were barred from the grounds and had to remain in a nearby village when the family was in residence. Hungry for copy, some filed what stories of family activities they could ferret out. When some of those were fanciful, the president acted. He wrote Paul Dana, editor of the *New York Sun,* one of the offending papers, to ask that the reporter in question be recalled from Oyster Bay (Morison 1951, 3:303). Dana complied.

One kind of writer seemed to upset the president. More than once he lashed out at the "muckrakers" who stirred up stories about corrupt politicians and unsavory business practices. He accused them of exaggerating and distorting to advance themselves (see Document 5.1). Whether his protests were sincere or merely useful is difficult to tell. They could have been intended to placate the business community and some of the leaders of his party in Congress who were targets of the muckraker stories. Nevertheless, the work of the muckrakers was helpful in advancing some of the regulatory and antitrust policies he championed. Certainly Steffens was one of these crusading writers. Reflecting on the role of the press in a speech in Milwaukee in 1910, Roosevelt acknowledged the important role of reporters in exposing corruption, but even in that role they must be scrupulous about telling the truth (see Document 5.2).

The responses of publishers and editorial writers were not as helpful or appealing to Roosevelt as the work of their staff on the scene. He regarded the work of reporters as more important than that of the editorial writers or their publishers, who often angered him. He despised William Randolph Hearst, who, he believed, inflamed evil passions, and described his publications as a malign influence on the country (Brands 1997, 413). After sharp criticism by Joseph Pulitzer's *New York World,* he considered suing and wrote to New York district attorney Henry Stimson, "Pulitzer is one of these creatures of the gutter of such unspeakable degradation that to him even eminence on a dunghill seems enviable" (Morison 1952, 6:1415–1417).

After he left office his romance with the working press continued. He did ban reporters from his African safari; that was to be a private adventure, and he, himself, had contracted to write about his experience. But on his return to politics he welcomed the reporters who flocked to cover his quest for office. William Allen White was an active supporter of his candidacy in 1912. The faithful Riis was there to help and made several campaign speeches for his friend. In the years that followed, Roosevelt could be assured that his press releases would get wide circulation, and he took advantage of this, especially in his assaults on Wilsonian policies. Roosevelt was, in a sense, a member of the press when he resumed his own writing career with political commentary in *Outlook* magazine, *Metropolitan* magazine, and later in syndication through the *Kansas City Star*. Recalling his presidential experiences with the press years later, Roosevelt thought newspaper correspondents had been "as a whole [a] singularly able, trustworthy, and public-spirited body of men, and the most useful of all agents in the fight for efficient and decent government" (Roosevelt 1926, 20:344–345).

THE CABINET

When Roosevelt hurriedly took the oath of office in Buffalo, New York, after President William McKinley's assassination, he wanted to calm the fears of a nation in shock. He quickly announced that he would ask McKinley's cabinet to stay on, sending the country a signal of continuity and stability. Their tenure, of course, was not to be enduring, and he gradually replaced McKinley's men with his own choices. Some carried on longer than others, but only Secretary of Agriculture James Wilson remained in the Roosevelt cabinet for the full length of his stay in office. The president sought out men of integrity and accomplishment and was generally successful in drawing the talented and intelligent to his service.

The cabinet met regularly with the president on Tuesdays and Fridays. Tradition ruled in the seating order of the members, the leaders of the oldest established departments seated closest to the president. But the atmosphere of these meetings tended to be informal. At meetings, members offered reports of department activities and discussed administration policy. The president liked to use the cabinet as a sounding board for his messages to Congress. As indicated by the great length and the stream of recommendations of his annual messages, Roosevelt kept himself current and engaged in the details of government operations in all areas. Nevertheless, he gave cabinet officers broad freedom of action in their departments.

Although Roosevelt was a master at engineering useful leaks to support administration goals, he was impatient when untimely news sometimes escaped from cabinet discussions. Thus, when, in 1902, he decided to prosecute the Northern Securities trust, the president told only Attorney General Philander Knox, keeping the matter out of the cabinet. He was concerned about the timing and public impact of the move and perhaps also worried about the likely adverse reaction from Secretary of State John Hay and Secretary of War Elihu Root, who, he knew, would disapprove the action. Many important issues and especially the most politically sensitive were reserved for more private conferences with trusted advisers, only some of whom were members of the cabinet. The variety of personalities in the cabinet and its size made it unappealing as a forum for decision making. Like many presidents Roosevelt looked outside the cabinet meetings for governing advice in which he had confidence. Root and Hay he often consulted in private; outside the cabinet, Gifford Pinchot served, especially for conservation policy; and Sen. Henry Cabot Lodge was among his closest confidants.

Roosevelt engineered the creation of a new cabinet department. In his first message to Congress he urged the establishment of a Department of Commerce and Industries to deal with both business and labor issues. He repeated the plea in his second annual message and succeeded in 1903 when Congress established the Department of Commerce and Labor (see Document 5.3). He appointed his trusted secretary George B. Cortelyou to head the new department. A measure of his confidence in Cortelyou was evident when, soon after elevating him to cabinet rank, he insisted, against resistance from the leadership of the party, that Cortelyou be made chairman of the Republican National Committee for the election of 1904. After the election Roosevelt made Cortelyou postmaster general, wanting a firm hand in the distribution of that patronage-rich department. Cortelyou closed out his service in the administration as treasury secretary, playing a key role in resolving the financial crisis of 1907.

The most important and influential men serving in the Roosevelt cabinet were John Hay and Elihu Root. Hay was a personal friend who had for some years socialized with Roosevelt in that Washington circle. Hay had been a close friend of Roosevelt's father, and he represented a link to Roosevelt's hero, Abraham Lincoln, whom Hay served as a personal secretary. The two men genuinely liked each other, although Hay often had reservations about Roosevelt's manner and about his more progressive ideas. Hay was increasingly ill during his service to the president, but he stayed on until his death in July 1905. Roosevelt privately complained that Hay was too infirm to do much work and that he himself had to take on foreign policy chores during Hay's last years in office. His lament should not be taken too seriously, for Roosevelt liked to act as his own secretary of state.

It was Elihu Root, as the most senior cabinet officer present, who administered the oath of office to Roosevelt in Buffalo. Root knew the president well from their contact in New York politics. It was Root who handled the legal arguments about Roosevelt's eligibility to run for governor in 1898 because of a dispute over his legal residence. He began his service in the Roosevelt administration as secretary of war; he returned to his law practice in New York in 1904, but after Hay's death in 1905 he responded to the president's appeal to return to Washington to become secretary of state. Like Hay, Root was staunchly conservative and sometimes regarded Roosevelt with paternal amusement and sometimes with alarm. Roosevelt acknowledged Root's intelligence and experience, regarded him as his most able adviser, and turned to him often. Root liked the president and supported him even on some issues with which he personally disagreed. He often acted as a go-between to smooth over the frequently bumpy relations with conservatives of the party and the business community. Root defended Roosevelt's candidacy for reelection in 1904, when more than a few party regulars would have preferred a different candidate.

Their relationship was a close one and Roosevelt's respect for Root was strong enough for the older man to tease the young president when occasion warranted. The story is told of one such event at a cabinet meeting in which Roosevelt asked if he had successfully defended himself against charges that he had treated Colombia badly in the dispute over Panama. The president looked to Root for reassurance, but the secretary of state replied, "You certainly have, Mr. President. You have shown that you were accused of seduction and you have conclusively proved that you were guilty of rape" (Jessup 1964, 1:404–405). The reporter of the story, Root's biographer, doubted the authenticity of the account, but he regarded it as typical of Root's wit and of his relationship with Roosevelt.

As dependable as Root was in the cabinet, William Howard Taft and Hay were also the elder statesmen of that body, and Roosevelt's relationship with them was marked by the respect of a younger man for the age, experience, and the quasi-paternal care they showed him. Taft responded generously to every presidential request, and their relationship grew quickly into a genuine friendship. Roosevelt referred to Taft as Will and praised his service in the warmest language. After the war with Spain Taft served with distinction as high commissioner in the Philippines. Taft's deepest political ambition was for an appointment to the Supreme Court. A measure of his commitment to Roosevelt is evident when Roosevelt offered to nominate him to the Court, but Taft declined to leave his post in the Philippines because he was still needed there. Roosevelt called him back to Washington as secretary of war when Root left for his private law practice in 1904. Taft served as troubleshooter, counselor, and confidant and was probably the most important and reliable figure in the administration next to Root. As early as 1905, Roosevelt thought of Taft as a possible successor, and that idea soon became firm enough for the president to work his influence to ensure his nomination in 1908. That they were once so close made the later break between them so painful, especially to Taft. It also stands as testimony to the intensity of Roosevelt's ambition to return to the presidency.

THE CONGRESS

When Theodore Roosevelt became president the political makeup of the United States Congress was thoroughly conservative. There were few progressives yet in either the House or the Senate. The Republican Party dominated both chambers, and the leadership was held by men who were largely satisfied with things as they were. They saw little need for social reform and none for harnessing the muscular power of corporate interests. They regarded the trusts as efficient and productive; they thought regulatory legislation unnecessary and even mischievous. The country had recovered from the economic collapse of 1894, the Populist movement had disintegrated, and all was well in their political world. All that was needed was vigilance to control labor unrest and to avoid the threat to American prosperity posed by radicals. The new president had a different vision of the country's needs. Nevertheless, Roosevelt, always politically acute, knew the men he had to work with and strove for good relations with Congress.

Steering the course of the Senate was a group of Republicans known as "The Four," who worked together to control the legislative agenda. Nelson W. Aldrich of Rhode Island was a millionaire businessman who said little in debate but wielded decisive influence on his colleagues. John

C. Spooner of Wisconsin came from a career as a railroad lobbyist and was a bitter foe of the Wisconsin reformer Robert M. La Follette. Orville H. Platt of Connecticut, an expansionist in foreign policy, played the "stand-pat" conservative in domestic matters. And William B. Allison of Iowa, more open to occasional compromise, was slightly less dogmatic in his conservatism than the other three. In addition to the dominant "Four," Mark Hanna of Ohio, President McKinley's mentor, was still powerful, had no affection for Roosevelt, and was a possible rival for the 1904 Republican Party presidential nomination.

An Aldrich biographer suggests that Roosevelt and the "Four" reached an understanding at a meeting in Oyster Bay in September 1902. If the president did not trouble their designs in economic matters, he could have a free hand in other areas of national politics (Stephenson 1971, 196). Although Roosevelt's principal biographers do not confirm such a deal, it gains some credibility from a reading of his first term. He did not press very hard on issues like a lower tariff, and aside from antitrust vigor there was little to threaten the economic status quo. Nevertheless, Roosevelt was much more assertive and independent in his conduct of foreign policy.

In the House, conservatives also reigned with little challenge. Speaker David B. Henderson was not a strong leader, but he was replaced in 1903 by Joseph G. Cannon, who ruled with an iron will and sought to make the House as influential as the Senate. Cannon was second to none in his devotion to the interests of corporate America. Republicans controlled the House with a comfortable majority against a weak Democratic contingent. The Democrats in Congress were not well organized or effectively united and could offer little discomfort to their rivals.

Given the cast, Roosevelt realized he had to move discreetly. He consulted with the leadership frequently, offered them advanced notice of the contents of his official messages, and invited their comments. His first annual message was comparatively restrained in its demands and clearly sensitive to the prejudices of his audience. Even as his messages grew bolder, his relations with Congress remained circumspect. When Taft complained to him about congressional resistance to administration policy, the president replied with a statement of respect for Aldrich, Cannon, and other conservatives in Congress and reminded Taft that these men were "the most powerful factors in Congress" with whom he had to work (Morison 1951, 3:450–451). In his autobiography Roosevelt reflected on his experience in dealing with Congress. "I made a resolute effort to get on with [the leadership]. . . . We succeeded in working together, although with increasing friction, for some years, I pushing forward and they hanging back" (see Document 5.4).

Realism dictated the maintenance of good relations with the congressional bosses if Roosevelt hoped to move his own ideas to adoption. Early on he was also aware that alienating the leaders of his own party could jeopardize his nomination in 1904. His measured pace and willingness to compromise accounts for much of the impatience and disappointment of progressives, who shared many of his reform ideas but chafed at his caution. The struggle for passage of the Hepburn Act (1906) to regulate the railroads perhaps best illustrates his skill in moving a reluctant legislature to adopt a reform measure (see Chapter 3). Despite the important victory, the more fervent among the progressives, including Sen. Robert La Follette of Wisconsin, remained disappointed over the compromises that made passage possible.

After the election of 1904 the makeup of Congress became somewhat more progressive, promising more support for the administration. With his own landslide election as a mandate, Roosevelt's posture toward Congress stiffened. His messages grew more demanding, and his last annual message in 1908 struck conservatives as radical in its insistence on sweeping social and economic reform. The reading of that message was interrupted repeatedly by applause from progressives of both parties while the old guard sat grimly silent.

Inevitably the tensions of his sparring with congressional leaders led to unpleasant confrontations from time to time. In 1908 Congress restricted the powers and jurisdiction of the Secret Service to presidential protection and to hunting down counterfeiters. Behind this was the concern of some that the investigating energies of the service might turn toward the activities of members of Congress. An irate Roosevelt struck back by publicly agreeing that the action of Congress was a measure of self-protection and that the restrictions on the Secret Service would only benefit the "criminal classes." Congressmen did not appreciate the implied association. The House voted 212 to 35 to censure the president for disrespect of Congress (Pringle [1931] 1956, 339–340).

Given the conservative nature of his party and Congress, Roosevelt's legislative record, especially in his second term, was a remarkable achievement. He worked with progressives of both parties, pressured conservatives, enlisted the press, and toured the country to ignite pub-lic support for his reforms. William Harbaugh, one of Roosevelt's most astute biographers, offers a keen assessment of the president's relation-ship with Congress: "[H]is bold and imaginative leadership had forged the Grand Old Party into a crude instrument of reform. By feinting and threatening, by advancing and retreating, by inciting the people and cooperating with the opposition he had wrenched from its leaders legis-lation that many of them bitterly opposed" (Harbaugh 1966, 244).

Theodore Roosevelt did not satisfy either those on the stolid right or the more avid left in Congress. But he did transform the relationship between the presidency and Congress and compiled a creditable record of reform by working with great skill in the pragmatic center.

THE COURTS

As he assumed the duties of the presidency Roosevelt was concerned about the influence of the courts on the success of his administration. During the late nineteenth century, the heyday of big-business expan-sion, the Supreme Court developed constitutional interpretations that favored the power of capital over labor and that insulated business enter-prise from government regulation. It was as close to an era of thoroughly free enterprise as American capitalism has ever enjoyed. The Court con-sistently struck down efforts by the states to regulate railroads and other businesses. Then in 1895 the high court delivered a sharp blow against federal regulation of the trusts. In the case of *United States v. E. C. Knight,* the Court distinguished between manufacturing and commerce and held a monopoly of sugar refining immune from prosecution as a trust. This struck at the heart of the Sherman Anti-Trust Act of 1890 and dimmed the prospects for effective antitrust suits. Roosevelt understood clearly that his plans for strengthening the hand of the government to stem the excesses of big business could be frustrated by an unfriendly judiciary.

The president acknowledged that a justice of the Supreme Court should be above partisanship, but he should "keep in mind also his rela-tion with his fellow statesmen who are striving in cooperation with him to advance the ends of government" (Lodge 1925, 1:518). In regard to labor he thought the Court should show some consideration for the workers who most needed it. Although the *Northern Securities* case

(1904) was a great victory for his administration, his frustration with narrowly conservative court decisions mounted. In a speech to the elite Union League Club of Philadelphia, he warned that a constitutional amendment might be necessary if the courts continued to rule against the federal regulation of corporations. He was convinced that the founders intended such a role for the government.

The constitutional separation of powers blocks direct presidential influence on the decisions of the Supreme Court. The appointing power does give the president some leverage in shaping the character of the Court, but he has no guarantee that an appointee will consistently reflect the views of his benefactor. This, Roosevelt would learn. He was able to name three men to the high court during his presidency. The first opportunity came in 1902 with the resignation of Justice Horace Gray. He had been a progressive voice in the Court whose majority usually acted as guarantors of the rights of property. The search for a replacement focused on the chief justice of the Massachusetts Supreme Judicial Court, Oliver Wendell Holmes Jr.

Holmes was a legal realist. He read the law not as a body of fixed principles but as a flexible instrument restrained only by the Constitution. His views were shaped by Darwinian ideas applied to society, an outlook of enormous impact on American thought in the late nineteenth century. This popular philosophy argued that life is a struggle for power and survival through unrelenting competition. Although he held conservative economic views, his idea of competition embraced the notion that organized labor was a legitimate player for advantage in the struggle against capital. As a result his decisions in Massachusetts did occasionally shock his patrician friends. For example, he defended the right of labor to employ boycotts, to insist on closed union shops, and, in one of his most famous decisions, he held that picketing during a strike was a legal means by which labor could challenge management. He also defended the right of the state to regulate business enterprise. But Holmes was no progressive partisan, and his reading of the law could fall firmly against government regulations at times. In his work on the bench, Holmes demonstrated a powerful immunity to political and popular pressures.

Roosevelt knew Holmes's writings and was encouraged by those decisions, which he interpreted as showing sympathy for labor and support for broader powers of government regulation. He was impressed that Holmes could make decisions that were not consistent with the interests of that privileged class he had served in his practice. Expecting that Holmes would help to offset the staunchly probusiness bias of the Court, the president announced his appointment in August 1902. After Senate confirmation in December, he entertained Holmes at a grand White House dinner in January and looked forward to the new justice's joining his coterie of Washington friends.

The first important test of the wisdom of his choice came in the *Northern Securities* case. By his reading of the temper of the nine justices, Roosevelt hoped for a favorable decision and counted Holmes on his side in light of his record in Massachusetts and, perhaps, in the expectation that his appointee would cooperate in his design to strengthen the government's powers. Although the government did win, the vote was a close five to four with Holmes drafting a vigorous dissent. Competition, he argued, fostered growth, and trusts were a product of successful competition. The Constitution did not give Congress the power to reconstruct society, however well intentioned (see Document 3.3). That the majority gave Roosevelt the victory could not dampen his rage at Holmes; he felt betrayed. In the years that followed, the two continued to meet socially, but what began as a warm friendship dissolved into correct formality. To this, Holmes was indifferent. Remembering Roosevelt years later he described the president as "a likeable, a big figure, a rather ordinary intellect, with extraordinary gifts, a shrewd and I think pretty unscrupulous politician" (Harbaugh 1966, 162).

In 1903 Roosevelt made his second appointment, appeals court judge William Rufus Day. He knew Day well and counted on him to support the government in the Northern Securities case. Day did so, but eventually he, too, would disappoint. In 1906 he sided with the majority in striking down a workmen's compensation law, the Employers Liability Act, which Roosevelt counted as one of his important victories when he squeezed the measure out of a reluctant Congress. He later sent Day a book on the subject and warned that intolerable working conditions could lead the country to revolution (Morison 1952, 6:103–104).

His third appointment came in 1906. He named William H. Moody, who had served in the administration as secretary of the navy and as attorney general. For his work on the bench, Roosevelt had high praise.

By the end of his presidency Roosevelt regarded the judiciary with frustration and a disappointment bordering on anger. In 1908 he called the reversal of a fine of $29 million against Standard Oil a miscarriage of justice. A lower court had imposed the fine for the company's violation of the Elkins Anti-rebate Act, forbidding carriers from giving large shippers rebates from published rates. In his last year in office Roosevelt accused the courts of abusing the use of the injunction against labor unions (see Documents 5.5 and 5.6). Later, during his 1912 campaign to return to the presidency, he advocated popular recall of judges at the state level (see Document 6.6). Speaking in 1913 he charged that the courts had recklessly abused their powers for the past fifty years. "The result has been a lamentably large number of cases to make the courts the bulwarks of special privilege against justice" (Roosevelt 1926, 17:376). They had, he charged, given in to pressure to serve the privileged classes.

Given the conservative disposition of the judiciary and of much of the often recalcitrant Congress during his presidency, Roosevelt's achievement in redirecting the energies of the government toward conservation, regulation, and social reform becomes magnified. It took all of his great energy and political skill to weave through these obstacles to a transformed presidency and a more effective government.

THE MILITARY

Theodore Roosevelt was more knowledgeable about military matters and devoted more direct attention to the military establishment of the United States than most presidents. His study of the War of 1812, his years of lobbying in support of Alfred Thayer Mahan's call for stronger naval forces, his work as assistant secretary of the navy, and his service in Cuba helped to shape his convictions about the important role of the military, especially the navy, in American national life. Hemispheric security inevitably depended on the United States, and fulfillment of that obligation he understood to demand a much stronger navy than existed when he came into office. From the earliest days of his presidency he campaigned for naval buildup as essential "to the honor and material welfare, and above all the peace, of our nation in the future" (Roosevelt 1926, 15:117). Every annual message to Congress carried a plea for more appropriations or praise for progress made, coupled with a warning that to stop meant to retreat. The need was not only to enlarge the battle fleet with more ships but also to replace ships grown obsolete. The president supported and made allies of reformers in the navy who were working for the same ends. Among these were officers like William S.

Simms, whose intensity offended some of his colleagues, but whose campaign to improve gunnery technology and practice and to raise shipbuilding standards to keep pace with potential enemies won Roosevelt's hearty approval. This kind of support made the president a hero to many navy men in and out of the service (see Document 5.7).

Most of the naval power of the United States at the turn of the century was concentrated in Atlantic waters, and Roosevelt was acutely aware of the growing strength of Japan in the Pacific. He was determined to shift some of that naval power to the Pacific and to demonstrate that the American navy was fit for operations in two oceans. Without consulting his cabinet he settled on the idea of sending the battle fleet on a round-the-world cruise. There was some resistance in Congress and from East Coast interests and newspapers, which feared the Atlantic seaboard would be rendered vulnerable. There were doubts that a full battle fleet could sail around the world without serious breakdowns. He brushed aside the objections, including the fear that the action would provoke Japan. Indeed, one of his intentions was to impress the Japanese and other world powers with a show of American strength. His purpose, he said, was peace not war. There were other motives. The trip would give the navy valuable training and experience in operations far from home ports. Also important was the expectation that news reports of a successful voyage would stimulate public support for a larger navy. When the chairman of the Senate Committee on Naval Affairs, Eugene Hale of Maine, threatened to hold back appropriations, Roosevelt said he would send the fleet anyway, and Congress could leave it stranded in the Pacific (Roosevelt 1926, 20:540). The appropriation was promptly voted.

On December 16, 1907, from the deck of the presidential yacht, *Mayflower,* at Hampton Roads, Virginia, a delighted Roosevelt received a twenty-one-gun salute as he saw the Great White Fleet off on its historic voyage. Sixteen battleships steamed around Cape Horn to San Francisco and on to New Zealand, Australia, the Philippines, China, and Japan. The Japanese greeted the visit with great courtesy and hospitality, the fears of giving offense unrealized. The voyage continued through the Indian Ocean, passed through the Suez Canal, and crossed the Mediterranean to the Atlantic. After a fifteen-month journey without serious incident, the ships returned to Hampton Roads, where Roosevelt again greeted the fleet on Washington's Birthday in 1909. Once again a bold move against skeptical resistance gave the president a public triumph.

The need for growth in the army was deemed less urgent than strengthening the navy. In fact, after the Spanish-American War in 1898 the army had been reduced in strength to the legal minimum of 60,000 men. Under Roosevelt that number was increased to 100,000, and the Militia Act of 1903 reorganized and increased support for the National Guard. The most important contribution of the Roosevelt administration to the army was the reorganization of its command structure. With Roosevelt's strong backing, this was the work of Secretary of War Elihu Root.

Root had been thinking about such a reorganization for several years, going back to his service in the McKinley cabinet. Supply and command confusion during the Spanish-American War demonstrated that divided authority had hampered military operations and endangered the troops. After much study and consultation with experienced officers, Root prepared legislation for congressional action. The plan eliminated the post of commanding general of the army and substituted the chief of staff, who was to serve as the direct agent of the president. It also established a General Staff Corps, a group of more than forty officers assigned full time to the development of military policy and planning. Military education was bolstered by the creation of the Army War College for advanced training of officers. Against the resistance of some old army hands and their allies in Congress, Roosevelt urged passage of the reforms. His persistence and Root's stature and political skill prevailed. Congress approved the reorganization in 1903, establishing the basis of the modern command structure of the American military. Before leaving office Roosevelt recommended a similar plan for the reorganization of the naval command structure.

The president's service record, his unstinting support for the armed forces, and his expertise in military matters made him a favorite among officers and troops alike. But there were some unhappy incidents during his tenure. Roosevelt strained to defend his draconian action in the Brownsville incident (see Chapter 3). A more personal conflict troubled the president when Gen. Nelson A. Miles, commanding general of the army, challenged his authority. Miles disliked Roosevelt and was thought to have presidential ambitions of his own. Roosevelt had little regard for Miles, holding him responsible for some of the command confusion he witnessed during his days in Cuba. In December 1901 Miles violated protocol by making a public statement critical of a naval inquiry into the conduct of two admirals during the Spanish-American War, implying administration interference. For this he was censured by Root, with Roosevelt's backing. In addition, Roosevelt publicly scolded Miles at a White House reception. "I will have no criticism of my administration from you or any other officer in the Army" (quoted in Morris 2001, 79). The setting of the rebuke humiliated Miles and ensured lasting enmity. He opposed administration plans for army reorganization and so testified in congressional hearings. In 1902 he told a reporter he had been ordered not to go to the Philippines to investigate the suppression of the insurrection there. He implied that the administration wanted to suppress reports of atrocities committed by American troops. Although Roosevelt would have liked to dismiss Miles, he knew the general had important friends in Congress and decided to temper his anger. He allowed Miles to continue in his post, knowing that his mandatory retirement was due in 1903. At that time Miles retired without receiving the customary presidential statement of commendation for his long service.

Another source of embarrassment for Roosevelt was the behavior of the military in dealing with the Philippine insurrection. Brutality marked the fighting on both sides and atrocities were committed. Especially onerous was the work of Gen. Jacob Smith, who told his officers he wanted no prisoners. When reports of his actions spread, Roosevelt ordered an investigation in 1902. With more than enough evidence available, Roosevelt ordered Smith dismissed from the army.

Realism marked Roosevelt's understanding of world affairs, and at the start of the twentieth century realism dictated to him that military strength was imperative. He insisted repeatedly that military preparedness would make peace more likely than war. This theme was the centerpiece of his policy as president and one that he continued to preach in his political commentaries after he left office (see Document 5.8).

BUSINESS AND LABOR

The attitude of the business community toward Roosevelt ranged from cool to bitterly hostile. The *Northern Securities* case shocked the business barons, who had never had to give much serious thought to government interference with their affairs. His support for the coal miners in 1902 struck the owners as more like betrayal than arbitration. Business leaders taunted the president by attributing every disturbance in the economy and every dip in the stock market to the uncertainties generated by his progressive talk and action. Much as they mistrusted Roosevelt, they had nowhere else to turn. His popularity precluded any serious challenge to his nomination or election in 1904. To men like J. P. Morgan, John D. Rockefeller, and Henry Frick his calls for a new and powerful regulatory role for government was as welcome as a Populist crusade and more repulsive coming from the man to whose campaign chest they had contributed so generously. Once reelected Roosevelt entered the most legislatively productive years of his presidency, and when he left office the business community looked forward with relief to the presidency of the more dependable William Howard Taft.

Organized labor did not have high hopes for the new administration when Roosevelt became president. His past record and much of his earlier rhetoric were not encouraging. But as Roosevelt's views about the role of unions and the needs of working people evolved, so too did the response of labor. His role in the coal strike, his repeated calls for prolabor measures like workmen's compensation, and his criticism of the courts for rejecting federal and state laws protecting workers gave labor a voice of support in the White House that was unprecedented (see Documents 5.5 and 5.9). He supported labor's demand for a law that would limit the judicial use of the injunction against striking workers, a tool the courts ingeniously discovered in the Sherman Act, which was originally designed to attack the trusts. Unlike earlier presidents, he welcomed labor leaders into the White House and conferred repeatedly with labor men like Samuel Gompers, leader of the American Federation of Labor, the country's largest labor organization. His relations with labor leaders were not without tensions. Gompers, like some of the progressives, could be testy about the president's willingness to compromise with conservatives. But labor's needs were great and a Congress led by Sen. Nelson Aldrich and Speaker of the House Joseph Cannon was reluctant to offend its business-class patrons. This the president understood better than most of his critics. Roosevelt's conversion to the cause of the laboring classes was completed in his Bull Moose campaign in 1912. His platform, touting better wages, hours, and working conditions; old-age pensions; opposition to child labor; and other labor reforms echoed the perennial demands of the nation's labor leaders and confirmed the conservatives' suspicions about his "radicalism."

CONCLUSION

By the time Roosevelt left the White House, the institution most directly affected by his work was the presidency itself. Woodrow Wilson, writing as a political scientist, had lamented the lack of effective executive leadership in *Congressional Government,* his analysis of the American political system. For many years presidents had acted largely as administrators of the congressional will. The presidential voice was muted, and initiatives for major changes rarely came from the White House. Roosevelt made the presidency a powerful force in the political life of the nation. His famous "bully pulpit" energized public opinion with telling influence on the legislature. The precedents he set and the agenda he broadcast focused the nation's attention on the office of president and demonstrated the larger potential of executive leadership. His influence on the character of the presidency endured long after he left it and constitutes an important part of his political legacy.

BIBLIOGRAPHIC ESSAY

Among the works helpful in understanding Roosevelt's relations with major institutions are the following principal biographies: H. W. Brands, *T.R.: The Last Romantic* (New York: Basic Books, 1997), a careful study focusing principally on his political career; Kathleen Dalton, *Theodore Roosevelt: A Strenuous Life* (New York: Alfred A. Knopf, 2002), the most recent biography, with special attention paid to the influence of women in Roosevelt's personal and political life; Lewis L. Gould, *The Presidency of Theodore Roosevelt* (Lawrence: University Press of Kansas, 1991), one of the best compact histories of the Roosevelt presidency; William Henry Harbaugh, *The Life and Times of Theodore Roosevelt* (New York: Collier Books, 1963), among the most scholarly of the biographies and still very useful; and Nathan Miller, *Theodore Roosevelt: A Life* (New York: William Morrow, 1992), a generally sympathetic biography. Edmund Morris's *Theodore Rex* (New York: Random House, 2001), the second volume of a projected three-volume biography, is a finely detailed history of the presidential years. George E. Mowry, *The Era of Theodore Roosevelt* (New York: Harper and Row, 1958), offers a broad picture of the United States during the Roosevelt years and a friendly interpretation of his performance. Henry Pringle's *Theodore Roosevelt: A Biography* (1931; reprint, New York:

Harcourt Brace, 1956) is a prize-winning biography dating from the 1930s that is often critical of the president's policies and politics.

For Roosevelt's relations with the press see Elmer Cornwell Jr., *Presidential Leadership of Public Opinion* (Bloomington: Indiana University Press, 1966), a study of twentieth-century presidents in their press and public relations. Jacob Riis, *Theodore Roosevelt the Citizen* (New York: Outlook, 1904), provides an intimate look at TR by a loyal friend of many years who taught Roosevelt about the lives of the "other half"; Lincoln Steffens, *The Autobiography of Lincoln Steffens* (New York: Grosset and Dunlap, 1931), is another work that offers firsthand details of Roosevelt's relations with the press and attitudes toward reform. John Tebbel and Sarah M. Tebbel, *The Press and the Presidency* (New York: Oxford University Press, 1985), is a more recent look at presidential press relations.

Helpful for understanding the president's relations with cabinet members are Kenton J. Clymer, *John Hay: The Gentleman as Diplomat* (Ann Arbor: University of Michigan Press, 1975) and Philip C. Jessup, *Elihu Root*, 2 vols. (New York: Anchor Books, 1964), an aging but still authoritative biography. Also helpful is Richard W. Leopold, *Elihu Root and the Conservative Tradition* (Boston: Little, Brown, 1954). William Manners, *TR and Will* (New York: Harcourt Brace, 1969), studies the friendship and later break with Taft. William Roscoe Thayer, *John Hay*, 2 vols. (Boston: Houghton Mifflin, 1916) is an admiring biography by a contemporary.

For relations with leaders of Congress see: John Morton Blum, *The Republican Roosevelt* (Cambridge: Harvard University Press, 1977), which offers a detailed analysis of legislative politics. John A. Garraty, *Henry Cabot Lodge: A Biography* (New York: Alfred A. Knopf, 1953), discusses TR's relations with his close friend. George E. Mowry, *Theodore Roosevelt and the Progressive Movement* (Madison: University of Wisconsin Press, 1946), is a brilliant analysis of the role of TR in the Progressive movement; and Nathaniel Wright Stephenson, *Nelson Aldrich* (Port Washington, N.Y.: Kennikat Press, 1971), describes the important conservative influence of the Rhode Island senator.

Roosevelt reflected on his relations with the courts in his autobiography in 1913, which was published in several editions and appears as volume 20 in the national edition of Theodore Roosevelt, *The Works of Theodore Roosevelt*, national ed., 20 vols. (New York: Charles Scribner's Sons, 1926). Offering some insight into his association with Justice Oliver Wendell Holmes is Catherine Drinker Bowen, *The Yankee from Olympus* (Boston: Little, Brown, 1943).

Concerning relations with the military see William R. Braisted, *The United States Navy in the Pacific, 1897–1909* (Austin: University of Texas Press, 1958); Gordon V. O'Gara, *Theodore Roosevelt and the Rise of the Modern Navy* (Princeton, N.J.: Princeton University Press, 1943); and Kenneth Wimmel, *Theodore Roosevelt and the Great White Fleet* (Washington, D.C.: Brassey's, 1998). Also see the biographies of Root listed above for treatment of the administration's reorganization of the army.

Works dealing with Roosevelt's relations with labor and business leaders include Robert J. Cornell, *The Anthracite Coal Strike of 1902* (Washington, D.C.: Catholic University Press, 1957); Irving Greenberg, *Theodore Roosevelt and Labor: 1900–1918* (New York: Garland, 1988); and Jean Strouse, *Morgan: American Financier* (New York: Random House, 1999), a report on exchanges between Roosevelt and the most important figure in American finance.

Document 5.1   The Man with the Muck-Rake, April 14, 1906

On more than one occasion Roosevelt chided the press when some of its number exaggerated or distorted accounts of public corruption. Some of these stories accused members of Congress of cooperating in the corruption. Although the exposés helped in his efforts to increase government regulation of business, it was perhaps with an eye toward distancing himself from the "muckrakers" and placating the men he had to work with in Congress that the president publicly rebuked that kind of reporting. The address excerpted here comes from a cornerstone ceremony for a House office building.

In Bunyan's "Pilgrim's Progress" you may recall the description of the Man with the Muck-rake, the man who could look no way but downward, with the muck-rake in his hand; who was offered a celestial crown for his muck-rake, but who would neither look up nor regard the crown he was offered, but continued to rake to himself the filth of the floor.

In "Pilgrim's Progress" the Man with the Muck-rake is set forth as the example of him whose vision is fixed on carnal instead of on spiritual things. Yet he also typifies the man who in this life consistently refuses to see aught that is lofty, and fixes his eyes with solemn intentness only on that which is vile and debasing. Now, it is very necessary that we should not flinch from seeing what is vile and debasing. There is filth on the floor, and it must be scraped up with the muck-rake; and there are times and places where this service is the most needed of all the services that can be performed. But the man who never does anything else, who never thinks or speaks or writes, save of his feats with the muck-rake, speedily becomes, not a help to society, not an incitement to good, but one of the most potent forces for evil.

There are, in the body politic, economic and social, many and grave evils, and there is urgent necessity for the sternest war upon them. There should be relentless exposure of and attack upon every evil man whether politician or business man, every evil practice, whether in politics, in business, or in social life. I hail as a benefactor every writer or speaker, every man who, on the platform, or in book, magazine, or newspaper, with merciless severity makes such attack, provided always that he in his turn remembers that the attack is of use only if it is absolutely truthful. The liar is no whit better than the thief, and if his mendacity takes the form of slander, he may be worse than most thieves. It puts a premium upon knavery untruthfully to attack an honest man, or even with hysterical exaggeration to assail a bad man with untruth. An epidemic of indiscriminate assault upon character does not good, but very great harm. The soul of every scoundrel is gladdened whenever an honest man is assailed, or even when a scoundrel is untruthfully assailed.

Now, it is easy to twist out of shape what I have just said, easy to affect to misunderstand it, and, if it is slurred over in repetition, not difficult really to misunderstand it. Some persons are sincerely incapable of understanding that to denounce mud-slinging does not mean the indorsement of whitewashing; and both the interested individuals who need whitewashing, and those others who practice mud-slinging, like to encourage such confusion of ideas. One of the chief counts against those who make indiscriminate assault upon men in business or men in public life, is that they invite a reaction which is sure to tell powerfully in favor of the unscrupulous scoundrel who really ought to be attacked, who ought to be exposed, who ought, if possible, to be put in the penitentiary. If Aristides is praised overmuch as just, people get tired of hearing it; and over censure of the unjust finally and from similar reasons results in their favor. . . .

To assail the great and admitted evils of our political and industrial life with such crude and sweeping generalizations as to include decent men in the general condemnation means the searing of the public conscience.

There results a general attitude either of cynical belief in and indifference to public corruption or else of a distrustful inability to discriminate between the good and the bad. Either attitude is fraught with untold damage to the country as a whole. The fool who has not sense to discriminate between what is good and what is bad is well-nigh as dangerous as the man who does discriminate and yet chooses the bad. There is nothing more distressing to every good patriot, to every good American, than the hard, scoffing spirit which treats the allegation of dishonesty in a public man as a cause for laughter. Such laughter is worse than the crackling of thorns under a pot, for it denotes not merely the vacant mind, but the heart in which high emotions have been choked before they could grow to fruition.

There is any amount of good in the world, and there never was a time when loftier and more disinterested work for the betterment of mankind was being done than now. The forces that tend for evil are great and terrible, but the forces of truth and love and courage and honesty and generosity and sympathy are also stronger than ever before. It is a foolish and timid, no less than a wicked, thing to blink the fact that the forces of evil are strong, but it is even worse to fail to take into account the strength of the forces that tell for good. Hysterical sensationalism is the very poorest weapon wherewith to fight for lasting righteousness. The men who with stern sobriety and truth assail the many evils of our time, whether in the public press, or in magazines, or in books, are the leaders and allies of all engaged in the work for social and political betterment. But if they give good reason for distrust of what they say, if they chill the ardor of those who demand truth as a primary virtue, they thereby betray the good cause, and play into the hands of the very men against whom they are nominally at war. . . .

The first requisite in the public servants who are to deal in this shape with corporations, whether as legislators or as executives, is honesty. This honesty can be no respecter of persons. There can be no such thing as unilateral honesty. The danger is not really from corrupt corporations; it springs from the corruption itself, whether exercised for or against corporations.

The eighth commandment reads: "Thou shalt not steal." It does not read: "Thou shalt not steal from the rich man." It does not read: "Thou shalt *not* steal from the poor man." It reads simply and plainly: "Thou shalt not steal." No good whatever will come from that warped and mock morality which denounces the misdeeds of men of wealth and forgets the misdeeds practiced at their expense; which denounces bribery, but blinds itself to blackmail; which foams with rage if a corporation secures favors by improper methods, and merely leers with hideous mirth if the corporation is itself wronged. The only public servant who can be trusted honestly to protect the rights of the public against the misdeed of a corporation is that public man who will just as surely protect the corporation itself from wrongful aggression. If a public man is willing to yield to popular clamor and do wrong to the men of wealth or to rich corporations, it may be set down as certain that if the opportunity comes he will secretly and furtively do wrong to the public in the interest of a corporation.

But, in addition to honesty, we need sanity. No honesty will make a public man useful if that man is timid or foolish, if he is a hot-headed zealot or an impracticable visionary. As we strive for reform we find that it is not at all merely the case of a long up-hill pull. On the contrary, there is almost as much of breeching work as of collar work; to depend only on traces means that there will soon be a runaway and an upset. The men of wealth who today are trying to prevent the regulation and control of their business in the interest of the public by the proper government authorities will not succeed, in my judgment, in checking the progress of the movement. But if they did succeed they would find that they had sown the wind and would surely reap the whirlwind, for they would ultimately provoke the violent excesses which accompany a reform coming by convulsion instead of by steady and natural growth.

On the other hand, the wild preachers of unrest and discontent, the wild agitators against the entire existing order, the men who act crookedly, whether because of sinister design or from mere puzzle-headedness, the men who preach destruction without proposing any substitute for what they intend to destroy, or who propose a substitute which would be far worse than the existing evils—all these men are the most dangerous opponents of real reform. If they get their way they will lead the people into a deeper pit than any into which they could fall under the present system. If they fail to get their way they will still do incalculable harm by provoking the kind of reaction which, in its revolt against the senseless evil of their teaching, would enthrone more securely than ever the very evils which their misguided followers believe they are attacking. . . .

Source: Theodore Roosevelt, *The Works of Theodore Roosevelt,* national ed. (New York: Charles Scribner's Sons, 1926), 16:415–423.

Document 5.2   The Public Press, Address at Milwaukee, Wisconsin, September 7, 1910

Concern for the role of the press continued to engage the president after he left office. That era of what today is referred to as "investigative reporting" exposed many scandals, especially concerning the collusion of politicians in corrupt business practices. Roosevelt endorsed the exposure of public corruption, but insisted on the need for accuracy.

. . . The newspaper men—publishers, editors, reporters—are just as much public servants as are the men in the government service themselves, whether those men be elected or appointed officers. Now, we have always held in higher honor the public man who did his duty, and we have always felt that the public man who did not do his duty was deserving of a peculiar degree of reprobation. And just the same way about the newspaper man. The editor, the publisher, the reporter, who honestly and truthfully puts the exact facts before the public, who does not omit for improper reasons things that ought to be stated, who does not say what is not true, who does not color his facts so as to give false impressions, who does not manufacture his facts, who really is ready, in the first place, to find out what the truth is, and, in the next place, to state it accurately—that man occupies one of the most honorable positions in the community. . . .

Exactly as I put as the first requisite of the man in public life that he should be honest, so I put as the first requisite of the man writing for the newspaper that he should tell the truth. Now, it is important that he should tell the whole truth, for there can be no greater service rendered than the exposure of corruption in either public life or in business, or in that intricate web of public life and business which exists too often in America today, I cannot say with sufficient emphasis how earnestly I hope that corruption will be exposed wherever found, and that a man ought to be especially anxious to expose it in his own class or in his own party. I will draw no distinction between corrupt men of my own party and those of the opposite party, excepting that I will be just a trifle more anxious to get at those of my own party, because I feel a little more responsible for it.

If an article is published in a magazine, exposing corruption, and the article tells the truth, I do not care what it is, the writer has rendered the greatest possible service by writing it; but I want to be certain that he is telling the truth, and if he does not tell the truth he does wrong in more than one way. It is not only that he wrongs one individual; he wrongs the public, because he deprives them of the chance to discriminate between honest men and scoundrels. The greatest service that can be rendered to the scoundrel in public life is to attack the honest man untruthfully. If the honest man is lied about, either the lies are believed, and he and the scoundrel are put on the same plane of scoundrelism, or else the lies themselves tend to produce the impression in the public mind that no statements about public men are true, and that, therefore, the truth when told about corrupt men in public life can be disregarded also. Incessant falsehood inevitably produces in the public mind a certain disbelief in good men and a considerable disbelief in the charges against bad men; so that there results the belief that there are no men entirely good and no men entirely bad, and that they are all about alike and colored gray. Now, that is the worst possible frame of mind that can be induced in a democracy like ours. It is essential that the public should know the character of its servants; and it is essential that the public should not be misled into believing a dishonest public servant honest and an honest public servant dishonest. Those who mislead them are doing as much damage as the dishonest men themselves. Mark Twain, who was not only a great humorist, but a great philosopher, in his proverbs by Pudd'nhead Wilson, said that there are eight hundred and sixty-nine different kinds of lies, but that the only one authoritatively prohibited is bearing false witness against your neighbor. The politician—I am a politician—and the writer for periodicals or the press—and I am one again—should bear steadily in mind that the eighth and ninth commandments are equally binding: "Thou shalt not steal; Thou shalt not bear false witness against thy neighbor."

Source: Theodore Roosevelt, *The Works of Theodore Roosevelt,* national ed. (New York: Charles Scribner's Sons, 1926), 13:544–548.

Document 5.3   Calls for a New Cabinet Department of Commerce and Industries

Among the first requests Roosevelt made of Congress was a call for the establishment of a new cabinet department. The growth of industry and the increasing importance of labor organization convinced him of the need. After repeated requests, he won the creation of the Department of Commerce and Labor in 1903.

From Annual Message, December 3, 1901

. . . There should be created a Cabinet officer, to be known as secretary of commerce and industries, as provided in the bill introduced at the last session of the Congress. It should be his province to deal with Commerce in its broadest sense; including among many other things whatever concerns labor and all matters affecting the great business corporations and our merchant marine.

The course proposed is one phase of what should be a comprehensive and far-reaching scheme of constructive statesmanship for the purpose of broadening our markets, securing our business interests on a safe basis, and making firm our new position in the international industrial world; while scrupulously safeguarding the rights of wage-worker and capitalist, or investor and private citizen, so as to secure equity as between man and man in this Republic. . . .

From Annual Message, December 2, 1902

. . . It is earnestly hoped that a secretary of commerce may be created, with a seat in the Cabinet. The rapid multiplication of questions affecting labor and capital, the growth and complexity of the organizations through which both labor and capital now find expression, the steady tendency toward the employment of capital in huge corporations, and the wonderful strides of this country toward leadership in the international business world justify an urgent demand for the creation of such a position. Substantially all the leading commercial bodies in this country have united in requesting its creation. It is desirable that some such measure as that which has already passed the Senate be enacted into law. The creation of such a department would in itself be an advance toward dealing with and exercising supervision over the whole subject of the great corporations doing an interstate business; and with this end in view, the Congress should endow the department with large powers, which could be increased as experience might show the need. . . .

From Annual Message, December 7, 1903

. . . The establishment of the Department of Commerce and Labor, with the Bureau of Corporations thereunder, marks a real advance in the direction of doing all that is possible for the solution of the questions vitally affecting capitalists and wage-workers. The act creating the department was approved, on February 14, 1903, and two days later the head of the department was nominated and confirmed by the Senate. Since then the work of organization has been pushed as rapidly as the initial appropriations permitted, and with due regard to thoroughness and the broad purposes which the department is designed to serve. After the transfer of the various bureaus and branches to the department at the beginning of the current fiscal year, as provided for in the act, the personnel comprised 1,289 employees in Washington and 8,836 in the country at large. The scope of the department's duty and authority embraces the commercial and industrial interests of the nation. It is not designed to restrict or control the fullest liberty of legitimate business action, but to secure exact and authentic information which will aid the Executive in enforcing existing laws, and which will enable the Congress to enact additional legislation if any should be found necessary, in order to prevent the few from obtaining privileges at the expense of diminished opportunities for the many. . . .

Source: Theodore Roosevelt, *The Works of Theodore Roosevelt,* national ed. (New York: Charles Scribner's Sons, 1926), 15:93, 149, 169–170.

Document 5.4   Reflections on Relations with Congress (1913)

The legislative achievements of his presidency required Roosevelt to work with a conservative and often uncooperative Congress. His political agility and willingness to compromise wrung substantial victories, but not without tension and some bitterness. Here, as written in his autobiography, he candidly comments about the experience and the men with whom he sparred.

For the reasons I have already given in my chapter on the governorship of New York, the Republican party, which in the days of Abraham Lincoln was founded as the radical progressive party of the nation, had been obliged during the last decade of the nineteenth century to uphold the interests of popular government against a foolish and ill-judged mock-radicalism. It remained the Nationalist as against the particularist or States'-rights party, and in so far it remained absolutely sound; for little permanent good can be done by any party which worships the States'-rights fetish or which fails to regard the State, like the county or the municipality, as merely a convenient unit for local self-government, while in all national matters, of importance to the whole people, the nation is to be supreme over State, county, and town alike. But the States'-rights fetish, although still effectively used at certain times by both courts and Congress to block needed national legislation directed against the huge corporations or in the interests of working men, was not a prime issue at the time of which I speak. In 1896, 1898, and 1900 the campaigns were waged on two great moral issues: (1) the imperative need of a sound and honest currency; (2) the need, after 1898, of meeting in manful and straightforward fashion the extraterritorial problems arising from the Spanish War. On these great moral issues the Republican party was right, and the men who were opposed to it, and who claimed to be the radicals, and their allies among the sentimentalists, were utterly and hopelessly wrong. This had, regrettably but perhaps inevitably, tended to throw the party into the hands not merely of the conservatives but of the reactionaries; of men who, sometimes for personal and improper reasons, but more often with entire sincerity and uprightness of purpose, distrusted anything that was progressive and dreaded radicalism. These men still from force of habit applauded what Lincoln had done in the way of radical dealing with the abuses of his day; but they did not apply the spirit in which Lincoln worked to the abuses of their own day. Both houses of Congress were controlled by these men. Their leaders in the Senate were Messrs. Aldrich and Hale. The Speaker of the House when I became President was Mr. Henderson, but in a little over a year he was succeeded by Mr. Cannon, who, although widely differing from Senator Aldrich in matters of detail, represented the same type of public sentiment. There were many points on which I agreed with Mr. Cannon and Mr. Aldrich, and some points on which I agreed with Mr. Hale. I made a resolute effort to get on with all three and with their followers, and I have no question that they made an equally resolute effort to get on with me. We succeeded in working together, although with increasing friction, for some years, I pushing forward and they hanging back. Gradually, however, I was forced to abandon the effort to persuade them to come my way, and then I achieved results only by appealing over the heads of the Senate and House leaders to the people, who were the masters of both of us. I continued in this way to get results until almost the close of my term; and the Republican party became once more the progressive and indeed the fairly radical progressive party of the nation. When my successor was, chosen, however, the leaders of the House and Senate, or most of them, felt that it was safe to come to a break with me, and the last or short session of Congress, held between the election of my successor and his inauguration four months later, saw a series of contests between the majorities in the two houses of Congress and the President— myself— quite as bitter as if they and I had belonged to opposite political parties. However, I held my own. I was not able to push through the legislation I desired during these four months, but I was able to prevent them doing anything I did not desire, or undoing anything that I had already succeeded in getting done.

There were, of course, many senators and members of the Lower House with whom up to the very last I continued to work in hearty accord, and with a growing understanding. I have not the space to enumerate, as I would like to, these men. For many years Senator Lodge had been my close personal and political friend, with whom I discussed all public questions that arose, usually with agreement; and our intimately close relations were of course unchanged by my entry into the White House. He was of all our public men the man who had made the closest and wisest study of our foreign relations, and more clearly than almost any other man he understood the vital fact that the efficiency of our navy conditioned our national efficiency in foreign affairs. Anything relating to our international relations, from Panama and the navy to the Alaskan boundary question, the Algeciras negotiations, or the peace of Portsmouth, I was certain to discuss with Senator Lodge and also with certain other members of Congress, such as Senator Turner, of Washington, and Representative Hitt, of Illinois. Anything relating to labor legislation and to measures for controlling big business or efficiently regulating the giant railway systems, I was certain to discuss with Senator Dolliver, or Congressman Hepburn or Congressman Cooper. With men like Senator Beveridge, Congressman (afterward Senator) Dixon, and Congressman Murdock, I was apt to discuss pretty nearly everything relating to either our internal or our external affairs. There were many, many others. The present president of the Senate, Senator Clark, of Arkansas, was as fearless and high-minded a representative of the people of the United States as I ever dealt with. He was one of the men who combined loyalty to his own State with an equally keen loyalty to the people of all the United States. He was politically opposed to me; but when the interests of the country were at stake, he was incapable of considering party differences; and this was especially his attitude in international matters—including certain treaties which most of his party colleagues, with narrow lack of patriotism, and complete subordination of national to factional interest, opposed. I have never anywhere met finer, more faithful, more disinterested, and more loyal public servants than Senator O. H.

Platt, a Republican, from Connecticut, and Senator Cockrell, a Democrat, from Missouri. They were already old men when I came to the presidency; and doubtless there were points on which I seemed to them to be extreme and radical; but eventually they found that our motives and beliefs were the same, and they did all in their power to help any movement that was for the interest of our people as a whole. . . .

Source: Theodore Roosevelt, *The Works of Theodore Roosevelt,* national ed. (New York: Charles Scribner's Sons, 1926), 20:341–344.

Document 5.5   On the Relation of the Courts to the Wage-Earner, Message to Congress, December 8, 1908

After praising judges as valuable public servants, Roosevelt launched into a critique of their work as shortsighted and narrow in its defense of corporate interests. Coming near the end of his term, the message reflected his frustration with the courts, his understanding of corporate power, and his growing sympathy for the needs of labor.

. . . I most earnestly urge upon the Congress the duty of increasing the totally inadequate salaries now given to our judges. On the whole there is no body of public servants who do as valuable work, nor whose moneyed reward is so inadequate compared to their work. Beginning with the Supreme Court, the judges should have their salaries doubled. It is not befitting the dignity of the nation that its most honored public servants should be paid sums so small compared to what they would earn in private life that the performance of public service by them implies an exceedingly heavy pecuniary sacrifice. . . .

The judges who have shown themselves able and willing effectively to check the dishonest activity of the very rich man who works iniquity by the mismanagement of corporations, who have shown themselves alert to do justice to the wage-worker, and sympathetic with the needs of the mass of our people, so that the dweller in the tenement-houses, the man who practices a dangerous trade, the man who is crushed by excessive hours of labor, feel that their needs are understood by the courts—these judges are the real bulwark of the courts; these judges, the judges of the stamp of the President-elect [Taft], who have been fearless in opposing labor when it has gone wrong, but fearless also in holding to strict account corporations that work iniquity, and farsighted in seeing that the working man gets his rights, are the men of all others to whom we owe it that the appeal for such violent and mistaken legislation has fallen on deaf ears, that the agitation for its passage proved to be without substantial basis. The courts are jeopardized primarily by the action of those Federal and State judges who show inability or unwillingness to put a stop to the wrong-doing of very rich men under modern industrial conditions, and inability or unwillingness to give relief to men of small means or wage-workers who are crushed down by these modern industrial conditions; who, in other words, fail to understand and apply the needed remedies for the new wrongs produced by the new and highly complex social and industrial civilization which has grown up in the last half-century.

The rapid changes in our social and industrial life which have attended this rapid growth have made it necessary that, in applying to concrete cases the great rule of right laid down in our Constitution, there should be a full understanding and appreciation of the new conditions to which the rules are to be applied. What would have been an infringement upon liberty half a century ago may be the necessary safeguard of liberty today. What would have been an injury to property then may be necessary to the enjoyment of property now. . . .

There are certain decisions by various courts which have been exceedingly detrimental to the rights of wage-workers. This is true of all the decisions that decide that men and women are, by the Constitution, "guaranteed their liberty" to contract to enter a dangerous occupation, or to work an undesirable or improper number of hours, or to work in unhealthy surroundings; and therefore cannot recover damages when maimed in that occupation and cannot be forbidden to work what the legislature decides is an excessive number of hours, or to carry on the work under conditions which the legislature decides to be unhealthy. . . . Decisions such as those alluded to above nullify the legislative effort to protect the wage-workers who most need protection from those employers who take advantage of their grinding need. They halt or hamper the movement for securing better and more equitable conditions of labor. The talk about preserving to the misery-hunted beings who make contracts for such service their "liberty" to make them, is either to speak in a spirit of heartless irony or else to show an utter lack of knowledge of the conditions of life among the great masses of our fellow countrymen, a lack which unfits a judge to do good service just as it would unfit any executive or legislative officer. . . .

The power of injunction is a great equitable remedy, which should on no account be destroyed. But safeguards should be erected against its abuse. I believe that some such provisions as those I advocated a year ago for checking the abuse of the issuance of temporary injunctions should be adopted. . . .

The chief lawmakers in our country may be, and often are, the judges, because they are the final seat of authority. Every time they interpret contract, property, vested rights, due process of law, liberty, they necessarily enact into law parts of a system of social philosophy; and as such interpretation is fundamental, they give direction to all lawmaking. The decisions of the courts on economic and social questions depend upon their economic and social philosophy; and for the peaceful progress of our people during the twentieth century we shall owe most to those judges who hold to a twentieth-century economic and social philosophy and not to a long outgrown philosophy, which was itself the product of primitive economic conditions. . . .

The huge wealth that has been accumulated by a few individuals of recent years, in what has amounted to a social and industrial revolution, has been as regards some of these individuals made possible only by the improper use of the modern corporation. A certain type of modern corporation, with its officers and agents, its many issues of securities, and its constant consolidation with allied undertakings, finally becomes an instrument so complex as to contain a greater number of elements that, under various judicial decisions, lend themselves to fraud and oppression than any device yet evolved in the human brain. Corporations are necessary instruments of modern business. They have been permitted to become a menace largely because the governmental representatives of the people have worked slowly in providing for adequate control over them. . . .

Our great clusters of corporations, huge trusts and fabulously wealthy multimillionaires, employ the very best lawyers they can obtain to pick flaws in these statutes after their passage; but they also employ a class of secret agents who seek, under the advice of experts, to render hostile legislation innocuous by making it unconstitutional, often through the insertion of what appear on their face to be drastic and sweeping provisions against the interests of the parties inspiring them. . . . A very striking illustration of the consequences of carelessness in the preparation of a statute was the employers' liability law of 1906. In the cases arising under that law, four out of six courts of first instance held it unconstitutional; six out of nine justices of the Supreme Court held that its subject-matter was within the province of congressional action; and four of the nine justices held it valid. It was, however, adjudged unconstitutional by a bare majority of the court—five to four. It was surely a very slovenly piece of work to frame the legislation in such shape as to leave the question open at all.

Real damage has been done by the manifold and conflicting interpretations of the interstate commerce law. Control over the great corporations doing interstate business can be effective only if it is vested with full power in an administrative department, a branch of the Federal executive, carrying out a Federal law; it can never be effective if a divided responsibility is left in both the States and the nation; it can never be effective if left in the hands of the courts to be decided by lawsuits. . . .

In no other nation in the world do the courts wield such vast and far-reaching power as in the United States. All that is necessary is that the courts as a whole should exercise this power with the far-sighted wisdom already shown by those judges who scan the future while they act in the present. Let them exercise this great power not only honestly and bravely, but with wise insight into the needs and fixed purposes of the people, so that they may do justice and work equity, so that they may protect all persons in their rights, and yet break down the barriers of privilege, which is the foe of right.

Source: Theodore Roosevelt, *The Works of Theodore Roosevelt,* national ed. (New York: Charles Scribner's Sons, 1926), 15:504–516.

Document 5.6   On Judges and the "Criminal Rich," January 2, 1908

Writing Attorney General Charles Joseph Bonaparte, Roosevelt defended his criticism of the courts and lashed out at the "criminal rich." His occasional use of such language infuriated the business barons, who thought of him as unreliable and even dangerous.

My dear Bonaparte:

. . . It is difficult to speak about the judges, for it behooves us all to treat with the utmost respect the high office of judge; and our judges as a whole are brave and upright men. But there is need that those who go wrong should not be allowed to feel that there is no condemnation of their wrongdoing. A judge who on the bench either truckles to the mob or bows down before a corporation; or who, having left the bench to become a corporation lawyer, seeks to aid his clients by denouncing as enemies of property all those who seek to stop the abuses of the criminal rich; such a man performs an even worse service to the body politic than the Legislator or Executive who goes wrong. In no way can respect for the courts be so quickly undermined as by teaching the public thru the action of a judge himself that there is reason for the loss of such respect. The judge who by word or deed makes it plain that the corrupt corporation, the law-defying corporation, the law-defying rich man, has in him a sure and trustworthy ally, the judge who by misuse of the process of injunction makes it plain that in him the wage-worker has a determined and unscrupulous enemy, the judge who when he decides in an employer's liability or a tenement house factory case shows that he has neither sympathy for nor understanding of those fellow citizens of his who most need his sympathy and understanding; these judges work as much evil as if they pandered to the mob, as if they shrank from sternly repressing violence and disorder. The judge who does his full duty well stands higher, and renders a better service to the people, than any other public servant; he is entitled to greater respect; and if he is a true servant of the people, if he is upright, wise and fearless he will unhesitatingly disregard even the wishes of the people if they conflict with the eternal principles of right as against wrong. He must serve the people; but he must serve his conscience first. All honor to such a judge; and all honor cannot be rendered him if it is rendered equally to his brethren who fall immeasurably below the high ideals for which he stands. There should be a sharp discrimination against such judges. They claim immunity from criticism, and the claim is heatedly advanced by men and newspapers like those of whom I speak. Most certainly they can claim immunity from untruthful criticism; and their champions, the newspapers and the public men I have mentioned, exquisitely illustrate by their own actions mendacious criticism in its most flagrant and iniquitous form.

But no servant of the people has a right to expect to be free from just and honest criticism. It is the newspapers and the public men whose thoughts and deeds show them to be most alien to honesty and truth who themselves loudly object to truthful and honest criticism of their fellow servants of the great monied interests.

We have no quarrel with the individuals, whether public men, lawyers or editors, to whom I refer. These men derive their sole power from the great, sinister offenders who stand behind them. They are but puppets who move as the strings are pulled by those who control the enormous masses of corporate wealth which if itself left uncontrolled threatens dire evil to the Republic. It is not the puppets, but the strong, cunning men and the mighty forces working for evil behind, and to a certain extent, thru the puppets with whom we have to deal. We seek to control law-defying wealth, in the first place to prevent its doing evil, and in the next place to avoid the vindictive and dreadful radicalism which if left uncontrolled it is certain in the end to arouse. Sweeping attacks upon all property, upon all men of means, without regard to whether they do well or ill, would sound the death knell of the Republic; and such attacks become inevitable if decent citizens permit rich men whose lives are corrupt and evil to domineer in swollen pride, unchecked and unhindered, over the destinies of this country. We act in no vindictive spirit, and we are no respecters of persons. If a labor union does what is wrong we oppose it as fearlessly as we oppose a corporation that does wrong; and we stand with equal stoutness for the rights of the man of wealth and for the rights of the wage-workers; just as much so for one as for the other. We seek to stop wrongdoing; and we desire to punish the wrongdoer only so far as is necessary in order to achieve this end. We are the staunch upholders of every honest man, whether businessman or wage-worker. I do not for a moment believe that our actions have brought on business distress; so far as this is due to local and not world-wide causes, and to the actions of any particular individuals, it is due to the speculative folly and flagrant dishonesty of a few men of great wealth, who now seek to shield themselves from the effects of their own wrongdoings by ascribing its results to the actions of those who have sought to put a stop to the wrongdoing. But if it were true that to cut out rottenness from the body politic meant a momentary check to an unhealthy-seeming prosperity, I should not for one moment hesitate to put the knife to the cancer. On behalf of all our people, on behalf no less of the honest man of means than of the honest man who earns each day's livelihood by that day's sweat of his brow, it is necessary to insist upon honesty in business and politics alike, in all walks of life, in big things and in little things; upon just and fair dealing as between man and man. . . .

Source: Theodore Roosevelt, *The Works of Theodore Roosevelt,* national ed. (New York: Charles Scribner's Sons, 1926), 20:448–451.

Document 5.7   On the Need for a Strong Navy, Address to the Naval War College, July 22, 1908

Always a proponent of preparedness based on effective naval power (see Documents 1.1 and 1.9), Roosevelt made his case to Congress and carried his message to the public repeatedly. He responds here to critics who resisted his military policies, including the buildup of the navy and the world tour of the fleet. His appearance at the Naval War College in Newport, Rhode Island, he knew, would be widely reported and draw national attention.

There are only a few things that I desire to say today to the conference, and what I have to say really is said less to the officers present than to the great bulk of my fellow countrymen outside. I could not speak to you technically. I can speak to my fellow countrymen who are deeply interested in the American navy, but who sometimes tend to be misled as to the kind of navy we should have and as to what the navy can and ought to do.

For instance, there are always a certain number of well-meaning, amiable individuals—coupled with others not quite so well-meaning—who like to talk of having a navy merely for defense, who advocate a coast-defense navy. Such advocacy illustrates a habit of mind as old as human nature itself—the desire at the same time to do something, and not to do it, than which there is no surer way of combining the disadvantages of leaving it undone and of trying to do it. A purely defensive navy, a mere coast-defense navy, would be almost worthless. To advocate a navy merely for coast defense stands in point of rational intelligence about on a par with advocating the creation of a school of prize-fighters in which nobody should do anything but parry. No fight was ever won yet except by hitting; and the one unforgivable offense in any man is to hit soft. Don't hit at all if it can possibly be avoided; but if you do hit, hit as hard as you know how. That applies to the individual and it applies to the nation; and those who advocate a merely defensive navy, a mere coast-defense navy, are advocating that we shall adopt as a national principle the principle of hitting soft. I hope with all my heart that never will this nation of ours hit unless it cannot possibly be helped. I believe that the nation should do everything honorable at all times to avoid any trouble; that it should scrupulously refrain from wronging or insulting any other nation; that it should put up with a good deal in the way of misconduct on the part of others before going to war. But when this nation does have to go to war, such war will only be excusable if the nation intends to hammer its opponent until that opponent quits fighting. You don't hammer an opponent if you keep your fleet along the coast waiting until the opponent takes the initiative and hammers you.

For the protection of our coasts we need fortifications; we need to have these fortifications not merely to protect the salient points of our possessions, but we need them so that the navy can be foot-loose. A year ago at the time that it was announced that the fleet was to go around the world there were a certain number of newspapers, especially in my own city of New York, that raised a clamorous protest against it. Exactly how close the connection was between this protest against the fleet going around the world and dissatisfaction with the economic policies of the Administration, it is not necessary at this moment to discuss; but the protest was made. It took at one time the form of a mistaken prophecy to the effect that the fleet would not be allowed to go around the world, and one of the reasons alleged was that to let it go around the world would leave New York defenseless in the event of war; the theory evidently being that the fleet, or a portion of it, would be used especially to protect New York and other cities in the event of war. If war comes at any time in the future, that Administration under which it comes will indeed be guilty of folly if they use the fleet to protect any port. Let the port be protected by the fortifications; the fleet must be foot-loose to search out and destroy the enemy's fleet. That is the function of the fleet; that is the only function that can justify the fleet's existence; and that function cannot exist in the case of such a ridiculous fleet as the fleet would be if it were only possible to use it for coast-defense purposes.

Again, as a question of national policy. When statesmen, when the people behind political leaders, embark on any given policy, they build up for themselves a time of humiliation and disaster in the future if they do not prepare to make that policy effective. There is something to be said (from my standpoint, gentlemen, not much, but still something) for the theory that this nation shall never have any interests outside its own borders and shall assume toward other nations an attitude of such meekness that no trouble can ever possibly come. As I say, something can be said for that policy. It would not appeal to me; but still it is a defensible policy. But a wholly indefensible policy would be consistently to work for the assumption of responsibilities without making any provision for meeting the demands necessarily entailed by those responsibilities. To be rich, aggressive, and unarmed, is to invite certain disaster and annihilation. . . .

I have spoken of our needing an efficient navy because of our possessions that are separated from us by water; because of our advocacy of the
Monroe Doctrine; because of our being engaged in building the Isthmian
Canal. But constituted as this people is, if we did not have a foreign possession; if we abandoned the Monroe Doctrine; if we handed over to some
other power the Panama Canal, it would still be necessary for us to have a
navy, and a strong, fighting navy. We do not want any navy at all if it is not
a first-class one; and such a navy will be necessary for us just so long as we
demand the right to administer our internal affairs as we think best. . . .

Now, gentlemen, the possibilities of misapprehension, of misconstruc-
tion, of what one says are infinite, especially when they are accompanied
with something of design. I wish to reiterate, and to say with just as much
earnestness as I have spoken today on other subjects, that I want a first-
class fighting navy because it is the most effective guaranty of peace that
this country can have. Uncle Sam can well afford to pay for his peace and
safety so cheap an insurance policy as is implied in the maintenance of the
United States navy. There is not a more paying investment that he makes.
All of the leaders of our people are fond of assuring this people that it is
a great people; they are fond of assuring it of that fact even when they are
advocating policies that if carried out would assuredly make the fact merely
a memory. We are a great people. That ought not to be a subject for boastfulness; it ought to be a subject for serious consideration because of the
heavy responsibilities that go with it. We cannot help playing a great part
in the world, but we can very easily help playing that part well; and to be
a great people and make a great failure is as unattractive a spectacle as
history affords. We are one of the great world-powers—in situation, in
population, in wealth. We are such a power because of the spirit and purpose of our people. It is not open to us to decide whether or not the career
that we lead shall be important; it has got to be important. All we can
decide is as to whether our success shall be great or our failure great; we
are sure to make either a great failure or a great success. I would not pre-
tend for a moment, gentlemen, to you or to anyone else that merely military proficiency on land or sea would by itself make this or any other
nation great. First and foremost come the duties within the gates of our
own household; first and foremost our duty is to strive to bring about a
better administration of justice, cleaner, juster, more equitable methods
in our political, business, and social life, the reign of law, the reign of
that orderly liberty, which was the first consideration in the minds of the

founders of this Republic. Our duties at home are of the first importance. But our duties abroad are of vital consequence also. This nation may fail, no matter how well it keeps itself prepared against the possibility of disaster from abroad; but it will certainly fail if we do not thus keep ourselves prepared. And I ask our people to take the keenest and most intelligent interest in the affairs of the navy and to watch closely those at Washington, in the Executive Department and in the Legislative Department as well, who are concerned with the affairs of the navy, because as a nation we need greatly in the interest of peace, in the interest of true national greatness, that the United States navy, with its ships, its officers, its enlisted men, shall at every point be kept in the highest possible condition of efficiency and well-being.

Source: Theodore Roosevelt, *The Works of Theodore Roosevelt,* national ed. (New York: Charles Scribner's Sons, 1926), 16:250–257.

Document 5.8   Preparedness against War, June 1915

Roosevelt issued calls for military preparedness repeatedly in the years after he left the White House. He was especially forceful in his appeals after the start of World War I in Europe. The following example appeared in Metropolitan *magazine, to which he was a regular contributor. As so often in the war years, Roosevelt could not resist the temptation to assail President Woodrow Wilson and his administration.*

Military preparedness meets two needs. In the first place, it is a partial insurance against war. In the next place, it is a partial guaranty that if war comes the country will certainly escape dishonor and will probably escape material loss. . . .

The first and most essential form of preparedness should be making the navy efficient. Absolutely and relatively, our navy has never been at such a pitch of efficiency as in February, 1909, when the battle fleet returned from its voyage around the world. Unit for unit, there was no other navy in the world which was at that time its equal. During the next four years we had an admirable secretary of the navy, Mr. Meyer—we were fortunate in having then and since good secretaries of war in Mr. Stimson and Mr. Garrison. Owing to causes for which Mr. Meyer was in no way responsible, there was a slight relative falling off in the efficiency of the navy, and probably a slight absolute falling off during the following four years. But it remained very efficient.

Since Mr. Daniels came in, and because of the action taken by Mr. Daniels under the direction of President Wilson, there has been a most lamentable reduction in efficiency. If at this moment we went to war with a first-class navy of equal strength to our own, there would be a chance not only of defeat but of disgrace. It is probably impossible to put the navy in really first-class condition with Mr. Daniels at its head, precisely as it is impossible to conduct our foreign affairs with dignity and efficiency while Mr. Bryan is at the head of the State Department.

But the great falling off in naval efficiency has been due primarily to the policy pursued by President Wilson himself. . . . The fleet has had no maneuvering for twenty-two months. It has had almost no gun practice by division during that time. There is not enough powder; there are not enough torpedoes; the bottoms of the ships are foul; there are grave defects in the submarines; there is a deficiency in aircraft; the under-enlistments indicate a deficiency of from ten thousand to twenty thousand men; the whole service is being handled in such manner as to impair its fitness and morale.

Congress should summon before its committees the best naval experts and provide the battleships, cruisers, submarines, floating mines, and aircraft that these experts declare to be necessary for the full protection of the United States. It should bear in mind that while many of these machines of war are essentially to be used in striking from the coasts themselves, yet that others must be designed to keep the enemy afar from these coasts. Mere defensive by itself cannot permanently avail. The only permanently efficient defensive arm is one which can act offensively. Our navy must be fitted for attack, for delivering smashing blows, in order effectively to defend our own shores. Above all, we should remember that a highly trained personnel is absolutely indispensable, for without it no material preparation is of the least avail.

Source: Theodore Roosevelt, *The Works of Theodore Roosevelt,* national ed. (New York: Charles Scribner's Sons, 1926), 18:117–139.

Document 5.9   On Protection for Wage-Earners, Message to Congress, December 8, 1908

By the end of Roosevelt's presidency he was much more intense in his advocacy of improved working conditions and benefits for workers. His last annual message to Congress left no doubt about his commitment to that cause. He would carry these ideas into his 1912 Progressive Party campaign.

. . . There should no longer be any paltering with the question of taking care of the wage-workers who, under our present industrial system, become killed, crippled, or worn out as part of the regular incidents of a given business. The majority of wage-workers must have their rights secured for them by State action; but the National Government should legislate in thoroughgoing and far-reaching fashion not only for all employees of the National Government, but for all persons engaged in interstate commerce. The object sought for could be achieved to a measurable degree, as far as those killed or crippled are concerned, by proper employers' liability laws. As far as concerns those who have been worn out, I call your attention to the fact that definite steps toward providing old-age pensions have been taken in many of our private industries. These may be indefinitely extended through voluntary association and contributory schemes, or through the agency of savings-banks, as under the recent Massachusetts plan. To strengthen these practical measures should be our immediate duty; it is not at present necessary to consider the larger and more general governmental schemes that most European governments have found themselves obliged to adopt.

Our present system, or rather no system, works dreadful wrong, and is of benefit to only one class of people—the lawyers. When a workman is injured what he needs is not an expensive and doubtful lawsuit, but the certainty of relief through immediate administrative action. The number of accidents which result in the death or crippling of wage-workers, in the Union at large, is simply appalling; in a very few years it runs up a total far in excess of the aggregate of the dead and wounded in any modern war. No academic theory about "freedom of contract" or "constitutional liberty to contract" should be permitted to interfere with this and similar movements. Progress in civilization has everywhere meant a limitation and regulation of contract. I call your especial attention to the bulletin of the Bureau of Labor which gives a statement of the methods of treating the unemployed in European countries, as this is a subject which in Germany, for instance, is treated in connection with making provision for worn-out and crippled workmen.

Pending a thoroughgoing investigation and action there is certain legislation which should be enacted at once. The law, passed at the last session of the Congress, granting compensation to certain classes of employees of the government, should be extended to include all employees of the government, and should be made more liberal in its terms. There is no good ground for the distinction made in the law between those engaged in hazardous occupations and those not so engaged. If a man is injured or killed in any line of work, it was hazardous in his case. Whether one per cent or ten per cent of those following a given occupation actually suffer injury or death ought not to have any bearing on the question of their receiving compensation. It is a grim logic which says to an injured employee or to the dependents of one killed that he or they are entitled to no compensation because very few people other than he have been injured or killed in that occupation. Perhaps one of the most striking omissions in the law is that it does not embrace peace officers and others whose lives may be sacrificed in enforcing the laws of the United States. The terms of the act providing compensation should be made more liberal than in the present act. A year's compensation is not adequate for a wage-earner's family in the event of his death by accident in the course of his employment. And in the event of death occurring, say, ten or eleven months after the accident, the family would only receive as compensation the equivalent of one or two months' earnings. In this respect the generosity of the United States toward its employees compares most unfavorably with that of every country in Europe—even the poorest.

The terms of the act are also a hardship in prohibiting payment in cases where the accident is in any way due to the negligence of the employee. It is inevitable that daily familiarity with danger will lead men to take chances that can be construed into negligence. So well is this recognized that in practically all countries in the civilized world, except the United States, only a great degree of negligence acts as a bar to securing compensation. Probably in no other respect is our legislation, both State and national, so far behind practically the entire civilized world as in the matter of liability and compensation for accidents in industry. It is humiliating that at European international congresses on accidents the United States should be singled out as the most belated among the nations in respect to employers' liability legislation. This government is itself a large employer of labor, and in its dealings with its employees it should set a standard in this country which would place it on a par with the most progressive countries in Europe. The laws of the United States in this respect and the laws of European countries have been summarized in a recent Bulletin of the Bureau of Labor, and no American who reads this summary can fail to be struck by the great contrast between our practices and theirs—a contrast not in any sense to our credit.

The Congress should without further delay pass a model employers' liability law for the District of Columbia. The employers' liability act recently declared unconstitutional, on account of apparently including in its provisions employees engaged in intrastate commerce as well as those engaged in interstate commerce, has been held by the local courts to be still in effect so far as its provisions apply to the District of Columbia. There should be no ambiguity on this point. If there is any doubt on the subject, the law should be re-enacted with special reference to the District of Columbia. This act, however, applies only to employees of common carriers. In all other occupations the liability law of the District is the old common law. The severity and injustice of the common law in this matter has been in some degree or another modified in the majority of our States, and the only jurisdiction under the exclusive control of the Congress should be ahead and not behind the States of the Union in this respect. A comprehensive employers' liability law should be passed for the District of Columbia.

Source: Theodore Roosevelt, *The Works of Theodore Roosevelt,* national ed. (New York: Charles Scribner's Sons, 1926), 15:501–504.

"Can a Champion Come Back?" 1910.

CHAPTER SIX

After the White House

Roosevelt in Retirement

The decision not to run for reelection in 1908 was a painful one for Theodore Roosevelt. He felt bound in honor to respect his 1904 election-night pledge to forgo a third term, but he deeply regretted leaving the office. The thought of retirement was made worse by knowing he would be nominated if he allowed it, and with his popularity at its peak, he would very likely win the election. Only forty-nine years old and full of vigor, he enjoyed being president. He had always wanted to be at the center of the action, and there was no more active center than the White House. He wanted to stay and said so, but in the end he could not. Still, if he could not accept another nomination, he could decide who did. The president's influence was such that his endorsement would settle the matter. His choice was William Howard Taft.

Taft had served Roosevelt loyally and well as governor-general of the Philippines and then secretary of war, and the two became close friends. Taft was generous with support and advice, on which Roosevelt frequently called. He saw Taft as staunchly committed to his policies, an important influence on his selection as successor. By 1906 the president, confident that his ideas would continue to shape national policy, was clear in his choice. His influence and control of the party machinery closed out the chances of other hopefuls.

At the Republican convention in June 1908, Taft was nominated on the first ballot. That year the Democrats returned to William Jennings

Bryan as standard-bearer for the third time. Bryan remained very popular among Democrats and die-hard supporters, but he could not shake the image of populist radicalism. This the election results amply confirmed. Taft captured 321 electoral votes to Bryan's 162 and beat his popular vote by more than 1.2 million. Roosevelt was more than pleased. He had anointed Taft and the country affirmed his choice. Although not clear at the time, the exchange of congratulations between the president and the president-elect carried the seeds of future unhappiness. Writing to the president to thank him, Taft linked Roosevelt to his own brother Charley, who heavily funded the campaign, as the two men who made his election possible. A sensitive Roosevelt deeply resented being given equal standing with a mere supplier of campaign cash (Miller 1992, 492). In the days that followed, Taft displayed an unexpected independence in naming the members of his cabinet. An annoyed Roosevelt said little about it to Taft but complained in private. More substantial misgivings about Taft came later. But in March 1909, accompanying Taft to his inauguration, Roosevelt was pleased with his choice, and a few days later he left the country for a new adventure.

ON AFRICAN SAFARI

With his son Kermit as a partner, Roosevelt traveled to Africa for a year-long hunting trip. Many months earlier he began to plan for a safari to pursue African big game. Family and friends worried about the wisdom of risking health and safety on such a dangerous trek. The perils of the hunt were matched by the risk of disease, but no persuasion could deflect the president's hunger for this new experience. Roosevelt had confronted and conquered the largest and most dangerous animals in the United States, but he longed for the thrill of an African hunt, which promised to be so much more novel and exciting. He, himself, dealt with the logistics for the trip, and he made a pact with the Smithsonian Museum to bring back specimens of African game. This gave the hunt the look of a scientific expedition and deflected the criticism of those who objected to killing animals simply for sport. Contributions, the largest of which came from Andrew Carnegie, financed a substantial part of the cost of the trip. Roosevelt also arranged with *Scribner's Magazine* to write a series of articles about his adventure, for which he was to be paid $50,000. Later he collected those reports for his book *African Game Trails* (see Document 6.1).

After a long journey the huntsman disembarked at Mombasa in what was then called British East Africa, now Kenya. With a large company of guides and porters the safari set out into the interior, winding through forests and grasslands. At times sleeping in tents in the wild, at times resting comfortably at the homes of local planters and officials, Roosevelt reveled in the excitement and the danger of the hunt. Keeping close track of his kills, he later reported that he personally shot an amazing 296 animals and birds. Among them were 9 lions, 5 elephants, 13 rhinoceroses, and a great assortment of African fauna. By April 1910 Roosevelt had worked his way up to the Nile River and on to Khartoum, where he was reunited with his beloved Edith, whom he had missed terribly. From there they traveled on to Cairo and departed Egypt at Alexandria for a tour of Europe.

A YANKEE IN EUROPE

Everywhere he went in Europe Roosevelt was feasted as a world celebrity. He was literally treated royally as monarchs and heads of state went out of their way to dine and entertain the Roosevelts as honored guests. In what became a tiring but splendid routine, receptions, parades, and formal dinners greeted the president in Austria, Belgium, Denmark, France, Germany, Holland, and Italy. In Norway he gave a speech acknowledging the Nobel Peace Prize he was awarded in 1906 for his role in ending the Russo-Japanese War (see Chapter 4). Then it was on to England to receive honorary degrees from Cambridge and Oxford. While at Oxford he delivered the prestigious Romanes Lecture, outlining the achievements and the limits of Western imperialism (see Document 6.2). The address ranged across the history of peoples and empires, concluding with the idea that imperialism could not be justified unless it worked in the interests of the other races as well as the imperialists. Empire building should be guided by justice and the moral law. The argument expressed his view that imperialist activity by nations like Britain and the United States spread the benefits of civilization, not an uncommon view among expansionists. During his stay in England King Edward VII died suddenly, and Roosevelt stayed on representing Taft at the state funeral. Even then, people famous and ordinary sought out the president, and wags croaked that Roosevelt was the star even at the funeral of the dead king.

Finally it was home to New York City on June 18. The city's welcome was a measure of his stature and popularity at home. His ship was greeted by dozens of harbor craft and a twenty-one-gun salute from a navy ship. He landed to a ceremony at Battery Park before an estimated 100,000 spectators, followed by a parade up Broadway and Fifth Avenue with thousands more lining the streets. Astute observers wondered whether that kind of adulation might draw the ex-president out of political retirement. By this time Roosevelt was already unhappy with Taft's performance as president and anxious to get back into politics.

As he assumed the role of private citizen, Roosevelt gave some thought to his finances. He enjoyed a comfortable income from a trust fund left him by his father, but he was not a wealthy man as measured by the standards of the day, and now he was out of a job. Writing was a passion with him, but it also contributed substantially to his income. In addition to books, such as his autobiography, *African Game Trails,* and *Through the Brazilian Wilderness,* Roosevelt wrote essays on many subjects throughout the years of his retirement. He became a contributing editor of *Outlook* magazine immediately on leaving the presidency. The association continued for five years and served as a vehicle for political commentary as well as entertaining articles on a variety of topics, including what became the early chapters of his autobiography. He offered book reviews, social commentary, and even a critique of the famous Armory Show in 1913, the first large exhibition of modern art in the United States. He enjoyed the show. In 1914 he shifted his writing to *Metropolitan* magazine, which lured him with a lucrative contract for his work. Many of his attacks on Wilsonian neutrality and war policies appeared in that journal. From October 1917 until his death he also contributed editorials to the *Kansas City Star* that were syndicated in dozens of newspapers around the country. The last of these he dictated to his secretary just three days before his death.

THE LURE OF POLITICS

Serious doubts about the Taft presidency disturbed Roosevelt while he was still on the hunt in Africa. During the year-long safari and the European tour that followed, politics and ideology strained the relationship between Taft and Roosevelt to the point of conflict. The mails were able to reach the former president even in the African wilds. News from friends in Washington carried disturbing reports about a struggle in the Taft administration over conservation issues. When Richard A. Ballinger replaced James R. Garfield, a Roosevelt holdover as secretary of the interior, a debate over western lands raised a storm of bickering between the new secretary and Roosevelt's loyal chief forester Gifford Pinchot. Ballinger sought to reopen more than a million acres of public lands to commercial use, and Taft sided with him, rejecting Pinchot's protests. An infuriated Pinchot, who once had hoped to head the Interior Department, began a campaign of public criticism of his superiors and even charged Ballinger with corruption in the matter (Mowry 1958, 253). A congressional investigation cleared Ballinger of the charges, and an irate Taft fired Pinchot in the fall of 1909. All of this was reported to Roosevelt by Pinchot and other friends already disenchanted with Taft. Their version of the affair now moved Roosevelt to question the wisdom of choosing Taft to succeed him. In the long run Taft compiled a creditable record in building on Roosevelt's conservation legacy. But in 1909 Roosevelt loyalists portrayed Taft as backsliding to please conservatives.

That image was sharpened when Taft disappointed progressives repeatedly in their reform struggles. When progressive Republicans in the House organized an effort to oust the archconservative Joseph Cannon as Speaker of the House, Taft, although apparently sympathetic, thought it inappropriate to lend support. He also expressed sympathy for a major progressive push to lower tariff rates. But when that legislation was altered in committee by Sen. Nelson Aldrich of Rhode Island, rates on important items were actually raised even higher. Taft not only signed the Payne-Aldrich Tariff Act but also defended the measure in speeches. This Roosevelt noted with distaste.

Roosevelt's attraction to progressive causes grew with each year in office and now advanced even further. While in London he read a new book, *The Promise of American Life*, by Herbert Croly. The book did not transform his thinking as much as it confirmed some ideas about government he had developed as president and some he held instinctively. Croly's work was both supportive of progressive aims and critical of progressive ideology. For him, progressives were still too closely tied to the ideas of Thomas Jefferson. Government that governed least, a federal government of very limited powers, may have been appropriate a hundred years earlier, but that kind of government could not meet the challenges of a modern industrial nation. There could not be, for example, a return to the days of small enterprise. Trusts were efficient and productive instruments; they should not be dismantled. Rather, they should be harnessed and regulated by a government strong enough to control them. Important reforms could not be won by the states or by a feeble national government. The United States required a powerful government with strong leaders if it were to achieve its destiny.

The former president was impressed. He was severely critical of Jefferson in his own historical writing. Nor was he daunted by the idea of strong government headed by effective leaders. Despite dozens of lawsuits, breaking up the trusts had not been successful; more and larger holding companies were created year by year. And government regulation was an important focus of his administration. Indeed, Croly could have been describing the temper of his own presidency. How much the book whetted his appetite to return to active politics cannot be measured, but Croly's phrase a "new nationalism" became the slogan of Roosevelt's return to presidential politics in 1912. Settling in at Oyster Bay on his return, Roosevelt was host to a parade of political figures, many of whom used their visit to attack Taft. Newspapers carried reports of these visits, and in Washington a concerned Taft was hurt by what appeared to be a courting of his enemies (Pringle [1931] 1956, 377). Late in June, Roosevelt visited Taft while the president was vacationing in Beverly, Massachusetts. The visit was cordial but marked by awkward moments and an air of tension.

His return from his extended trip overseas to a hero's welcome had shown the ex-president's public appeal to be still strong, and it was not long before the flow of invitations to speak before admiring crowds became too tempting to resist. In August 1910 he began a speaking tour of western states, which, beyond the ceremonials, was uneventful until his speech at Osawatomie, Kansas. There he unveiled a progressive political agenda that would have shocked a younger Roosevelt. He invoked Abraham Lincoln's dictum that labor was prior to and superior to capital; workers deserved decent treatment and a square deal. He conceded that property rights merited protection, but only in balance with human rights; corporations should be subject to effective government control; the federal government needed enhanced powers to support and protect the common good. Some ideas he revived from earlier statements as president, but the details and context of the program he presented were electrifying. Cleverly transforming the focus of his call for change from himself to the public, he echoed Croly, punching out the climactic sentence, "The American people are right in demanding a New Nationalism, without which we cannot hope to deal with new problems" (see Document 6.3).

The speech caused a sensation and immediately stimulated speculation about another presidential bid. For a leader of a major political party in 1910, it was a radical statement. Progressives across the country applauded joyfully, and party regulars, as expected, were bitter. Taft, whom Roosevelt had so far declined to endorse for reelection, was furious and assumed that his predecessor meant to challenge his nomination. If Roosevelt aimed to capture control of the Republican rank and file, he also risked splitting the party into warring factions. His old friend Henry Cabot Lodge, innocent of Roosevelt's progressive enthusiasms, worried. He warned his friend that such speeches were casting him as a radical, if not a revolutionary. Roosevelt cooled his rhetoric for a time but remained alert to the possibility of a presidential run.

"MY HAT IS IN THE RING"

As the congressional elections approached, Roosevelt walked a political tightrope. He entered into New York Republican Party politics, perhaps hoping to have some influence in the selection of delegates to the next national convention. He made conciliatory gestures to the regulars but in doing so risked criticism from progressives. State Republicans, despite blocking efforts by Taft men, chose him as state convention keynote speaker, and in that role he held out an olive branch of praise for the president. This neither satisfied the conservatives nor pleased the progressives. Ever the campaigner, he also toured the country in behalf of Republican candidates, all the while trying carefully to avoid alienating one or the other wing of the party.

In November the Republicans lost control of the House to the Democrats for the first time since 1896 and lost seats in the Senate. Progressives took this as a sign of public disenchantment with Taft and the conservative domination of the party. It was in the more conservative eastern states that Republicans lost most seats, and those Republicans in the West who won were often from the progressive side of the party. Although progressive gains were encouraging, Roosevelt was disappointed at the defeat of Henry L. Stimson, whom he supported in the race for governor in New York, and he worried that his pulling power with the electorate did not match his popularity. He confessed his disappointment to Henry Cabot Lodge and thought that the loss in New York would end speculation about his candidacy in 1912, which he claimed, somewhat ingenuously, was making him uneasy (Lodge 1925, 2:394).

Although he believed his own chances for the nomination were remote, he refrained from a public endorsement of Taft. Neither did he endorse Sen. Robert M. La Follette, who was leading a progressive Republican revolt against Taft, and he declined to state categorically that he would not be a candidate himself. With a Roosevelt campaign still a possibility, important supporters of La Follette, like Hiram Johnson, governor of California, declared for Roosevelt. When La Follette's inept campaign faltered, the temptation to enter the race was too strong for Roosevelt to resist. He insisted, however, that his candidacy had to be, or appear to be, a response to popular demand. On February 10, 1912, it was arranged that a group of Republican governors who had already urged him to run would write to Roosevelt insisting he was being called to run by a majority of Republicans. Late in February his reply was published. Responding as if to a draft, he said he would accept if nominated by the party convention (see Documents 6.4 and 6.5). When reminded of his no-third-term pledge of 1904, he brushed the problem aside saying the pledge concerned a third *consecutive* term.

While Republicans across the country cheered, some of Roosevelt's closest friends were miserably unhappy, if not surprised. Elihu Root and Lodge were party loyalists whose instincts and politics would not permit them to bolt from the party's sitting president. Lodge was particularly distressed by Roosevelt's speech in Columbus, Ohio, attacking the judicial system for killing reform legislation in the states in the name of property rights (Lodge 1925, 2:423–424). Even worse was his proposal to establish the right of the people to remove judges by a recall vote (see Document 6.6). For Lodge this was too extreme and his commitment to Taft too strong. Taft himself was distraught, perhaps less by the political challenge than by the fact that it came from his old and dear friend.

Knowing that the party machinery would produce delegates to the national convention pledged to Taft, Roosevelt looked to the primaries, relatively new to American politics. By 1912 about a dozen states provided for primary elections. He campaigned at an exhausting pace across the country with gratifying results. In the primary states Roosevelt polled over one million votes, more than the total for Taft and La Follette combined, and he won in Taft's home state of Ohio. Of the 362 delegate seats at stake, Roosevelt won 272, an embarrassment for the president and a humiliation for La Follette. The primary results seemed to confirm that the former president was indeed responding to the popular will.

By the time the Republican delegates gathered in convention at Chicago in June, the party was bitterly divided, and events were soon to make the split irrevocable. As a result of acrimonious battles for delegates at state conventions there were a few more than 250 disputed seats at the convention. The numbers suggested that Roosevelt needed about 70 of those disputed delegates for a chance at nomination. But Taft men controlled the convention committees, and after the petitions and arguments were heard, all but a handful of the disputed seats were filled with Taft delegates. Roosevelt could hardly contain his rage and ranted about a "saturnalia of fraud and larceny" (Brands 1997, 714). But the issue was settled. The roll call of the states gave Taft the nomination by a slim majority.

As the convention drew to a close, Roosevelt addressed his supporters at a hastily assembled rally elsewhere in the city. He called on them to join a moral struggle against the party bosses who had stolen the nomination for Taft. It was the Taft men who fractured the party, and he exhorted his audience to join together in a new party, nominate a new candidate, and launch a progressive campaign to wrest control of the government from the corrupt special interests who blocked reform (Roosevelt 1926, 17:204ff.). Roosevelt gave a classic performance, casting himself in the role of commander responding to the call of his troops to war against evil forces. The troops roared their assent, and so was born the Bull Moose Progressive Party. The 1912 election was to be a three-way race.

The faithful gathered again in Chicago in the first week of August. Their leader treated them to a long "Confession of Faith," combining renewed charges against the corrupt with a program of reform that thrilled the most avid progressives. Adding to the atmosphere of what seemed like a religious revival meeting, Roosevelt brought the convention to its feet when he closed his speech proclaiming, "We stand at Armageddon, and we battle for the Lord" (see Document 6.7). The convention quickly nominated Roosevelt by acclamation and chose Hiram

Johnson for vice president. When the delegates crafted their party plat-form, they listed an array of reforms that remained the liberal political agenda for years to come. The list offered benefits for labor that included an eight-hour day, a minimum wage, prohibition of child labor, safety regulations in the workplace, and more. They also revived other peren-nial progressive favorites, including banking reform, lower tariffs, an income tax, women's suffrage, and campaign finance reform. Those with an eye to history would have noted that many of these ideas had been trumpeted by the Populists (whom Roosevelt had ridiculed) in the 1890s, but they were now sanitized and deemed more acceptable com-ing from middle-class reformers.

The Democrats watched the rupture of the Republican Party with undisguised pleasure. As the minority party they could not have written a more congenial script for the election. In their turn they chose Woodrow Wilson, renowned scholar and former Princeton University president, whose political career consisted of one successful term as reform governor of New Jersey. Wilson's political views were firmly con-servative for most of his academic career, but by the time he entered the race for governor of New Jersey, he had gravitated toward more liberal views. Now Wilson and the Democrats embraced a distinctly progressive program. Roosevelt, who had met and expressed admiration for Wilson in the past, now declared he was not fit to be president (Morison 1954, 7:591–593).

The three-way race quickly became a two-man contest. In speeches across the country, Roosevelt broadcast the Progressive platform dressed in the rhetoric of the New Nationalism. Reform was long past due. The trust powers must be trumped and made to serve the commonweal. It would take an active government propelled by a leader unafraid of wield-ing power to counter the influence of the monied special interests. Wil-son also proffered liberal reforms, but his vision of government still reflected a more Jeffersonian image. His slogan was the New Freedom. He warned that Roosevelt's big government might bring beneficent change, but what if it did not; once created how could such a powerful engine ever be dismantled? The difference was more theoretical than real and proved to be so when President Wilson himself greatly enlarged the range and power of federal action. Both candidates promised reform, and much of the argument was about means to that end. Meanwhile, Taft lagged behind, a defender of the status quo. Willing or not, he was the icon of conservatism at a moment when the electorate was looking for change.

A spectacle of high drama in the campaign came on the evening of October 14 in Milwaukee. As he left his hotel for a scheduled rally, Roosevelt turned to greet a group of waiting supporters. Out of the crowd a shot rang out and the bullet struck him squarely in the chest. The assailant was quickly nabbed and dragged away to a long prison term. A deranged Frank F. Schrank later offered that he acted to avenge Roosevelt's assassination of McKinley and to prevent him from serving a third term. Roosevelt's life was spared because the slug first drove through a metal eyeglass case and the folded pages of his speech before penetrating his chest and lodging in a rib just short of his heart. Stunned and bleeding he insisted on continuing on to the auditorium. When he reached the podium he explained to the audience that he had been shot and, to the despair of his aides, delivered his full speech. Only then did he consent to go to a hospital for treatment. Doctors removed the slug and were gratified to find little damage, and the patient quickly returned to Oyster Bay for some rest. Recuperation interrupted, but did not stop, the campaign.

Always the keen political analyst, Roosevelt understood that the party split raised the odds against victory, probably beyond reach. The results confirmed the analysis. Wilson polled 6.3 million votes; Roosevelt won 4.1 million; and Taft totaled a weak 3.5 million. The electoral count was even more decisive: 435 votes for Wilson, 88 for Roosevelt, and an embarrassing 8 votes for Taft, who won only Utah and Vermont. Clearly, Wilson profited from Roosevelt's bolt, but it is not clear that Taft could have won even with a united party. Many of the progressive Republicans who followed Roosevelt would likely have switched to Wilson or sat out the election. The national mood favored reform, and Taft was not its champion.

BACK INTO RETIREMENT

After the election a somewhat subdued Roosevelt resumed his writing chores, producing his autobiography and essays for *Outlook* magazine. The American Historical Association recognized his status as a historian when it elected him to be its president. In December 1912, a month after the election, he delivered the presidential address to the association gathered in Boston (see Document 6.8). This long address was a scholarly examination of the nature of historical writing. Roosevelt took pains to insist that the historian's work not only must be accurate but also must appeal to the reader. Good writing and good science should both inform the work of the successful historian. The speech was well received, but this was a different inaugural from the one he had sought. In the summer of 1913, Roosevelt accepted invitations from several South American governments for a lecture tour. Always restless and easily tempted by adventure, he decided to expand the trip to include an expedition to explore an uncharted region of the Amazon in Brazil.

In January 1914, with his son Kermit again accompanying him, Roosevelt joined a Brazilian explorer, Candido Rondon, and set out into the interior to explore a recently discovered river called the River of Doubt. The journey proved much more arduous than his well-supplied and carefully prepared African safari. For two months the party suffered the dangers of river rapids, tangled jungle terrain, biting insects, and disease. Under the strain of these terrible conditions, an argument led one member of the party to shoot and kill another, the murderer fleeing into the jungle never again to be seen. Roosevelt himself suffered a badly infected leg and malarial fever that left him delirious. The party did, however, manage to chart the river for 1,500 miles, and to his delight, the Brazilian government renamed the river Rio Roosevelt (see Document 6.9).

TAKING AIM AT WILSON

Roosevelt needed time to recover from his ordeal, but it was not long before he again became embroiled in national and world affairs. He watched with frustration as President Woodrow Wilson impressed the nation by compiling a solid record of progressive reforms in his first two years in office, including lower tariffs, banking reform creating the Federal Reserve System, and stronger antitrust action. Despite the caution of his New Freedom campaign, Wilson strengthened the regulatory powers of the national government with the establishment of the Federal Trade Commission and other legislative victories. The former president's frustration turned to anger when the Wilson administration negotiated a treaty with Colombia in 1913 that included the payment of $25 million as a kind of reparation for the American role in the revolt of Panama. Roosevelt was insulted and enraged at the implication that he had done something wrong, and he railed at Wilson. He called the treaty a "crime against the United States" and thought it shameful "to put ourselves in the wrong by the payment of blackmail" (Morison 1954, 7:778). He told Lodge he considered Wilson ridiculous and intellectually dishonest. His opinion did not improve with the passing of time, but his language grew steadily more extreme.

When Colonel Roosevelt, as he liked to be called, returned from South America, Wilson was deeply embroiled in troubles with Mexico. A revolution turned into a civil war that pitted Victoriano Huerta against Venustiano Carranza for control of the country. Wilson refused to recognize Huerta's claim to power, favoring Carranza as the best hope for a democratic regime in Mexico. An incident in which Huerta's forces briefly arrested a group of American sailors seeking supplies ashore resulted in an American attack on Vera Cruz and a real danger of war with Mexico. Conflict was averted in large part because the diplomacy of Wilson and his secretary of state, William Jennings Bryan, was generally restrained and patient. Roosevelt's assessment painted Wilson as inept and Bryan as contemptible. He called Wilson's restraint and openness to mediation disgusting, and in an essay published in the *New York Times* in December 1916, he denounced Wilson's policies in Mexico.

When war broke out in Europe in August 1914, Wilson called on Americans to be neutral in thought as in action. Roosevelt at first endorsed neutrality but soon changed his mind. He labeled Germany a criminal aggressor and opposed the president's call for American neutrality. A British blockade of Germany effectively ended significant American trade with that country. But holding strictly to the rights of a neutral country, the administration continued to trade with the Allied powers and even allowed loans to the Allies for the purchase of supplies in the United States. American ships were free to deliver nonmilitary goods to Britain and France; the sale but not the delivery of military goods was also allowed under the rules of international law governing neutral powers. This was not enough for Roosevelt. He argued for open support of the Allied powers against Germany. Using his platform as a regular contributor to the *Outlook,* he also campaigned for a vigorous military buildup to prepare for the possibility of war. Again, Wilson was his target for his failure to act quickly. When Wilson did press Congress for major increases in land and naval forces, Roosevelt pronounced Wilson "all wrong on the navy and ninety-five per-cent wrong on the army" (Morison 1954, 8:1012).

On May 7, 1915, the British liner *Lusitania* was sunk by a German submarine as it approached the British Isles. More than 1,200 civilians lost their lives, including 128 Americans. Roosevelt called it murder and insisted it was cause for war. A few days after the sinking, *Metropolitan*, the journal to which he was now under contract for a series of articles, published a piece by him titled "Murder on the High Seas" (see Document 6.10). He called for the seizure of all German ships in American ports and a ban on trade with Germany. He told his readers he did not think this action would mean war, but "there are things worse than war." Until the entry of the United States into the war in 1917, Roosevelt continued to excoriate Wilson publicly and privately without restraint on his temptation to extreme language.

Meanwhile another presidential election approached and the old warhorse imagined he could hear the trumpet call. His dream of a return to the presidency was not dead and at least in part accounted for his obsessive hatred and abuse of Wilson. He had returned to the Republican fold and campaigned for party candidates in 1914. He was convinced, as always, that most party members favored his nomination, but primaries alone could not amass enough delegates to nominate, and the leadership of the GOP was not ready to forgive his revolt in 1912. Nevertheless, he plotted a comeback. Although he remained silent about the nomination in public, he encouraged the loyal to advance his name as a candidate, and he refused to endorse any of the likely prospects, including the former governor of New York and justice of the Supreme Court Charles Evans Hughes.

In March of the election year, when the Massachusetts primary endorsed Roosevelt, he was on a visit to Trinidad. When news of efforts on his behalf in Massachusetts reached him, he released a statement to the press that constituted a "non-denial" denial of interest in the nomination. First he said he would not be a candidate; then he added, "it would be a mistake to nominate me unless the country has in its mood something of the heroic." He took another slap at Wilson and concluded with several paragraphs that read remarkably like a campaign speech (see Document 6.11).

Many of the progressives who followed Roosevelt out of the Republican Party in 1912 were unable or unwilling to go back to that party. Some, like Herbert Croly, admired Wilson's accomplishments, and they were ready to support him for reelection. The influential journalist William

Allen White, a progressive and past supporter of Roosevelt, confessed he could not be enthusiastic about the potential Republican nominee, Charles Evans Hughes, in view of Wilson's accomplishments. Clearly, some of Roosevelt's friends did not share his assessment of the president. Some progressives wanted to try again in 1916 with a third party. In June the remnants of the Bull Moose Progressives met in Chicago to nominate a presidential candidate, even as the Republicans were meeting in the same city to make their choice. Roosevelt tried to keep all roads open as he held on to the hope that he might yet head the ticket of both parties. The Progressives did indeed nominate Roosevelt, but the Republicans, the scars of 1912 still visible, turned decisively to Hughes. Tempted though he was and soberly aware of the likely outcome of another three-way race for president, Roosevelt declined the Progressive nomination to the bitter disappointment of his loyalists (see Document 6.12). Instead, he finally endorsed Hughes. As with any potential competitor, Roosevelt had been sharply critical of Hughes in the past, but now he urged his partisans to vote for the justice. With a faint, sad echo of the statement he released in Trinidad earlier, a dejected Roosevelt wrote to his sister Anna, "Well the country wasn't in a heroic mood!" (Morison 1954, 8:1063).

Unable to sit out an election season, Roosevelt devoted much time and energy in the fall to campaigning across the country for Hughes. On election night the early returns were so favorable to Hughes that eastern newspapers declared him elected, and Wilson retired that evening believing he had lost. But the president pulled close by winning the western states, and when returns from California were reported in the early morning hours, Wilson found he had been reelected. A disconsolate Roosevelt reflected on his party's mistake: the chance for victory was lost when the party failed to nominate him (Morison 1954, 8:1127–1128).

As the war in Europe ground on, Roosevelt continued to editorialize about the lack of adequate preparedness and grew increasingly anti-German. In addition to his conviction that the Germans had caused the war and committed atrocities in their invasion of neutral Belgium, other influences may have colored his views. He had always harbored warm feelings toward the British, and his writing years earlier emphasized the kinship of the English-speaking peoples. The British ambassador to the United States during the war, Cecil Spring-Rice, was his lifelong friend, correspondent, and a guest at Sagamore Hill and had, in fact, served as best man at his wedding to Edith. Roosevelt believed that Britain and the United States represented the best of civilization, and their power in concert could serve the peace of the world (Tilchin 1997, 241). These connections and beliefs made it difficult for Roosevelt to be detached in his analysis, and he read the war as a struggle between the forces of good and evil. Accordingly, he believed that the United States should be much more actively committed to the good.

OVER THERE

In the early weeks of 1917 Germany decided on a policy of unrestricted submarine warfare combined with a land offensive for a great push to victory. This called for the sinking of American ships and certain war with the United States, but the Germans calculated that strangling supplies to Britain and France and victory in land battles would win the war before American aid could be effective. In this they miscalculated. In March, German submarines began sinking American merchant ships, and on April 2 Wilson went to Congress for a declaration of war. It was one act by Wilson that Roosevelt did not feel compelled to attack.

In fact, for a short time Roosevelt suspended his merciless assaults on Wilson. He praised his address to Congress and called on Americans to back the president. Patriotism certainly moved him, but the Colonel of the Rough Riders had something else in mind as well. Even before the formal declaration of war Roosevelt appealed to Secretary of War Newton D. Baker for approval to raise a volunteer division to fight in France. Baker made excuses and delayed, so on April 10 the Colonel visited the White House to plead with Wilson directly. Given their rivalry and the history of Roosevelt's attacks on the president, the meeting was surprisingly cordial. Roosevelt was on his best behavior as a supplicant, and Wilson confessed that he found a compelling sweetness and charm in his visitor. Roosevelt made his case for leading the volunteers into battle, and he left the meeting with some hope but not a great deal of confidence that Wilson would grant his request.

Any hope was misplaced. It was argued by some, including the French, that a Roosevelt-led division arriving in France would provide a great boost to Allied morale. The French premier, Georges Clemenceau, sent a statement to several American newspapers encouraging the idea of a Roosevelt division in France. But there were weighty reasons against such a plan. Military leaders were opposed; there was concern that the conduct of the military draft would be disrupted and supplies diverted. Technical reasons aside, Wilson was not likely to provide his rival, consistently unkind to him and still a potential candidate for office, a commission for heroic action. Then, too, Roosevelt, in addition to being fifty-eight years old and blind in one eye, had never fully recovered from the damage to his health suffered in Brazil. Wilson's refusal added yet another reason to hate that "gray rat in the White House," and the assaults on Wilson soon resumed.

Despite his eagerness to taste the thrill of battle again, Roosevelt sensed the decline in his health by late 1917. He suffered a variety of ailments, lost hearing in his left ear, and felt older than his fifty-eight years. In February 1918, he underwent surgery for an abscessed leg and was confined to the hospital for a month. He recovered well from the surgery and was soon back at his writing chores, attuned to the political scene, and blasting Wilson at every opportunity.

If Roosevelt could not go to war, his sons could, and all four, Archie, Theodore Jr., Kermit, and Quentin served with distinction on the front lines. Their father was naturally proud of his men but worried that it was unlikely that all four would return safely. His fear was justified. Archie was seriously wounded in action and received the Croix de Guerre from the French government. But worse was to come. Twenty-year-old Quentin trained as a pilot, and on July 17, 1918, his fighter was shot down behind enemy lines. The Germans recovered his body, and word reached Roosevelt that he had been buried with military honors, an odd decency amid the ugliness of an indecent war. Roosevelt's grief was mitigated only by the pride in his son's sacrifice. He regretted that it was not he who had died in France, and the pain of Quentin's loss never left him.

THE LAST ACT

When President Wilson announced his Fourteen Points as a set of war aims and guide for negotiating a just peace, he was hailed around the world. But from Oyster Bay, Roosevelt said, "Let us dictate peace by the hammering of guns and not chat about peace to the accompaniment of the clicking of typewriters" (Morison 1954, 8:1380). His preference was for unconditional surrender and harsh punishment for Germany. The severe terms of the eventual treaty, insisted upon by Britain and France over Wilson's objections, proved to be disastrous for the world.

But in 1918, Roosevelt was thinking of another run for the presidency. The Republicans gained control of both houses of Congress in the 1918 elections, and Roosevelt thought his chances for nomination in 1920 were good. He had reconciled with Taft. By coincidence the two men met in a hotel dining room when both were visiting Chicago. It was a highly emotional meeting that brought cheers from the other patrons when the two clasped hands and sat at a table together. The bitterness of party leaders over the 1912 election was fading, and Roosevelt's name was the one most often mentioned for 1920. Whether Wilson would be his rival for a third term or not, it was prudent to prepare, and he never let up on his criticism.

One of the less admirable performances by Roosevelt was his role in conspiring with Henry Cabot Lodge to kill Wilson's plans for the United States to join the League of Nations. Both men had been international-ists all their political lives, frequently advocating a greater role for the United States in world affairs and rejecting isolationism. Roosevelt had written in the past about the need for an organization of nations joined to punish aggressors. In his Nobel Prize address in 1910, he called for arms limitation, as Wilson did in the Fourteen Points; he also suggested the formation of a league of peace to prevent aggression by force if nec-essary (see Document 6.13). Now that Wilson championed a League of Nations, it was a bad idea.

On the question of joining the League, Roosevelt announced he would accept American membership but only if strong reservations were incorporated into the charter. In December 1918, he conferred with Lodge, who was chairman of the Senate Foreign Relations Committee and determined to block the ratification of the peace treaty and with it American membership in the League. Lodge visited the ailing Roosevelt at his bedside, and the two worked on a broad list of reservations. This planning went on before Wilson went to Paris for the treaty negotiations. In the end Lodge succeeded in killing the treaty and Wilson's dream for the United States in the League.

Roosevelt did not witness the defeat of the treaty by the Senate, nor did he realize his hopes for 1920. By the time Roosevelt met with Lodge in December, he was seriously ill. Ever since suffering the injuries and disease during his Brazilian expedition, he had developed mysterious infections that assaulted him with high fevers. One of these bouts sent him to the hospital for several weeks in November and December, and with less than full health doctors allowed him to return home to Sagamore Hill for Christmas. There he continued to write and correspond with friends, but his old energy failed to return. On the evening of January 5, 1919, he complained of feeling ill and went to bed. Shortly after 4 a.m. the champion of the strenuous life died quietly in his sleep.

When Theodore Roosevelt left the presidency behind, he filled his life with adventure and action: hunting, exploration, politics, and a massive production of writing. It was a life of leadership, achievement, and excitement, in all of which he thrived. It was also a life of failed ambition and frustrated hopes. Although he never won public office again, he encouraged progressive reforms and inspired a generation to public service. That his party still looked to him in anticipation of the election of 1920 is evidence of his enduring appeal.

In his post-presidential career Roosevelt can also be read as a man driven to follow the spotlight. His ego suffered criticism badly, and his ambition at times pushed his otherwise generous personality to be unkind and even ruthless toward those he saw as competitors. Too often he counted among his enemies anyone who was not a committed supporter. Historians still struggle to understand and measure this side of his personality (Mowry 1958, 110–111). Was his break with Taft primarily motivated by political differences or by his unquenchable desire to return to the White House? Taft made the progressives unhappy, but his record was not nearly as conservative as Roosevelt claimed. Was his brutal treatment of Wilson in public and private writings entirely a matter of principle and honest opposition, or was it driven by self-interest and perhaps envy? Wilson was vulnerable on several counts, and his conduct of neutrality policy is still controversial. But the language and passion of Roosevelt's attacks strike the reader as needlessly extreme. Roosevelt enjoyed great powers of persuasion, and he doubtless convinced himself of the rightness of his actions and motives. He served his country tirelessly and well as an ex-president. But his style and intensity to some degree obscured the legacy of his life after the presidency.

LEGACY

In his performance as president Theodore Roosevelt left a legacy to his successors and to the nation that endures a century later. The elements of that gift include his example of confident leadership, his understanding of the uses of power, and his vision of the office of the presidency as a source of political and diplomatic initiative beyond the mere administration of the congressional will. With imagination and skill he invested the office with a mission to shape the national will and awaken the electorate to urgent national needs. In this recast role he embraced and promoted a progressive vision of government action for economic and social justice. Roosevelt made explicit his idea of the presidency for his successors, urging a combination of power and accountability. "I think it should be a very powerful office, and I think the President should be a very strong man who uses without hesitation every power that the position yields; but because of this fact I believe he should be sharply watched by the people and held to a strict accountability by them" (Lodge 1925, 2:304).

Woodrow Wilson was the first beneficiary of Roosevelt's notion of the presidency, despite the fact that he campaigned in 1912 still bearing a Jeffersonian wariness about big government. Once in office he successfully pursued progressive objectives by wielding effective presidential power and influence. He lobbied legislators on critical bills, broke precedent by addressing Congress in person, and in the end he expanded the powers and functions of the federal government dramatically.

For the rest of the century, successful presidents continued to draw on the Roosevelt legacy. The vision of Franklin Roosevelt in attacking the Great Depression owed much to the hopes "quickened in the progressive era" of his distant cousin (Kennedy 1999, 247–248). The younger Roosevelt understood well the uses of power and the public platform. Years later John Kennedy "fully shared Theodore Roosevelt's concept of the White House as a 'bully pulpit.'" Kennedy thought the admonition to "speak softly and carry a big stick" was sound advice. Echoing Roosevelt he said, "If we are strong, our strength will speak for itself. If we are weak, words will be of no help" (Sorensen 1965, 336, 515).

At the end of the century American presidents continued to acknowledge the debt to Roosevelt. George H. W. Bush spoke of Roosevelt often and described him as a "visionary" (Bush 1990, 2:1005). Bill Clinton also invoked his predecessor frequently and understood clearly the significance of the Roosevelt presidency. "At the end of the 19th century, the White House was weak; the Congress was at the mercy of special interests. Roosevelt's genius was to redefine the role of Government and the role of the President, to protect the public interest and to act as an accountable agent of change" (Clinton 2001, 2:2039).

The influence of only a small coterie of American presidents endures much beyond their years in office. Roosevelt's transformation of the presidency, his understanding of the emerging importance of the United States in world affairs, and his initiative in enlarging the role of the federal government in the life of the nation contributed much to what has been called the American Century. In the new century Americans and their leaders continue to draw on the legacy of Theodore Roosevelt.

BIBLIOGRAPHIC ESSAY

The following books focus on the post-presidential years. H. W. Brands, *T.R.: The Last Romantic* (New York: Basic Books, 1997), is a solid and reliable biography. For a comparison of careers and comment on the interaction between Wilson and Roosevelt, see John Milton Cooper Jr., *The Warrior and the Priest: Woodrow Wilson and Theodore Roosevelt* (Cambridge: Harvard University Press, 1983). Kathleen Dalton's *Theodore Roosevelt: A Strenuous Life* (New York: Alfred A. Knopf, 2002) is the most recent biography and pays special attention to the influence of women in Roosevelt's personal and political life. The post-presidential years receive careful treatment from John A. Gable, *The Bull Moose Years: Theodore Roosevelt and the Progressive Party* (New York: Kennikat Press, 1978), and Joseph Gardner, *Departing Glory: Theodore Roosevelt as ex-President* (New York: Charles Scribner's Sons, 1973). Aloysius Norton, *Theodore Roosevelt* (Boston: Twayne Publishers, 1980), summarizes and analyzes Roosevelt's work as a writer. For his own perspective on life and politics see *Theodore Roosevelt: An Autobiography,* vol. 20 of *The Works of Theodore Roosevelt,* national ed. (New York: Charles Scribner's Sons, 1926). William Roscoe Thayer, *Theodore Roosevelt: An Intimate Biography* (New York: Grosset and Dunlap, 1919), is an admiring narrative by an old friend and Harvard classmate.

Document 6.1   *African Game Trails*

As an avid hunter, Roosevelt had dreamed of stalking the big game of Africa. Months before leaving office, he laid plans for a safari that would wind through hundreds of miles of eastern Africa and bring him face to face with an array of exotic and dangerous game. Before he left he arranged for the serial publication of stories of the hunt, and these he later collected for the book African Game Trails. *The following is a sample of his work.*

At last we came in sight of the mighty game. The trail took a twist to one side, and there, thirty yards in front of us, we made out part of the gray and massive head of an elephant resting his tusks on the branches of a young tree. A couple of minutes passed before, by cautious scrutiny, we were able to tell whether the animal was a cow or a bull, and whether, if a bull, it carried heavy enough tusks. Then we saw that it was a big bull with good ivory. It turned its head in my direction and I saw its eye; and I bred a little to one side of the eye, at a spot which I thought would lead to the brain. I struck exactly where I aimed, but the head of an elephant is enormous and the brain small, and the bullet missed it. However, the shock momentarily stunned the beast. He stumbled forward, half falling, and as he recovered I bred with the second barrel, again aiming for the brain. This time the bullet sped true, and as I lowered the rifle from my shoulder, I saw the great lord of the forest come crashing to the ground.

But at that very instant, before there was a moment's time in which to reload, the thick bushes parted immediately on my left front, and through them surged the vast bulk of a charging bull elephant, the matted mass of tough creepers snapping like packthread before his rush. He was so close that he could have touched me with his trunk. I leaped to one side and dodged behind a tree trunk, opening the rifle, throwing out the empty shells, and slipping in two cartridges. Meanwhile Cuninghame [a professional safari manager accompanying Roosevelt] fired right and left, at the same time throwing himself into the bushes on the other side. Both his bullets went home, and the bull stopped short in his charge, wheeled, and immediately disappeared in the thick cover. We ran forward, but the forest had closed over his wake. We heard him trumpet shrilly, and then all sounds ceased.

The 'Ndorobo, who had quite properly disappeared when this second bull charged, now went forward, and soon returned with the report that he had fled at speed, but was evidently hard hit, as there was much blood on the spoor. If we had been only after ivory we should have followed him at once; but there was no telling how long a chase he might lead us; and as we desired to save the skin of the dead elephant entire, there was no time whatever to spare. It is a formidable task, occupying many days, to preserve an elephant for mounting in a museum, and if the skin is to be properly saved, it must be taken off without an hour's unnecessary delay.

So back we turned to where the dead tusker lay, and I felt proud indeed as I stood by the immense bulk of the slain monster and put my hand on the ivory. The tusks weighed a hundred and thirty pounds the pair. There was the usual scene of joyful excitement among the gun-bearers—who had behaved excellently—and among the wild bush people who had done the tracking for us; and, as Cuninghame had predicted, the old Masai Dorobo, from pure delight, proceeded to have hysterics on the body of the dead elephant. The scene was repeated when Heller and the porters appeared half an hour later. Then, chattering like monkeys, and as happy as possible, all porters, gun-bearers, and 'Ndorobo alike, began the work of skinning and cutting up the quarry, under the leadership and supervision of Heller and Cuninghame, and soon they were all splashed with blood from head to foot. One of the trackers took off his blanket and squatted stark naked inside the carcass the better to use his knife. Each laborer rewarded himself by cutting off strips of meat for his private store, and hung them in red festoons from the branches round about. There was no let-up in the work until it was stopped by darkness.

Our tents were pitched in a small open glade a hundred yards from the dead elephant. The night was clear, the stars shone brightly, and in the west the young moon hung just above the line of tall tree-tops. Fires were speedily kindled and the men sat around them, feasting and singing in a strange minor tone until late in the night. The flickering light left them at one moment in black obscurity, and the next brought into bold relief their sinewy crouching figures, their dark faces, gleaming eyes and flashing teeth. When they did sleep, two of the 'Ndorobo slept so close to the fire as to burn themselves; an accident to which they are prone, judging from the many scars of old burns on their legs. I toasted slices of elephant's heart on a pronged stick before the fire, and found it delicious; for I was hungry, and the night was cold. We talked of our success and exulted over it, and made our plans for the morrow; and then we turned in under our blankets for another night's sleep.

Source: Theodore Roosevelt, *The Works of Theodore Roosevelt*, national ed. (New York: Charles Scribner's Sons, 1926), 4:210–213.

Document 6.2   Romanes Lecture, Oxford University, June 7, 1910

During his triumphal tour of Europe in 1910 the universities of Cambridge and Oxford conferred honorary degrees on Roosevelt, and at Oxford he was invited to deliver the prestigious Romanes Lecture. He took the occasion to defend and to challenge great power imperialism, insisting on the need for just and humane rule.

. . . You belong to a nation which possesses the greatest empire upon which the sun has ever shone. I belong to a nation which is trying, on a scale hitherto unexampled, to work out the problems of government for, of, and by the people, while at the same time doing the international duty of a great power. But there are certain problems which both of us have to solve, and as to which our standards should be the same. The Englishman, the man of the British Isles, in his various homes across the seas, and the American, both at home and abroad, are brought into contact with utterly alien peoples, some with a civilization more ancient than our own, others still in, or having but recently arisen from, the barbarism which our people left behind ages ago. The problems that arise are of well-nigh inconceivable difficulty. They cannot be solved by the foolish sentimentality of stay-at-home people, with little patent recipes and those cut-and-dried theories of the political nursery which have such limited applicability amid the crash of elemental forces. Neither can they be solved by the raw brutality of the men who, whether at home or on the rough frontier of civilization, adopt might as the only standard of right in dealing with other men, and treat alien races only as subjects for exploitation.

No hard-and-fast rule can be drawn as applying to all alien races, because they differ from one another far more widely than some of them differ from us. But there are one or two rules which must not be forgotten. In the long run there can be no justification for one race managing or controlling another unless the management and control are exercised in the interest and for the benefit of that other race. This is what our peoples have in the main done, and must continue in the future in even greater degree to do, in India, Egypt and the Philippines alike. In the next place, as regards every race, everywhere, at home or abroad, we cannot afford to deviate from the great rule of righteousness which bids us treat each man on his worth as a man. He must not be sentimentally favored because he belongs to a given race; he must not be given immunity in wrong-doing or permitted to cumber the ground, or given other privileges which would be denied to the vicious and unfit among ourselves. On the other hand, where he acts in a way which would entitle him to respect and reward if he was one of our own stock, he is just as entitled to that respect and reward if he comes of another stock, even though that other stock produces a much smaller proportion of men of his type than does our own. This has nothing to do with social intermingling, with what is called social equality. It has to do merely with the question of doing to each man and each woman that elementary justice which will permit him or her to gain from life the reward which should always accompany thrift, sobriety, self-control, respect for the rights of others, and hard and intelligent work to a given end. To more than such just treatment no man is entitled, and less than such just treatment no man should receive.

The other type of duty is the international duty, the duty owed by one nation to another. I hold that the laws of morality which should govern individuals in their dealings one with the other are just as binding concerning nations in their dealings one with the other. The application of the moral law must be different in the two cases, because in one case it has, and in the other it has not, the sanction of a civil law with force behind it. The individual can depend for his rights upon the courts, which themselves derive their force from the police power of the state. The nation can depend upon nothing of the kind; and therefore, as things are now, it is the highest duty of the most advanced and freest peoples to keep themselves in such a state of readiness as to forbid to any barbarism or despotism the hope of arresting the progress of the world by striking down the nations that lead in that progress. It would be foolish indeed to pay heed to the unwise persons who desire disarmament to be begun by the very peoples who, of all others, should not be left helpless before any possible foe. But we must reprobate quite as strongly both the leaders and the peoples who practice, or encourage, or condone, aggression and iniquity by the strong at the expense of the weak. We should tolerate lawlessness and wickedness neither by the weak nor by the strong; and both weak and strong we should in return treat with scrupulous fairness. The foreign policy of a great and self-respecting country should be conducted on exactly the same plane of honor, for insistence upon one's own rights and of respect for the rights of others that marks the conduct of a brave and honorable man when dealing with his fellows. Permit me to support this statement out of my own experience. For nearly eight years I was the head of a great nation, and charged especially with the conduct of its foreign policy; and during those years I took no action with reference to any other people on the face of the earth that I would not have felt justified in taking as an individual in dealing with other individuals.

I believe that we of the great civilized nations of today have a right to feel that long careers of achievement lie before our several countries. To each of us is vouchsafed the honorable privilege of doing his part, however small, in that work. Let us strive hardily for success, even if by so doing we risk failure, spurning the poorer souls of small endeavor, who know neither failure nor success. Let us hope that our own blood shall continue in the land, that our children and children's children to endless generations shall arise to take our places, and play a mighty and dominant part in the world. But whether this be denied or granted by the years we shall not see, let at least the satisfaction be ours that we have carried onward the lighted torch in our own day and generation. If we do this, then, as our eyes close, and we go out into the darkness, and others' hands grasp the torch, at least we can say that our part has been borne well and valiantly.

Source: Theodore Roosevelt, *The Works of Theodore Roosevelt,* national ed. (New York: Charles Scribner's Sons, 1926), 12:57–60.

Document 6.3   "New Nationalism" Speech, August 31, 1910

Unable to resist the lure of politics and increasingly disenchanted with President William Howard Taft, Roosevelt launched a speaking tour of western states in the summer of 1910. His speech to a group of Republicans at Osawatomie, Kansas, shocked conservatives and delighted progressives by calling for an array of reforms and nothing less than a new role for the federal government in the life of the nation.

We come here today to commemorate one of the epoch-making events of the long struggle for the rights of man—the long struggle for the uplift of humanity. Our country—this great Republic—means nothing unless it means the triumph of a real democracy, the triumph of popular government, and, in the long run, of an economic system under which each man shall be guaranteed the opportunity to show the best that there is in him. That is why the history of America is now the central feature of the history of the world;

for the world has set its face hopefully toward our democracy; and, O my fellow citizens, each one of you carries on your shoulders not only the burden of doing well for the sake of your own country, but the burden of doing well and of seeing that this nation does well for the sake of mankind.

There have been two great crises in our country's history: first, when it was formed, and then, again, when it was perpetuated; and, in the second of these great crises—in the time of stress and strain which culminated in the Civil War, on the outcome of which depended the justification of what had been done earlier, you men of the Grand Army, you men who fought through the Civil War, not only did you justify your generation, not only did you render life worth living for our generation, but you justified the wisdom of Washington and Washington's colleagues. If this Republic had been founded by them only to be split asunder into fragments when the strain came, then the judgment of the world would have been that Washington's work was not worth doing. It was you who crowned Washington's work, as you carried to achievement the high purpose of Abraham Lincoln. . . .

Of that generation of men to whom we owe so much, the man to whom we owe most is, of course, Lincoln. Part of our debt to him is because he forecast our present struggle and saw the way out. He said: "I hold that while man exists it is his duty to improve not only his own condition, but to assist in ameliorating mankind."

And again: "Labor is prior to, and independent of, capital. Capital is only the fruit of labor, and could never have existed if labor had not first existed. Labor is the superior of capital, and deserves much the higher consideration."

If that remark was original with me, I should be even more strongly denounced as a Communist agitator than I shall be anyhow. It is Lincoln's. I am only quoting it; and that is one side; that is the side the capitalist should hear. Now, let the working man hear his side.

"Capital has its rights, which are as worthy of protection as any other rights. . . . Nor should this lead to a war upon the owners of property. Property is the fruit of labor; . . . property is desirable; is a positive good in the world."

And then comes a thoroughly Lincoln-like sentence:

"Let not him who is houseless pull down the house of another, but let him work diligently and build one for himself, thus by example assuring that his own shall be safe from violence when built."

It seems to me that, in these words, Lincoln took substantially the attitude that we ought to take; he showed the proper sense of proportion in his relative estimates of capital and labor, of human rights and property rights. Above all, in this speech, as in many others, he taught a lesson in wise kindliness and charity; an indispensable lesson to us of today. But this wise kindliness and charity never weakened his arm or numbed his heart. We cannot afford weakly to blind ourselves to the actual conflict which faces us to-day. The issue is joined, and we must fight or fail.

In every wise struggle for human betterment one of the main objects, and often the only object, has been to achieve in large measure equality of opportunity. In the struggle for this great end, nations rise from barbarism to civilization, and through it people press forward from one stage of enlightenment to the next. One of the chief factors in progress is the destruction of special privilege. The essence of any struggle for healthy liberty has always been, and must always be, to take from some one man or class of men the right to enjoy power, or wealth, or position, or immunity, which has not been earned by service to his or their fellows. That is what you fought for in the Civil War, and that is what we strive for now. . . .

I stand for the square deal. But when I say that I am for the square deal, I mean not merely that I stand for fair play under the present rules of the game, but that I stand for having those rules changed so as to work for a more substantial equality of opportunity and of reward for equally good service. . . . Now, this means that our government, national and State, must be freed from the sinister influence or control of special interests. . . .

There can be no effective control of corporations while their political activity remains. To put an end to it will be neither a short nor an easy task, but it can be done.

We must have complete and effective publicity of corporate affairs, so that people may know beyond peradventure whether the corporations obey the law and whether their management entitles them to the confidence of the public. It is necessary that laws should be passed to prohibit the use of corporate funds directly or indirectly for political purposes; it is still more necessary that such laws should be thoroughly enforced. Corporate expenditures for political purposes, and especially such expenditures by public-service corporations, have supplied one of the principal sources of corruption in our political affairs.

It has become entirely clear that we must have government supervision of the capitalization, not only of public-service corporations, including, particularly, railways, but of all corporations doing an interstate business. I do not wish to see the nation forced into the ownership of the railways if it can possibly be avoided, and the only alternative is thoroughgoing and effective regulation, which shall be based on a full knowledge of all the facts, including a physical valuation of property. This physical valuation is not needed, or, at least, is very rarely needed, for fixing rates; but it is needed as the basis of honest capitalization.

We have come to recognize that franchises should never be granted except for a limited time, and never without proper provision for compensation to the public. It is my personal belief that the same kind and degree of control and supervision which should be exercised over public-service corporations should be extended also to combinations which control necessaries of life, such as meat, oil, and coal, or which deal in them on an important scale. I have no doubt that the ordinary man who has control of them is much like ourselves. I have no doubt he would like to do well, but I want to have enough supervision to help him realize that desire to do well.

I believe that the officers, and, especially, the directors, of corporations should be held personally responsible when any corporation breaks the law.

Combinations in industry are the result of an imperative economic law which cannot be repealed by political legislation. The effort at prohibiting all combination has substantially failed. The way out lies, not in attempting to prevent such combinations, but in completely controlling them in the interest of the public welfare. For that purpose the Federal Bureau of Corporations is an agency of first importance. Its powers, and, therefore, its efficiency, as well as that of the Interstate Commerce Commission, should be largely increased. We have a right to expect from the Bureau of Corporations and from the Interstate Commerce Commission a very high grade of public service. We should be as sure of the proper conduct of the interstate railways and the proper management of interstate business as we are now sure of the conduct and management of the national banks, and we should have as effective supervision in one case as in the other. The Hepburn Act, and the amendment to the act in the shape in which it finally passed Congress at the last session, represent a long step in advance, and we must go yet further. . . .

Of conservation I shall speak more at length elsewhere. Conservation means development as much as it does protection. I recognize the right and duty of this generation to develop and use the natural resources of our land; but I do not recognize the right to waste them, or to rob, by wasteful use, the generations that come after us. I ask nothing of the nation except that it so behave as each farmer here behaves with reference to his own children. That farmer is a poor creature who skins the land and leaves it worthless to his children. The farmer is a good farmer who, having enabled the land to support himself and to provide for the education of his children leaves it to them a little better than he found it himself. I believe the same thing of a nation.

Moreover, I believe that the natural resources must be used for the benefit of all our people, and not monopolized for the benefit of the few, and here again is another case in which I am accused of taking a revolutionary attitude. People forget now that one hundred years ago there were public men of good character who advocated the nation selling its public lands in great quantities, so that the nation could get the most money out of it, and giving it to the men who could cultivate it for their own uses. We took the proper democratic ground that the land should be granted in small sections to the men who were actually to till it and live on it. Now, with the water-power, with the forests, with the mines, we are brought face to face with the fact that there are many people who will go with us in conserving the resources only if they are to be allowed to exploit them for their benefit. That is one of the fundamental reasons why the special interest should be driven out of politics. Of all the questions which can come before this nation, short of the actual preservation of its existence in a great war, there is none which compares in importance with the great central task of leaving this land even a better land for our descendants than it is for us, and training them into a better race to inhabit the land and pass it on. Conservation is a great moral issue for it involves the patriotic duty of insuring the safety and continuance of the nation. Let me add that the health and vitality of our people are at least as well worth conserving as their forests, waters, lands, and minerals, and in this great work the national government must bear a most important part. . . .

National efficiency has many factors. It is a necessary result of the principle of conservation widely applied. In the end it will determine our failure or success as a nation. National efficiency has to do, not only with natural resources and with men, but is equally concerned with institutions. The State must be made efficient for the work which concerns only the people of the State; and the nation for that which concerns all the people. There must remain no neutral ground to serve as a refuge for lawbreakers, and especially for lawbreakers of great wealth, who can hire the vulpine legal cunning which will teach them how to avoid both jurisdictions. It is a misfortune when the national legislature fails to do its duty in providing a national remedy, so that the only national activity is the purely negative activity of the judiciary in forbidding the State to exercise power in the premises.

I do not ask for over-centralization; but I do ask that we work in a spirit of broad and far-reaching nationalism when we work for what concerns our people as a whole. We are all Americans. Our common interests are as broad as the continent. I speak to you here in Kansas exactly as I would speak in New York or Georgia, for the most vital problems are those which affect us all alike. The national government belongs to the whole American people, and where the whole American people are interested, that interest can be guarded effectively only by the national government. The betterment which we seek must be accomplished, I believe, mainly through the national government.

The American people are right in demanding that New Nationalism, without which we cannot hope to deal with new problems. The New Nationalism puts the national need before sectional or personal advantage. It is impatient of the utter confusion that results from local legislatures attempting to treat national issues as local issues. It is still more impatient of the impotence which springs from over-division of governmental powers, the impotence which makes it possible for local selfishness or for legal cunning, hired by wealthy special interests, to bring national activities to a deadlock. This New Nationalism regards the executive power as the steward of the public welfare. It demands of the judiciary that it shall be interested primarily in human welfare rather than in property, just as it demands that the representative body shall represent all the people rather than any one class or section of the people.

Source: Theodore Roosevelt, *The Works of Theodore Roosevelt,* national ed. (New York: Charles Scribner's Sons, 1926), 17:5–20.

Document 6.4   Governors' Letter Urging Roosevelt Candidacy, February 10, 1912

Intent on countering the influence of President William Howard Taft's supporters on the nominating process, Roosevelt hoped to create the impression that the party faithful were demanding that he run in 1912. By pre-arrangement with a group of Republican governors anxious to see him nominated, this letter was sent to Roosevelt to cast his candidacy in 1912 as a response to a groundswell of demand.

To Theodore Roosevelt

We, the undersigned Republican Governors, assembled for the purpose of considering what will best insure the continuation of the Republican Party as a useful agency of good government, declare it our belief, after a careful investigation of the facts, that a large majority of the Republican voters of the country favor your nomination, and a large majority of the people favor your election as the next President of the United States.

We believe that your candidacy will insure success in the next campaign. We believe that you represent as no other man represents those principles and policies upon which we must appeal for a majority of the votes of the American people, and which, in our opinion, are necessary for the happiness and prosperity of the country.

We believe that, in view of this public demand, you should soon declare whether, if the nomination for the presidency comes to you unsolicited and unsought, you will accept it.

In submitting this request we are not considering your personal interests. We do not regard it as proper to consider either the interests or the preference of any man as regards the nomination for the presidency. We are expressing our sincere belief and best judgment as to what is demanded of you in the interests of the people as a whole, and we feel that you would be unresponsive to a plain public duty if you should decline to accept the nomination coming as the voluntary expression of the wishes of a majority of the Republican voters of the United States through the action of their delegates in the next National Convention.

Yours truly,
William E. Glasscock, West Virginia.
Chester H. Aldrich, Nebraska.

Robert P. Bass, New Hampshire.

Joseph M. Cary, Wyoming.

Chase S. Osborn, Michigan.

W. R. Stubbs, Kansas.

Herbert S. Hadley, Missouri.

Source: Theodore Roosevelt, *The Works of Theodore Roosevelt,* national ed. (New York: Charles Scribner's Sons, 1926), 17:149–150.

Document 6.5   The Reply to the Republican Governors, February 24, 1912

Having arranged for the governors' appeal to him, Roosevelt was ready with his response, agreeing to bear the burden in the "interests of the people as a whole."

Gentlemen:

I deeply appreciate your letter, and I realize to the full the heavy responsibility it puts upon me, expressing as it does the carefully considered convictions of the men elected by popular vote to stand as the heads of government in their several States.

I absolutely agree with you that this matter is not one to be decided with any reference to the personal preferences or interests of any man, but purely from the standpoint of the interests of the people as a whole.

I will accept the nomination for President if it is tendered to me, and I will adhere to this decision until the convention has expressed its preference.

One of the chief principles for which I have stood, and for which I now stand, and which I have always endeavored and always shall endeavor to reduce to action, is the genuine rule of the people, and therefore I hope that so far as possible the people may be given the chance, through direct primaries, to express their preference as to who shall be the nominee of the Republican Presidential Convention.

Very truly yours,

Theodore Roosevelt.

Source: Theodore Roosevelt, *The Works of Theodore Roosevelt,* national ed. (New York: Charles Scribner's Sons, 1926), 17:149–150.

Document 6.6   Speech to the Ohio Constitutional Convention, February 21, 1912

Roosevelt's criticism of the Taft administration and the progressive reforms he broadcast rattled conservatives and even some of his friends, who feared a party split. Nothing disturbed conservatives more than his attack on the courts as excessively solicitous of property rights. At Columbus he went as far as advocating the removal of judges from office by popular vote.

. . . We stand for the rights of property, but we stand even more for the rights of man.

We will protect the rights of the wealthy man, but we maintain that he holds his wealth subject to the general right of the community to regulate its business use as the public welfare requires. . . .

Moreover, shape your constitutional action so that the people will be able through their legislative bodies, or, failing that, by direct popular vote, to provide workmen's compensation acts to regulate the hours of labor for children and for women, to provide for their safety while at work, and to prevent overwork or work under unhygienic or unsafe conditions. See to it that no restrictions are placed upon legislative powers that will prevent the enactment of laws under which your people can promote the general welfare, the common good. Thus only will the "general welfare" clause of our Constitution become a vital force for progress, instead of remaining a mere phrase. This also applies to the police powers of the government. Make it perfectly clear that on every point of this kind it is your intention that the people shall decide for themselves how far the laws to achieve their purposes shall go, and that their decision shall be binding upon every citizen in the State, official or non-official, unless, of course, the Supreme Court of the nation in any given case decides otherwise. . . .

There remains the question of the recall of judges. . . .

I do not believe in adopting the recall save as a last resort, when it has become clearly evident that no other course will achieve the desired result.

But either the recall will have to be adopted or else it will have to be made much easier than it now is to get rid, not merely of a bad judge, but of a judge who, however virtuous, has grown so out of touch with social needs and facts that he is unfit longer to render good service on the bench. . . .

There are sound reasons for being cautious about the recall of a good judge who has rendered an unwise and improper decision. Every public servant, no matter how valuable—and not omitting Washington or Lincoln or Marshall—at times makes mistakes. Therefore we should be cautious about recalling the judge, and we shall be cautious about interfering in any way with the judge in decisions which he makes in the ordinary course as between individuals. But when a judge decides a constitutional question, when he decides what the people as a whole can or cannot do, the people should have the right to recall that decision if they think it wrong. We should hold the judiciary in all respect; but it is both absurd and degrading to make a fetish of a judge or of anyone else. . . .

Again and again in the past justice has been scandalously obstructed by State courts declaring State laws in conflict with the Federal Constitution, although the Supreme Court of the nation had never so decided or had even decided in a contrary sense.

When the supreme court of the State declares a given statute unconstitutional, because in conflict with the State or the National Constitution, its opinion should be subject to revision by the people themselves. Such an opinion ought always to be treated with great respect by the people, and unquestionably in the majority of cases would be accepted and followed by them. But actual experience has shown the vital need of the people reserving to themselves the right to pass upon such opinion. If any considerable number of the people feel that the decision is in defiance of justice, they should be given the right by petition to bring before the voters at some subsequent election, special or otherwise, as might be decided, and after the fullest opportunity for deliberation and debate, the question whether or not the judges' interpretation of the Constitution is to be sustained. If it is sustained, well and good. If not, then the popular verdict is to be accepted as final, the decision is to be treated as reversed, and the construction of the Constitution definitely decided—subject only to action by the Supreme Court of the United States. . . .

Source: Theodore Roosevelt, *The Works of Theodore Roosevelt,* national ed. (New York: Charles Scribner's Sons, 1926), 17:119–140.

Document 6.7   Acceptance Speech at the National Convention of the Progressive Party, August 6, 1912

Roosevelt justified his bolt from the Republican Party in 1912 by charging fraud in the nominating process when the regulars chose William Howard

Taft. When he accepted the nomination of the Bull Moose Progressive Party, he made an impassioned "Confession of Faith" and laid out a program of reform, much of which remained on the liberal agenda for years to come.

. . . Neither the Republican nor the Democratic platform contains the slightest promise of approaching the great problems of to-day either with understanding or good faith; and yet never was there greater need in this nation than now of understanding and of action taken in good faith, on the part of the men and the organizations shaping our governmental policy. Moreover, our needs are such that there should be coherent action among those responsible for the conduct of national affairs and those responsible for the conduct of State affairs; because our aim should be the same in both State and nation; that is, to use the government as an efficient agency for the practical betterment of social and economic conditions throughout this land. There are other important things to be done, but this is the most important thing. It is preposterous to leave such a movement in the hands of men who have broken their promises as have the present heads of the Republican organization (not of the Republican voters, for they in no shape represent the rank and file of the Republican voters). These men by their deeds give the lie to their words. There is no health in them, and they cannot be trusted. But the Democratic party is just as little to be trusted. . . .

If this country is really to go forward along the path of social and economic justice, there must be a new party of nation-wide and non-sectional principles, a party where the titular national chiefs and the real State leaders shall be in genuine accord, a party in whose counsels the people shall be supreme, a party that shall represent in the nation and the several States alike the same cause, the cause of human rights and of governmental efficiency. At present both the old parties are controlled by professional politicians in the interests of the privileged classes, and apparently each has set up as its ideal of business and political development a government by financial despotism tempered by make-believe political assassination. Democrat and Republican alike, they represent government of the needy many by professional politicians in the interests of the rich life. This is class government, and class government of a peculiarly unwholesome kind.

It seems to me, therefore, that the time is ripe, and over-ripe, for a genuine Progressive movement, nation-wide and justice-loving, sprung from and responsible to the people themselves, and sundered by a great gulf from both of the old party organizations, while representing all that is best in the hopes, beliefs, and aspirations of the plain people who make up the immense majority of the rank and file of both the old parties. . . .

In the last twenty years an increasing percentage of our people have come to depend on industry for their livelihood, so that to-day the wage-workers in industry rank in importance side by side with the tillers of the soil. As a people we cannot afford to let any group of citizens or any individual citizen live or labor under conditions which are injurious to the common welfare. Industry, therefore, must submit to such public regulation as will make it a means of life and health, not of death or inefficiency. We must protect the crushable elements at the base of our present industrial structure.

The first charge on the industrial statesmanship of the day is to prevent human waste. The dead weight of orphanage and depleted craftsmanship, of crippled workers and workers suffering from trade diseases, of casual labor, of insecure old age, and of household depletion due to industrial conditions are, like our depleted soils, our gashed mountainsides and flooded river-bottoms, so many strains upon the national structure, draining the reserve strength of all industries and showing beyond all peradventure the public element and public concern in industrial health. . . .

We hold that under no industrial order, in no commonwealth, in no trade, and in no establishment should industry be carried on under conditions inimical to the social welfare. The abnormal, ruthless, spendthrift industry of establishment tends to drag down all to the level of the least considerate.

Here the sovereign responsibility of the people as a whole should be placed beyond all quibble and dispute. The public needs have been well summarized as follows:

1. We hold that the public has a right to complete knowledge of the facts of work.

2. On the basis of these facts and with the recent discoveries of physicians and neurologists, engineers and economists, the public can formulate minimum occupational standards below which, demonstrably, work can be prosecuted only at a human deficit.

3. In the third place, we hold that all industrial conditions which fall below such standards should come within the scope of governmental action and control in the same way that subnormal sanitary conditions are subject to public regulation and for the same reason—because they threaten the general welfare.

To the first end, we hold that the constituted authorities should be empowered to require all employers to file with them for public purposes such wage scales and other data as the public element in industry demands. The movement for honest weights and measures has its counterpart in industry. All tallies, scales, and check systems should be open to public inspection and inspection of committees of the workers concerned. All deaths, injuries, and diseases due to industrial operation should be reported to public authorities.

To the second end, we hold that minimum wage commissions should be established in the nation and in each State to inquire into wages paid in various industries and to determine the standard which the public ought to sanction as a minimum; and we believe that, as a present installment of what we hope for in the future, there should be at once established in the nation and its several States minimum standards for the wages of women, taking the present Massachusetts law as a basis from which to start and on which to improve.

We pledge the Federal Government to an investigation of industries along the lines pursued by the Bureau of Mines with the view to establishing standards of sanitation and safety; we call for the standardization of mine and factory inspection by interstate agreement or the establishment of a Federal standard. We stand for the passage of legislation in the nation and in all States providing standards of compensation for industrial accidents and death, and for diseases clearly due to the nature of conditions of industry, and we stand for the adoption by law of a fair standard of compensation for casualties resulting fatally which shall clearly fix the minimum compensation in all cases.

In the third place, certain industrial conditions fall clearly below the levels which the public to-day sanction.

We stand for a living wage. Wages are subnormal if they fail to provide a living for those who devote their time and energy to industrial occupations. The monetary equivalent of a living wage varies according to local conditions, but must include enough to secure the elements of a normal standard of living—a standard high enough to make morality possible, to provide for education and recreation, to care for immature members of the family, to maintain the family during periods of sickness, and to permit of reasonable saving for old age.

Hours are excessive if they fail to afford the worker sufficient time to recuperate and return to his work thoroughly refreshed. We hold that the night labor of women and children is abnormal and should be prohibited; we hold that the employment of women over forty-eight hours per week is abnormal and should be prohibited. We hold that the seven-day working week is abnormal, and we hold that one day of rest in seven should be provided by law. We hold that the continuous industries, operating twenty-four hours out of twenty-four, are abnormal, and where, because of public necessity or of technical reasons (such as molten metal), the twenty-four hours must be divided into two shifts of twelve hours or three shifts of eight, they should by law be divided into three of eight.

Safety conditions are abnormal when, through unguarded machinery, poisons, electrical voltage, or otherwise, the workers are subjected to unnecessary hazards of life and limb; and all such occupations should come under governmental regulation and control.

Home life is abnormal when tenement manufacture is carried on in the household. It is a serious menace to health, education, and childhood, and should therefore be entirely prohibited. Temporary construction camps are abnormal homes and should be subjected to governmental sanitary regulation.

The premature employment of children is abnormal and should be prohibited; so also the employment of women in manufacturing, commerce, or other trades where work compels standing constantly; and also any employment of women in such trades for a period of at least eight weeks at time of childbirth.

Our aim should be to secure conditions which will tend everywhere toward regular industry, and will do away with the necessity for rush periods, followed by out-of-work seasons, which put so severe a strain on wage-workers.

It is abnormal for any industry to throw back upon the community the human wreckage due to its wear and tear, and the hazards of sickness, accident, invalidism, involuntary unemployment, and old age should be provided for through insurance. This should be made a charge in whole or in part upon the industries, the employer, the employee, and perhaps the people at large to contribute severally in some degree. Wherever such standards are not met by given establishments, by given industries, are unprovided for by a legislature, or are balked by unenlightened courts, the workers are in jeopardy, the progressive employer is penalized, and the community pays a heavy cost in lessened efficiency and in misery. What Germany has done in the way of old-age pensions or insurance should be studied by us, and the system adapted to our uses, with whatever modifications are rendered necessary by our different ways of life and habits of thought.

Working women have the same need to combine for protection that working men have; the ballot is as necessary for one class as for the other; we do not believe that with the two sexes there is identity of function; but we do believe that there should be equality of right; and therefore we favor woman suffrage. Surely, if women could vote, they would strengthen the hands of those who are endeavoring to deal in efficient fashion with evils such as the white-slave traffic; evils which can in part be dealt with nationally, but which in large part can be reached only by determined local action, such as insisting on the wide-spread publication of the names of the owners, the landlords, of houses used for immoral purposes. . . .

We Progressives stand for the rights of the people. When these rights can best be secured by insistence upon States' rights, then we are for States' rights; when they can best be secured by insistence upon national rights, then we are for national rights. Interstate commerce can be effectively controlled only by the nation. The States cannot control it under the Constitution, and to amend the Constitution by giving them control of it would amount to a dissolution of the government. The worst of the big trusts have always endeavored to keep alive the feeling in favor of having the States themselves, and not the nation, attempt to do this work, because they know that in the long run such effort would be ineffective. . . .

I believe in a protective tariff, but I believe in it as a principle, approached from the standpoint of the interests of the whole people, and not as a bundle of preferences to be given to favored individuals. In my opinion, the American people favor the principle of a protective tariff, but they desire such a tariff to be established primarily in the interests of the wage-worker and the consumer. . . . To accomplish this the tariff to be levied should as nearly as is scientifically possible approximate the differential between the cost of production at home and abroad. This differential is chiefly, if not wholly, in labor cost. No duty should be permitted to stand as regards any industry unless the workers receive their full share of the benefits of that duty. In other words, there is no warrant for protection unless a legitimate share of the benefits gets into the pay-envelope of the wage-worker. . . .

Now, friends, this is my confession of faith. I have made it rather long because I wish you to know what my deepest convictions are on the great questions of today, so that if you choose to make me your standard-bearer in the fight you shall make your choice understanding exactly how I feel— and if, after hearing me, you think you ought to choose some one else, I shall loyally abide by your choice. . . .

Surely there never was a fight better worth making than the one in which we are engaged. It little matters what befalls anyone of us who for the time being stands in the forefront of the battle. I hope we shall win, and I believe that if we can wake the people to what the fight really means we shall win. But, win or lose, we shall not falter. Whatever fate may at the moment overtake any of us, the movement itself will not stop. Our cause is based on the eternal principle of righteousness; and even though we who now lead may for the time fail, in the end the cause itself shall triumph. Six weeks ago, here in Chicago, I spoke to the honest representatives of a convention which was not dominated by honest men; a convention wherein sat, alas! a majority of men who, with sneering indifference to every principle of right, so acted as to bring to a shameful end a party which had been founded over a half-century ago by men in whose souls burned the fire of lofty endeavor. Now to you men, who, in your turn, have come together to spend and be spent in the endless crusade against wrong, to you who face the future resolute and confident, to you who strive in a spirit of brotherhood for the betterment of our nation, to you who gird yourselves for this great new fight in the never-ending warfare for the good of humankind, I say in closing what in that speech I said in closing: We stand at Armageddon, and we battle for the Lord.

Source: Theodore Roosevelt, *The Works of Theodore Roosevelt,* national ed. (New York: Charles Scribner's Sons, 1926), 17:254–299.

Document 6.8   Inaugural as President of the American Historical Association, December 27, 1912

Roosevelt was well respected for his historical writing, especially for his naval history of the War of 1812. In 1912 he was elected to a term as president of the American Historical Association and delivered this presidential address about the task of the historian.

. . . Many learned people seem to feel that the quality of readableness in a book is one which warrants suspicion. Indeed, not a few learned people seem to feel that the fact that a book is interesting is proof that it is shallow. This is particularly apt to be the attitude of scientific men. Very few great scientists have written interestingly, and these few have usually felt apologetic about it. Yet sooner or later the time will come when the mighty sweep of modern scientific discovery will be placed, by scientific men with the gift of expression, at the service of intelligent and cultivated laymen. Such service will be inestimable. Another writer of "Canterbury Tales," another singer of "Paradise Lost," could not add more to the sum of literary achievement than the man who may picture to us the phases of the age-long history of life on this globe, or make vivid before our eyes the tremendous march of the worlds through space. . . .

Do not misunderstand me. In the field of historical research an immense amount can be done by men who have no literary power whatever. Moreover, the most painstaking and laborious research, covering long periods of years, is necessary in order to accumulate the material for any history worth writing at all. There are important by-paths of history, moreover, which hardly admit of treatment that would make them of interest to any but specialists. All this I fully admit. In particular I pay high honor to the patient and truthful investigator. He does an indispensable work. My claim is merely that such work should not exclude the work of the great master who can use the materials gathered, who has the gift of vision, the quality of the seer, the power himself to see what has happened and to make what he has seen clear to the vision of others. My only protest is against those who believe that the extension of the activities of the most competent mason and most energetic contractor will supply the lack of great architects. If, as in the Middle Ages, the journeymen builders are themselves artists, why this is the best possible solution of the problem. But if they are not artists, then their work, however much it represents of praiseworthy industry, and of positive usefulness, does not take the place of the work of a great artist. . . .

This does not mean that good history can be unscientific. So far from ignoring science, the great historian of the future can do nothing unless he is steeped in science. He can never equal what has been done by the great historians of the past unless he writes not merely with full knowledge, but with an intensely vivid consciousness, of all that of which they were necessarily ignorant. He must accept what we now know to be man's place in nature. He must realize that man has been on this earth for a period of such incalculable length that, from the standpoint of the student of his development through time, what our ancestors used to call "antiquity" is almost indistinguishable from the present day. If our conception of history takes in the beast-like man whose sole tool and weapon was the stone fist-hatchet, and his advanced successors, the man who etched on bone pictures of the mammoth, the reindeer, and the wild horse, in what is now France, and the man who painted pictures of bison in the burial caves of what is now Spain; if we also conceive in their true position our "contemporaneous ancestors," the savages who are now no more advanced than the cave-dwellers of a hundred thousand or two hundred thousand years back, then we shall accept Thothmes and Caesar, Alfred and Washington, Timoleon and Lincoln, Homer and Shakespeare, Pythagoras and Emerson, as all nearly contemporaneous in time and in culture.

The great historian of the future will have easy access to innumerable facts patiently gathered by tens of thousands of investigators, whereas the great historian of the past had very few facts, and often had to gather most of these himself. The great historian of the future can not be excused if he fails to draw on the vast storehouses of knowledge that have been accumulated, if he fails to profit by the wisdom and work of other men, which are now the common property of all intelligent men. He must use the instruments which the historians of the past did not have ready to hand. Yet even with these instruments he can not do as good work as the best of the elder historians unless he has vision and imagination, the power to grasp what is essential and to reject the infinitely more numerous nonessentials, the power to embody ghosts, to put flesh and blood on dry bones, to make dead men living before our eyes. In short, he must have the power to take the science of history and turn it into literature.

Source: Theodore Roosevelt, *The Works of Theodore Roosevelt,* national ed. (New York: Charles Scribner's Sons, 1926), 12:3–11.

Document 6.9   Exploring in Brazil

After his election defeat in 1912 a dejected Roosevelt escaped to a new adventure. He was past fifty now, and joining an expedition to Brazil, he said, was his last chance to be a boy again. The trip was dangerous and damaged his health but, in the end, was a proud success. He recorded the progress and perils of the trek and published his account in periodical and book form. Here he recounts some of the hardships his party endured.

. . . The men were growing constantly weaker under the endless strain of exhausting labor. Kermit [TR's son] was having an attack of fever, and Lyra [a Brazilian army lieutenant] and [naturalist George K.] Cherrie had touches of dysentery, but all three continued to work. While in the water trying to help with an upset canoe I had by my own clumsiness bruised my leg against a boulder; and the resulting inflammation was somewhat bothersome. I now had a sharp attack of fever, but thanks to the excellent care of the doctor, was over it in about forty-eight hours; but Kermit's fever grew worse and he too was unable to work for a day or two. We could walk over the portages, however. A good doctor is an absolute necessity on an exploring expedition in such a country as that we were in, under penalty of a frightful mortality among the members; and the necessary risks and hazards are so great, the chances of disaster so large, that there is no warrant for increasing them by the failure to take all feasible precautions.

The next day we made another long portage round some rapids, and camped at night still in the hot, wet, sunless atmosphere of the gorge. The following day, April 6, we portaged past another set of rapids, which proved to be the last of the rapids of the chasm. For some kilometers we kept passing hills, and feared lest at any moment we might again find ourselves fronting another mountain gorge; with, in such case, further days of grinding and perilous labor ahead of us, while our men were disheartened, weak, and sick. Most of them had already begun to have fever. Their condition was inevitable after over a month's uninterrupted work of the hardest kind in getting through the long series of rapids we had just passed; and a long further delay, accompanied by wearing labor, would have almost certainly meant that the weakest among our party would have begun to die. There were already two of the camaradas who were too weak to help the others, their condition being such as to cause us serious concern.

However, the hills gradually sank into a level plain, and the river carried us through it at a rate that enabled us during the remainder of the day to reel off thirty-six kilometers, a record that for the first time held out promise. Twice tapirs swam the river while we passed, but not near my canoe. However, the previous evening Cherrie had killed two monkeys and Kermit one, and we all had a few mouthfuls of fresh meat; we had already had a good soup made out of a turtle Kermit had caught. We had to portage by one short set of rapids, the unloaded canoes being brought down without difficulty. At last, at four in the afternoon, we came to the mouth of a big river running in from the right. We thought it was probably the

Ananis, but, of course, could not be certain. It was less in volume than the one we had descended, but nearly as broad; its breadth at this point being ninety-five yards as against one hundred and twenty for the larger river. There were rapids ahead, immediately after the junction, which took place in latitude ten degrees fifty-eight minutes south. We had come two hundred and sixteen kilometers all told, and were nearly north of where we had started. We camped on the point of land between the two rivers. It was extraordinary to realize that here about the eleventh degree we were on such a big river, utterly unknown to the cartographers and not indicated by even a hint on any map. We named this big tributary Rio Cardozo, after a gallant officer of the commission who had died of beriberi just as our expedition began. We spent a day at this spot, determining our exact position by the sun, and afterward by the stars, and sending on two men to explore the rapids in advance. They returned with the news that there were big cataracts in them, and that they would form an obstacle to our progress. They had also caught a huge siluroid fish, which furnished an excellent meal for everybody in camp. This evening at sunset the view across the broad river, from our camp where the two rivers joined, was very lovely; and for the first time we had an open space in front of and above us, so that after nightfall the stars, and the great waxing moon, were glorious overhead, and against the rocks in midstream the broken water gleamed like tossing silver. . . .

Accordingly, it was a rather sorry crew that embarked the following morning, April 15. But it turned out a red-letter day. The day before, we had come across cuttings, a year old, which were probably but not certainly made by pioneer rubber men. But on this day—during which we made twenty-five kilometers—after running two hours and a half we found on the left bank a board on a post with the initials J. A., to show the farthest-up point which a rubber man had reached and claimed as his own. . . .

In mid-afternoon we stopped at another clean, cool, picturesque house of palm thatch. The inhabitants all fled at our approach, fearing an Indian raid; for they were absolutely unprepared to have anyone come from the unknown regions upstream. They returned and were most hospitable and communicative; and we spent the night there. . . . We had come over three hundred kilometers in forty-eight days, over absolutely unknown ground; we had seen no human being, although we had twice heard Indians. Six weeks had been spent in steadily slogging our way down through the interminable series of rapids. It was astonishing before, when we were on a river of about the size of the upper Rhine or Elbe, to realize that no geographer had any idea of its existence. But, after all, no civilized man of any grade had ever been on it. Here, however, was a river with people dwelling along the banks, some of whom had lived in the neighborhood for eight or ten years; and yet on no standard map was there a hint of the river's existence. . . .

We had passed the period when there was a chance of peril, of disaster, to the whole expedition. There might be risk ahead to individuals, and some difficulties and annoyances for all of us; but there was no longer the least likelihood of any disaster to the expedition as a whole. We now no longer had to face continual anxiety, the need of constant economy with food, the duty of labor with no end in sight, and bitter uncertainty as to the future. . . .

Source: Theodore Roosevelt, *The Works of Theodore Roosevelt,* national ed. (New York: Charles Scribner's Sons, 1926), 5:253–261.

Document 6.10　　Essay on the Sinking of the *Lusitania,* May 9, 1915

Roosevelt wrote this essay, "Murder on the High Seas," for Metropolitan *magazine, blasting Germany for the* Lusitania *sinking and criticizing President Woodrow Wilson for what he thought was an inadequate response. His hostility to Germany and to Wilson grew as the war continued.*

The German submarines have established no effective blockade of the British and French coast lines. They have endeavored to prevent the access of French, British, *and neutral* ships to Britain and France by attacks upon them which defy every principle of international law as laid down in innumerable existing treaties, including The Hague conventions. Many of these attacks have represented pure piracy; and not a few of them have been accompanied by murder on an extended scale. In the case of the *Lusitania* the scale was so vast that the murder became wholesale. . . .

The day after the tragedy the newspapers reported in one column that in Queenstown there lay by the score the bodies of women and children, some of the dead women still clasping the bodies of the little children they held in their arms when death overwhelmed them. In another column they reported the glee expressed by the Berlin journals at this "great victory of German naval policy." It was a victory over the defenseless and the unoffending, and its signs and trophies were the bodies of the murdered women and children.

Our treaties with Prussia in 1785, 1799, and 1828, still in force in this regard, provide that if one of the contracting parties should be at war with any other power the free intercourse and commerce of the subjects or citizens of the party remaining neutral with the belligerent powers shall not be interrupted. Germany has treated this treaty as she has treated other scraps of paper.

But the offense goes far deeper than this. The action of the German submarines in the cases cited can be justified only by a plea which would likewise justify the wholesale poisoning of wells in the path of a hostile army, or the shipping of infected rags into the cities of a hostile country; a plea which would justify the torture of prisoners and the reduction of captured women to the slavery of concubinage. Those who advance such a plea will accept but one counter-plea—strength, the strength and courage of the just man armed.

When those who guide the military policy of a state hold up to the soldiers of their army the Huns, and the terror once caused by the Huns, for their imitation, they thereby render themselves responsible for any Hunnish deed which may follow. The destruction of cities like Louvain and Dinant, the scientific vivisection of Belgium as a warning to other nations, the hideous wrong-doing to civilians, men, women, and children in Belgium and northern France, in order thereby to terrorize the civilian population—all these deeds, and those like them, done on the land, have now been paralleled by what has happened on the sea.

In the teeth of these things, we earn as a nation measureless scorn and contempt if we follow the lead of those who exalt peace above righteousness, if we heed the voices of those feeble folk who bleat to high heaven that there is peace when there is no peace. For many months our government has preserved between right and wrong a neutrality which would have excited the emulous admiration of Pontius Pilate—the arch-typical neutral of all time. We have urged as a justification for failing to do our duty in Mexico that to do so would benefit American dollars. Are we now to change faces and advance the supreme interest of American dollars as a justification for continuance in the refusal to do the duty imposed on us in connection with the World War?

Unless we act with immediate decision and vigor we shall have failed in the duty demanded by humanity at large, and demanded even more clearly by the self-respect of the American Republic.

We did not act with immediate decision and vigor. We did not act at all. The President immediately after the sinking made a speech in which occurred his sentence about our "being too proud to fight." . . .

I see it stated in the despatches from Washington that Germany now offers to stop the practice of murder on the high seas, committed in violation of the neutral rights she is pledged to preserve, if we will now abandon further neutral rights, which by her treaty she has solemnly pledged herself to see that we exercise without molestation.

Such a proposal is not even entitled to an answer. The manufacture and shipment of arms and ammunition to any belligerent is moral or immoral, according to the use to which the arms and munitions are to be put. If they are to be used to prevent the redress of hideous wrongs inflicted on Belgium then it is immoral to ship them. If they are to be used for the redress of those wrongs and the restoration of Belgium to her deeply wronged and unoffending people, then it is eminently moral to send them.

Without twenty-four hours' delay this country should and could take effective action. It should take possession of all the interned German ships, including the German war-ships, and hold them as a guaranty that ample satisfaction shall be given us. Furthermore it should declare that in view of Germany's murderous offenses against the rights of neutrals all commerce with Germany shall be forthwith forbidden and all commerce of every kind permitted and encouraged with France, England, Russia, and the rest of the civilized world.

I do not believe that the firm assertion of our rights means war, but, in any event, it is well to remember there are things worse than war.

Let us as a nation understand that peace is worth having only when it is the handmaiden of international righteousness and of national self-respect.

Source: Theodore Roosevelt, *The Works of Theodore Roosevelt,* national ed. (New York: Charles Scribner's Sons, 1926), 18:377–381.

Document 6.11   Statement to the Press on 1916 Candidacy, March 9, 1916

Roosevelt never entirely abandoned his hope of returning to the White House. Although he knew the chances for a Republican nomination in 1916 were remote, when pressed by reporters while on vacation in Trinidad, he released this ambiguous statement. It said he was not a candidate, but then again . . .

I am deeply sensible of the honor conferred on me and of the good-will shown me by the gentlemen who have announced themselves as delegates to be elected in my interest in the Massachusetts presidential primary. Nevertheless I must request, and I now do request and insist, that my name be not brought into the Massachusetts primaries, and I emphatically decline to be a candidate in the primaries of that or of any other State. Months ago I formally notified the authorities of Nebraska, Minnesota, and Michigan to this effect.

I do not wish the nomination. I am not in the least interested in the political fortunes—either of myself or any other man.

I am interested in awakening my fellow countrymen to the need of facing unpleasant facts. I am interested in the triumph of the great principles for which with all my heart and soul have striven and shall continue to strive.

I will not enter into any fight for the nomination and I will not permit any factional fight to be made in my behalf. Indeed, I will go further and say that it would be a mistake to nominate me unless the country has in its mood something of the heroic—unless it feels not only devotion to ideals but the purpose measurably to realize those ideals in action. . . .

Nothing is to be hoped for from the present administration, and the struggles between the President and his party leaders in Congress are today merely struggles as to whether the nation shall see its governmental representatives adopt an attitude of a little more or a little less hypocrisy and follow a policy of slightly less baseness. All that they offer us is a choice between degrees of hypocrisy and degrees of infamy.

But disgust with the unmanly failure of the present administration, I believe, does not, and I know ought not to, mean that the American people will vote in a spirit of mere protest. They ought not to, and I believe they will not, be content merely to change the present administration for one equally timid, equally vacillating, equally lacking in vision, in moral integrity and in high resolve. They should desire, and I believe they do desire, public servants and public policies signifying more than adroit cleverness in escaping action behind clouds of fine words, in refusal to face real internal needs, and in complete absorption of every faculty in devising constantly shifting hand-to-mouth and day-to-day measures for escape from our international duty by the abandonment of our national honor—measures due to sheer dread of various foreign powers, tempered by a sometimes harmonizing and sometimes conflicting dread of various classes of voters, especially hyphenated voters, at home. . . .

June is a long way off. Many things may occur between now and then. It is utterly impossible to say now with any degree of certainty who should be nominated at Chicago. The crying, the vital need now is that the men who next June assemble at Chicago from the forty-eight States, and express the view of the entire country shall act with the sane and lofty devotion to the interest of our nation as a whole which was shown by the original Continental Congress. They should approach their task unhampered by any pledge except to bring to accomplishment every ounce of courage, intelligence, and integrity they possess.

Source: Theodore Roosevelt, *The Works of Theodore Roosevelt,* national ed. (New York: Charles Scribner's Sons, 1926), 17:410–413.

Document 6.12   Telegram to the Progressive National Convention, June 10, 1916

To the bitter disappointment of die-hard partisans, Roosevelt declined the nomination of the Progressive Party in 1916. He saw no hope in another three-way race and decided to support the Republican nominee, Charles Evans Hughes.

TO THE PROGRESSIVE CONVENTION:

I am very grateful for the honor you confer upon me by nominating me as President. I cannot accept at this time. I do not know the attitude of the candidate of the Republican Party toward the vital questions of the day. Therefore, if you desire an immediate decision, I must decline the nomination. But if you prefer it, I suggest that my conditional refusal to run be placed in the hands of the Progressive National Committee.

If Mr. Hughes's statements, when he makes them, shall satisfy the committee that it is for the interest of the country that he be elected, they can act accordingly and treat my refusal as definitely accepted. If they are not satisfied they can so notify the Progressive Party, and at the same time they can confer with me and then determine on whatever action we may severally deem appropriate to meet the needs of the country.

Source: *New York Times*, June 11, 1916; also available in Elting E. Morison, ed., *The Letters of Theodore Roosevelt* (Cambridge: Harvard University Press, 1954), 8:1062–1063.

Document 6.13   Nobel Peace Prize Acceptance Speech, May 5, 1910

During a tour of Europe following his African safari, Roosevelt stopped in Stockholm to deliver his Nobel Peace Prize address, which he had been unable to do as president when he won the prize for his role in ending the Russo-Japanese War. Speaking of ways to promote and keep peace, Roosevelt suggested the creation of a league of peace among nations. When the idea of a League of Nations came from President Woodrow Wilson, however, Roosevelt worked to block American participation.

It is with peculiar pleasure that I stand here today to express the deep appreciation I feel of the high honor conferred upon me by the presentation of the Nobel Peace Prize. The gold medal which formed part of the prize I shall always keep, and I shall hand it on to my children as a precious heirloom. The sum of money provided as part of the prize by the wise generosity of the illustrious founder of this world-famous prize system, I did not, under the peculiar circumstances of the case, feel at liberty to keep. I think it eminently just and proper that in most cases the recipient of the prize should keep for his own use the prize in its entirety. But in this case, while I did not act officially as President of the United States, it was nevertheless only because I was President that I was enabled to act at all; and I felt that the money must be considered as having been given me in trust for the United States. I therefore used it as a nucleus for a foundation to forward the cause of industrial peace, as being well within the general purpose of your Committee; for in our complex industrial civilization of today the peace of righteousness and justice, the only kind of peace worth having, is at least as necessary in the industrial world as it is among nations. There is at least as much need to curb the cruel greed and arrogance of part of the world of capital, to curb the cruel greed and violence of part of the world of labor, as to check a cruel and unhealthy militarism in international relationships.

We must ever bear in mind that the great end in view is righteousness, justice as between man and man, nation and nation, the chance to lead our lives on a somewhat higher level, with a broader spirit of brotherly good-will one for another. Peace is generally good in itself, but it is never the highest good unless it comes as the handmaid of righteousness; and it becomes a very evil thing if it serves merely as a mask for cowardice and sloth, or as an instrument to further the ends of despotism or anarchy. We despise and abhor the bully, the brawler, the oppressor, whether in private or public life, but we despise no less the coward and the voluptuary. No man is worth calling a man who will not fight rather than submit to infamy or see those that are dear to him suffer wrong. No nation deserves to exist if it permits itself to lose the stern and virile virtues; and this without regard to whether the loss is due to the growth of a heartless and all-absorbing commercialism, to prolonged indulgence in luxury and soft, effortless ease, or to the deification of a warped and twisted sentimentality. . . .

I feel that I have the right to have my words taken seriously when I point out where, in my judgment, great advance can be made in the cause of international peace. I speak as a practical man, and whatever I now advocate I actually tried to do when I was for the time being the head of a great nation and keenly jealous of its honor and interest. I ask other nations to do only what I should be glad to see my own nation do.

The advance can be made along several lines. First of all there can be treaties of arbitration. There are, of course, states so backward that a civilized community ought not to enter into an arbitration treaty with them, at least until we have gone much further than at present in securing some kind of international police action. But all really civilized communities should have effective arbitration treaties among themselves. . . .

Secondly, there is the further development of the Hague Tribunal, of the work of the conferences and courts at The Hague. It has been well said that the first Hague Conference framed a Magna Charta for the nations; it set before us an ideal which has already to some extent been realized, and towards the full realization of which we can all steadily strive. The second Conference made further progress; the third should do yet more.

Meanwhile the American government has more than once tentatively suggested methods for completing the Court of Arbitral Justice constituted at the second Hague Conference and for rendering it effective. It is earnestly to be hoped that the various governments of Europe, working with those of America and of Asia, shall set themselves seriously to the task of devising some method which shall accomplish this result. . . .

Finally, it would be a masterstroke if those great powers honestly bent on peace would form a League of Peace, not only to keep the peace among themselves, but to prevent, by force if necessary, its being broken by others. The supreme difficulty in connection with developing the peace work of The Hague arises from the lack of any executive power, of any police power to enforce the decrees of the court. In any community of any size the authority of the courts rests upon actual or potential force: on the existence of a police, or on the knowledge that the able-bodied men of the country are both ready and willing to see that the decrees of judicial and legislative bodies are put into effect. In new and wild communities where there is violence, an honest man must protect himself; and until other means of securing his safety are devised, it is both foolish and wicked to persuade him to surrender his arms while the men who are dangerous to the community retain theirs. He should not renounce the right to protect himself by his own efforts until the community is so organized that it can effectively relieve the individual of the duty of putting down violence. So it is with nations. Each nation must keep well prepared to defend itself until the establishment of some form of international police power, competent and willing to prevent violence as between nations. As things are now, such power to command peace throughout the world could best be assured by some combination between those great nations which sincerely desire peace and have no thought themselves of committing aggressions. The combination might at first be only to secure peace within certain definite limits and on certain definite conditions; but the ruler or statesman who should bring about such a combination would have earned his place in history for all time and his title to the gratitude of all mankind.

Source: Theodore Roosevelt, *The Works of Theodore Roosevelt,* national ed. (New York: Charles Scribner's Sons, 1926), 16:305–309.

Appendix A
Notable Figures of the Roosevelt Presidency

Adams, Henry (1838–1918 b. Boston, Massachusetts)
Historian and author
After serving as secretary to his father, Charles Francis Adams, U.S. minister to Britain during the Civil War, Adams taught history at Harvard University until 1877. Moving to Washington, he devoted himself to historical studies and social and political criticism. He and John Hay built homes at Lafayette Square, close to the White House, and often included Roosevelt in their coterie, which included the artist John La Farge and the geologist Clarence King. Adams admired Roosevelt's energy but could also be caustically critical of the president.

Aldrich, Nelson W. (1841–1915 b. Foster, Rhode Island)
U.S. Senate, Rhode Island, 1881–1911
After a successful business career, Aldrich was elected as a Republican senator from Rhode Island and rose to the leadership of the conservative old guard. He was one of the "Four" who dominated the Senate during the administrations of William McKinley and Roosevelt. Aldrich resisted many of Roosevelt's domestic policies and staunchly defended corporate interests against regulation. He was strongly protectionist in trade policy, and as sponsor of the Payne-Aldrich Act in 1909, he deflected progressive efforts to lower tariff rates. His Senate investigation of the banking industry during the Taft administration was influential in shaping the Federal Reserve System enacted under Woodrow Wilson.

Allison, William Boyd (1829–1908 b. Perry Township, Ohio)
U.S. House of Representatives, Iowa, 1862–1871; U.S. Senate, Iowa, 1873–1908
Allison made his fortune as a corporate lawyer before being elected to the House of Representatives in 1862. After he rose to the Senate he became one of the conservative "Four" who dominated the upper house during Roosevelt's presidency, although he was somewhat less rigid than his colleagues and more responsive to Roosevelt's persuasive efforts. Allison introduced a compromise amendment that helped Roosevelt win passage of the Hepburn Act for railroad regulation in 1906.

Baer, George F. (1842–1914 b. Lavansville, Pennsylvania)
Attorney and railroad executive
Baer was appointed counsel to the Philadelphia and Reading Railroad in 1870, and in 1901 he became president when J. P. Morgan took control of Reading. He acted

as representative of management in the coal mine strike of 1902 and stubbornly resisted concessions to the workers. Baer's rudeness and intransigence sorely tried Roosevelt's patience.

Ballinger, Richard A. (1858–1922 b. Boonesboro, Iowa)
Mayor, Seattle, 1904–1906; secretary of the interior, 1909–1911
Ballinger was a reforming mayor of Seattle from 1904 to 1906 before becoming President William H. Taft's secretary of the interior, where he was accused by progressives of reversing Roosevelt's conservation policies on public lands. This conflict, in which Roosevelt's friend Gifford Pinchot, the zealous chief of the Bureau of Forestry, played a leading role, contributed to Roosevelt's break with Taft.

Beveridge, Albert J. (1862–1927 b. Highland County, Ohio)
U.S. Senate, Indiana, 1899–1911
Beveridge was a strong supporter of Roosevelt's reform initiatives, campaigning against child labor and supporting antitrust legislation and lower tariffs. He was one of the leaders of the Progressive revolt of 1912 and backed Roosevelt's candidacy. He lost his bid to return to the Senate in the election of 1914 and opposed the fusion of the Progressive and Republican Parties in 1916. A historian of distinction, he wrote biographies of John Marshall and Abraham Lincoln.

Cannon, Joseph G. (1836–1926 b. New Garden, North Carolina)
U.S. House of Representatives, Illinois 1873–1891, 1893–1913, 1915–1923; Speaker of the House, 1903–1911
As Speaker, Cannon, a Republican, was noted for his arbitrary, dictatorial behavior that gave rise to the term *Cannonism*. He was fiercely defensive of corporate interests and opposed most progressive reform efforts. Yet he aided Roosevelt in the passage of the Pure Food and Drug bill in 1906. His opposition to tariff reform forced Roosevelt to abandon the issue. The failure of President William H. Taft to support progressive congressmen in their effort to oust Cannon as Speaker in 1909 contributed to the estrangement of progressives from Taft.

Carnegie, Andrew (1835–1919 b. Dunfermline, Scotland)
Industrialist and philanthropist
Carnegie lived one of the "rags-to-riches" stories of the Gilded Age. After immigrating to the United States, he began as a worker in a cotton factory in Allegheny, Pennsylvania, in 1848 and rose to success in the railroad and oil industries. By the 1890s he came to dominate the American steel industry, accumulating a vast fortune. He sold his company in 1901 to devote his life to philanthropy. Among his beneficiaries was Theodore Roosevelt, when Carnegie contributed to the funding of Roosevelt's African safari for the collection of big-game specimens.

Cortelyou, George B. (1862–1940 b. New York, New York)
Secretary to President Roosevelt, 1901–1903; secretary of commerce and labor, 1903–1904; postmaster general, 1905–1907; secretary of the Treasury, 1907–1909
Cortelyou won Roosevelt's confidence and was appointed his first secretary of commerce and labor. Later he served in other important positions, including chairman of the Republican Party for the 1904 election campaign. Roosevelt entrusted Cortelyou with sensitive assignments and gave him a key role in negotiations with Wall Street financiers during the banking panic of 1907.

Croly, Herbert (1869–1930 b. New York, New York)
Progressive author and critic
Croly was the author of *The Promise of American Life,* a critique of progressivism admired by Roosevelt and influential in shaping his "New Nationalism" ideas in 1912. Croly rejected the Jeffersonian fear of strong central government and called for vigorous leadership to solve the problems of modern industrial society. In 1914 he became the founding editor of the journal of political opinion the *New Republic.* He was an early critic of the Versailles Treaty, and in the 1920s he became disillusioned over the decline of progressivism.

Davis, Richard Harding (1864–1916 b. Philadelphia, Pennsylvania)
Journalist
An influential newspaper reporter, feature writer, and foreign correspondent for *Harper's Weekly* and the *New York Evening Sun,* Davis specialized in war coverage. He provided much friendly copy about Roosevelt, especially of his exploits with the Rough Riders in Cuba. He remained a friend and supporter of Roosevelt to the end of his life.

Dewey, George (1837–1917 b. Montpelier, Vermont)
Naval officer
As a young officer Dewey participated in several naval battles during the Civil War. A commodore in command of the Pacific squadron, he was ordered to Hong Kong by Assistant Secretary of the Navy Roosevelt in case of war with Spain in 1898. His victory over the Spanish fleet at Manila signaled the growth of American power in the Pacific and won him promotion to the rank of admiral of the navy. On Roosevelt's orders, Dewey commanded a battleship squadron to waters off Venezuela in 1902 during tensions with Germany. By a special accommodation, he remained on active duty long past the normal retirement age and served until his death.

Fairbanks, Charles Warren (1852–1918 b. Unionville Center, Ohio)
U.S. Senate, Indiana, 1897–1905; vice president, 1905–1909; chair, Republican platform committee, Republican National Convention, 1912
One of the last of the American politicians born in a log cabin, Fairbanks, a conservative, was chosen to balance the Republican ticket in 1904. Although at

opposite ends of the Republican Party spectrum, Roosevelt and Fairbanks maintained cordial relations during Roosevelt's second term.

Foraker, Joseph (1846–1917 b. Rainsboro, Ohio)
Governor, Ohio, 1885–1889; U.S. Senate, Ohio, 1897–1908
An old guard Republican, Foraker frequently clashed with Roosevelt on regulatory policies and strongly opposed the Hepburn Act of 1906. He also publicly challenged the president's judgment in the Brownsville soldiers incident that same year. He resigned from the Senate in 1908 after charges of financial corruption related to the Standard Oil Company.

Garfield, James R. (1865–1950 b. Hiram, Ohio)
Civil service commissioner, 1902–1903; commisioner, Bureau of Corporations, Department of Commerce and Labor, 1903–1907; secretary of the interior, 1907–1909
The son of the former president, James A. Garfield, Garfield was a favorite of Roosevelt and his frequent tennis partner. Garfield served under Roosevelt in the Civil Service Commission. As head of the Bureau of Corporations he investigated antitrust violations. Roosevelt was deeply disappointed when President William H. Taft named Richard Ballinger to replace Garfield as secretary of the interior. Especially bitter was Gifford Pinchot, who had been given a free hand in the forestry service by Garfield. Garfield joined Pinchot in attacking Ballinger's conservation policies. He joined the Progressive revolt in 1912 in support of Roosevelt.

Hanna, Marcus Alonzo (1837–1904 b. New Lisbon, Ohio)
U.S. Senate, Ohio, 1897–1904; Republican Party chairman, 1900
Hanna became wealthy through industrial and banking interests and remained a strong supporter of business interests throughout his political career. He was instrumental in the election of William McKinley as governor of Ohio in 1891 and in his election to the presidency in 1896 and again in 1900, raising unprecedented sums for the presidential campaigns. He was McKinley's most trusted adviser and close friend. Elected to the Senate in 1897, Hanna opposed Roosevelt's nomination as vice president and worked against his reformist policies in the Senate. For a time he considered challenging Roosevelt for the Republican presidential nomination in 1904.

Hay, John (1838–1905 b. Salem, Indiana)
Assistant secretary of state, 1878–1880; ambassador to Britain, 1897; secretary of state, 1898–1905
A man of many talents, Hay was at various times in his life a journalist, poet, historian, and diplomat. With John Nicolay, he was private secretary to Abraham Lincoln, and together they wrote the ten-volume *Abraham Lincoln: A History.* Hay

served in several diplomatic postings abroad before becoming assistant secretary of state under President Rutherford B. Hayes. Among his important contributions as secretary of state were his crafting of the Open Door Policy concerning China and his negotiation of the Hay-Pauncefote Treaty, which opened the way for American control of the Panama Canal. He was Roosevelt's counselor and, with his close friend Henry Adams, a White House neighbor with whom the president socialized.

Hepburn, William (1833–1916 b. Wellsville, Ohio)
U.S. House of Representatives, Iowa, 1881–1887, 1893–1909
Hepburn was a Union soldier during the Civil War. As a Republican congressman he was the principal sponsor of the 1906 act to regulate railroads that bears his name, an important achievement of the Roosevelt administration. He was also a sponsor and strong supporter of the Pure Food and Drug law of 1906.

Holmes, Oliver Wendell, Jr. (1841–1935 b. Boston, Massachusetts)
Associate justice, Massachusetts supreme judicial court, 1882–1899; chief justice, Massachusetts supreme judicial court, 1899–1902; associate justice, U.S. Supreme Court, 1902–1932
An eminent Boston attorney who wrote extensively on the law, Holmes was editor of the *American Law Review* (1870–1873) and became a professor of law at Harvard in 1882. After serving for twenty years on the Massachusetts supreme judicial court, he became Roosevelt's first appointment to the U.S. Supreme Court. He bitterly disappointed the president, however, with his dissent in the *Northern Securities* case in 1904. Famous for his dissenting opinions, he continued to serve on the court until 1932, retiring at the age of ninety-one.

Hughes, Charles Evans (1862–1948 b. Glens Falls, New York)
Governor, New York, 1906–1910; associate justice, U.S. Supreme Court, 1910–1916; Republican presidential candidate, 1916; secretary of state, 1921–1925; judge, Permanent Court of International Justice, 1928–1930; chief justice, U.S. Supreme Court, 1930–1941
Hughes was elected governor of New York as a reform candidate and championed the passage of anticorruption and labor legislation. Appointed to the Supreme Court by President William H. Taft in 1910, he resigned to run for president in 1916, losing to Woodrow Wilson in a close election. He was not a Roosevelt favorite, although the president campaigned for him against Wilson. He later served as secretary of state under Presidents Warren G. Harding and Calvin Coolidge and as chief justice of the U.S. Supreme Court.

Kaneko, Baron Kentaro (1853–1942 b. Fukuoka domain, Kyushu, Japan)
Diplomat
Serving in several influential government positions in Japan in the 1880s and 1890s, Kaneko also lectured at Tokyo University. Kaneko had attended Harvard

University while the young Roosevelt was a student there. He was sent to Washington to represent Japanese interests during the Russo-Japanese War (1904–1905) and became a friend of Roosevelt. He conferred with him during California school and immigration crises.

Knox, Philander C. (1853–1921 b. Brownsville, Pennsylvania)
Attorney general, 1901–1904; U.S. Senate, Pennsylvania, 1904–1909, 1917–1921; secretary of state, 1909–1913
A talented corporation lawyer, Knox was appointed attorney general in 1901 by President William McKinley and continued in that position under Roosevelt. At Roosevelt's direction, Knox instituted and successfully prosecuted the *Northern Securities* antitrust suit in 1902. He resigned as attorney general when he was elected to the Senate. Despite his faithful service in the administration, in the Senate he opposed some of Roosevelt's important reform initiatives. President William H. Taft named him secretary of state. After returning to the Senate in 1917, he joined Henry Cabot Lodge in leading the opposition to the ratification of the Versailles Treaty.

La Follette, Robert M. (1855–1925 b. Primrose, Wisconsin)
Governor, Wisconsin, 1901–1906; U.S. Senate, Wisconsin, 1906–1925; Progressive Party presidential candidate, 1924
La Follette was a progressive senator who was disappointed by Roosevelt's willingness to compromise on issues like the Hepburn Act. Elected to the Senate in early 1905, he deferred taking his seat until early 1906 so that he could finish his work as governor. He participated in founding the National Progressive Republican League in 1911, hoping to replace President William H. Taft as the party nominee in 1912. Roosevelt, however, displaced him as the progressive favorite for the nomination. He remained a leading progressive voice in American politics and ran for president on the Progressive Party ticket in 1924, finishing a weak third behind the Republican Calvin Coolidge and the Democrat John W. Davis.

Lodge, Henry Cabot (1850–1924 b. Boston, Massachusetts)
U.S. Senate, Massachusetts, 1893–1924
Lodge taught history at Harvard University as a young man. He edited the influential *North American Review* and wrote several historical works, including biographies of Daniel Webster and George Washington. He was a lifelong intimate friend and confidant of Roosevelt despite his more conservative leanings. He campaigned with Roosevelt for a stronger navy and lobbied for Roosevelt's appointments to the Civil Service Commission and as assistant secretary of the navy. He often served as a mediator between Roosevelt and the old guard Republicans. Lodge supported President William H. Taft in the 1912 presidential election, but his friendship with Roosevelt survived. Like Roosevelt he was a bitter enemy of Woodrow Wilson and led the fight against the United States joining the League of Nations.

Long, John D. (1838–1915 b. Buckfield, Maine)
Governor, Massachusetts, 1880–1882; U.S. House of Representatives, Massachusetts, 1883–1889; secretary of the navy, 1897–1902
Long was appointed secretary of the navy by President William McKinley. Roosevelt's superior in the Navy Department during the buildup preceding the Spanish-American War, Long was gently tolerant of the independent initiatives of Roosevelt, his assistant secretary.

Mahan, Alfred Thayer (1840–1914 b. West Point, New York)
Naval officer and historian
A Union naval officer during the Civil War, Mahan later served as president of the Newport Naval War College. He gained worldwide attention with his books *The Influence of Sea Power upon History, 1660–1783* (1890) and *The Influence of Sea Power upon the French Revolution and Empire, 1793–1812* (1892). Roosevelt endorsed his ideas enthusiastically, and they were allies in pressing for a buildup of U.S. naval armaments.

Mitchell, John (1870–1919 b. Braidwood, Illinois)
President, United Mine Workers of America, 1898–1908; vice president, American Federation of Labor, 1899–1914; commissioner of labor, New York State, 1914; chairman, New York State Industrial Commission, 1915–1919
A mine worker from the age of twelve, Mitchell joined the United Mine Workers of America at its inception in 1890. As the union's president Mitchell represented the miners in the anthracite coal strike of 1902. During negotiations at the White House, Roosevelt grew to respect his integrity and reasoned arguments.

Morgan, J. P. (1837–1913 b. Hartford, Connecticut)
Financier
The most successful financier of the Gilded Age and Progressive Era, Morgan dominated American banking and exerted worldwide influence. He was challenged by Roosevelt in the *Northern Securities* suit of 1902 and was deeply disturbed by the president's efforts in antitrust prosecutions and corporate regulation. Nevertheless, he contributed to Roosevelt's 1904 campaign and sought and won presidential cooperation in the banking crisis of 1907.

Pinchot, Gifford (1865–1946 b. Simsbury, Connecticut)
Chief forester, 1898–1910
As a young man Pinchot traveled to Europe to study forestry and applied his ideas at the Vanderbilt estate in North Carolina in 1892. As the chief of the forestry division of the Interior Department, he was the key architect of the Roosevelt administration's conservation policy and enjoyed the complete confidence of the president. For his criticism of the conservation policies of Secretary of the Interior Richard Ballinger, he was fired by President William H. Taft in 1910. That

conflict with Ballinger and Pinchot's consequent dismissal contributed to Roosevelt's disenchantment with Taft.

Platt, Orville (1827–1905 b. Washington, Connecticut)
U.S. Senate, Connecticut, 1879–1905
Platt, a conservative Republican, opposed Roosevelt on domestic issues but offered strong support in foreign and military policy. He was one of the "Four," a group of old guard senators who dominated the Senate during the Roosevelt years. He was the author of the Platt Amendment, a rider to an appropriations bill in 1901 that gave the United States important rights in Cuba, including leasing rights to establish a naval base there.

Platt, Thomas Collier (1833–1910 b. Oswego, New York)
New York State Republican Party boss; U.S. Senate, New York, 1881, 1897–1909
Platt, a member of the conservative faction of the Republican Party, became a powerful force in New York State politics and built an effective but ethically dubious Republican machine there, exercising great control over patronage and policy in the state. He was instrumental in Roosevelt's nomination and election as governor in 1898 but resistant to Roosevelt's reformist policies in office. Platt worked assiduously to exile Roosevelt by making him the vice presidential nominee in 1900. With Roosevelt's ascension to the presidency, Platt's influence in New York receded.

Riis, Jacob (1849–1914 b. Ribe, Denmark)
Author and reformer
Riis's work as a police reporter for the *New York Evening Sun* and the *Tribune* exposed him to the bitter conditions of the city's slums and led him to combine journalism with a struggle for social reform for the rest of his life. His best-known book, *How the Other Half Lives* (1890), was an important influence on progressive reformers and admired by Roosevelt, who became a close friend. Roosevelt brought Riis into his inner circle during his tenure as New York City police commissioner, and the reporter remained a loyal supporter through the presidential years and in the campaign of 1912.

Root, Elihu (1845–1937 b. Clinton, New York)
Secretary of war, 1899–1903; secretary of state, 1905–1909
In building a successful and lucrative law practice, Root earned a reputation as a leader of the profession in New York and beyond. Active in New York politics in the 1890s, he led the state's constitutional convention in 1894. His legal agility settled the residency dispute that cleared the way for Roosevelt's campaign for governor in 1898. President William McKinley appointed him secretary of war, and he continued in that office under Roosevelt until 1903, when he returned briefly to the practice of law. He rejoined the administration in 1905, replacing John Hay

as secretary of state. As secretary of war he effected the reorganization of the army in 1902, and as secretary of state he negotiated the Root-Takahira Agreement with Japan in 1908, strengthening friendly relations with that country. He remained a firm supporter of President William H. Taft in 1912, leading to several years of estrangement from Roosevelt.

Spooner, John C. (1843–1919 b. Lawrenceburg, Indiana)
U.S. Senate, Wisconsin, 1885–1891, 1897–1907
Spooner was a successful railroad lawyer before his election to the Senate. As a leader of conservative Republicans in the Senate, he was a foe of Robert La Follette in both Wisconsin politics and the Senate. He worked closely with Sen. Nelson Aldrich in defense of corporate interests and against reform during the Roosevelt years.

Steffens, Lincoln (1866–1936 b. San Francisco, California)
Journalist
Steffens wrote muckraking articles about political corruption for *McClure's Magazine*. He used much of this material in his most important book, *The Shame of the Cities*. With Jacob Riis he assisted Roosevelt as police commissioner and became a friend and occasional adviser to the president.

Taft, William Howard (1857–1930 b. Cincinnati, Ohio)
U.S. solicitor general, 1890–1892; circuit court judge, 1892–1900; president, U.S. Philippine Commission, 1900–1901; governor, Philippine Islands, 1901–1904; secretary of war, 1904–1908; president, 1909–1913; chief justice, U.S. Supreme Court, 1921–1930
A successful lawyer and superior court judge in Ohio, Taft was named solicitor general by President Benjamin Harrison. After some years as a federal circuit court judge, he was appointed to lead the Philippine Commission by President William McKinley. He continued in that position under Roosevelt until his appointment as secretary of war. He was a faithful friend and trusted adviser to the president and became Roosevelt's choice to succeed him. Elected president in 1908, Taft relied more on the conservatives of the party and could not satisfy growing progressive demands for reform. By 1910 Roosevelt was speaking out against administration policies. Roosevelt challenged the president's renomination in 1912, and failing in that, opposed him in the election. After several years of estrangement, the two were reconciled at a chance meeting in Chicago in 1918. In 1921 President Warren Harding appointed Taft chief justice of the Supreme Court.

Washington, Booker T. (1856–1915 b. Hale's Ford, Virginia)
Educator and African American leader
Rising from his birth in slavery to success as a teacher and administrator at the Hampton Institute, Washington became the head of the Tuskegee Institute in

Alabama in 1881, building it into a distinguished institution. He urged industrial education and training for black Americans as their path to economic success and advancement. His outlook clashed with that of W. E. B. DuBois and other black leaders, who insisted on fighting for immediate recognition of black civil rights and equality. Recognizing him as a leader of African Americans, Roosevelt invited him to dine in the White House in 1901, causing widespread outrage, especially in the South. Roosevelt often consulted Washington on political policy and federal appointments in the South.

White, William Allen (1868–1944 b. Emporia, Kansas)
Journalist

Publisher of the Emporia *Gazette*, White gained a national reputation as a political analyst and wrote for *McClure's Magazine* and the *Saturday Evening Post*. A friend, and consistent supporter of Roosevelt, his own views followed Roosevelt's shift from conservative to progressive politics. White strongly backed Roosevelt's effort to return to the presidency in 1912. He continued as a leading voice in American journalism until his death.

Wood, Leonard (1860–1927 b. Winchester, New Hampshire)
General, U.S. Army

An army surgeon and soldier, Wood joined his close friend Theodore Roosevelt in organizing the Rough Riders in 1898. He led the regiment with Roosevelt as his second-in-command. He was the military governor of Cuba from 1899 to 1902 and governor of the Moro Province in the Philippines from 1903 to 1906. From 1910 to 1914 he served as chief of staff of the army and urged military preparedness after the outbreak of World War I. Wood joined Roosevelt as critic of Wilsonian neutrality policy. In 1920 he was a leading but unsuccessful candidate for the Republican presidential nomination.

Key Events in Roosevelt's Life

1858

October 27 Roosevelt is born in New York City. He is the eldest son of Theodore, a wealthy merchant and philanthropist, and Martha Bulloch Roosevelt, a southern aristocrat.

1861

The Civil War begins.

1865

Roosevelt watches Abraham Lincoln's funeral cortege from his grandfather's house in New York City.

1876

September Roosevelt enrolls at Harvard University.

1878

February 9 Roosevelt's father, whom his son idolizes, dies of stomach cancer at the age of forty-six.

1880

June 30 Roosevelt graduates from Harvard University, *magna cum laude* and Phi Beta Kappa.

Early October Roosevelt enrolls at Columbia Law School; he leaves in 1882 without graduating.

October 27 Roosevelt marries Alice Hathaway Lee, the daughter of a wealthy Bostonian family.

1881

November Running as a Republican, Roosevelt becomes the youngest man ever elected to the New York State Assembly. Although initially a conservative, he eventually becomes the leader of reform-minded members of the party. He is reelected in 1882 and 1883.

December Roosevelt publishes *The Naval War of 1812,* which he had begun in college. The work, a study of naval strategy and a call for naval readiness, becomes required reading at the U.S. Naval Academy at Annapolis, Maryland, for many years.

1883

Roosevelt becomes minority leader of the New York State Assembly.

May Roosevelt works with New York Democratic governor Grover Cleveland to pass civil service reform.

1884

February 12 Roosevelt's first child, Alice, is born.

February 14 Roosevelt's mother dies of typhoid fever on the same day that his wife dies of Bright's disease. In his diary, he writes, "The light has gone out of my life."

April As chairman of the City Investigating Committee, Roosevelt investigates corruption in New York City government. The committee's final report results in several reforms, including centralizing authority in New York City in the hands of the mayor.

June Roosevelt is introduced to national politics at the Republican National Convention, where he unsuccessfully promotes reform candidate George Edmunds. Later this month, he departs for his ranch in the Dakotas. For the next three years ranching will be his primary occupation.

1886

November 2 Roosevelt comes in third in the New York mayoral race that pits him against the highly respected Democrat Abram Hewitt and the radical reformer Henry George.

December 2 Roosevelt marries his childhood friend Edith Kermit Carow in a London ceremony.

1887

September 13 Roosevelt's first son, Theodore, is born at Sagamore Hill, Roosevelt's estate on Long Island.

1889

May 7 President Benjamin Harrison appoints Roosevelt as one of the three members of the U.S. Civil Service Commission. At the post he becomes nationally visible as spokesman for the Republican Party on good government and the merit system. He serves on the commission until May 1895.

October 10 Roosevelt's son Kermit is born at Sagamore Hill.

1891

August 13 Roosevelt's daughter Ethel is born at Sagamore Hill.

1894

April 10 Roosevelt's son Archibald is born in Washington, D.C.

1895

May 6 Roosevelt becomes president of the Police Commission of New York City. During two tumultuous years on the job, he receives national attention for reforming and professionalizing the department.

1897

April 6 President William McKinley appoints Roosevelt assistant secretary of the navy. While in office Roosevelt advocates war against Spain, then trying to suppress an independence movement in its colony of Cuba.

November 19 Roosevelt's son Quentin is born in Washington, D.C.

1898

February 15 The U.S. battleship *Maine* blows up in Havana harbor.

April 25 The Spanish-American War begins as the United States declares war on Spain.

May 6 Roosevelt resigns his navy post to help organize the First U.S. Volunteer Cavalry Regiment (the Rough Riders).

July 1 Roosevelt's "crowded hour" comes as he leads the Rough Riders in fighting at Kettle Hill and San Juan Hill in Cuba. He is later nominated for, but denied, the Medal of Honor. Roosevelt's heroism establishes his national reputation.

November 8 Roosevelt is elected governor of New York. Although disdainful of reformers, the new governor's administration will be characterized by reforms designed to improve education and housing conditions for the poor, curb government corruption, and preserve the environment. His attempts to regulate and tax business alienate conservative interests.

1899

April 1 Roosevelt approves two measures designed to improve the working conditions of the poor: the Costello Anti-Sweatshop Act, which provides for the inspection of work in tenements, and an amendment to the labor law limiting working hours of women and children and increasing the authority of factory inspectors.

April 4 Roosevelt approves an act prohibiting elected city officials from also holding appointive offices the salaries for which are paid by the city.

April 19 Roosevelt approves the Civil Service Act reforming New York's civil service system.

May 5 Roosevelt approves the Raines-Mazet Police Act, forbidding police officers from soliciting money for political funds or attempting to influence public opinion.

May 26 Roosevelt signs the Ford Franchise Tax Act, providing for the taxing of corporations that held public franchises. The same day he signs a bill forbidding the pollution of waters used by state fish hatcheries.

1900

January 3 In his annual message to the legislature, Roosevelt deems forest preservation "of the utmost importance" and calls for the creation of state parks.

March 14 Roosevelt signs a bill providing for the opening of corporation books for inspection by investors and creditors.

April 18 Roosevelt signs legislation prohibiting racial discrimination in public education.

June 21 Roosevelt is nominated for vice president at the Republican National Convention.

November 6 The McKinley-Roosevelt ticket wins the general election.

1901

March 4 Roosevelt takes office as vice president.

September 6 President William McKinley is shot by an anarchist in Buffalo, New York.

September 14 Roosevelt becomes president following McKinley's death. At age forty-two he is the youngest man ever to become president.

October 16 President and Mrs. Roosevelt dine privately with African American educator Booker T. Washington at the White House. Washington is the first black American to dine with a president in the executive mansion.

November 18 The United States and Great Britain conclude the second Hay-Pauncefote Treaty, giving the United States exclusive control over an interoceanic canal on the Central American isthmus.

1902

February 19 Roosevelt orders attorney general Philander C. Knox to file an antitrust suit against the Northern Securities Company under the terms of the Sherman Act.

May 5 Henry Cabot Lodge, chair of a Senate committee investigating reports of atrocities by American troops during the Philippine insurrection, confirms that crimes were committed.

May 22 Crater Lake National Park (Oregon) is established. During Roosevelt's presidency the number of national parks doubles, 125 million acres are added to forest reserves, 16 national monuments are created, and 51 wildlife refuges founded.

June 17 Roosevelt signs the Newlands Reclamation Act, which provides for the use of money from western land sales to finance federal irrigation projects.

July 14 Reacting to stories of atrocities committed by American troops during the Philippine insurrection, Roosevelt overrules the judgment of a court martial and orders the dismissal of Gen. Jacob H. Smith, who had been accused of using torture and brutal methods to subdue the rebellion.

October Roosevelt intervenes to help settle the anthracite coal strike. This was the first time an American president had become actively involved in the details of a labor dispute.

December When Britain, Germany, and Italy send warships to the coast of Venezuela to pressure it for payment of debts, Roosevelt successfully persuades the parties to agree to arbitration to settle the matter.

1903

January 22 The Hay-Herran Convention settles the terms by which the United States will receive a ninety-nine-year lease on a six-mile-wide canal zone in Panama.

February 14 Roosevelt wins the establishment of the Department of Commerce and Labor. The department includes a Bureau of Corporations empowered to investigate corporations involved in interstate commerce.

February 19 Roosevelt signs the Elkins Anti-Rebate Act, forbidding carriers from giving large shippers rebates from published rates and investing courts with the power to issue injunctions against violators.

August 12 The Colombian Senate rejects the Hay-Herran Convention.

September 3–October 20 During deliberations between the United States and Great Britain over the boundary between Alaska and Canada, Roosevelt suggests he might send troops to occupy the disputed area if the results of the conference are disappointing. A joint U.S.-British commission sustains U.S. claims.

November 2 Roosevelt orders warships to Panama to maintain free transit across the isthmus.

November 6 The United States recognizes the Republic of Panama following its secession from Colombia.

November 18 The United States and Panama sign the Hay-Bunau-Varilla Treaty, granting the United States the right to build the Panama Canal.

1904

February 7 Roosevelt orders U.S. naval forces to the Dominican Republic to protect American life and property following an insurrection.

February 10 The Russo-Japanese War begins.

March 14 In *Northern Securities Co. v. United States,* the Supreme Court rules the company in violation of the Sherman Anti-Trust Act.

November 8 Roosevelt wins landslide election for a second term and announces he will not run again in 1908.

December 6 In his annual message to Congress, Roosevelt issues the "Roosevelt Corollary" to the Monroe Doctrine, asserting the U.S. right to intervene in the affairs of Latin American states.

1905

February 1 The National Forest Service is established.

February 7 The Dominican and U.S. governments sign an accord under which Santo Domingo agrees to American control of its customs offices in return for the U.S. government's assuming responsibility for all Dominican debt.

March 17 Roosevelt gives away his niece Eleanor Roosevelt at her wedding to distant cousin Franklin Delano Roosevelt.

August 9 The Portsmouth Peace Conference, brokered by Roosevelt, concludes with a peace treaty between Russia and Japan. Roosevelt is awarded the Nobel Peace Prize in 1906 for his work as a mediator.

1906

Upton Sinclair publishes *The Jungle,* exposing conditions in the Chicago stockyards and meat packing plants.

January 16 As a result of Roosevelt's intervention, a diplomatic conference convenes in Algeciras, Spain, to discuss the partition of Morocco. Roosevelt had intervened in the dispute among France, England, and Germany for fear that the Moroccan crisis might precipitate a European war.

February 17 Roosevelt's daughter Alice marries Rep. Nicholas Longworth of Ohio in a magnificent ceremony at the White House.

June 8 Roosevelt signs the Act for the Preservation of American Antiquities, designed to protect prehistoric and other national treasures. Roosevelt uses the law to designate as national monuments such natural wonders as Muir Woods and the Grand Canyon.

June 29 Roosevelt signs the Hepburn Act, giving the Interstate Commerce Commission the power to regulate railroad rates and prohibit discrimination among shippers. The same day Roosevelt signs a bill authorizing the construction of a lock canal in Panama.

June 30 Roosevelt signs the Pure Food and Drug Act, forbidding the manufacture and sale of adulterated or fraudulently labeled foods and drugs, and the Meat Inspection Act, providing for the federal inspection of meat packers and sellers.

August The president of Cuba, Tomás Estrada Palma, facing insurrection, requests U.S. intervention. Under the terms of the Platt Amendment, Roosevelt sends a Marine contingent to maintain order. American forces remain until 1909.

October 11 The San Francisco Board of Education orders the segregation of all Japanese, Chinese, and Korean children.

November 5 Roosevelt orders dishonorable discharges for 167 black soldiers accused of involvement in the Brownsville affair.

1907

February Roosevelt persuades the San Francisco Board of Education to rescind its segregation order.

February 24 In the gentlemen's agreement, Roosevelt promises no official discrimination against the Japanese living in the United States, and Japan agrees to restrain the emigration of Japanese workers.

July 31 U.S. troops withdraw from the Dominican Republic.

October 22 The Knickerbocker Trust Company, a major New York bank, is forced to close its doors when nervous depositors, agitated by rumors of impending collapse, create a run on the bank. In response, the stock market drops steeply and other banks tremble.

November 4 To avoid a general economic collapse, Roosevelt permits the U.S. Steel Company to acquire the troubled Tennessee Coal and Iron Company with the assurance that he will not launch an antitrust suit against U.S. Steel, the nation's largest trust.

December 16 The Great White Fleet begins its journey around the world, in part to demonstrate American power and in part as a friendly gesture.

1908

April 22 Congress passes the Employers Liability Act, demanded by Roosevelt. The act provides compensation to workers injured on the job in areas of federal jurisdiction.

May 13 Roosevelt hosts a White House conference on conservation, which includes cabinet members, members of Congress, state governors, and members of the Supreme Court. It succeeds in bringing the issue to national attention.

June 8 Roosevelt appoints a National Conservation Commission, headed by Gifford Pinchot, to study the nation's natural resources systematically.

May 30 The Aldrich-Vreeland Act establishes the National Monetary Commission, authorized to investigate and report on foreign and domestic banking systems.

November 3 William Howard Taft, Roosevelt's chosen successor, wins the presidential election.

November 20 Roosevelt personally helps formulate the Root-Takahira Agreement in which the United States and Japan commit themselves to peaceful commerce in the Pacific, continuation of the open door in China, and respect for the territorial integrity of China.

1909

March 23 Roosevelt departs for a year-long African safari.

1910

Spring Roosevelt is hailed as a world celebrity and feted in the capitals of Europe.

May 20 Roosevelt represents the United States at the funeral of British king Edward VII.

June 18 Roosevelt and his family return to New York.

August 31 Roosevelt delivers the "New Nationalism" speech in Osawatomie, Kansas. The speech, calling for greatly expanded welfare and regulatory programs—including closer government supervision of business, tariff reduction, a progressive income tax, and the passage of laws regulating working conditions—launches his return to politics.

1912

February 12 Roosevelt announces his candidacy for the Republican presidential nomination.

June 18–22 Although Roosevelt outpolled Taft in the primaries and caucuses, Taft wins the presidential nomination at the Republican National Convention.

August 5–7 Roosevelt's supporters form the National Progressive Party and nominate him for president.

October 14 Roosevelt is shot at a rally in Milwaukee, Wisconsin. He delivers a ninety-minute speech before seeking medical help.

November 5 Roosevelt outpolls Taft in the general election, but the Democratic candidate, Woodrow Wilson, wins the presidency.

1913

Roosevelt publishes *Theodore Roosevelt: An Autobiography.*

October 4 TR sails to Latin America for a lecture tour and to lead an expedition up Brazil's River of Doubt.

1914

February 27–April 27 Roosevelt nearly dies of malarial fever while exploring the River of Doubt. The river is later renamed Rio Roosevelt in his honor.

June 28 The assassination of Archduke Franz Ferdinand of Austria precipitates World War I.

August 4 President Woodrow Wilson issues a proclamation of American neutrality in the world war.

August 14 The Panama Canal opens to traffic.

1915

Roosevelt publishes *America and the World War,* condemning the Wilson administration, and particularly Woodrow Wilson, for its policies toward the war in Europe.

February 4 Germany declares the waters around the British Isles a war zone and announces it will destroy any enemy merchant ship in the area.

May 7 A German submarine sinks the British liner *Lusitania,* killing 128 Americans.

1916

June 10 Roosevelt declines the Progressive Party's nomination for president and campaigns for the Republican candidate, Charles Evans Hughes.

1917

January 31 Germany announces a policy of unrestricted submarine warfare off Allied shores.

February and March German submarines sink six U.S. merchant ships.

April 6 The United States declares war on Germany.

May 19 President Wilson refuses Roosevelt's request to raise and lead a company of American volunteers to fight in France.

1918

July 14 Roosevelt's son Quentin, a fighter pilot, is shot down and killed in France.

November–December Roosevelt joins Sen. Henry Cabot Lodge to oppose Wilson's plan for a League of Nations.

1919

January 6 Roosevelt dies of a blood clot in his sleep at Sagamore Hill.

Appendix C
Roosevelt's Cabinet, 1901–1909

Title	Officeholder	Dates of service
Attorney general	Philander C. Knox	1901–1904
	William H. Moody	1904–1906
	Charles J. Bonaparte	1906–1909
Postmaster general	Charles Emory Smith	1901–1902
	Henry C. Payne	1902–1904
	Robert J. Wynne	1904–1905
	George B. Cortelyou	1905–1907
	George von L. Meyer	1907–1909
Secretary of the navy	John D. Long	1901–1902
	William H. Moody	1902–1904
	Paul Morton	1904–1905
	Charles J. Bonaparte	1905–1906
	Victor H. Metcalf	1906–1908
	Truman H. Newberry	1908–1909
Secretary of the Treasury	Lyman J. Gage	1901–1902
	Leslie M. Shaw	1902–1907
	George B. Cortelyou	1907–1909
Secretary of state	John M. Hay	1901–1905
	Elihu Root	1905–1909
	Robert Bacon	1909
Secretary of war	Elihu Root	1901–1904
	William H. Taft	1904–1908
	Luke E. Wright	1908–1909
Secretary of the interior	Ethan A. Hitchcock	1901–1907
	James R. Garfield	1907–1909
Secretary of commerce and labor	George B. Cortelyou	1903–1904
	Victor H. Metcalf	1904–1906
	Oscar S. Straus	1906–1909
Secretary of agriculture	James Wilson	1901–1909

Works Cited

Beale, Howard K. 1956. *Theodore Roosevelt and the Rise of America to World Power.* Baltimore: Johns Hopkins University Press.

Brands, H. W. 1997. *T.R.: The Last Romantic.* New York: Basic Books.

Bush, George H. W. Bush. 1990. *Public Papers of the Presidents of the United States: George H. W. Bush, 1989.* 2 vols. Washington, D.C.: Government Printing Office.

Clements, Kendrick A., and Eric A. Cheezum. 2003. *Woodrow Wilson.* Washington, D.C.: CQ Press.

Clinton, William J. 2001. *Public Papers of the Presidents of the United States: William J. Clinton, 2000–2001.* 3 vols. Washington, D.C.: Government Printing Office.

Collin, Richard H. 1990. *Theodore Roosevelt's Caribbean.* Baton Rouge: Louisiana State University Press.

Cornwell, Elmer, Jr. 1966. *Presidential Leadership of Public Opinion.* Bloomington: Indiana University Press.

Dallek, Robert. 1983. *The American Style of Foreign Policy.* New York: Alfred A. Knopf.

Dalton, Kathleen. 2002. *Theodore Roosevelt: A Strenuous Life.* New York: Alfred A. Knopf.

Dulles, Foster Rhea. 1955. *America's Rise to World Power, 1898–1954.* New York: Harper Brothers.

Harbaugh, William Henry. 1966. *The Life and Times of Theodore Roosevelt.* New York: Collier Books.

Hofstadter, Richard. 1954. *The American Political Tradition and the Men Who Made It.* New York: Vintage Books.

Jessup, Philip C. 1964. *Elihu Root.* 2 vols. New York: Anchor Books.

Kennedy, David. 1999. *Freedom from Fear: The American People in Depression and War, 1929–1945.* New York: Oxford University Press.

Lodge, Henry Cabot, ed. 1925. *Selections from the Correspondence of Theodore Roosevelt and Henry Cabot Lodge, 1884–1918.* 2 vols. New York: Charles Scribner's Sons.

McCullough, David. 1981. *Mornings on Horseback*. New York: Simon and Schuster.

Marks, Frederick W., III. 1979. *Velvet on Iron: The Diplomacy of Theodore Roosevelt*. Lincoln: University of Nebraska Press.

Miller, Nathan. 1992. *Theodore Roosevelt: A Life*. New York: William Morrow.

Morison, Elting E., ed. 1951–1954. *The Letters of Theodore Roosevelt*. 8 vols. Cambridge: Harvard University Press.

Morris, Edmund. 1979. *The Rise of Theodore Roosevelt*. New York: Ballantine Books.

———. 2001. *Theodore Rex*. New York: Random House.

Mowry, George E. 1958. *The Era of Theodore Roosevelt*. New York: Harper and Brothers.

Pringle, Henry. [1931] 1956. *Theodore Roosevelt: A Biography*. New York: Harcourt Brace.

Riis, Jacob. 1904. *Theodore Roosevelt the Citizen*. New York: Outlook.

Roosevelt, Theodore. 1926. *The Works of Theodore Roosevelt*. National ed. 20 vols. New York: Charles Scribner's Sons.

Sorensen, Theodore. 1965. *Kennedy*. New York: Harper and Row.

Steffens, Lincoln. 1931. *The Autobiography of Lincoln Steffens*. New York: Grosset and Dunlap.

Stephenson, Nathaniel Wright. 1971. *Nelson Aldrich*. Port Washington, N.Y.: Kennikat Press.

Strouse, Jean. 1999. *Morgan: American Financier*. New York: Random House.

Sullivan, Mark. 1936. *Our Times: 1900–1925*. Vol. 2, *America Finding Herself*. New York: Charles Scribner's Sons.

Tilchin, William N. 1997. *Theodore Roosevelt and the British Empire*. New York: St. Martin's Press.

Woodward, C. Van. 1971. *Origins of the New South*. Baton Rouge: Louisiana State University Press.

Index